The Hidden 1970s

The Hidden 1970s

Histories of Radicalism

EDITED BY

DAN BERGER

RUTGERS UNIVERSITY PRESS

NEW BRUNSWICK, NEW JERSEY, AND LONDON

LIBRARY OF CONGRESS CATALOGING-IN-PUBLICATION DATA

The hidden 1970s : histories of radicalism / edited by Dan Berger.
   p. cm.
Includes bibliographical references and index.
ISBN 978–0–8135–4873–9 (hardcover : alk. paper) — ISBN 978–0–8135–4874–6
(pbk. : alk. paper)
   1. Radicalism—United States—History—20th century.   2. Social movements—
United States—History—20th century.   3. Political culture—United States—
History—20th century.   4. United States—Social conditions—1960–1980.
I. Berger, Dan, 1981–
   HN90.R3H53   2010
   303.48′4097309047—dc22   2009052305

A British Cataloging-in-Publication record for this book is available
from the British Library.

Gil Scott-Heron, "Bicentennial Blues" and "A Poem for Jose Campos Torres,"
from *Now and Then: The Poems of Gil Scott-Heron* (Canongate, 2000), reprinted
by permission of the publisher.

Visit our Web site: http://rutgerspress.rutgers.edu

Manufactured in the United States of America

For B. Loewe and in memory of Alan Berkman
−conjurers of freedom and possibility

CONTENTS

Acknowledgments   ix

List of Abbreviations: North American Leftist Organizations in the 1970s   xi

Introduction: Exploding Limits in the 1970s   1
    DAN BERGER

PART ONE
Insurgency

1   Improvising on Reality: The Roots of Prison Abolition   21
        LIZ SAMUELS

2   Sick of the Abuse: Feminist Responses to
    Sexual Assault, Battering, and Self-Defense   39
        VICTORIA LAW

3   "The Struggle Is for Land!": Race, Territory,
    and National Liberation   57
        DAN BERGER, WITH ROXANNE DUNBAR-ORTIZ

4   Canada's Other Red Scare: The Anicinabe Park
    Occupation and Indigenous Decolonization   77
        SCOTT RUTHERFORD

PART TWO
Solidarity

5   "A Line of Steel": The Organization of the Sixth
    Pan-African Congress and the Struggle for
    International Black Power, 1969–1974   97
        FANON CHE WILKINS

6   How Indigenous Peoples Wound Up at the United Nations   115
         ROXANNE DUNBAR-ORTIZ

7   "Hit Them Harder": Leadership, Solidarity, and
         the Puerto Rican Independence Movement   135
         MEG STARR

8   Unorthodox Leninism: Workplace Organizing and
         Anti-Imperialist Solidarity in the Sojourner Truth Organization   155
         MICHAEL STAUDENMAIER

                              PART THREE
                              Community

9   Play as World-making: From the Cockettes to the Germs,
         Gay Liberation to DIY Community Building   177
         BENJAMIN SHEPARD

10   "We Want Justice!": Police Murder, Mexican American
         Community Response, and the Chicano Movement   195
         BRIAN D. BEHNKEN

11   Rising Up: Poor, White, and Angry in the New Left   214
         JAMES TRACY

12   The Movement for a New Society: Consensus,
         Prefiguration, and Direct Action   231
         ANDREW CORNELL

13   Hard to Find: Building for Nonviolent Revolution
         and the Pacifist Underground   250
         MATT MEYER AND PAUL MAGNO

14   "The Original Gangster": The Life and Times of
         Red Power Activist Madonna Thunder Hawk   267
         ELIZABETH CASTLE

         Notes on Contributors   285
         Index   289

ACKNOWLEDGMENTS

Well before we had ever met, Daniel Burton-Rose called me out of the blue in August 2006 to talk about the hidden histories of the 1970s. This book emerges out of that conversation and the many he and I have had since. I thank him for that, even if our attempts at co-editing the project did not pan out. I thank him as well for helping cover the costs of copyediting an early version of the manuscript.

An enormous thank you to the contributors for their research, patience, and commitment. Regardless of the stage at which they joined the project, everyone shared an excitement for their work and the bigger project of which it is now a part. Likewise, Leslie Mitchner was wonderfully devoted to the book from conception to completion. It was a pleasure to work with her and all the fine folks at Rutgers University Press. Felicia Kornbluh and Dylan Rodríguez proved gracious and critical readers for Rutgers, and I thank them for the many ways their comments strengthened the manuscript. Special thanks to Felicia for reading two different versions with great precision. Natasha Zaretsky assured me that the introduction was ready for the outside world. Suzy Subways tackled a penultimate draft of the manuscript with her unparalleled skills as both copyeditor and critical reader. Bob Brown copyedited the final version for the press with extreme care. I'm grateful to Laurie Prendergast for preparing the index. Josh MacPhee of the Just Seeds artist cooperative (www.justseeds.org) designed the cover with speed, skill, and humor. I thank him for his prodigious efforts to make and celebrate people's history.

For trying, successfully or otherwise, to connect me with potential authors, I thank Daniel Burton-Rose, Roxanne Dunbar-Ortiz, Bill Fletcher, Matt Meyer, Lorena Oropeza, Meg Starr, and James Tracy, along with Bob Brown, Trevor Griffey, Tommi Avicolli Mecca, Paul Longmore, Akinyele Umoja, and Linda Watts, whose work and wisdom have much to offer those interested in the 1970s. Dana Barnett won my heart long before she helped solve an ongoing title conundrum, but I thank her for that as well, along with the incredible support she has given me and many others in our community.

Gil Scott Heron deserves special mention for providing the soundtrack for the book. Along with Suzanne Hitchman, Rob McBride wonderfully provided me with a sampling of other music from the decade as I was finishing the project. He also commented on my contributions to the book and immersed me in the natural beauty of the San Francisco Bay Area. He and Donna Willmott have proven themselves rare beings: friends that have become family and mentors who have provided me with both a political and a physical home.

I hope the introduction appropriately records my gratitude to at least some of the many scholars and memoirists who have already taken up the difficult work of trying to make sense of the 1970s. Thanks also to several colleagues whose work and generosity have provided valuable role models as scholars, teachers, and public intellectuals: Matthew Countryman, Mike Foley, Peniel Joseph, George Katsiaficas, Matthew Lassiter, José López, John McMillian, Gina Morantz-Sanchez, Louise Newman, Adolph Reed, David Roediger, Dylan Rodríguez, Andrea Smith, Tom Sugrue, Becky Thompson, Heather Thompson, Tim Tyson, and Jeremy Varon. Barbie Zelizer, John Jackson, Barbara Savage, and Michael Delli Carpini have consistently encouraged me—both to work on this project and to not let it come between me and my dissertation. I did not always listen, but I hope I have not disappointed them.

I am so fortunate to be part of a broad and supportive community of friends, colleagues and comrades. They continue to ground me in history—including, perhaps most importantly, the present—while indulging my obsession with other histories. I thank them for their loving inspiration. A partial list: Kazembe Balagun, Dana Barnett, Diana Block, Andy Cornell, Chris Dixon, Nava EtShalom, David Gilbert, Rob Goldberg, Sha Grogan-Brown, Walidah Imarisha, Alex Knight, Toussaint Losier, Matthew Lyons, Claude Marks, Molly McClure, Claire McGuire, Leo McGuire, Bernadine Mellis, Matt Meyer, Layne Mullett, Jalil Muntaqim, Mendal Polish, Joshua Kahn Russell, gabriel sayegh, Aishah Simmons, Michael Simmons, Zoharah Simmons, Sarah Small, Riley Snorton, Meg Starr, David Stein, Suzy Subways, Max Toth, Maggie Von Vogt, Laura Whitehorn, Andrew Willis-Garcés. "Thank you" hardly seems enough.

Finally, I dedicate this book to two people who have brought much beauty and joy to the world. Dr. Alan Berkman (1945–2009), was a man I admired but did not know, whose courage and commitment carried him, as both a doctor and an organizer, throughout many of the hidden and visible battles of the 1970s and well beyond, from Wounded Knee to the South Bronx and many points in between. He challenged racial and economic injustice in fighting AIDS, apartheid, and his own two-decade battle with cancer. He was a prison activist and a former prisoner, and I count myself among the many who admired his resilience. His death is a major loss. But his example lives on. I see it in the visionary thinking, inspired organizing, and loving empathy of B. Loewe, my beloved twin. For them, this book.

LIST OF ABBREVIATIONS: NORTH AMERICAN LEFTIST ORGANIZATIONS IN THE 1970S

This list of organizations is meant to help the reader navigate the plethora of acronyms that appear in the text and which scattered the political landscape at the time. While making no claims at being exhaustive, this directory provides a provisional map of groups active in the 1970s North American Left. Some of these groups started before 1970; others stopped and started at various points throughout the decade, and others still exist today.

AFSC	American Friends Service Committee
AIM	American Indian Movement
AQAG	A Quaker Action Group
BHA	Black Hills Alliance
BLA	Black Liberation Army
BPP	Black Panther Party
CAMP	Chicago Area Military Project
CBE	Center for Black Education
CISA	South American Indian Council
FALN	Fuerzas Armadas de Liberación Nacional / Armed Forces of National Liberation
GJB	George Jackson Brigade
GLF	Gay Liberation Front
HRUM	Health Revolutionary Movement
IITC	International Indian Treaty Council
IWK	I Wor Kuen
LSP	Liga Socialista Puertorriqueña / Puerto Rican Socialist League
LRBW	League of Revolutionary Black Workers
LULAC	League of United Latin American Citizens
MAYO	Mexican American Youth Organization
MIRA	Movimiento Independentista Revolucionario Armado / Armed Revolutionary Independence Movement

MLN	Movimiento de Liberación Nacional / National Liberation Movement
MNS	Movement for a New Society
NAPO	New Afrikan Prisoners Organization
NIYC	National Indian Youth Council
NRG	Nonviolent Revolutionary Group
O4O	October 4th Organization
OL	October League [later, the Communist Party Marxist-Leninist, CPM-L]
OWS	Ojibway Warriors Society
PFOC	Prairie Fire Organizing Committee
PRRWO	Puerto Rican Revolutionary Workers Organization
PRSC	Puerto Rican Solidarity Committe
PSP	Partido Socialista Puertorriqueño / Puerto Rican Socialist Party
RNA	Republic of New Afrika [later the Provisional Government of the Republic of New Afrika, PG-RNA]
RUA	Rising Up Angry
RUP	La Raza Unida Party
RU	Revolutionary Union [later, the Revolutionary Communist Party, RCP]
SAIS	Survival of American Indians
Sixth PAC	Sixth Pan-African Congress
SOL	Spirit of Logos
STO	Sojourner Truth Organization
UNA	United Native Americans
VVAW	Vietnam Veterans Against the War
WARN	Women of All Red Nations
WFHC	Women's Feminist Health Collective
WKLD/OC	Wounded Knee Legal Defense/Offense Committee
WL	White Lightning
WRL	War Resisters League
WUO	Weather Underground Organization
WWRSS	We Will Remember Survival School

The Hidden 1970s

America has got the blues and the blues is
in the street looking for three principles—
justice, liberty, equality.
We would do well to join the blues looking for
justice, liberty, and equality.
The blues is in the street.
America has got the blues but don't let it get by us.
—Gil Scott-Heron, "Bicentennial Blues" (1976)

Introduction

Exploding Limits in the 1970s

DAN BERGER

Barack Obama's successful 2008 presidential campaign generated much attention to the many barriers broken by his candidacy and subsequent election. His campaign energized many people who previously had been disinterested in or, by virtue of their age, ineligible from participating in national electoral politics. Several pundits and Democratic Party insiders openly hoped, and some even proclaimed, that the ascendance of Obama—two years old when Kennedy was killed and nineteen when Reagan was elected—would herald the end of the long-running 1960s-backlash culture wars.

But the sixties era, which extended well into the 1970s, still loomed large in the election. Most directly, of course, John McCain ran on his status as a Vietnam War veteran and former prisoner of war. The decade of the 1970s in particular was also central to Republican criticism of Obama, first through the sensationalist response to the incendiary, if not especially unique, views of his former pastor, Jeremiah Wright, and then through his association with former Weather Underground leader (now Distinguished Professor of Education at the University of Illinois at Chicago) Bill Ayers, with whom he sat on a board of directors for a Chicago philanthropic organization. This combination revived two standard 1970s bogeymen: fiery black nationalists and violent New Leftists. As is often the case with the media-fueled pseudo-scandals of a campaign season, these controversies were long on shock and short on substance. Yet both Wright and Ayers proved salient symbols for a conservative attack on Obama. Controversial in their heyday, both black nationalism in general and the Weather Underground in particular were repackaged and resold as even more dangerous commodities in the days of a global war on terror.[1] That these tactics failed to defeat Obama's presidential bid should not distract us from the many ways in which the 1960s and 1970s remain malleable and potent reference points in U.S. politics.

The 1970s seems not only to inform the current era but strangely to be reappearing in it. Since the turn of the century, more than a dozen partisans of 1970s

1

radical groups have been brought up on charges emanating from that period.[2] The activists who have been arrested or convicted in the twenty-first-century prosecutions of sixties-era acts participated in the militant wings of the Black Power and antiwar movements, which, with increasing frequency throughout the 1970s, embraced illegal, violent, or underground tactics and strategies. Beyond these legal cases, the political and cultural context of the early twenty-first century would seem to herald the second coming of the 1970s. Barack Obama, like Jimmy Carter, campaigned for the presidency on being an outsider able to change the culture of Washington. And, like Carter, he pledged to restore human rights stripped away by a criminal predecessor (George W. Bush and Richard Nixon, respectively).[3] The major issues Obama confronted upon assuming the presidency on January 20, 2009, seemed to combine several of the dominant political issues of the 1970s: war, economic devastation, and an energy crisis. And as gay marriage continued to inflame passions throughout the country, one of the most popular films of 2008 was a bio-pic of Harvey Milk, the first openly gay politician in the United States and a man who opposed the homophobia of the burgeoning Christian Right. Milk was murdered in 1978.

Scholars searching for proof of how the country got to its current point of polarization have increasingly turned to the 1970s as "the Big Bang" moment of modern American conservatism, when many of what we now recognize to be its current dimensions came together in a coherent and increasingly coordinated force.[4] Yet acknowledging the importance of the 1970s to the Right should not remove the Left from view. The Right's emergence and success appeared after decades of organizing, done in a conscious effort to defeat the ideologies and policies of the Left—not just the New Deal and Great Society federal programs, but the initiative displayed by a myriad of grassroots social movements. Left and Right cannot be viewed in isolation from each other. This book intends to contribute to filling this gap by refocusing attention on leftwing movements in the shifting terrain of the era.

All historic moments are rife with contingency, and perhaps none in recent history are more so than the 1970s. It was a decade that saw an openly imperial president preside over a range of liberal or progressive domestic policies—including several environmental reforms and an attempt to provide universal health care—even as he sought to wipe out radical protest and then was destroyed by his own paranoid, egomaniacal zeal.[5] It was a decade that gave political liberalism one last chance through the presidency of Jimmy Carter, while allowing economic neoliberalism and an attack on government regulation as a response to widespread fears of national decline. This combination yielded a free-market anticommunism that avoided large-scale military combat but supported a range of interventions abroad while attacking unions and other traditionally Democratic constituencies domestically. When Carter's neoliberal approach and folksy charm failed to end the energy crisis, free hostages held in Iran, halt the decay of American cities, or rally the nation to its former sense of divine mission,

Americans voted overwhelmingly for the triumphant nationalism and aggrandized militarism of Ronald Reagan.[6]

In the early part of the decade, more and more working-class people, disproportionately doing the fighting in Vietnam, came out against the war while media coverage, to Nixon's delight, emphasized street battles between resentful construction workers and antiwar students.[7] The 1970s saw the death penalty outlawed and then reinstated, as a range of new antidrug measures and law-and-order campaigns yielded the steady rise of a highly racialized mass incarceration that especially affected urban black communities. The end of the decade witnessed a national investigation, through the Church Committee, of domestic spying and foreign intervention by American intelligence agencies aiming to crush leftist opposition at home and abroad. This investigation was sparked by the 1971 leak of documents taken by radicals who had broken into an FBI office in Pennsylvania. It resulted in the indictment and conviction of two of the FBI's top officials, the highest-ranking FBI officials to ever have been convicted in court. In his first hundred days as president, Ronald Reagan pardoned both men, Special Agent Edward Miller and Assistant FBI Director Mark Felt.[8] (In 2005, Felt admitted his role as one of the enigmatic supporting actors of the ultimate 1970s drama, when he told a *Vanity Fair* journalist that he was "Deep Throat," the secret informant who helped *Washington Post* reporters Bob Woodward and Carl Bernstein develop the Watergate story.) The 1970s also witnessed the rise of blockbuster summer movies, punk rock, and reality television, to say nothing of the cultural products that did not thrive beyond the decade, like disco and the pet rock.[9]

What, then, are we to make of the 1970s? It was a deeply ambivalent and contentious moment, simultaneously moving in multiple directions. The Vietnam War, finally over by 1975, continued to provide the framework through which diverse forms of political and cultural opposition circulated.[10] Recent studies have usefully shown the decade to be a time that was "up for grabs," the moment when many of the reforms that social movements had pushed for finally came to fruition, in the context of a resurgent conservative movement.[11] Even more than the reforms, the 1970s witnessed the diffusion of certain 1960s values and mores, especially to those places that were not epicenters of New Left militancy. Scholars have shown the uneven ascension of conservative politicians and reactionary ideologies throughout American political culture—uneven because they never achieved hegemonic status, despite the appearance to the contrary.[12] These historians have demonstrated the salience of the era's cultural products, from naturalizing surveillance, fear, and cynicism to the many ways that different musical genres expressed certain hopes and fears of the generation.[13] Challenging the belief, popular even at the time, that the 1970s was bleak, boring, or both—poet-radical Gil Scott-Heron said in 1973 that it was "winter in America," and Peter Carroll titled his 1982 book on the decade *It Seemed like Nothing Happened*[14]—such studies have shown the 1970s to be a moment of fierce contestation. Yet these texts have largely treated radical social movements as irrelevant to shaping the

1970s, with one historian asserting that the decade witnessed "the virtual disappearance of the radical Left as an organized political force."[15]

A separate group of scholars, including some activist veterans of the era, have found their way to the 1970s almost accidentally. Challenging any neat decade-based periodizations, these texts emphasize the grassroots politics of the so-called "long sixties." This long sixties stretches from the 1950s to the 1970s, bookended by the flourishing and decline of social movements for racial justice and against the war in Vietnam.[16] By emphasizing women's liberation, Black Power, and anti-imperialism, among other movements of the time, these scholars have shown that some of the most significant aspects of "the sixties" actually occurred in the 1970s. These studies challenge an earlier historiography which, obsessed with the decline of the 1960s, argues that social movements destroyed themselves by the end of an activist decade in a fit of solipsistic rage. The picture revealed in this newer work is a decidedly more complex view of the period, as case studies and memoirs follow a number of political actors of the sixties, from their origins in the 1940s or 1950s through the many paths they took during and since the 1960s and 1970s. These studies have started to uncover the many ways that the 1970s was a moment in which activism continued, changed, or, with some movements, grew.[17]

As these scholarly accounts and activist memoirs have shown, the 1970s was when many of the hallmark events and issues of "the sixties" actually transpired—the Attica prison riot (1971), Vietnam veterans angrily returning their medals to the White House in protest (1971), the Wounded Knee standoff (1973), the Seabrook Nuclear Power Plant civil disobedience (1977), the "White Night" riots protesting the light sentence given to the man who murdered Harvey Milk (1979), and numerous other such events. Ruth Rosen argues that the 1970s, "arguably the most intellectually vital and exciting [period] in the history of American women, also witnessed an amazing array of revelations and changes in social, political, and public thought and policy."[18] The 1970s saw the legalization of abortion; liberalized gender roles; the expanded visibility of lesbians, gays, and transgender people; the near passage of the Equal Rights Amendment; and the rise of an explicitly women-of-color feminism, which introduced what became known as "intersectional" analyses of power and society. (This brand of feminism arose alongside the leadership that some women of color exercised in what has often been described as a white liberal or second-wave feminism).[19] Similarly, the 1970s witnessed the emergence on the national stage of powerful movements for Puerto Rican independence, disability rights, and environmentalism, among others.

This book is an effort to combine these two historical approaches. It takes root at the intersection of Scott-Heron's "winter in America" and what can be called the viewpoint of the 1970s as the sixties' second decade. The articles here see the 1970s as clearly and organically part of the sixties—understood here as an era, not simply a decade—but also as a distinctive period. As many have already demonstrated, the 1970s was a time when social movements were repressed and tore themselves asunder. But it was also a moment when movements experimented and expanded. For those radicals who remained strongly identified with the antiwar and antiracist movements of the 1960s, the 1970s was a time when they felt they had to walk their talk. Unable to hide further in their rhetorical pronouncements of impending revolution, these people readied themselves for the task at hand. That task varied widely; for activists involved in groups such as the October League (OL), Revolutionary Union (RU), or the Puerto Rican Socialist Party (PSP), it meant attempts at consolidating revolutionary organizations, usually in the form of a communist party or its protean precursors. For others, it meant armed struggle building for "people's war," and indeed the 1970s witnessed hundreds of armed attacks as well as the emergence of clandestine organizations such as the Black Liberation Army (BLA), the Fuerzas Armadas de Liberación Nacional (FALN), the George Jackson Brigade (GJB), and, of course, the Weather Underground.[20]

These various groupings shared an idiom shaped, in turn, by Marxism, revolutionary nationalism, and above all a belief in vanguard political formations or strategies. Others, including many who were newly politicized in this polarized environment, learned *new* languages. Their politics emerged from widespread efforts, capitalizing on newly available political space and rejecting what they saw as failed directions of the recent past, to experiment with alternative praxes. Radicals attempted to redefine political affinity in ways frequently messier and often smaller than the beloved community of the previous decade. These alternative political communities were led by people whose voices or perspectives had often been unheard a few years earlier: women, indigenous peoples, gays, lesbians, bisexuals and transgender people, Puerto Ricans, environmentalists, people with disabilities, and others. More so than their 1960s counterparts, many of these groups were committed to addressing the ways power inequalities reproduced themselves within social movements and not just outside of them. Nevertheless these movements still identified community as their goal, as they sought to build from the ground up organizations and institutions able both to meet people's needs and to withstand the reaction of state institutions.

Inspired by the movements they helped build or in whose shadow they worked, some radicals in the 1970s committed to trying new things. They established intentional communities, secular and faith-based, out of which they organized against war, tried to confront interpersonal violence without relying on police or the criminal justice system, and injected a playful culture into otherwise stern political spaces. Such examples were often in dialogue with the much-maligned therapeutic solutions that were said to mark the 1970s "retreat" from political engagement.[21] But, as several articles included here make clear, not all who embraced spirituality were fleeing political action. Many viewed their spiritual practice as inseparable from their quest to form deeply engaged political communities. They comprise vital dimensions of left-wing practice in this era—some of the many hidden histories of 1970s radicalism.

Acknowledging the ways that the Left grew and changed in the 1970s is not meant to overlook or downplay its fracturing in that era. Those who criticize solipsism and arrogance, rigidity and reclusiveness have ample evidence in the 1970s Left, especially after the end of the Vietnam War stripped the Left of its most shared platform. Taking seriously the claim that politics and culture in the 1970s were up for grabs means acknowledging the ways in which the Left's many weaknesses rendered activists less effective than they could have been—or even counterproductive, in more than a few cases. Within the Left, political rigidity and personal transformation were two sides of the same coin that served to marginalize some 1960s activists from 1970s realities. The latter approach, together with those who traded social change for capitalist advance, has become clichéd evidence of what Tom Wolfe called in 1976 the "Me Decade." By the end of the 1970s, Yippie Jerry Rubin and troubadour Bob Dylan were two of the most well known former rebels to have embraced spiritual and personal transformation instead of politics: Rubin published a biography mid-decade celebrating meditation, Erhard Seminars Training (EST), and New Age practices, while Dylan recorded a gospel album and became a born-again Christian.[22] Surveying this cultural landscape, Gil Scott-Heron said America in the 1970s was trying to decide between *Gunsmoke* sheriff Matt Dillon and counterculture icon Bob Dylan. But perhaps a more fitting choice was between the rebellious Bob Dylan of the 1960s and the newly religious, largely apolitical Bob Dylan of the 1970s.[23] (The Dillon of *Gunsmoke* did not become America's choice until 1980.)

These shifts became visible culturally, politically, and economically throughout the 1970s. As a result, journalists and others in a rush to label the decade as it was in progress turned increasingly to discourses of confusion, transformation, and, above all, *limits*. Numerous observers, both during and since the 1970s, have described the decade through the framework of limits. From U.S. defeat in Vietnam to the 1973–1974 OPEC boycott, the energy crisis to the 1979 seizure of American diplomats in Iran, global developments showed that the country was not invincible and that it faced challenges for its disproportionate resource usage and conservative political allegiances.[24] Faced with challenges to the affluence that bolstered postwar economic growth, Americans in the 1970s had to confront the limitations of their power. Attempting to instill and install limits as a paradigm of U.S. foreign policy, Henry Kissinger pioneered détente as a plan to minimize direct U.S. military involvement and emphasize economic self-interest, especially regarding resource allocation, in dealing with the rest of the world.[25] As president, Jimmy Carter spoke of American limits in regard to energy usage, long lines at gas stations, and a general "crisis of confidence."[26] More recent historical studies have embraced this framework, saying that the 1970s conceded to a belief, politically and culturally, economically and socially, that the country needed to learn to live within limits.[27] This perspective sees the 1970s as a moment of transition marked largely by failure—American affluence and idealism created problems that could not be solved by either military might or political will, and so limits were needed.

As the essays in this collection demonstrate, the 1970s can be seen not only as a time of limits but equally as one of extremes. To argue that the 1970s is best understood by its limits is to miss how profoundly radical the period was—not just or even primarily for the Left. Indeed, the 1970s housed radicals of all stripes, leading Michael Harrington to declare in 1976 that the United States was "moving vigorously left, right, and center, all at once."[28] The U.S. government in the 1970s faced challenges from the Left, from the Right, and from within—be they whistleblowers like Daniel Ellsberg, who leaked what became known as the Pentagon Papers in 1971, or politicians such as Daniel Patrick Moynihan and Gerald Ford, who sought to dismantle various aspects of the government while holding official positions within it. The far Left attacked the U.S. state for its imperialism, repression, and undemocratic nature. Some in the Left, as several of the essays collected here show, attempted to move beyond the state form itself. The Right, meanwhile, leveraged a critique of liberalism to attack the role of government in providing social services and to support the role of government in fighting crime and communism. This conservative attack, aided by various Republican and Democratic politicians, joined free-market economics with the growing conservative groundswell opposing taxes, social spending, desegregation busing, homosexuality, unionization, affirmative action, feminism, secularism, and a general culture of disorder.[29] Reagan's 1980 presidential victory owed its success to an ability to combine these various strains into a political platform—one that famously defined government as the problem, free-market militarism as the solution. His successful appeal to American nationalism, signaling a disregard for détente and the framework of limits, showed that many in the United States did not care to operate within or appreciate a perspective of limits.[30] Reagan and the sector of the Right for which he became a spokesman identified free-market economics and strident militarism as necessary antidotes to liberalism's limits.

The 1970s was, in short, the ultimate exploder of limits, the end of the Keynesian economic system that had dictated U.S. policy since the 1930s.[31] The neoliberal political economy that ascended in this period facilitated the widespread deindustrialization of the United States, the turn to a service-and-information economy, the privatization of public services, and the rise of a credit-based economy. For most of the 1970s, the U.S. economy experienced a drop in profit alongside high taxes. Executive salaries rose while workers' pay stagnated or dropped in the context of a systemic attack on the welfare state. Neoliberalism gained increasing support from all three presidents of the 1970s, from Ford's consistent support for deregulation and decreased federal spending to Carter's chilly response to public-sector unionism.[32] Nixon was, in fact, the least neoliberal when it came to domestic economic policy, even if he oversaw the turn to stagflation and was the most hawkish in the realm of foreign policy. On the local level, the first black mayor of Atlanta, Democrat Maynard Jackson, fired striking sanitation workers in 1977—a move Reagan would nationalize in 1981 when air traffic controllers went on strike.[33]

Beyond these epochal shifts, developments of the 1970s exploded limits by crossing the boundaries of traditional political allegiances. Some of the decade's towering politicians—such as Richard Nixon and Ronald Reagan at the national level, and Philadelphia's Frank Rizzo at the local level—mobilized various forms of resentment, often appealing to white racial solidarity and "law and order," to woo traditionally Democratic voters over to the Republican ticket. The success of this approach could be seen in the 1972 election, where many traditional members of the Democratic Party coalition, led by AFL-CIO president George Meany, abandoned presidential candidate George McGovern. This disarray within the Democratic Party coalition gave Nixon a sweeping reelection victory, even as news of his illegal acts began to crescendo.[34] Abortion access and a new gay visibility gave politicians occasion to mobilize previously apolitical or moderate Christian communities. Building on the racial pride emphasized by the Black Power movement and associated phenomena in Mexican/Chicano, Puerto Rican, and Native American communities, Italians, Irish, Jews, and other white people emphasized pride in their ethnic heritage. Nixon sought to exploit this development among both blacks and whites, speaking in favor of black capitalism as "black power" and trumpeting white ethnicity.[35] The political mobilization of white ethnicity fed into two of the touchstone examples of racial strife in the 1970s: massive white violence and opposition to desegregation busing in Boston and the 1978 Supreme Court ruling which determined that the affirmative-action policies of the Regents of the University of California endangered the constitutional commitment to equal protection.[36]

The attack on limits was a profound undercurrent of 1970s culture. While some on the Left promised "revolution in our lifetime," New Age spirituality and Christian evangelism offered paths to reach nirvana or avoid apocalypse in our lifetime. The millennial nature of 1970s cultural anxiety was perhaps most clearly expressed in the best-selling book of the decade, made into a movie in 1979, Hal Lindsey and Carole Carlson's *The Late Great Planet Earth*, a Christian tale of the coming Rapture. Others sought to create their own rapture: A white former community organizer named Jim Jones had built a large, mostly black, following for his organization, the People's Temple, which moved from California in 1974 to establish a socialist paradise in Guyana. In 1978, Jones's followers killed five people, including a senator; Jones then persuaded more than nine hundred of his followers to drink poisoned Kool-Aid.[37] Surveying the 1970s, several cultural critics feared that the public sphere had been obviated by narcissism, post-industrialism, and consumer culture.[38] These critics were responding to other developments of the 1970s that attempted to transcend the limits of politics or even consciousness itself through meditation, jogging, Scientology, the human potential movement, reevaluation counseling, and Eastern religions.

While these cultural forms persist in myriad ways, perhaps the greatest legacy of mainstream 1970s political culture was the wide spread of an ironic or cynical detachment when it came to formal power. Upon seeing the depths of Nixon's corruption, his resignation, and his immediate pardoning by Ford, alongside the widespread illegal and unethical actions entertained by U.S. law enforcement domestically and abroad, many Americans wanted little to do with the institutions governing their lives. This cynicism emerged as television and other media gained even greater dominance in facilitating political spectacles—moving toward flashier images and more dramatic stories, away from things that did not produce a high market value, such as news.

Limits were exploding on the Left as well—often quite literally, given the hundreds of armed attacks that occurred in the decade by and against clandestine groups. Most of these actions were bombings targeting U.S. government buildings or corporate offices, a tactic not utilized widely in the American Left since the turn of the twentieth century.[39] These bombings were sometimes financed by bank robberies, another well-worn tactic of leftist insurrection internationally that this country had not seen regularly for decades. This turn to left-wing spectacular violence generated what is, perhaps, the most iconic if confounding aspect of 1970s militancy: the 1974 kidnapping of heiress Patricia Hearst and her subsequent affiliation with her captors, the Symbionese Liberation Army.[40] Latin American guerrilla groups had staged several kidnappings by the mid-1970s, but militants in the United States had never done so. Two highly visible prison breaks in 1979—by alleged FALN member William Morales (arrested in 1978) and alleged BLA member Assata Shakur (arrested in 1973)—showed that the full panoply of insurgent techniques had come home.[41] These and other leftist guerrillas emerged in England, Germany, Italy, and the United States, among elsewhere, in the 1970s by explicitly rejecting the implicitly agreed-upon limits of acceptable political action in Western democracies.

Other leftists rejected limits in the 1970s by building nonviolent underground networks for draft resisters and antiwar sabotage, turning to the land in large numbers through communal living or quasi-secessionist attempts to build alternative forms of governance, or attempting to organize workers outside of the union or party model. In an era of increasing globalization, radicals in the United States attempted to develop their own foreign policy by appealing for indigenous rights at the United Nations, working for the independence of Puerto Rico, and trying to foster Pan-African networks of Black Power. These and other challenges to conventional political forms suggest, as Van Gosse has argued in a somewhat different vein, that the time period of and since the 1970s has been profoundly postmodern.[42] This partial list is not to deny that many leftists continued working for social change through a variety of tried-and-true methods. On balance, however, the 1970s Left fought against the limits of traditional American politics.

Viewing the decade from these alternate vantage points recasts our view of the 1970s. It also gets us closer to understanding the shape of radical politics since that time. Even if conservative forces proved far more successful in seizing and maintaining the reins of formal political power, the Left today is partly a product of the debates and paradigms that emerged in the 1970s. Certainly, Obama's election builds on the rise of black mayors and other politicians of color in the 1970s—including Shirley Chisholm's 1972 presidential run, the first such attempt by an African American and the second by a woman.[43] But the legacies are both more local and more diffuse. Since the 1970s nonprofit organizations have become the dominant entities providing social services and advancing liberal causes. Although many such organizations existed before then, the political shifts of the 1970s made them more prominent. Nonprofits have emerged as new economic forces that have provided jobs for thousands of progressives, while generating spirited critiques from the Left for providing a safety valve, keeping grassroots organizations loyal to foundations or the state rather than their political vision, and isolating them from the communities they ostensibly serve or of which they are said to be a part.[44] Angela Davis, an icon of the 1970s for her antiprison activism and her friendship with black militant prison organizer-author George Jackson, helped start an organization in 1998 dedicated to abolishing the prison industrial complex. The group, Critical Resistance, republished a primer of prison abolition written in 1976 by a collective of radical pacifists.[45] Although surveillance, policing, and incarceration have all expanded exponentially since *Instead of Prisons* was first published, the original document's framework of community responses to social problems informs the work of Critical Resistance and other abolitionist groups in the twenty-first century.

The anti-imperialist and anti-interventionist movements of the 1970s, which upheld self-determination in opposition to U.S. support for brutal dictatorships in the Third World, has informed the widespread protests of global financial institutions such as the World Trade Organization (WTO), the International Monetary Fund, and the World Bank since the 1999 demonstration against the WTO in Seattle.[46] Indigenous militancy, so central to the 1970s political and cultural landscape, has been a driving force of the recent leftism in Latin America and the U.S. Left's support for it in places like Bolivia and Mexico.[47] The "poor people's movement" model of organizing, embraced by Dr. Martin Luther King, Jr. toward the end of his life and taken up by his associates afterward, has, alongside the welfare rights movement of that era, similarly informed contemporary urban social movements.[48] Perhaps more elusively but no less significantly, the efforts of some 1970s radicals to organize in ways that confronted injustice within social-justice movements while simultaneously responding to outside forces have shaped several contemporary political endeavors among grassroots activists. These contemporary examples, while often small and as plagued with problems as their forerunners, borrow from the organizing models of feminists, pacifists, and anarchists in the 1970s.

Studying the Left of the 1970s, then, is an opportunity to do more than counter the declension narrative that sees the end of the 1960s as the beginning of an undifferentiated conservative era.[49] Leftists in the 1970s, in no less of a transitional state than other sectors of society, tried a series of experiments. These experiments looked different based on how one defined the transition. This book gathers professionally trained and independent scholars of the 1970s, almost entirely people who, like me, did not live through the period they describe but who are engaged in ongoing research about the movements they chronicle. While it proved unfeasible to combine scholarly essays with first-person reflections, the essays gathered here strive to center the voices and experiences of that era's partisans through oral histories alongside traditional archival research. This project is not an attempt to cover all things radical about the 1970s in the United States, but rather to emphasize several political phenomena distinctive to the period that have yet to receive significant attention in the historical record. Such a project necessitates creating a certain, if provisional, political cartography, mapping as it does diverse streams of grassroots organizing. Therefore, to aid readers in following these varied histories, a listing of acronyms of the organizations described in this book appears preceding the introduction.

The articles in Part One chronicle those who saw the 1970s as a time of moving rapidly toward revolution. Trying to expose fundamental power imbalances in the United States, some prepared for battle. This insurgency emanated, in the words of the prison rebels at Attica, from "the fury of those who are oppressed."[50] Throughout the 1970s, this fury could be heard resounding from behind prison walls, where, Liz Samuels describes (chapter 1), prisoners and others began organizing to abolish confinement. This movement was a rare venue in which radical black nationalists and white pacifists converged around a shared set of demands. Insurgency could be found in the growing number of black and Native American militants who turned toward land reclamation as a political strategy (Dan Berger with Roxanne Dunbar-Ortiz, chapter 3; Scott Rutherford, chapter 4), as well as the campaigns in defense of women of color who had killed the men who sexually assaulted them or tried to (Victoria Law, chapter 2).

There were varied sources and strategies for making revolutionary change possible. The essays in Part Two emphasize the radical organizing that saw solidarity as the linchpin for political advancement. Solidarity was multivalent: it was global, and global organizing was one arena in which activism often grew rather than receded over the course of the 1970s. Roxanne Dunbar-Ortiz describes (chapter 6) how indigenous people used the United Nations to advance sovereignty claims. In chapter 7, Meg Starr studies the Puerto Rican independence movement as one of the most dynamic projects of that era, combining insurgency, internationalism, and community organizing in the service of decolonization. Consciously diasporic activism could be found elsewhere in this period. By examining the 1974 Sixth Pan-African Congress, its organizing and its results, Fanon Che Wilkins (chapter 5) uncovers the debates percolating among black radicals in the post–civil rights era, when Africa was a privileged ideal but a complicated reality. The politics of solidarity manifested in the fusion of global struggles with grassroots organizing. Out of this space came groups such as the Sojourner Truth Organization (Michael Staudenmaier, chapter 8), a mostly white organization which, from 1969 through the early 1980s, attempted to organize workers outside of unions and in solidarity with national liberation struggles.

The book concludes with several case studies describing those who tried to fashion new political forms out of community bonds. Ever an elusive and elastic term, community was found in localism, in shared identities, and often in a combination of the two. Brian Behnken (chapter 10) describes how Chicano activists tried to build community power in fighting police brutality in Texas, and James Tracy (chapter 11) chronicles the hidden history of radical organizing in urban, white, working-class communities wrought by deindustrialization and an ethnic revival that often resorted to open white supremacy. Community was a place and a practice, an ideal and a reality, for many in the politicized counterculture. Militant atheists, radical Quakers, devout Catholics, and others joined forces in all-out assault on the mechanisms of war, racial oppression, and environmental devastation. Their efforts, as Andrew Cornell shows in his study of Movement for a New Society (chapter 12) and Matt Meyer and Paul Magno argue in their examination of the white pacifist underground (chapter 13), positioned community as the oppositional antidote to capitalism and militarism. While these projects were often small in scale, the value assigned to community and its often implicit attributes—sustainability, democracy, cohesion—continue to exert powerful influence in the political imagination since that time, and thus they have had an impact beyond their size. Despite its connotative attachment to tradition, community in its 1970s variants was also the hallmark of attempts to craft a new brand of politics. It was the synonym for the most wild experimentation, bridging cultural expression with newly politicized populations and newly politicized practices, as Benjamin Shepard argues in his study of the "queer politics of play" (chapter 9). Finally, because many 1970s activists continue to work for social justice, the book closes with Elizabeth Castle's biographical article about the enduring political life of Madonna Thunder Hawk (chapter 14).

Insurgency. Solidarity. Community. These were the beacons followed by the 1970s Left, and they shape the structure of this book. As with any categorization, this one should not be mistaken for firm boundaries in viewing either the book or the projects covered herein. Even the category of "the Left" was up for grabs in the 1970s, as it was later. Many of these projects and experiments openly sought to reinvigorate or redefine what constituted radicalism. Numerous activists and groups moved among various practices of insurgency, solidarity, and community. Many tried to combine them in the search for an effective and sustaining political practice. Whether veteran activists of the rapidly changing world of the 1960s or political neophytes coming of age in the often confusing 1970s, many of the activists examined here explored these three poles as they tried to change the world while the world changed.

ACKNOWLEDGMENTS

Thanks to Daniel Burton-Rose, Felicia Kornbluh, Rob McBride, Dylan Rodríguez, Suzy Subways, and Natasha Zaretsky for their comments on earlier drafts.

NOTES

1. Former members of the Weather Underground have also revisited the group through a string of memoirs, books, and articles. These recollections differ widely in their assessment of the group. See, for instance, Bill Ayers, *Fugitive Days: Memoir of an Antiwar Activist* (Boston: Beacon Press, 2008); Bill Ayers, Bernardine Dohrn, and Jeff Jones, *Sing a Battle Song: The Revolutionary Poetry, Statements, and Communiqués of the Weather Underground, 1970–1974* (New York: Seven Stories Press, 2006); Howie Machtinger, "You Say You Want a Revolution," *In These Times* online edition, February 18, 2009, available at http://www.inthesetimes.com/article/4251/you_say_you_want_a_revolution/ (accessed April 12, 2009); Jonah Raskin, "Looking Backward: Reflections on Language, Gesture and Mythology in the Weather Underground," *Socialism and Democracy* 20: 2 (July 2006): 121–135; Mark Rudd, *Underground: My Life with SDS and the Weathermen* (New York: William Morrow, 2009); and Cathy Wilkerson, *Flying Close to the Sun: My Life and Times as a Weatherman* (New York: Seven Stories Press, 2007). This climate has also led to the republication of one of the early memoirs. See Susan Stern, *With the Weathermen: The Personal Journal of a Revolutionary Woman*, edited by Laura Browder (New Brunswick, NJ: Rutgers University Press, 2007).

2. Dan Berger, "Rescuing Civil Rights from Black Power: Collective Memory and Saving the State in Twenty-first Century Prosecutions of 1960s-Era Cases," *Journal for the Study of Radicalism* 3: 1 (2009): 1–27. This contemporary prosecution of former Black Panthers and other militant activists of that time period coincides, perhaps deliberately, with the prosecution of former Klansmen charged with murders of civil rights activists in the 1950s and early 1960s. Some left-wing radicals imprisoned since that era have also been paroled from prison in recent years.

3. Burton I. Kaufman and Scott Kaufman, *The Presidency of James Earl Carter, Jr.* (Lawrence: University Press of Kansas, 2006).

4. Bruce J. Schulman and Julian E. Zelizer, "Introduction," in *Rightward Bound: Making America Conservative in the 1970s*, ed. Schulman and Zelizer (Cambridge, MA: Harvard University Press, 2008), 2.

5. The literature on Richard Nixon is vast and growing. For one examination of his contradictory presidency, see James T. Patterson, *Grand Expectations: The United States, 1945–1974* (New York: Oxford University Press, 1996), 710–742. Rick Perlstein's massive book is, he says, not about Richard Nixon as much as it is about the political polarization he nurtured, but the book remains an excellent source on Nixon's campaigns and political life. See Rick Perlstein, *Nixonland: The Rise of a President and the Fracturing of America* (New York: Scribner, 2008).

6. Cf. Edward D. Berkowitz, *Something Happened: A Political and Cultural Overview of the Seventies* (New York: Columbia University Press, 2006); James T. Patterson, *Restless Giant: The United States from Watergate to Bush v. Gore* (New York: Oxford University Press, 2005); Schulman and Zelizer, eds., *Rightward Bound*; and Bruce J. Schulman, *The Seventies: The Great Shift in American Culture, Society, and Politics* (New York: De Capo Press, 2001).

7. Natasha Zaretsky, *No Direction Home: The American Family and the Fear of National Decline, 1968–1980* (Chapel Hill: University of North Carolina Press, 2007), 120.

8. David Cunningham, *There's Something Happening Here: The New Left, the Klan, and FBI Counterintelligence* (Berkeley: University of California Press, 2004), 198. The text of Reagan's pardon is available online: http://www.reagan.utexas.edu/archives/speeches/1981/41581d.htm (accessed July 12, 2009). The pardon was made on April 15, 1981.

9. Many of these cultural shifts are described in greater detail in Andreas Killen, *1973 Nervous Breakdown: Watergate, Warhol, and the Birth of Post-Sixties America* (New York: Bloomsbury, 2006), and Schulman, *The Seventies*.

10. The United States continued to be involved in Vietnam's political and economic affairs after withdrawing troops in 1975, and the war was a salient point of contention within American domestic political culture. For one accounting of the war after the war, see Edwin A. Martini, *Invisible Enemies: The American War on Vietnam, 1975–2000* (Amherst: University of Massachusetts Press, 2007).

11. Killen, *1973*, 7–8; and Beth Bailey and David Farber, "Introduction," in *America in the Seventies*, ed. Bailey and Farber (Lawrence: University Press of Kansas, 2004), 2.

12. Schulman and Zelizer, "Introduction"; and Patterson, *Restless Giant*, 13–44.

13. Cf. Philip Jenkins, *Decade of Nightmares: The End of the Sixties and the Making of Eighties America* (Oxford: Oxford University Press, 2006); Stephen Paul Miller, *The Seventies Now: Culture as Surveillance* (Durham, NC: Duke University Press, 1999); Lester D. Friedman, ed., *American Cinema in the 1970s: Themes and Variations* (New Brunswick, NJ: Rutgers University Press, 2007); and Schulman, *The Seventies*.

14. Gil Scott-Heron, *Now and Then: The Poems of Gil Scott-Heron* (New York: Canongate, 2000), 62–63; Peter N. Carroll, *It Seemed Like Nothing Happened: The Tragedy and Promise of America in the 1970s* (1982; rpt. New Brunswick, NJ: Rutgers University Press, 2000).

15. Patterson, *Restless Giant*, 77.

16. The literature here is particularly vast. For a good overview of this approach, see Jeremy Varon, Michael S. Foley, and John McMillian, "Time is an Ocean: the Past and Future of the Sixties," *The Sixties: A Journal of History, Politics and Culture* 1: 1 (2008), 1.

17. There are many monographs to point to, including my own book on the Weather Underground. For overviews, see Van Gosse and Richard Moser, eds., *The World the 60s Made: Politics and Culture in Recent America* (Philadelphia: Temple University Press, 2003); Peniel E. Joseph, ed., *The Black Power Movement: Rethinking the Civil Rights–Black Power Era* (New York: Routledge, 2006); Andrés Torres and José E. Velázquez, eds., *The Puerto Rican Movement: Voices from the Diaspora* (Philadelphia: Temple University Press, 1998). In terms of memoirs, see, for examples, Roxanne Dunbar-Ortiz, *Outlaw Woman: A Memoir of the War Years, 1960–1975* (San Francisco: City Lights Books, 2001); Miguel "Mickey" Melendez, *We Took the Streets: Fighting for Latino Rights with the Young Lords* (New York: St. Martin's Press, 2003); and Diana Block, *Arm the Spirit: A Woman's Journey Underground and Back* (Oakland, CA: AK Press, 2009).

18. Ruth Rosen, *The World Split Open: How the Modern Women's Movement Changed America* (New York: Penguin Books, 2000), 195.

19. Besides Rosen, see Cherríe Moraga and Gloria Anzaldúa, eds., *This Bridge Called My Back: Writings by Radical Women of Color* (New York: Kitchen Table Press, 1981); Kimberly Springer, *Living for the Revolution: Black Feminist Organizations, 1968–1980* (Durham, NC: Duke University Press, 2005); and Becky Thompson, *A Promise and a Way of Life: White Antiracist Activism* (Minneapolis: University of Minnesota Press, 2001), 113–227. For the leading roles women of color played in second-wave feminism, see, for instance, Nancy MacLean, *Freedom Is Not Enough: The Opening of the American Workplace* (Cambridge, MA: Harvard University Press, 2006), 117–154. I thank Natasha Zaretsky for bringing this point and source to my attention.

20. For overviews of these political polarities, see Max Elbaum, *Revolution in the Air: Sixties Radicals Turn to Lenin, Mao, and Che* (New York: Verso, 2002); and Dan Berger, *Outlaws of America: The Weather Underground and the Politics of Solidarity* (Oakland, CA: AK Press, 2006).

21. Christopher Lasch, *The Culture of Narcissism: American Life in an Age of Diminishing Expectations* (New York: W. W. Norton, 1978); and Tom Wolfe, "The 'Me' Decade and the Third Great Awakening." The essay was originally published in *New York* magazine in August

1976; it was reprinted in Wolfe's book *The Purple Decades* (New York: Farrar, Strauss and Giroux, 1983), 265–296. For contemporary journalistic and scholarly accounts, see David Frum, *How We Got Here: The 70s, the Decade that Brought You Modern Life (for Better or Worse)* (New York: Basic Books, 2000); and Zaretsky, *No Direction Home,* 183–221.

22. For Rubin's transformation, see his memoir *Growing (Up) at 37* (New York: M. Evans & Co., 1976). For Dylan's, see Howard Sounes, *Down the Highway: The Life of Bob Dylan* (New York: Grove, 2001), 323–327. For the growth of born-again Christianity, see Paul Boyer, "The Evangelical Resurgence in 1970s American Protestantism" in *Rightward Bound,* ed. Schulman and Zelizer, 29–51.

23. Quoted in Jefferson Cowie, "'Vigorously Left, Right, and Center': The Crosscurrents of Working-Class America in the 1970s," in *America in the Seventies,* ed. Bailey and Farber, 76–77. For the controversy over Dylan among counterculture musicians, journalists, and activists in the 1970s, see Peter Doggett, *There's a Riot Going On: Revolutionaries, Rock Stars, and the Rise and Fall of the '60s* (Edinburgh: Canongate, 2007) 459–463.

24. Zaretsky, *No Direction Home.*

25. Henry Kissinger, *The White House Years* (Boston: Little, Brown, 1979). See also Jeremi Suri, *Henry Kissinger and the American Century* (Cambridge, MA: Harvard University Press, 2007).

26. Berkowitz, *Something Happened,* 104–132; and Patterson, *Restless Giant,* 108–151.

27. Stephanie Slocum-Schaffer, *America in the 1970s* (Syracuse: Syracuse University Press, 2003).

28. Quoted in Cowie, "'Vigorously Left, Right, and Center,'" 76.

29. Thomas Byrne Edsall with Mary D. Edsall, *Chain Reaction: The Impact of Race, Rights and Taxes on American Politics* (New York: W. W. Norton, 1991); Lisa McGirr, *Suburban Warriors: The Origins of the New American Right* (Princeton, NJ: Princeton University Press, 2001); and Perlstein, *Nixonland.*

30. Cf. Jeremi Suri, "Détente and its Discontents," in *Rightward Bound,* ed. Schulman and Zelizer, 227–245; and Sean Wilentz, *The Age of Reagan: A History, 1974–2008* (New York: HarperCollins, 2008).

31. David Harvey, *A Brief History of Neoliberalism* (Oxford: Oxford University Press, 2005). This shift, however, actually bolstered the state in the form of rising military and law enforcement budgets. See Ruth Wilson Gilmore, "Globalization and U.S. Prison Growth: From Military-Keynesianism to Post-Keynesian Militarism," *Race and Class* 40: 2–3 (October 1998–March 1999): 171–187; and, more generally, Ruth Wilson Gilmore, *Golden Gulag: Prisons, Crisis, Surplus, and Opposition in Globalizing California* (Berkeley: University of California Press, 2007); and Marie Gottschalk, *The Prison and the Gallows: The Politics of Mass Incarceration in America* (Cambridge: Cambridge University Press, 2006).

32. Joseph A. McCartin, "'Fire the Hell Out of Them': Sanitation Workers' Struggles and the Normalization of the Striker Replacement Strategy in the 1970s," *Labor: Studies in the Working Class History of the Americas* 2: 3 (2005): 67–92; Joseph A. McCartin, "'A Wagner Act for Public Workers': Labor's Deferred Dream and the Rise of Conservatism, 1970–1976," *Journal of American History* 95: 1 (2008): 123–148.

33. For Ford's neoliberalism, see Patterson, *Restless Giant,* 96–98; and, more generally, John Robert Greene, *The Presidency of Gerald R. Ford* (Lawrence: University Press of Kansas, 1995). For Carter, see Joseph A. McCartin, "Turnabout Years: Public Sector Unionism and the Fiscal Crisis," in *Rightward Bound,* ed. Schulman and Zelizer, 210–226. For Reagan and the PATCO strike, see Paul L. Butterworth, James T. Schultz, and Marian C. Schultz, "More than a Labor Dispute: The PATCO Strike of 1981," *Essays in Economic and Business History* 23 (2005): 125–139.

34. Perlstein, *Nixonland*, 541–748.

35. Thomas J. Sugrue and John D. Skrentny, "The White Ethnic Strategy," in *Rightward Bound*, ed. Schulman and Zelizer, 171–192; Matthew Frye Jacobson, *Roots Too: White Ethnic Revival in Post-Civil Rights America* (Cambridge, MA: Harvard University Press, 2006); and John D. Skrentny, *The Minority Rights Revolution* (Cambridge, MA: Harvard University Press, 2002).

36. Eric Porter, "Affirming and Disaffirming Actions: Remaking Race in the 1970s," in *America in the Seventies*, ed. Bailey and Farber, 50–74.

37. Rebecca Moore, Anthony B. Pinn, and Mary R. Sawyer, *Peoples Temple and Black Religion in America* (Bloomington: Indiana University Press, 2004); Tim Reiterman and John Jacobs, *Raven: The Untold Story of Rev. Jim Jones and His People* (New York: Dutton, 1982).

38. Hal Lindsey and Carole Carlson, *The Late Great Planet Earth* (1970; rpt. Grand Rapids, MI: Zondervan, 1998); Lasch, *The Culture of Narcissism*; Daniel Bell, *The Coming of Post-Industrial Society: A Venture in Social Forecasting* (New York: Basic Books, 1976); and Richard Sennett, *The Fall of Public Man* (New York: Alfred A. Knopf, 1976).

39. For accounts of its usage in the early 1900s, see Louis Adamic, *Dynamite: The Story of Class Violence in America* (1934; rpt. Oakland, CA: AK Press, 2008); Mike Davis, *Buda's Wagon: A Brief History of the Car Bomb* (New York: Verso, 2007).

40. William Graebner, *Patty's Got a Gun: Patricia Hearst in 1970s America* (Chicago: University of Chicago Press, 2008). The SLA spectacle produced a myriad of books at the time but has yet to be revisited by scholars in a major way. The SLA has, however, been the subject of an opera and a documentary film. Graebner's book sees the Hearst trial as indicative of the cultural shifts of the 1970s, although his book does not offer new information in describing the SLA or its activities. Among the most significant of the accounts that appeared at the time, see John Bryan, *This Soldier Still at War* (New York: Harcourt Brace Jovanovich, 1975); and Les Payne and Tim Findley, with Carolyn Craven, *The Life and Death of the SLA* (New York: Ballantine Books, 1976).

41. The Morales and Shakur escapes were high-profile prison breaks. Morales was the first person arrested as part of the FALN and was found after a bomb he was said to have been making exploded in his hands. He lost almost all of his fingers but escaped out a third-floor window in Bellevue Hospital. Shakur was arrested on the New Jersey Turnpike in 1973, following a shootout with state troopers that wounded her and killed one trooper and former Black Panther Zayd Shakur. Prosecutors described her as the "soul of the BLA." She escaped from Clinton Correctional Facility for Women in New Jersey. Despite their prominence, they were not the first revolutionaries to attempt or to achieve an escape from prison in the 1970s. Several other alleged BLA members made similar attempts throughout the decade. In Seattle, the George Jackson Brigade freed one of its members, John Sherman, as police took him to a hospital visit in 1976. See Daniel Burton-Rose, *Guerilla USA: The George Jackson Brigade and the Anticapitalist Underground of the 1970s* (Berkeley: University of California Press, 2010); Akinyele Umoja, "Repression Breeds Resistance: The Black Liberation Army and the Radical Legacy of the Black Panther Party," in *Liberation, Imagination and the Black Panther Party: A New Look at the Panthers and Their Legacy*, ed. Kathleen Cleaver and George Katsiaficas (New York: Routledge, 2001), 3–19; and Jan Susler, "Unreconstructed Revolutionaries," in *The Puerto Rican Movement*, ed. Torres and Velázquez, 144–152.

42. Van Gosse, "Postmodern America: A New Democratic Order in the Second Gilded Age," in *The World the 60s Made*, ed. Gosse and Moser, 1–36. David Harvey sees the 1970s as defined by the rise of postmodernism, aided by the 1973 end of Fordist economic production and increasing globalization. See David Harvey, *The Condition of Postmodernity* (Cambridge: Blackwell, 1990).

43. See Shola Lynch, director, *Chisholm '72: Unbought & Unbossed* (New York, NY: Realside Productions, 2004).

44. INCITE! Women of Color Against Violence, ed., *The Revolution Will Not Be Funded: Beyond the Non-Profit Industrial Complex* (Cambridge, MA: South End Press, 2006).

45. Prison Research Education Action Project, *Instead of Prisons* (Syracuse: PREAP, 1976). Critical Resistance republished the book in 2005.

46. Cf. Notes from Nowhere, ed., *We Are Everywhere: The Irresistible Rise of Global Anti-Capitalism* (London: Verso, 2003); and Eddie Yuen, Daniel Burton-Rose, and George Katsiaficas, eds., *Confronting Capitalism: Dispatches from a Global Movement* (New York: Soft Skull, 2004).

47. Ben Dangl, *The Price of Fire: Resource Wars and Social Movements in Bolivia* (Oakland, CA: AK Press, 2007); and Jan Rus, Rosalva Aída Hernández Castillo, and Shannon L. Mattiace, eds., *Mayan Lives, Mayan Utopias: The Indigenous Peoples of Chiapas and the Zapatista Movement* (Lanham, MD: Rowman & Littlefield, 2003).

48. For more on poor people's movements historically and theoretically, see Frances Fox Piven and Richard Cloward, *Poor People's Movements: Why They Succeed, How They Fail* (New York: Pantheon, 1977); Felicia Kornbluh, *The Battle for Welfare Rights: Politics and Poverty in Modern America* (Philadelphia: University of Pennsylvania Press, 2007); Annelise Orleck, *Storming Caesar's Palace: How Black Mothers Fought Their Own War on Poverty* (Boston: Beacon, 2005); and Michael K. Honey, *Going Down Jericho Road* (New York: W. W. Norton, 2007). Contemporary organizations and coalitions that describe themselves as attempting to use a similar model include the Coalition of Immokalee Workers, the Media Mobilizing Project, the Poor People's Economic Human Rights Campaign, and the Poverty Initiative at Union Theological Seminary. The Association of Community Organizations for Reform Now (ACORN) was an outgrowth of the National Welfare Rights Organization. The Right to the City Alliance also builds on the model of poor people's movement, even as it differs in some respects.

49. For an earlier critical discussion of the declension narrative, see Gosse, "Postmodern America: A New Democratic Order in the Second Gilded Age," in *The World the 60s Made*, ed. Gosse and Moser, 1–36.

50. Quoted in Tom Wicker, *A Time to Die* (New York: Ballantine Books, 1975), 35.

PART ONE

Insurgency

1

Improvising on Reality

The Roots of Prison Abolition

LIZ SAMUELS

> Improvising on reality is the key principle underlying the building of a united
> left and raising the consciousness of the people. It will give us our tactics.
>
> –George Jackson, *Blood in My Eye*, 1972

The five-day seizure of Attica Correctional Facility in 1971 by prisoners held there was pivotal for the development of what can be called prison abolitionist praxis. This political approach, at once an analysis and a strategy, held that "prison reform" was not just insufficient, but also counterproductive. It sought instead to remove entirely the system of imprisonment and policing through a revolutionary transformation that would render such institutions unnecessary. As the rebels at Attica made clear, abolition involved both direct confrontation with the prison system and building alternative practices to replace confinement and solve the social problems that the criminal justice system could not.

The "Attica rebellion," as it was known, also marked the beginning of the end of the revolutionary prisoners' movement—at least as an item of national attention. Over the previous decade, prisoners had become politicized alongside and as a part of radical movements of the time. By 1970 many prisoners across the country publicly identified themselves as revolutionaries organizing and fighting for prisoners' rights, often leading to confrontations with prison officials. Prisoners took control of Attica on September 9, 1971, after a year of rising tensions with the prison administration, led by newly forged alliances among Black Panther, Young Lord, Black Muslim, and white radical prisoners. Members of these groups and unaffiliated prisoners organized water and blankets for people in the yard as well as a negotiation team composed of two representatives from each cellblock. The Attica Brothers, as they came to be called, wanted improved conditions and rehabilitation programs, political and religious freedom, freedom from physical harm, and, in their initial demands, "speedy and safe transportation out of confinement, to a non-imperialistic country."[1] Negotiations began after the group of observers requested by the prisoners arrived at Attica on the night of September 10. By the morning of September 13, the negotiation team and New York State commissioner of corrections, Russell Oswald, had not reached resolution; Governor Nelson A. Rockefeller ordered the state police to flood the yard. Within five minutes, police had shot and killed twenty-nine prisoners and ten of the forty-three guard/hostages.[2]

News of the events at Attica saturated newspapers, television, and the alternative press for months. It was the focus of conversation among prisoners, leftist organizations, and national prison staff and administrators. Mainstream media broadcast the Attica standoff and subsequent police violence, which inspired, radicalized, startled, and infuriated people across the country. Prisoner newspapers buzzed with information about the uprising, connecting the events in upstate New York with struggles in their own prisons. Attica was every prison, and every prison was Attica; as the Attica Defense Committee put it, "Attica is all of us," and "Attica means fight back."[3] The prisoner organizing at Attica demonstrated the possibilities for a unified prison movement—specifically, prisoners' ability to self-organize and develop a social and political infrastructure—just as the subsequent state violence illustrated its risks in the context of America's growing dependence on prisons as a means of addressing problems in U.S. society. Organizing with people imprisoned at nearby Walpole State Prison, the Families and Friends of Prisoners Collective of Dorchester, Massachusetts, described prisons as a microcosm of power and oppression in the United States. Prison activists nationwide increasingly shared this analysis. The Dorchester collective wrote in its newsletter, "Walpole does not stand alone as a symbol of the institutionalized inhumanity of this country. Walpole is Attica is Angola is McAllister is Lewisburg is San Quentin is Deer Island and Charles St. All are pits of degradation and despair and all of their shame reflects on us."[4]

The violence prisoners experienced at Attica catalyzed similar actions. Despite persistent animosities, prisoners forged alliances. There were long work strikes at Alderson Federal Women's Prison in North Carolina, as well as in Vermont, Indiana, and California prisons.[5] Many of the actions organized in solidarity with the prisoners of Attica were led by multiracial coalitions that endeavored to erase racial divisions among prisoners by forming a united prisoner class consciousness. The organizational and ideological groundwork laid by Black Muslims, Black Panthers, and anticolonial and anti-imperialist prisoners throughout the preceding decade helped create the logistical coordination and political solidarity seen among prisoners in the immediate aftermath of Attica. Before the Attica uprising, a widespread prisoners' movement had pushed for reforms, but garnered minimal change. Having experienced the disappointment of reform, many activists on both sides of the walls were pushed by the repression at Attica and at other prisons to believe that only a complete overhaul—abolition—of American imprisonment would suffice. Abolitionist organizers in and outside of prisons shared a political analysis and praxis that rejected imprisonment, addressed interpersonal and community harm, and identified social problems as rooted in poverty, racism, and structural and interpersonal violence. A handful of sympathetic judges and prison officials aided some of these organizing efforts. Despite the strong foundation built by the prisoners' movement in general and the abolitionist movement in particular, both were in general decline by the late 1970s due to the mounting toll of repression, the decline of other social movements outside of prison, and an expanding acceptance of "law and order" approaches to imprisonment and surveillance. While the politics of law and order spurred massive prison expansion in the late 1970s and early 1980s, the foundation laid by abolitionist activists in and outside of prison continued to inform abolitionist organizing in the late twentieth and early twenty-first centuries.

Ideological Beginnings

Black Muslims were the earliest, and arguably most important, organizers for prisoners' rights in the 1960s. Black Muslims, including the Nation of Islam (NOI), spread an analysis of racism in the United States that linked the struggles of black people to the history of European colonialism and created strong black groupings that changed race relations within prison. This shift facilitated a mental shift for many black prisoners from individual to collective thinking.[6] The Black Muslims led struggles that went beyond asking for prison "improvements" to assert rights and freedoms for prisoners as a group. Drawing from the example set by the early civil rights movement, Black Muslims sought redress from the courts. From 1961 to 1978, there were sixty-six reported federal court decisions pertaining to religious and racial freedoms sought by Black Muslims in prison. Prior to this, the courts had rarely adjudicated issues surrounding prison conditions and the treatment of prisoners.[7] The litigation outside accompanied prisoners' political education inside. This organizing laid the groundwork for the development of prisoners' unions, study groups, councils, self-improvement groups, newspapers, revolutionary organizations, and national networks to fight for prisoners' political self-determination in the 1970s.[8]

Black Muslims helped create the space for a wide range of revolutionary literature and organizers to influence prisoner consciousness. The overlap of individuals and ideas from multiple movements fostered relationships and organizing within prisons and to some degree also brought these organizations together on the outside.[9] This cross-fertilization spread the idea, at least within the Left, that prisons were, in the words of former Black Panther Ashanti Alston, "an instrument of repression, part of a larger [repressive] society that was a capitalist society."[10] Imprisoned radicals brought with them their radical ideologies, which they shared in study groups and educational programs that taught cultural history and revolutionary theory from the writings of people such as Malcolm X, Karl Marx,

Che Guevara, Frantz Fanon, and Mao Zedong. Inmates for Action in Alabama, for example, established survival and political education programs in the mid-1970s that met every day of the week, covering topics such as black history and "Revolutionary theory and the truth of capitalism and its ill effects."[11]

Many individuals who had gone to prison for what the Left termed "social crimes" (i.e., street crime) were transformed by ideas introduced to them by literature sent in or given to them inside. A California prisoner named George Jackson became the most well known and influential prisoner-turned-revolutionary. In prison for armed robbery of seventy dollars from a gas station, Jackson became politicized and, ultimately, a field marshal of the Black Panther Party. Through him, Panther chapters sprung up throughout the California prison system. In his best-selling book, *Soledad Brother: The Prison Letters of George Jackson*, he articulated how black people were systematically oppressed and exploited in the United States, identifying a direct connection between imprisonment and anti-black racism.[12] This pernicious connection, as Jackson proclaimed in his posthumously published manifesto, *Blood in My Eye*, made prisoners "a mighty reservoir of revolutionary potential."[13] While Jackson became a cause célèbre, he was also training cadre within prison in a range of revolutionary theories and fighting techniques.[14] Jackson's growing popularity and the increasing number of leftists being incarcerated helped put prisoners at the center of the radical Left's agenda in the early 1970s. Prisoner activism built on the presence of militant organizations on the streets, especially among communities of color. Ralph Hamm, a leader in the National Prisoners Reform Association (NPRA) at MCI Walpole, described NPRA's program as "rooted within the Black Consciousness Movement of the time."[15] As with the Black Panthers, the work of the American Indian Movement, Brown Berets, Young Lords, and militant unionism contributed to widespread interest in and from radical prisoners.

Even more than revolutionaries outside of prison, organizers within prison faced violent repression. Radical prisoners, particularly radicals of color, endured additional physical and mental abuse, such as beatings and extended solitary confinement. After acts of resistance, including sit-ins and work strikes, participants were usually physically reprimanded.[16] Prisoners identified as leaders or political agitators were frequently kept in isolation or transferred to different cellblocks and between prisons.[17] In an attempt to squelch radical organizing of any kind, especially among black prisoners, prison officials also took away privileges, censored the mail, and banned books sent to prisoners identified as activists.[18]

Organizing

One of the ways prisoners tried to withstand prison administrators' repression was by forging a culture of solidarity. The main obstacle to building it was racial tension. Following World War II, the racial composition of prisons began to change from majority white to disproportionately black; yet in many places, prisons remained racially segregated until the 1960s.[19] While the Black Muslims and others challenged racial segregation, institutional integration did not address the pervasive racism among white prisoners, prison guards, and administrators. Prison administrators used racial divides to their advantage by favoring and privileging white prisoners over prisoners of color in order to maintain control, such that racial tensions at prisons often resulted in violent confrontations between prisoners.[20]

By the later 1960s, prisoners influenced by the ideologies of growing Third World movements in the United States and abroad asserted that prisoners constituted a separate political and economic class with common interests. Organizers tried to forge bonds among prisoners to build what they described as a united front that could engage in a common class struggle as an imprisoned class of people "subjected to [a] continuous cycle of poverty, prison, parole, and more poverty."[21] Organizations like the United Prisoners' Union, formed in 1970, sought to organize prisoners as a convicted class to break this cycle. A class-based approach did not define all of the growing prison movement, which was heavily shaped by racial nationalism, but there was a growing recognition that divisions among prisoners hampered organizing to effect change. Racial conflicts, such as a 1967 clash at San Quentin, began to be resolved through truces between white and black leaders and stated commitments to work together for unified goals.[22] At Walpole State Prison in Massachusetts, white prisoner Bobby Dellelo gained an "understanding that reform is impossible without racial equity" and if "Black prisoners were left behind, soon all prisoners would be right back with them."[23] Politicized prisoners argued that racial unity terrified prison officials—for, as Lorenzo Komboa Ervin, a Black Panther imprisoned at Terre Haute prison in Indiana, argued, "all prison officials know that if racism is surmounted, revolt is inevitable." Ervin considered the relationships between white radicals and black revolutionaries essential in dismantling the Klan's influence at Terre Haute.[24]

Imprisoned organizers increasingly called for (and often achieved) unity, which allowed them to organize successful strikes and protests surrounding specific demands. The uprisings at San Quentin in 1968 and at the Long Island branch of the Queens House of Detention in October 1970, and the work stoppages at Soledad, Folsom, and San Luis Obispo prisons in California in November of 1971, were organized by multiracial coalitions that attempted to breach racial divisions among prisoners with a united, cross-race, prisoner class consciousness. Heightened politicization of prisoners, support from outside organizations, and growing rejection of reform contributed to increasing organized prisoner resistance in the form of work strikes, sit-ins, and prison takeovers. Prison uprisings increased from five in 1967 to fifteen in 1968, thirty-seven in 1970, thirty-seven in 1971, and forty-eight in 1972, the most in any year of U.S. history.[25]

Prisoners across the country used work strikes to win gains in pay, improved conditions, and collective bargaining rights, as well as to express solidarity with other actions or events happening domestically and internationally. Perhaps as crucial, prisoner strikes aimed to garner visibility for prisoners as an oppressed but organized class. Between 1965 and 1975, prisoners went on strike in more than a dozen states, including Arizona, Ohio, Nebraska, Indiana, New Jersey, and Oklahoma.[26] Work strikes at women's prisons, such as the spring 1971 work strike at the California Institution for Women, Frontera, responded not only to labor practices but also to room and body searches.[27] Labor-centered organizing highlighted the ways the government profited from prisoner labor. By refusing to work, prisoners asserted their power as workers and challenged the perspective that prisoner labor was free and exploitable.[28] Nationwide, working prisoners were paid far below minimum wage, if at all. From the mid-1960s to the mid-1970s, unions were organized in California, Michigan, New York, Ohio, Washington, New England, North Carolina, Minnesota, and Washington.[29] Prisoner labor unions fought for prisoners' rights as workers whose labor was exploited by federal and state governments and unable to be used in and for their own communities. In the words of New Hampshire prisoners: "When prisoners rebel and demand to be treated as human beings; they are not only fighting the inhumane conditions; they are striking out against the state which maintains this situation by which each of us is robbed of the fruits of our labor every day."[30] Some unions utilized confrontational tactics, while others worked within legal and legislative channels. However, they shared a radical analysis of prison labor as central to American capitalism, and thus consistently pushed against the barriers set by prison authorities. NPRA had 80 percent of prisoners sign union cards when they requested recognition as a collective-bargaining unit for prisoners at MCI Walpole by the State Labor Relations committee. In addition to wanting to function as a collective bargaining unit, NPRA had goals to "exercise self-determination within the prison, and to demonstrate that the prison itself was unnecessary."[31] NPRA's organizing culminated in a three-month-long takeover of the prison in 1973, when the prisoners ran the institution after guards refused to work in protest of prisoner radicalism and what they saw as a lenient prison administration.[32]

Beyond Reform

Groups organizing inside and outside of prisons pushed for social programs, improved prison conditions, and a change in policies, such as indeterminate sentencing. Some liberal prison administrators tried to implement reforms as part of the prevailing "rehabilitation" correctional wisdom of the time, such as increased access to educational and technical training and the formation of "Inmate Grievance Councils." By design, these reforms were minor alterations to the existing system and were often used to dampen the fire of more radical critiques.[33] In Massachusetts, for example, reform legislation that sought to reduce the size of the prison system by linking state prisons in a step-wise "behavior modification program" that expanded work and community facilities resulted in significant prison expansion.[34] Former Department of Youth Services director Jerome Miller himself recognized these community corrections facilities as "not so much alternative as additional."[35] Even the granting of prison movement demands bolstered the prison system, as witnessed in the campaign against indeterminate sentencing. The reformers who had conceived of indeterminate sentencing in 1870 had viewed it as a "progressive" way to rehabilitate prisoners. But in practice, it was used to keep individuals imprisoned at the discretion of parole boards.[36] The 1970s prisoners' movement successfully overturned indeterminate sentencing; by the 1980s, however, individuals on the political Right had viewed this policy as too lenient and used its discontinuation as an opportunity to enact more repressive sentencing policies, such as mandatory minimums in the 1980s and three strikes laws in the 1990s.[37]

The combination of the disappointing reality of reform and the rapid radicalization of people inside, facilitated by the steady influx of radicals entering prison on politically motivated charges, led reformers and revolutionaries to start coupling demands for institutional changes with calls to overhaul or eliminate the entire system.[38] A radical analysis of imprisonment spread, identifying prisons as "warehouses of the poor" or weapons of "genocide" meant to oppress individuals and communities rather than promote safety. In this analysis, rather than being broken and in need of repair, U.S. prisons functioned as they were designed: to be tools for maintaining racial and class hierarchies. The United Prisoners Union wrote, "It is a gross political mistake to struggle for minimal reforms, because even when these reforms are granted, the Koncentration Kamps are still there for those who threaten the ruling class."[39] Jerome Miller agreed, characterizing reform as "innovation without threatening the institution's stability"[40] and "new language to cover old realities."[41]

The only solution, then, was to abolish prisons and develop new structures that dealt holistically with the root causes of societal harms. In a letter to one of his supporters, John Clutchette, one of the Soledad Brothers, wrote, "There is but one imperative—overhaul! [Reform] means changing the frame on the wall—but not the picture itself."[42]

It was in this context of a developing radical, prisoner-class consciousness and regional and local prison organizing that the prisoners at Attica occupied D Yard. The violence by New York State Troopers in response to the takeover (and subsequent self-organizing) of the facility by the prisoners at Attica proved to many the necessity of radical change. Calls for abolishing prisons were widespread. They intermingled with other approaches to prison organizing, including individual prisoner defense committees, prison moratorium organizing, legislative efforts, and insurrectionary appeals. Leftist media, such as the KPFA (Pacifica) radio show *Nothing Is More Precious Than*, covered news of prisoner organizing, promoted campaigns to free political prisoners, and circulated communiqués of underground groups such as the Black Liberation Army that challenged the prison system.[43] But even many in the prison movement did not view abolition as viable. It was not until after Attica that organizations explicitly focused on abolition

began to make concrete demands. They created programs that could effectively
abolish prisons by directly addressing the sources of social inequality and interpersonal and systemic violence. From the perspective of Angela Davis, herself a
political prisoner in 1971, "the Attica rebellion marked a moment within the history of this country when people started to take seriously the possibility of abolishing the prison."[44] Not masses of people, however, as the subsequent rise of mass
imprisonment well attests. But to some, Attica and its aftermath raised the specter
that the best prison was no prison at all.

Abolition was predicated on the idea that imprisonment was a means to control, maintain impoverishment among, and exert systemic violence upon, communities of color and poor whites. The demand to abolish prisons, and, more
recently, to abolish the prison industrial complex, emerged as a challenge to white
supremacy, economic inequality, and systemic violence. Activist Bettina Aptheker,
a supporter of the Soledad Brothers and active in the campaign to free Angela
Davis, wrote,

> The issue is not only reform, but also to mount a struggle to abolish the
> present functions and foundations of the prison system, an effort which can
> finally succeed only with the abolition of capitalism. . . . Of course, what
> reforms can be won in day-to-day battle on the legal and political front will
> be important concessions. But the point is to attack the whole foundation—
> all the assumptions—involved in maintaining [the] prison system.[45]

A variety of organizations, individuals, and means were employed to further the
cause of abolition. This included prisoner unions, prisoner support organizations,
revolutionary organizations, pacifists, and even a few judges and prison administrators. The broad politics of abolition provided one of very few places where black
nationalists, proponents of armed self-defense, and primarily white, radical pacifists came together in shared politics and practice. Self-identified abolitionists
considered themselves a part of a "living tradition of movements for social justice"
directly connected to movements to abolish slavery in the nineteenth century.
They saw the present-day terms of imprisonment as a different form of slavery that
was paradoxically enabled by the Thirteenth Amendment, which outlawed slavery
except as punishment for a crime, thereby writing (penal) slavery into law while
seeming to formally abolish it.[46]

Although initially dispersed, a common set of abolitionist ideas, strategies,
and tactics coalesced during the early to mid-1970s. Abolition was based on the
shared belief that social inequalities caused interpersonal violence. In the abolitionist handbook *Instead of Prisons* (1976), the Prison Research Education Action
Project (PREAP), a collective of abolitionist pacifists, defined crime "as a problem
with roots deep in the social structure, not just as a series of problems of individuals. Rather than punishing individual actors, collective response to the root
causes is needed."[47] These root causes, including racism, poverty, sexism, and
homophobia, were produced by society and the state and resulted in an unequal

distribution of power and wealth that benefited only a few.[48] Prisons were used to maintain this imbalance, failing to make the public safer and endangering the communities they targeted.[49] For PREAP, "the only meaningful way to change the prevailing American system of liberty for the free, justice for some, and inequality for all [was] through shifts in the distribution of power."[50]

Inmates for Action (IFA), an Alabama anti-prison prisoner group, and its allied organization on the outside, the Committee for Prisoner Support in Birmingham (CPSB), shared this perspective and connected abolition with the need for social change. Mafundi, a former IFA member who worked with the CPSB, wrote, "without the restructuring of society—its values, morals, priorities, etc.—there could never be a realistic effort to rid the country of crime and criminals."[51] Similarly, New England Prisoners Association members in New Hampshire held a "final and foremost objective to abolish prisons and the system which breeds them."[52] PREAP advocated a three-pronged abolitionist agenda that included "(1) economic and social justice for all, (2) concern for all victims and (3) rather than punishment, reconciliation in a caring community."[53] The handbook attempted to ground this tripartite strategy in concrete, community-based models of social change that connected revolutionary transformation of society to personal transformation of individuals and communities.

Maintaining the belief that imprisonment was "morally reprehensible and indefensible," as well as ineffective in actually promoting safety and the healing of interpersonal harms, abolitionists advocated for "reconciliation, not punishment [a]s a proper response to criminal acts"—what would grow to be called transformative justice. PREAP wrote,

> The present criminal (in)justice systems focus on someone to punish, caring little about the criminal's need or the victim's loss. The abolitionist response seeks to restore both the criminal and the victim to full humanity, to lives of integrity and dignity in the community. Abolitionists advocate the least amount of coercion and intervention in an individual's life and the maximum amount of care and services to all people in society.[54]

This perspective was shared by the American Friends Service Committee (AFSC), a Quaker peace and social justice organization; several members of PREAP were themselves Quakers.[55] While the Quakers had invented the penitentiary system in 1791, they became leaders in prison reform and, later, prison abolition organizing. AFSC ran a Criminal Justice Program that worked on prison reform and advocated for crisis centers and community empowerment as prison alternatives to more fully address the harm that people experienced and endured, as well as to improve living conditions and help people find employment and educational opportunities. They recommended "that a full range of therapy, counseling, and psychiatric and educational services be made available, free, on a voluntary basis, to the entire population, inside prisons and on the street."[56] The project of abolition, then, was just as much creative as it was for the destruction of the existing system

of punishment. Prisoner M. Sharon Smolick defined the task in the prologue to
Instead of Prisons:

> It is not enough to endorse a movement, support an issue or reach out among
> ourselves, inside and outside prisons. As abolitionists we must look to the
> future and examine the long term impact of their present reality. We must be
> creative and inquisitive. We must understand our direction and abolition
> must be that direction because the entire system of punishment has failed.[57]

Abolitionists understood that the development of such a community was a long-
term project, and while they advocated swift and massive change, they took steps
in the short term to build this new society. In its 1971 report on the state of prisons
and the criminal legal system in the United States, AFSC called for investment in
communities through funding for education, jobs, housing, and healthcare, as
well as an immediate moratorium on prison construction and an end to indeterminate sentencing.

> If the choice were between prisons as they now are and no prisons at all, we
> would promptly choose the latter. We are convinced that it would be far
> better to tear down all jails now than to perpetuate the inhumanity and
> horror being carried on in society's name behind prison walls. Prisons as
> they exist are more of a burden and disgrace to our society than they are a
> protection or a solution to the problem of crime.[58]

While urgently resisting the current prison system, abolitionists were strong critics of prison reform as it was then unfolding. Echoing Jackson's claim that reform
only meant greater repression, abolitionists argued that many reforms only
masked the true nature of prisons.[59] Abolitionists sought to expose prisons as
nothing more than the caging of humans, and advocated for "abolitionist reforms"
that took power out of the prison system, empowered communities, and created
opportunities for expanding abolitionist praxis. This praxis meant reducing and
eliminating prisons, most immediately, but it also entailed a broader assault on
the ideologies and institutions that made imprisonment possible. As PREAP
defined it, "Modern reforms attempt to mask the cruelty of caging. Our goals are
not diverted by handsome new facades, the language of 'treatment' and prison
managers who deftly gild the bars. Present reforms will not abolish the cage unless
they continue to move toward constant reduction of the function of prisons."[60]
Alongside avowed abolitionists, other organizations also worked for moratoriums
on prison construction. Abolitionists viewed moratorium as merely a first step,
and combined efforts to halt prison construction with programs that empowered
communities and furthered decarceration and excarceration.[61] Abolition reforms
ranged from expanding community-based services to funding housing and job-
creation programs, to improving prison visitation policies. These initiatives
sought to address the social problems that caused crime and tried to minimize the
isolation that prison imposed. Abolitionists worked to empower their communities

by designing and implementing solutions to problems of sexual violence, such as rape crisis centers, self-defense instruction, and provision of antirape education to people of all ages and genders. Prisoners also organized inside to prevent sexual assault and to empower survivors of sexual violence who were locked up. Prisoners Against Rape in Virginia and Washington, DC, focused on consciousness-raising, political education, and self-help, with the goal of eliminating rape.[62] Men Against Sexism (MAS), a gay prisoners' organization in Washington State Penitentiary in Walla Walla, linked an analysis of sexism, homophobia, and racism to organize against the sexual violence prevalent at the prison. MAS published a newspaper, the *Lady Finger*, provided physical protection for individuals targeted for assault, and fought for gay prisoners' rights.[63]

Decarceration strategies included fighting against indeterminate sentencing and parole, advocating for shorter sentences, and organizing community-restitution programs. Abolitionists advocated methods of excarceration to reduce dependency on prisons. These strategies included decriminalizing drug use and sex work, lowering bail fines, establishing community dispute and mediation centers, facilitating victim-offender reconciliation programs, alternative sentencing policies, and community probation that would be carried out by community organizations instead of "correctional" probation by probation officers.[64] Organizers utilized some prison administrators and government programs to make abolitionist gains. In Massachusetts, Commissioner of Corrections John Boone supported the development of community programs as alternatives to imprisonment and, although inconsistent, helped and supported prisoner- and community-led reforms at Walpole, including the formation of the NPRA.[65]

Abolitionist reforms aimed to transfer power from the courts and prisons to "the people." Organizations outside prisons, like the Ad Hoc Committee on Prison Reform in the Northeast, as well as inside prisons, like NPRA at Walpole, "were opposed to all treatment that was not demanded, developed, and self-selected by the prisoners, recognizing that 'normal' could also mean enforced compliance with societal ideals."[66] Instead, the abolitionist reforms that prisoners designed would improve immediate conditions while contributing to empowerment within their home communities outside of prison. Education was a vital element of this process, understood as a vital step in transformation rather than just a means of self-betterment. At Walpole, NPRA and Black African Nations Towards Unity (BANTU) organized classes in black history; remedial learning programs for reading, writing, and arithmetic; and classes to prepare imprisoned students for college.[67] BANTU organizer Ralph Hamm recalls,

> The Black prisoner population had far-reaching expectations that took from behind the prison walls, having entered as proverbial pariahs; back to our respective communities as educated and contributing members of the Consciousness Movement. We sought meaningful vocational and educational programs to transform us into productive human beings.[68]

Other abolitionist groups, such as Inmates for Action (IFA), The New England Prisoners Association (NEPA), and the Prisoners' Solidarity Committee (PSC), shared similar short-term goals as part of an effort to make prisons obsolete. In addition to better prison conditions, IFA advocated for an expansion of educational and vocational programs, "more humane and expanded visiting privileges," conjugal visits, union representation, and the "abolition of segregation (lock up/solitary confinement) and punitive isolation (hole/doghouse) cells, the termination of prison and jail construction, and the development of community-based treatment centers as alternatives to incarceration."[69]

Founded in Rhode Island, NEPA was a multiracial coalition of prisoners, ex-prisoners, and people outside of prison that initially came together to mobilize a national movement for prison reform. Between early 1973 and late 1974, they started to advocate for abolition. They organized for minimum wages for prison labor, a uniform penal code, and prisoner unions. NEPA also helped released prisoners find employment, edited and distributed a newspaper, *NEPA News*, and coordinated family visits at prisons throughout the Northeast. They wanted to "accomplish, promote, and cause creative, modern, progressive, and non-violent prison reform in the United States [that would]:

1. Abolish prisons as they exist and are used today
2. Replace prisons and imprisonment with an alternative that will work and phase out jails for awaiting trials
3. Deal with problems that are NOW facing prisoners, prisons, and the prison system.[70]

With chapters in a dozen states in the Northeast, Mid-Atlantic, and Midwest, the PSC organized for the abolition of prisons while providing concrete services in the form of legal assistance, transportation for family visits, and help with correspondence. The PSC also published a newspaper by the same name and publicized news in prisons through pamphlets, press releases, and demonstrations. While PSC activists worked for prison reforms, they consistently argued that justice and true change would only come through the abolition of the existing prison system.[71] "There is only one solution," wrote PSC organizer Tom Soto, "and that is to tear the prisons down."[72] That position was repeated by abolitionists across the country, including at the 1972 Prison Action Conference at the University of California, Berkeley, which adopted as its slogan, "Tear Down the Walls."[73]

In addition to these organizing projects, the call for abolition made its way, briefly and sometimes confusingly, into the broader public sphere. Beginning in 1971, Arthur Waskow at the Institute for Policy Studies called for a bicentennial without prisons or jails, a proposal he circulated informally but also published in the *Saturday Review*. Former attorney general Ramsey Clark published a book in 1970 that many journalists and others described as calling for abolition.[74] Yet some were skeptical of both Waskow's and Clark's proposals, seeing their abolitionism as too thin and not thought out. Jessica Mitford, a bestselling investigative reporter and longtime activist, challenged both men in her 1973 prison exposé *Kind and Usual Punishment*. In the book's conclusion, Mitford argued that Waskow and Clark both betrayed the principles of abolition by calling for the confinement of social deviants on enclosed farms—which would not be called prisons but, she argued, would serve the same purpose.[75] Abolition, therefore, was a contested concept, with a sweeping critique that appealed to a wide range of activists, intellectuals, and policy makers in the 1970s. Even when proponents disagreed on the specifics, the 1970s witnessed a widespread rejection of the existing prison system. Several reforms followed the wave of prisoner organizing and riots between 1968 and 1972. However, the Right and not the Left achieved greater success in massively overhauling the prison system—through its expansion rather than its retraction.

Backlash and Decreasing Momentum

Abolition efforts started to crystallize as the prison movement started to decline. In the mid-1970s, there were numerous calls and efforts to develop national organizations and a coordinated strategy to fight for prisoners' rights, prison reform, and prison abolition.[76] By the decade's end, these calls faced limited support. This waning support owed, in part, to a combination of limitations within the prison movement and expanded policing and retributive legislation. Recognizing the decline in the movement's appeal, some prison activists acknowledged that they had romanticized prisoners, failed to build popular support for their politics in a "law and order" climate, and responded to urgent crises rather than developing strategic priorities.[77] Many organizing efforts also depended, in part, on strategic, sympathetic key-holders, such as judges and prison administrators who were sympathetic to prisoners and prisoner advocates. Some of these power brokers made large-scale, if short-lived impacts, such as Jerome Miller, who closed juvenile prisons in Massachusetts in favor of decarceration and improved education because, in his words, "juvenile justice has always been and continues to be neglectful, demeaning, frequently violent, and largely ineffective."[78] With the increasing salience of law-and-order politics, however, there were fewer sympathetic officials like Miller to whom organizers could turn for support.

Law-and-order politics—which produced control units, created maximum-security prisons, and reintroduced the death penalty—made it more difficult for prisoners to organize. Increasingly punitive sentences were adopted, and an expanded drug war sent unprecedented numbers of people to prison. AFSC recognized that abhorrent practices, such as solitary confinement, were adopted "partially or minimally through the efforts of well-intentioned reformers," which led the organization to wonder whether "the changes we recommend turn out to be two-edged swords?"[79] Gains made by the prisoners' movement were often utilized or reinterpreted to expand the breadth and severity of the prison system, create more stringent sentencing policies, and "extend the net of social control" in communities most impacted by imprisonment—mostly poor and black.[80] Even with a certain liberalization of penal policies in the short term, the long-range-policy approach in the wake of prison radicalism was a massive extension of the prison system in American life.

The growth of the prison system was not just a set of policy decisions but a philosophical orientation toward punishment and control.[81] Abolitionist organizing in the mid-1970s had not only identified the limitations of prison reform but also laid the ideological and organizing foundations that abolitionists continued to use in the early twenty-first century. Twenty-nine years after *Instead of Prisons* was first published, the abolitionist organization Critical Resistance reprinted the handbook. Since the book first appeared, the U.S. prison population has grown from more than 200,000 to more than 2 million, with a massive increase in surveillance and policing, both in prison and in society as a whole.[82] Yet, according to Critical Resistance's introduction to the new edition, the fundamentals of abolition elucidated in the 1970s remain relevant to ending the current phenomenon of mass imprisonment. "While the climate in which we fight against imprisonment has certainly changed . . . *Instead of Prisons* is as timely and necessary as ever."[83]

ACKNOWLEDGMENTS

Much thanks and appreciation go to several individuals who provided generous assistance, support, and feedback in the production of this piece. In particular, Dan Berger contributed his own archival research and fabulous editing talent. Thanks also to Rachel Herzing, David Stein, and Geoff McNamara for their help and insight.

NOTES

1. Tom Wicker, *A Time to Die: The Attica Prison Revolt* (1975; rpt. Lincoln: University of Nebraska Press, 1994), 28.
2. For accounts of the Attica uprising, see Brad Lichtenstein, dir., *Ghosts of Attica* (New York: First Run/Icarus Films, 2001); Samuel Melville, *Letters from Attica* (New York: William Morrow, 1972); Wicker, *A Time to Die*. See also Heather Thompson, *Attica!* (New York: Pantheon, forthcoming).
3. See, for instance, Syracuse Attica Coalition, *Attica Is All of Us* (Syracuse, NY: Syracuse Attica Coalition, 1974).
4. Families and Friends of Prisoners Collective, "Introduction," in *Doing Time* (Dorchester, MA: Families and Friends of Prisoners Collective, August 1977). Attica was a common point of reference for prison activists throughout this period. For example, Inmates for Action, a prisoner group in Alabama prisons, called its 1974 update "Alabama's Atticas." *Midnight Special* 3:4 (April 1973): 5.
5. Daniel Burton-Rose, "War Behind Walls: Work Strikes and Prisoner Self-Organization in U.S. Prisons, 1967–76" (Bachelor's thesis, Oberlin College, 1998), 37–38.
6. Harvard Sitkoff, *The Struggle for Black Equality* (New York: Hill and Wang, 1981), 66; Bob Barber and John Pallas, "Riot to Revolution," in *Punishment and Penal Discipline: Essays on the Prison and Prisoners' Movement*, ed. Tony Platt and Paul Takagi (San Francisco: Crime and Social Justice Associates, 1980), 148–150.

7. James B. Jacobs, "The Prisoners' Rights Movement and Its Impacts, 1960–1980," *Crime and Justice* 2 (1980): 433–434.

8. The vast array of political organizing and cultural production to emerge from behind prison walls in the 1970s has yet to be fully documented. For preliminary overviews, see Ronald Berkman, *Opening the Gates: The Rise of the Prisoners' Movement* (Lexington, MA: Lexington Books, 1979), as well as the texts cited in notes 4 and 6 above, and note 13 below.

9. Outside groups came together around specific campaigns to free political prisoners. For example, the National United Committee to Free Angela Davis and All Political Prisoners (NUCFAD), and later the National Alliance Against Racist and Political Repression (NAARPR), included a wide range of Left groups, with members of the Black Panther Party, the Communist Party USA, and liberal sympathetic lawyers. See *Angela Davis: An Autobiography* (New York: International Publishers, 1988 [1974]), 397–398. NUCFAD co-edited the 1971 book *If They Come in the Morning*, which spotlighted dozens of cases then ongoing, including those of Black Panthers, antiwar activists, women of color feminists, and militants from the American Indian, Chicano, and Puerto Rican independence movements. See Angela Davis et al., eds., *If They Come in the Morning: Voices of Resistance* (San Francisco: The Third Press, 1971). The NAARPR files at the Schomburg Center for Research in Black Culture reveal the ongoing movement solidarity the group attempted throughout the 1970s, as it organized to support political prisoners from a range of causes and fought back against repressive legislation.

10. Ashanti Alston, interview with author, tape recording, Brooklyn, New York, January 5, 2004.

11. "Alabama's Atticas," *Midnight Special* 4:6 (August–September 1974): 8.

12. George Jackson, *Soledad Brother: The Prison Letters of George Jackson*, 2nd ed. (New York: Bantam Books, 1972).

13. George Jackson, "Toward the United Front," *Blood in My Eye* (New York: Random House, 1972 and Baltimore: Black Classics Press, 1990), 108.

14. See Jackson's self-description in *Blood in My Eye*. See also Lee Bernstein, "The Age of Jackson: George Jackson and the Culture of American Prisons in the 1970s," *Journal of American Culture* 30:3 (September 2007): 317, and Eric Cummins, *The Rise and Fall of California's Radical Prison Movement* (Stanford, CA: Stanford University Press, 1994), 151–186. The online journal *Proud Flesh: New Afrikan Journal of Culture, Politics, and Consciousness*—the title is taken from a letter by Jackson—shows one way in which Jackson continues to influence academic and activist discourse. See especially issue 5, available at: http://proudfleshjournal.com/issue5/toc5.htm.

15. Jamie Bissonette, *When the Prisoners Ran Walpole: A True Story in the Movement for Prison Abolition* (Cambridge, MA: South End Press, 2008), 129.

16. Cummins, *California's Radical Prison Movement*, 80.

17. Bo Brown, a former political prisoner and member of the George Jackson Brigade, an armed clandestine group in the mid-1970s, was frequently transferred from prison to prison. To limit her, Bo Brown recalled, they "kept me isolated and they moved me every year and a half to two years." Bo Brown, interview with author, tape recording, Oakland, CA, January 19, 2004.

18. The complaint of prison administration repression features prominently in prisoner writings at the time, as well as in the demands of rebelling prisoners, such as those at Folsom in 1970, Attica in 1971, and Marion in 1972. See, for instance, Alan Eladio Gómez, "Resisting Living Death at Marion Federal Penitentiary, 1972," *Radical History Review* 96 (2006): 58–86. Prisoner newsletters frequently spoke of such harassment; see Midnight

Special: Prisoners News, NYU Bobst Tamiment/Wagner Archives Main Collection (HV 6201. m53).

19. James B. Jacobs, "Race Relations and the Prisoner Subculture," *Crime and Justice* 1 (1979): 4–7.

20. Pallas and Barber, "Riot to Revolution," 150; Bernstein, "The Age of Jackson," 317.

21. "History of the U.P.U.," *Anvil* (March–April 1975): 1, Alternative Press Archives. Used with permission.

22. Pallas and Barber, "Riot to Revolution," 150; Cummins, *California's Radical Prison Movement*, 91.

23. Bissonette, *When the Prisoners Ran Walpole*, 28.

24. Lorenzo Komboa Ervin, "Behind the Walls of Prison," in *Race Traitor*, ed. Noel Ignatiev and John Garvey (New York: Routledge, 1996), 62.

25. Bert Useem and Peter Kimball, *States of Siege: U.S. Prison Riots 1971–1986* (Oxford: Oxford University Press, 1991), 18.

26. Arizona State Prison in Florence, 1972; Vermont, Lincoln, NE, October 18, 1971; Nebraska Penal Complex, October 18, 1971 (see *Penal Digest International* 1:5 [October 1971]: 4); Michigan City, IN, 1972; McAlester Prison, OK, May 1, 1970; Lucasville, OH, May 24, 1973; Framingham Women's Prison, MA, December 13, 1972; and Clinton Women's Prison, NJ, November 8, 1972.

27. Burton-Rose, "War Behind Walls," 26.

28. The Thirteenth Amendment of the United States made slavery or involuntary servitude illegal unless for punishment of a crime: "Amendment XIII Passed by Congress January 31, 1865. Ratified December 6, 1865. Section 1. Neither slavery nor involuntary servitude, except as a punishment for crime whereof the party shall have been duly convicted, shall exist within the United States, or any place subject to their jurisdiction." Available at www.archives.gov/exhibits/charters/constitution_amendments_11–27.html, see Amendment XIII (accessed May 31, 2009).

29. Ted Siegel, "Struggle in Ohio," *NEPA News* (October 1973): 3; Burton-Rose, "War Behind Walls," 41.

30. "Midnight Benefit," *Midnight Special: Prisoners News* 5:4 (July–August 1975): 1–3.

31. Bissonette, *When the Prisoners Ran Walpole*, 89.

32. For an account of the takeover of MCI Walpole, see Bissonette, *When the Prisoners Ran Walpole*.

33. Marie Gottschalk, *The Prison and the Gallows: The Politics of Mass Incarceration in America* (Cambridge: Cambridge University Press, 2006), 194.

34. Bob Martin, "The Massachusetts Correctional System: Treatment as an Ideology for Control," in *Punishment and Penal Discipline*, ed. Platt and Takagi, 156–164.

35. Jerome G. Miller, *Last One Over the Wall: The Massachusetts Experiment in Closing Reform Schools* (Columbus: Ohio State University Press, 1991), 4.

36. Perhaps the most famous indeterminate sentence at this time was that of George Jackson, who was given one year to life and whose militant presence inside led to repeated parole denial. His case, when it achieved notoriety, catalyzed the campaign against indeterminate sentencing.

37. See, for instance, Franklin E. Zimring, Gordon Hawkins, and Sam Kamin, *Punishment and Democracy: Three Strikes and You're Out in California* (New York: Oxford University Press, 2001), and Loïc Wacquant, *Punishing the Poor: The Neoliberal Government of Social Insecurity* (Durham, NC: Duke University Press, 2009).

38. Larry Sullivan, *The Prison Reform Movement: Forlorn Hope* (Boston: Twayne Publishers, 1990), 106–107.

39. "History of the U.P.U.," *The Anvil* (March–April 1975): 3.

40. Miller, *Last One Over the Wall*, 46.

41. Ibid., 4.

42. John Clutchette, "On Prison Reform," *If They Come in the Morning*, 136.

43. See "Nothing is More Precious Than . . ." archives, housed at The Freedom Archives, San Francisco, www.freedomarchives.org.

44. Angela Davis, interview with author, tape recording, Santa Cruz, CA, January 15, 2004.

45. Bettina Aptheker, "Social Functions of Prisons in Society," *If They Come in the Morning*, 57.

46. Prison Research Education Action Project (PREAP), "Time to Begin," in *Instead of Prisons: A Handbook for Abolitionists* (Syracuse, NY: Prison Research Education Action Project, 1976; and Oakland, CA: Critical Resistance, 2005), 16.

47. Ibid., 36.

48. Ibid., 20. At the time, of course, prison abolitionists discussed racism and poverty as structural causes of crime more than sexism and homophobia. Gendered analyses have become more prevalent among contemporary prison abolitionists. See Julia Sudbury, "Maroon Abolitionists: Black Gender-oppressed Activists in the Anti-Prison Movement in the U.S. and Canada," *Meridians* 9:1 (2009), 1–29; Critical Resistance and Incite! Women of Color Against Violence, "Gender Violence and the Prison-Industrial Complex," in Incite! Women of Color Against Violence, ed., *Color of Violence* (Cambridge: South End Press, 2006), 223–226.

49. *Instead of Prisons*, 38–45.

50. Ibid., 20.

51. Mafundi, "Understanding the Criminal Justice System," *Committee for Prisoner Support in Birmingham* 5 (April 1975). Alternative Press Archives. Used with permission.

52. "Plea for Unity," *NEPA News* (March 1974): 10–11.

53. PREAP, *Instead of Prisons*, 20.

54. Ibid., 11.

55. Sullivan, *The Prison Reform Movement*, 5; Scott Christianson, *With Liberty for Some: 500 Years of Imprisonment in America* (Boston: Northeastern University Press, 1998).

56. American Friends Service Committee (AFSC), *Struggle for Justice: A Report on Crime and Punishment in America* (New York: Hill and Wang, 1971, 1972), 170–173.

57. PREAP, *Instead of Prisons*, 9.

58. AFSC, *Struggle for Justice: A Report on Crime and Punishment in America*, 23.

59. Jackson, *Blood in My Eye*, 118. Jackson wrote, "But if one were forced for the sake of clarity to define [fascism] in a word simple enough for all to understand that word would be 'reform.'" Also see Karen Wald and Ward Churchill, "Remembering the Real Dragon: An Interview with George Jackson" in *Cages of Steel: The Politics of Imprisonment in America*, ed. Ward Churchill and Jim Vander Wall (College Park, MD: Maisonneuve Press, 1992), 178.

60. PREAP, *Instead of Prisons*, 23–25.

61. Ibid., 67.

62. Ibid., 152–153.

63. Daniel Burton-Rose, "The Anti-Exploits of Men Against Sexism, 1977–78," in *Prison Masculinities*, ed. Donald F. Sabo, Terry A. Kupers, and Willie London (Philadelphia: Temple

University Press, 2001), 224–229. Available at http://www.gjbip.org/ p4_c2_a_mas1.htm#_
ftnref1 (accessed January 3, 2009).

64. PREAP, *Instead of Prisons*, 114–127.

65. Bissonette, *When the Prisoners Ran Walpole*, 43–44, 78.

66. Ibid., 90.

67. Ibid., 142.

68. Ibid., 130.

69. "Alabama's Atticas," *Midnight Special* 3: 4 (April 1973): 5.

70. New England Prisoners Association, *NEPA News* 1:1, 1:3, 2:1–11. Alternative Press Archives. Used with permission.

71. *Prisoner Solidarity Committee* (September 30, 1971): 6. Alternative Press Archives. Used with Permission.

72. Tom Soto, "Tear the Prisons Down," *Prisoner Solidarity Committee* 3 (November 3, 1971): 4. Alternative Press Archives. Used with permission.

73. This conference took place at University of California, Berkeley, January 28–30, 1972. It featured workshops, films, and speakers. Cummins, *California's Radical Prison Movement*, 222.

74. See Arthur I. Waskow, "' . . . I Am Not Free,'" *Saturday Review*, January 8, 1972, 20–21; Ramsey Clark, *Crime in America: Observations on Its Nature, Causes, Prevention and Control* (New York: Simon and Schuster, 1970).

75. Jessica Mitford, *Kind and Usual Punishment: The Prison Business* (New York: Alfred A. Knopf, 1973), 299–300.

76. The 1972 National Prisoners Coalition was formed after a prisoners' conference in Portland; see "National Prisoners Coalition Formed," *Penal Digest International* 1: 10 (April–May 1972): 3. A national prison network formed briefly after the 1976 Hard Times Conference in Chicago; see "Build the Mass Prison Movement," *Midnight Special* 5:8 (June–July 1976): 12; and there was a call for a National Prisoner's Rights Coalition in 1977. See "Building a Mass Prison Movement," *Midnight Special* 5:12 (October 1977): 10–11.

77. "Announcement of NEPA Dissolution," stapled letter to final *NEPA News* (June 1976); "Building a Mass Prison Movement," *Midnight Special* 5:12 (October 1977): 10–11. This position was reflected in several memoirs or exposés by one-time prison activists that were also published in the late 1970s. See, for instance, Jo Durden-Smith, *Who Killed George Jackson? Fantasies, Paranoia and the Revolution* (New York: Alfred A. Knopf, 1976).

78. For a detailed account of the closure of Massachusetts juvenile prisons, see Miller, *Last One Over the Wall*.

79. AFSC, *Struggle for Justice*, 156.

80. Miller, *Last One Over the Wall*, 4.

81. More generally on this point, see David Garland, *The Culture of Control* (New York: Oxford University Press, 2001).

82. For an overview, see Christian Parenti, *Lockdown America: Police and Prisons in the Age of Crisis* (New York: Verso, 2000).

83. Critical Resistance, "Introduction to the Re-print," in PREAP, *Instead of Prisons*, iii.

2

Sick of the Abuse

Feminist Responses to Sexual Assault, Battering, and Self-Defense

VICTORIA LAW

By the early 1970s, the women's movement had popularized the idea that women had a right to defend themselves and their families from outside harm. The emergence of publications such as *The Woman's Gun Pamphlet* and groups like Women Armed for Self-Protection (both in 1975) attests to the growing acceptance, even popularity, of armed self-defense among segments of the women's movement.[1] As a result, feminists—both radical and more mainstream—began to rally around women arrested for self-defense. Several of these cases, such as those of Joan (Jo Ann) Little, Yvonne Wanrow, Inez Garcia, and Dessie Woods, became causes célèbre in the radical women's movement, prompting the formation of support committees that provided legal assistance and drew public attention to the cases. A woman's right to defend herself (and her children) from assault became a feminist rallying point throughout the 1970s. However, these same groups and individuals often ignored the issue of intimate violence and continued abuse, concentrating on higher-profile cases of self-defense against strangers. By comparing some of the most high-profile cases at the time to those given little to no attention, I argue that the larger radical women's movement failed to address battering with the same intensity devoted to more impersonal forms of violence, often leaving the issue to liberal feminists and the state to resolve.

Yvonne Wanrow

In 1972, Yvonne Wanrow, a Colville Indian and mother of two in Spokane, Washington, fatally shot a known child molester. On the afternoon of August 11, Wanrow's two children were at the home of her friend Shirley Hooper. While riding his bicycle, Wanrow's eleven-year-old son encountered William Wesler, who attempted to drag him into his house. The boy escaped. Wesler followed the boy to Hooper's house, repeating through the door, "I didn't touch the kid. I didn't touch the kid."[2]

Earlier that year, Hooper's seven-year-old daughter had been raped by an unidentified person, resulting in a sexually transmitted disease. When she saw Wesler, the girl told her mother, "He's the man who did it to me."[3] Hooper's landlord, Joseph Fah, also saw Wesler and told Hooper that Wesler had tried to molest a young boy who had previously lived there.[4]

Hooper called the police. Although they had arrested Wesler for child molestation on previous occasions and were familiar enough with him to nickname him "Chicken Bill," they refused to arrest him this time. Instead, they recommended that Hooper wait until after the weekend to file a complaint at the police station.[5] Fah suggested that Hooper hit Wesler with a baseball bat if he tried to enter the house. The police did not discourage this course of action, although their reply was less than comforting: "Yes, but wait until he gets in the house."[6] Hooper telephoned Wanrow, asking her to spend the night at Hooper's home. Wanrow, a five-foot, four-inch woman, had recently broken her leg and was on crutches. She brought her pistol. The two women also asked Angie and Chuck Michel, Wanrow's sister and brother-in-law, to spend the night.[7] They arrived with their own children.

At five in the morning, Chuck Michel went to Wesler's house with a baseball bat. He accused Wesler of molesting small children. Wesler, who was visibly intoxicated, suggested that they straighten the matter out at Hooper's house. Another man, David Kelly, was with Wesler and accompanied them. Wesler entered the house while Michel and Kelly remained outside.

The women demanded that Wesler leave. He refused. A shouting match ensued, waking Michel's young son, who had been asleep on the couch. Wesler approached the boy, stating, "My, what a cute little boy." Angie Michel stepped between them, while Wanrow went to the front door to yell for Chuck Michel. She turned to find the six-foot-two Wesler towering over her. Wanrow shot him. At her trial, the judge instructed the jury to consider only what had happened "at or immediately before the killing."[8] This omitted Wesler's record as a sex offender. Neither Hooper's daughter nor the doctor who had treated Wanrow's son after Wesler's kidnapping attempt was allowed to testify. Wanrow was convicted of murder and sentenced to twenty-five years in prison.[9]

Had this happened ten years earlier, Wanrow's story might have ended here. However, the women's movement took up her cause, turning her into a symbol of a woman's right to defend herself and her family from assault. Feminists in Seattle and Washington, DC, formed Yvonne Wanrow Defense Committees, hosting events to generate public interest and raise legal funds.[10] In Minnesota, supporters formed the Lesbian Feminist Organizing Committee to demonstrate support for Wanrow.[11] Members of the American Indian Movement, Women of All Red Nations, and the Native American Solidarity Committee organized a two-day benefit to raise money for her defense fund and educate the two hundred attendees about her case, the underlying issues of violence against women, and the history of systemic violence against Native people in the United States.[12]

In 1977, the Washington State Supreme Court granted Wanrow a new trial, partially on the basis that the original instructions to the jury on the law of self-defense were inaccurate. The judge's instructions had not allowed the jury to consider the relevant facts: Wesler was a known child molester; Wanrow had heard that he had previously raped her friend's daughter; and, less than twenty-four hours earlier, he had apparently attempted to assault her son. "The justification for self-defense is to be evaluated in light of ALL the facts and circumstances known to the defendant, including those known substantially before the killing," the court declared. The court also recognized that women's lack of access to self-defense training and to the "skills necessary to effectively repel a male assailant without resorting to the use of deadly weapons" made their circumstances different from those of men. The decision read, "Care must be taken to assure that our self-defense instructions afford women the right to have their conduct judged in light of the individual physical handicaps which are the product of sex discrimination."[13] The decision was hailed as a landmark case for a woman's right to self-defense.[14]

At her 1979 retrial, Wanrow pled guilty to reduced charges. She received suspended sentences on the manslaughter and assault charges, five years' probation, and one year of community service.[15] Without the pressure, publicity, and resources generated by her supporters, Wanrow would most likely have stayed in prison. The movement to free Yvonne Wanrow symbolized the women's movement's growing recognition of the right to self-defense in the context where some on the left celebrated violence by people of color.

Inez Garcia

On March 19, 1974, Miguel Jimenez and Luis Castillo arrived at the home of Inez Garcia, a thirty-year-old Cuban–Puerto Rican woman living in Soledad, California. They were drunk, belligerent, and looking for her roommate. They not only attacked him but also took Garcia to the alley outside. There, the three-hundred-pound Jimenez blocked the entrance while Castillo raped her.

Shortly after, the men called Garcia, threatening to kill her if she did not leave town.[16] In response, Garcia left the house to look for them, taking her gun. When she found them, Jimenez threw a knife at her. She shot and killed him.[17] Garcia was arrested and charged with first-degree (or premeditated) murder.

Garcia's case attracted considerable public support from the women's community. Local women formed the Inez Garcia Defense Committee and the Free Inez Committee.[18] In the weeks before her trial, supporters publicized Garcia's case at rock concerts, Chilean solidarity meetings, services at San Francisco's progressive Glide Memorial Church, the weekly women's night at the Starry Plough, a Berkeley bar run by IRA sympathizers, and other events where they might find potential sympathizers. The week before her trial began, the defense committee called a press conference at which Elaine Brown, then chair of the Black Panther Party, publicly affirmed party support for Garcia. This development drew media attention to the case; the following day, articles about Garcia appeared in local newspapers, and in the days that followed, the *New York Times*, television news, and wire services also picked up the story.[19]

The courtroom, however, remained a hostile environment. Stating "I do not see what rape has to do with the case," the judge instructed the jury not to consider Garcia's allegations of rape, because she had not physically resisted the assault.[20] However, he allowed the prosecutor to cross-examine her with explicit questions such as, "Did you take off your panties? Did you take off your bra? Did you like it?"[21] Garcia later said that the trial experience was "like being raped all over again."[22]

Charles Garry, a movement lawyer famous for his defense of the Black Panther Party, took Garcia's case. Rather than arguing her right to self-defense, Garry claimed that, suffering from shock, Garcia had little to no control over her own actions and had acted in a diminished capacity. Garry called psychiatrist Jane Oldden to testify that, after having been raped, Garcia "was not thinking about the consequences in the sense of the world around her or what the world around her would judge the consequences of her act, and she was in an impaired consciousness." Oldden compared Garcia's action to "sleep walking or periods of two or three hours of amnesia that people go through when the internal conflict is triggered off."[23] In addition, Garry stressed Garcia's lack of literacy and her history of emotional illnesses.

Garcia, however, undermined the "diminished capacity" argument. Frustrated by both the prosecution's demands for the details of her rape and her own lawyer's attempts to portray her as mentally incapacitated, Garcia walked off the witness stand, stating, "Another thing I want to say, I am not sorry that I did it and the only thing I am sorry is that I missed Louie."[24]

Garcia was convicted of second-degree murder and sentenced to five years to life in prison. Despite the judge's instructions to disregard Garcia's rape, the jurors obviously did consider it in their deliberations: After the trial, a juror told her defense team, "You can't kill someone for trying to give you a good time." Another bluntly told *Ms. Magazine*, "When I leave here I'll have less fear of raping a woman now than I did before. At least I know that if I got shot she won't get away."[25]

The women's movement did not drop Garcia's cause. On the day of her sentencing, more than one hundred women rallied in front of the jail where Garcia awaited transfer to the women's prison, chanting "Free Inez!" "Jail the judge!" and "Rape the judge—see how he likes it!"[26] Charles Garry filed an appeal based on the judge's refusal to allow testimony about rape. Four months later, thirty-eight protesters were arrested trying to present a petition demanding Garcia's freedom—signed by 1,600 people—to California governor Edmund Brown.[27] Defense committee members, unhappy with Garry's "diminished capacity" defense, asked feminist attorney Susan Jordan to take over Garcia's defense.[28]

Garcia spent two years in prison. In 1976, a California Court of Appeals reversed her conviction because the trial judge had instructed the jury not to consider the rape in their deliberations.[29]

There were several key differences in Garcia's retrial. In her *voir dire*, Jordan challenged potential jurors about their preconceptions of rape, thus making the assault an integral part of the case from the beginning. The judge allowed Jordan to present expert witnesses about both rape and its perception in Latino cultures. Garcia was acquitted.

Garcia's acquittal marked a change in the way that the legal system viewed rape victims. "No one had ever asked a jury to look at it that way, from a rape victim's point-of-view," Jordan stated.[30] A female juror told *off our backs* that, although the male jurors had been unable to put themselves in Garcia's shoes, they considered how they would feel if a wife or daughter had been raped.[31] A male juror confirmed this, stating that he had reacted negatively to expert testimony that Latina women respond more adversely to rape than women from other cultural backgrounds. His non-Latina wife would be just as upset. Although he had disagreed with the testimony, it had substantially impacted his understanding of women and rape.[32] The entire jury agreed that both rape and the threat of further harm were adequate provocation for Garcia's action. Like Wanrow's successful appeal, Garcia's acquittal established a legal precedent that extended the interpretation of imminent danger beyond the immediate time period of the assault, laying the foundation for what would later became known as the "battered woman's defense"—that a woman who kills her abuser is acting in self-defense even if she is not under attack at the time of the killing.[33]

Joan Little

Sixty-two-year-old Clarence Alligood, a white, male guard at North Carolina's Beaufort County Jail, was found dead in a cell on August 24, 1974. He was naked from the waist down. Eight days later, Joan Little, a twenty-one-year-old black woman and the jail's only female inmate, turned herself in.[34] She claimed that the guard had threatened her with an ice pick, forcing her to perform oral sex. Little killed the guard with the ice pick and fled the jail. Little was arrested and charged with first-degree murder, which, in North Carolina, carried a mandatory death penalty.[35]

Little's case raised the question of whether a black woman, particularly in the South, had a right to defend herself against sexual assault by a white man. It attracted the attention and support of many African American and feminist groups, including the Southern Christian Leadership Conference, the Black Panther Party, the Atlanta Lesbian Feminists Alliance (ALFA), North Carolina's Triangle Area Lesbian Feminists, and African American churches nationwide. Support committees emerged across the country.[36]

In North Carolina, social scientists volunteered their time and expertise. They collected newspaper coverage throughout the eastern region of the state and argued that this coverage would cause prejudice against Little. The defense presented this evidence in its argument for a change of venue, persuading the judge to move the trial from the state's eastern region to the more urban Wake County, where Raleigh, the state capital, is located. The social scientists also developed profiles of jurors with the most favorable opinions on race, rape, and the death penalty, which defense attorneys used in screening potential jurors.[37]

Little's defense exposed the chronic sexual abuse and harassment women endured in the jail and prison system. Countering the prosecution's argument that Little had enticed Alligood into her cell with promises of sex, the defense called on women who had previously been held at the jail. They testified that Alligood had a history of sexually abusing women in his custody. One woman stated that he had fondled her breasts while bringing her a late-night sandwich; another recalled that he had suggested that she had been in jail long enough to need a man.[38] Little testified that Alligood had come to her cell three times that night. After she refused his advances twice, he returned with an ice pick. "By then, I had changed into my nightgown. He was telling me I really looked nice in my gown, and he wanted to have sex with me," she stated. "He said he had been nice to me, and it was time I was nice to him. I told him I didn't feel like I should be nice to him that way."[39]

After seventy-eight minutes of deliberation, the jury acquitted Little, establishing a precedent for killing as justified self-defense against rape.[40]

Dessie Woods

On June 16, 1975, only months after Little's acquittal, another case involving rape and self-defense emerged. Dessie X. Woods and Cheryl Todd, two black women, were picked up by Ronnie Horne, a white salesman, while hitchhiking in Georgia. When Horne attempted to rape them, Woods killed Horne with his own gun. The pair then took the money from his wallet and fled. They were subsequently arrested.

During the trial, Judge James O'Connor ordered a "gag rule" that prevented the defendants or the lawyers from speaking to the press. He also prohibited demonstrations and literature distribution near the courthouse. On the opening day of the trial, however, defense attorneys challenged the gag order, forcing O'Connor to amend his order to allow demonstrators outside the courthouse. More than fifty people picketed, including many from the local black community.[41]

In 1976, Woods was convicted of voluntary manslaughter and, because she and Todd had taken the dead man's money, armed robbery. She was sentenced to twenty-two years. Todd was convicted of being an accomplice in the theft and received a five-year sentence.

Framing the case as an issue of colonial violence, black nationalist women particularly identified with and took up Woods's case. They formed the National Committee to Defend Dessie Woods (NCDDW) and the Dessie Woods Defense

Committee. Kai Lumumba Barrow, then a student in Atlanta involved with the Republic of New Afrika, said in a recent interview, "The feminist movement was not as visible as it is now and, particularly in terms of black women, it was really invisible. I was really young, so I was desperately looking for heroes, mentors, direction. I needed to see myself somewhere."[42] Like many other African American activist and nationalist women, Barrow saw herself in Dessie Woods. However, many of the white feminists who had rallied around Wanrow, Garcia, and Little remained relatively silent, as the bulk of support for Woods came from black nationalists.

"Dessie Woods's case was picked up by groups that were not necessarily welcoming to feminism," Barrow recalled. "There was an ongoing struggle within these groups in terms of the issue of feminism and in terms of how does feminism relate or not relate to black liberation. But neither the women nor the men [in these groups] were looking at white women in any kind of open manner. They would not have been welcomed into the work that we were doing."

One exception was the San Francisco–based Dessie Woods Support Coalition, a group of white women working under the leadership of the predominantly black NCDDW to provide support for the campaign to free Woods. Kathie Gottesman, a member of the coalition, explained that the NCDDW constantly challenged the white feminists to examine not only sexism and patriarchy but also racism and colonialism when viewing and promoting Woods's cause:

> We began to understand that when we as white women put the terms of our own oppression at the center we perpetuate a history of white people which fights for our advancement on the backs of African people. It continues to be a colonialist type of mentality which says, 'We'll accept only the part of the Dessie Woods struggle which is her right to defend herself as a woman, not the part that says she is an African freedom fighter fighting for the freedom of her people by refusing to submit to this white man who tried to assault her.[43]

Radical women's publications such as *off our backs* and *Aegis: Magazine on Ending Violence Against Women* also monitored Woods's case and urged readers to join her support movement. Woods remained a cause célèbre while imprisoned. In 1978, Sweet Honey in the Rock, a women's a cappella group that had earlier written a song about Joan Little, held a concert to remind the public about and raise funds for Woods's campaign.[44] Linda Leeks, a member of both the African People's Socialist Party and the Dessie Woods Defense Committee, spoke about Woods's case at a 1978 Take Back the Night rally in Washington, DC.[45] Damesha Blackearth, chairwoman of the NCDDW, traveled through Europe, speaking about Woods's case and the systematic human rights violations of black people in the United States.[46] Blackearth's tour garnered increased international attention: every July 4 until her release, protests demanding Woods's freedom were held throughout the United States and Europe, with "thousands of people marching, holding aloft drawings of Dessie."[47]

Despite continued public pressure, Woods was denied parole several times, transferred to the Georgia State Mental Hospital, and, at least once, physically assaulted by the prison's warden.[48] However, prolonged support eventually won her freedom: Woods was released in July 1981 after a lawyer from the People's Law Center filed a writ of habeas corpus challenging the use of circumstantial evidence and the use of a special prosecutor (hired by the dead man's family). The U.S. Court of Appeals determined that there had been insufficient evidence to convict and imprison her.[49]

And What About the Rest?

The cases of Yvonne Wanrow, Inez Garcia, Joan Little, and Dessie Woods are remarkable because they physically defended themselves or their children and participated in political movements on their behalf. Although some were convicted and imprisoned, they each garnered support from both radical feminist and people of color communities. The amount of public support—and the money raised from fundraisers, publicity, and appeals—gave these women better legal representation than they would otherwise have had and the ability to pursue various legal strategies. However, in each case, the man killed was not an intimate. Women's self-defense against abusive partners remained largely ignored by radical feminists and other groups. Why did these movements fail to support battered women's acts of self-defense?

Looking back, women involved in support committees recognize that the failure to accept battering as a legitimate issue influenced which cases were championed. "The real standard [for supporting a case] was around building a revolutionary movement—and what made one involved and how that was defined was very limiting,"[50] Barrow reflected recently. "The cases that were charged around race and class were seen as very political, as opposed to other personal, domestic issues. The battered women's movement has done a significant amount of work to make domestic violence a political and social issue as opposed to a personal issue. But back then, that wasn't happening. It was like, 'That's not something that we can take [on]. That's not something that we can get involved in. That's a personal situation, and so we can't build any sort of movement around that.'"[51] Diana Block, a cofounder of San Francisco Women Against Rape, agreed in a recent interview that the focus on building a revolutionary movement limited the range of cases that received widespread support: "There was a certain modeling to the cases of Inez Garcia and Joan Little. The whole movement was dealing with political prisoners as a very central issue, starting with the Panthers. They made that [issue] popular and provided more of an understanding of people who were unjustly incarcerated. Joan Little and Inez Garcia were the counterpart for the women's movement."

Although the women's movement had identified rape as a social problem around which to mobilize, many had yet to recognize battering as a feminist issue in the 1970s. Block argued that at the center of the women's movement in "the first part of the seventies was anti-rape work. People weren't even aware of domestic violence as a women's movement issue." With people only beginning to see rape as "a structural form of male violence," a political view of domestic violence was not widespread. Domestic violence, Block said, "was seen as an act that was codified by marriage. We just weren't talking in the early seventies about domestic violence."[52] Lois Ahrens, founder of the Center for Battered Women in Austin, Texas, offered a similar reflection on the time: "Back then, people knew that rape was a crime, but they did not know that battering—even where the woman barely escaped with her life—had anything much to do with committing a crime." She noted that in many women's liberation groups, "self-defense and solidarity with women who acted out of self-defense was keeping in line with what was the political agenda of the day . . . [Wanrow, Garcia, Little, and Woods] were not 'victims' in the sense that they were [not] the girlfriends or wives of the men that raped them, making embracing them all the more in line with [the idea of] fighting back." For Ahrens, the idea of "fighting back" was more powerful than the act of self-defense itself. In contrast, battered women "were in a less politically resonant category. Many had been married for many years, and it was a final act of desperation, rather than fighting back."[53]

However little attention the women's movement paid to the issue, battering and self-defense were not wholly invisible: In 1977, the *New York Times* published a study from Chicago's Cook County Jail, which found that 40 percent of the women charged with murdering their partners had been physically attacked on several occasions by these men.[54] The study also showed that each of these women had called the police at least five times, and that many had already separated from these men in attempts to escape the abuse.[55] However, many of the same individuals and organizations that had championed the rights of Wanrow, Garcia, Little, and Woods to defend themselves against assaults from strangers remained silent about those imprisoned for killing known (and intimate) abusers.[56] Thus, while some in the radical feminist movement attempted to publicize these cases, no mass mobilizations emerged.

In 1973, the same year that Wanrow was first convicted for killing "Chicken Bill," Jenna Kelsie shot and killed her ex-husband while he was beating her. Despite his history of abuse—including a nearly fatal incident in which he drove her car off the road with his truck—a jury found Kelsie guilty of second-degree murder. Unlike with Wanrow, no mass movement emerged to draw attention to her case or to provide better legal assistance. In 1976, having exhausted all of her requests for appeal on the grounds of trial irregularities, Kelsie began serving a fifteen-to-twenty-five-year sentence.[57]

In Maryland that same year, after seventeen years of abuse, Barbara Jean Gilbert killed her husband. She was convicted of first-degree murder and sentenced to life in prison. Lacking movement support, she nonetheless appealed her conviction and was granted a new trial. She was then convicted of manslaughter.

Although the prosecuting attorney had not asked for a prison sentence, and the parole and probation board recommended probation, the judge sentenced Gilbert to eight years, the maximum penalty for manslaughter. "You have inflicted pain and deprivation," Judge Samuel Meloy stated during sentencing. "You have snuffed out a life. Therefore the court has the right to inflict pain and deprivation on you."[58] Using prison to punish a woman for responding to violence with violence is not uncommon: in 1978, when sentencing Julia Parker Price to twenty years in prison for shooting her abusive husband, Judge John T. Gentry noted that he did so not because he believed she needed "rehabilitation," but to "get the word out to other wives in similar circumstances."[59]

Hostility did not pervade every courtroom. In a much less-publicized case in 1975 North Dakota, Katherine Rohrich was acquitted of shooting her abusive husband while he slept. The judge submitted the case to the jury on the grounds of self-defense and compulsion, defining the latter as "a force that would render a person of reasonable firmness incapable of resisting the pressure." The jury—after hearing evidence of the years of abuse endured by both Rohrich and her eleven children and the lack of assistance from the police—acquitted her.[60] In 1978, the Brooklyn Supreme Court dismissed a grand jury indictment against Agnes Scott, who had been charged with first-degree manslaughter of her abusive husband. Justice Julius Hellenbrand found that the district attorney had withheld the dead man's long history of abuse from the grand jury, despite several requests for this information.[61] That same year, Marlene Roan Eagle in South Dakota, Wanda Carr and Evelyn Ware in California, Sharon McNearney in Michigan, and Janice Hornbuckle in Washington were all acquitted of killing their abusive husbands on the grounds of self-defense.[62]

These acquittals occurred absent the popular support accorded Wanrow, Garcia, Little, and Woods. By the end of the decade, however, women were challenging the courts' hostility toward women who killed their abusers. In 1978, recognizing the need systematically to educate judges, jurors, and lawyers about the long-lasting effects of battering, Elizabeth Schneider, Yvonne Wanrow's appeal attorney, founded the Women's Self-Defense Law Project. During its two years of existence, the project worked on more than one hundred cases, developing case analysis, defense theory, and expert testimony.[63] The Women's Self-Defense Law Project signaled increasing awareness in the women's movement about abuse and the lack of support for survivors. It sought to achieve recognition of women's experiences and the different circumstances in which they killed, using the precedent set by Wanrow's successful challenge of the sex-bias in self-defense law.

Politicizing Battering

This is not to say that all individuals in the women's movement ignored or downplayed issues of battering and spousal abuse. Recognizing the need for and absence of safe spaces for women seeking to escape abusive relationships, many began opening their own homes. In 1973, Women's Advocates—an organization that originated as a consciousness-raising group in St. Paul, Minnesota—rented a small apartment as a refuge for women fleeing abuse. When the group was evicted three months later after neighbors complained, one member housed several women in her own home.[64] In 1976, two women who had both escaped abusive relationships opened their Boston apartment to other battered women before starting Transition House.[65] These early shelters utilized the self-help methods, egalitarian philosophies, and collective structures that had developed within the women's liberation movement, striving to be democratic alternatives in which women had the space to safely communicate, share experiences, examine the root causes of the violence against them, and begin to articulate a response.[66] However, these efforts received nowhere near the amount of attention, publicity, and support that the women's movement paid to Wanrow, Garcia, Little, and Woods.

By 1982, the number of battered women's shelters in the United States was estimated to be between three hundred and seven hundred. During that time, other resources, such as emergency crisis lines, counseling services, support groups, and victim advocacy for women seeking court intervention became available.[67] The existence of these resources resulted in a marked decline of women killing their batterers. Between 1979 and 1984, the number of men killed by their female partners decreased by more than 25 percent, although the rate of men killing their female partners remained stable during this time.[68]

The increased interest in the issue by those who did not identify with the women's liberation movement resulted in a watering down of the radical feminist analyses that led to the first refuges for battered women. These emerging institutions emphasized providing services without analyzing the political context in which abuse occurred. There was a shift from calling for broad social transformation to focusing on individual problems and demanding greater state intervention. As the issue became more prevalent in American consciousness, even shelters that had started as feminist alternatives became more like traditional social-service agencies. Lois Ahrens recounted that when the Center for Battered Women first opened in Austin in 1977, women integrated an understanding of the oppression and violence against women with a concern for those who sought their assistance. However, as the number of non-feminist staff members increased, they changed this approach: "The new leadership of the Center for Battered Women has said that it is very important to separate the issue of feminism and sexism from that of battered women," Ahrens reported in 1980. "With the new federal emphasis on the nuclear family, the center chooses to look at battered women as a 'family violence problem,' but refuses to consider the societal, cultural, and political implications of why women are the ones in the family so often beaten."[69]

This philosophical divide was not limited to Austin. Surveys taken in the late 1970s showed that fewer than half of battered women's shelters were founded by feminist groups or were explicitly feminist.[70] Shelters opened or taken over by nonpoliticized professionals began accepting money from sources that reshaped practices and policy. By 1980, the Law Enforcement Alliance of America (LEAA) had become one of the most significant sources of government funding, granting nearly three million dollars to battered women's shelters across the country on the condition that they work closely with the police, legal system, and medical and social service agencies.[71] Accompanying this shift was a change in how the issue of violence against women was identified. Violence became discussed as a problem rooted in individual behaviors and pathologies rather than analyses of domination, power, and societal structure.

Susan Jordan's watershed argument that a woman had the right to defend herself from assault became the Battered Woman's Syndrome, reinforcing negative stereotypes of women as passive, weak, and powerless, and stripping women of both their agency and their right to defend themselves from assault. Supporters argued that expert testimony about Battered Woman's Syndrome was needed to overcome judges' and juries' misconceptions that battered women provoke their abusers, invite or enjoy the abuse, and kill out of revenge rather than fear.[72] While Battered Woman's Syndrome explained why a woman did not leave her abuser, it failed to answer the question of whether she was reasonable in her actions to save her life. As Elizabeth Schneider pointed out, "If the testimony is limited, or perceived as limited to the issue of why the woman does not leave, it highlights a contradiction implicit in the battered woman syndrome—if the battered woman was so helpless and passive, why did she kill the batterer?"[73] Battered Woman's Syndrome reflected an emphasis on victimization rather than agency, and the diluting of feminist ideology through psychological rather than political explanations.

Battered Woman's Syndrome also proved problematic to those who did not appear submissive and domestic, such as women of color who were (and still are) often stereotyped as strong, masculine, and angry.[74] In the trials of Beverly Ibn-Tamas (1979) and Kathy Thomas (1978), both black women who had killed their batterers, the trial courts refused to admit testimony on Battered Woman's Syndrome. Thomas, who was further stigmatized as a welfare recipient and occasional drug user, was convicted of murder and sentenced to fifteen years. In 1981, the Ohio Supreme Court upheld her conviction; its decision became case law, barring the admission of Battered Woman's Syndrome for the next nine years.[75]

Many women and groups began shifting the focus from uprooting patriarchy to validating state-sanctioned responses, advocating for mandatory arrests and harsher penalties for men who battered women. Women's groups called attention to the murders of abused women, charging the police and court systems with indifference to the women's repeated pleas for assistance and protection and calling for increased police and state intervention.[76] At the same time, many of these same women refused to acknowledge a woman's right to defend herself physically against assault or the threat of assault. At the Center for Battered Women, a counselor who had been a vocal supporter of women's armed self-defense was one of the first people fired after a non-feminist faction took over control of the center.[77]

As early as 1980, battered women's advocates who identified as radical feminists questioned the push toward harsher state intervention, recognizing that these measures re-legitimized the state's agenda against poor people and communities of color.[78] "Laws are made by those in power to protect their own interest. Since wealthy white men are in power, the laws are made in their interests and against the interests of men and women of color and/or who are working class," noted Gail Sullivan, a former staff member of the Massachusetts Coalition of Battered Women's Service Groups. "We need to understand that under such a system, when men are punished for their behavior, it is not because the system is protecting women but because to do so supports and reflects an aspect of the system, such as racism and the isolation of Third World communities."[79]

Outside of the larger, better-funded, and more visible movement, women of color and others who recognized the danger of increased state intervention continued to organize within their own communities. In Boston, for example, black lesbian feminists formed the Combahee River Collective, naming themselves after the river where, in 1863, Harriet Tubman led a raid that freed 750 slaves. In response to the 1979 murders of several black women, police indifference, and black male leaders who urged women to either stay home or seek male protection, the collective wrote and distributed the pamphlet, "Six Black Women: Why Did They Have to Die?"[80] The pamphlet analyzed the murders as a result of the racism and sexism that devalued black women's lives. It galvanized diverse groups, including women from the larger white feminist community and black church groups, to begin recognizing, discussing, and working around the issue.[81] More generally, Combahee is widely recognized as one of the forerunners of women-of-color feminism.

While some white feminists worked with women-of-color-led groups, the racism of many other white feminists drove many women of color from the more visible feminist organizations, leading to the misperception that feminism was a white, middle-class movement.[82] However, as Combahee and similar organizations such as the National Black Feminist Organization and Third World Women's Alliance demonstrated, women of color were involved with feminist organizing in their own communities, including fighting sexual violence and other forms of violence against women. In addition, many women of color identified state violence as a central concern, one intimately connected to issues of interpersonal violence. In contrast, by the end of the decade, the politics and practices of the white feminist movements had been increasingly watered down by the increase in government funding (and accompanying restrictions), as well as a decrease in political analysis by those who were involved in this work.

The radical women's movement of the 1970s held that analyzing institutional sexism was integral to challenging and stopping violence against women, first by supporting women who physically defended themselves from assault, and later by launching the battered women's movement. By the 1980s, however, the battered women's movement focused more on institutional gains and state intervention

than on developing community-based solutions. The emphasis on state involvement posited policing and imprisonment as the best solutions to gender violence.
Women of color and other radical critics objected to this strategy, arguing that
these same institutions protected, promoted and perpetrated gender violence and
therefore should not be considered feminist responses. When their objections
were ignored or minimized, many activists left the battered women's and other
feminist movements to organize against abuse and violence in their own communities.[83] Their work has often been ignored by those studying the battered
women's movement; but their actions and criticisms paved the way for the analyses and actions of future women's groups toward solutions to end violence against
women without strengthening government control over women's lives or promoting incarceration as a solution to social problems.

NOTES

1. Women's Press Collective, *The Woman's Gun Pamphlet: A Primer on Handguns* (Oakland,
   CA: Women's Press Collective, 1975), 45.
2. *State v. Wanrow*, 88 Wn. 2d 221, 559 P.2d 548 (1977).
3. Vickie Leonard, "Wanrow Wins Retrial," *off our backs* 7 (1977): 5.
4. *State v. Wanrow*, 88 Wn. 2d 221, 559 P.2d 548 (1977).
5. "Colville Woman Appealing Murder Conviction in Death of Molester," *Akwesasne Notes*,
   August 31, 1975, 40.
6. *State v. Wanrow*, 88 Wn. 2d 221, 559 P.2d 548 (1977).
7. "Colville Woman Appealing Murder Conviction," 40.
8. *State v. Wanrow*, 88 Wn. 2d 221, 559 P.2d 548 (1977).
9. "Colville Woman Appealing Murder Conviction," 40.
10. Sherrie Cohen, "Second Trial for Yvonne Wanrow," *off our backs* 9:2 (February 1979): 10.
11. "Working in the Heart of the Monster: An Interview with Karen Clark," in *Fight Back!
    Feminist Resistance to Male Violence*, ed. Frederique Delacoste and Felice Newman
    (Minneapolis: Cleis Press, 1981), 316.
12. Terre Poppe, "Native American Benefit for Yvonne Swan Wanrow," *off our backs* 9:5 (May
    1979): 7.
13. Ibid.
14. In 1954, the Oklahoma Court of Appeals acknowledged gender differences and self-
    defense in *Easterling v. State*: "There may be such a difference in the size of the parties
    involved or disparity in their ages or physical condition which would give a person
    assaulted by fists reasonable grounds to apprehend danger of great bodily harm and thus
    legally justified in repelling the assault by the use of a deadly weapon. It is conceivable
    that a man might be so brutal in striking a woman with his fists as to cause her death."
    The court remanded the case for a new trial. *Easterling v. State*, OK CR 23, 267 P.2d
    185 (1954). Available at http://www.oscn.net/applications/oscn/deliverdocument.asp?
    citeid=50878 (accessed May 28, 2009).
15. Susan Madden, "Fighting Back with Deadly Force: Women Who Kill in Self-Defense," in
    Fight Back!, 147.
16. Kenneth Salter, *The Trial of Inez Garcia* (Berkeley, CA: Editorial Justa Publications, 1976),
    255–256.

17. Susan Rothaizer, "Inez Garcia Acquitted," *off our backs* 7:3 (April 1977): 5.

18. Danny Meyers, "Inez Garcia Wins Appeal for New Trial," *Sun Reporter* 33 (1976): 17.

19. Jim Wood, *The Rape of Inez Garcia* (New York: G. P. Putnam's Sons, 1976), 13–16, 19–20.

20. Nan Blitman and Robin Green, "Inez Garcia on Trial," *Ms. Magazine*, May 1975, 51, 53.

21. Jean Horan, "Executing the Enemy," *off our backs* 4:10 (October 1974): 8.

22. Rothaizer, "Inez Garcia Acquitted," 5.

23. Salter, *The Trial of Inez Garcia*, 341.

24. Ibid., 281.

25. Women's Press Collective, *The Woman's Gun Pamphlet*, 45.

26. Blitman and Green, "Inez Garcia on Trial," 86.

27. George Murphy, "38 Arrested in Protest," *San Francisco Chronicle*, February 8, 1975.

28. Susan Jordan, telephone interview with author, June 18, 2007.

29. Jean Horan, "New Trial for Inez," *off our backs* 11 (February 1976): 7.

30. "The Case of Inez Garcia: Interview with Susan Jordan," in *Dear Sisters: Dispatches from the Women's Liberation Movement*, ed. Rosalyn Baxandall and Linda Gordon (New York: Basic Books, 2000), 203.

31. Rothaizer, "Inez Garcia Acquitted," 5.

32. Elizabeth M. Schneider, Susan B. Jordan, Cristina C. Arguedas, "Representation of Women Who Defend Themselves in Response to Physical or Sexual Assault," in *Women's Self-Defense Cases: Theory and Practice*, ed. Elizabeth Bochnak (Charlottesville, VA: The Michie Co. [Law Publishers], 1981), 37.

33. Angela Browne, *When Battered Women Kill* (New York: Free Press, 1987), 172.

34. "Rape: Motive for Murder," *The Economist*, April 12, 1975, 71.

35. Jerrold K. Footlick, "Joan Little's Defense," *Newsweek*, February 24, 1975, 86.

36. Genna Rae McNeil, "'Joanne Is You and Joanne Is Me': A Consideration of African American Women and the 'Free Joan Little' Movement, 1974–75," in *Sisters in the Struggle: African-American Women in the Civil Rights–Black Power Movement*, ed. Bettye Collier (New York: NYU Press, 2001) 262–263; Dave Ottalini, "Chicken as a Vehicle to Power: Interview with Maryland American Studies Assistant Professor Psyche Williams-Forson," *Outlook Online: The University of Maryland Faculty and Staff Newsletter*, November 7, 2006 Available at http://www.outlook.umd.edu/article.cfm?id=2328 (accessed May 28, 2009).

37. John B. McConahay, Courtney J. Mullin, and Jeffrey Frederick, "The Uses of Social Science in Trials with Political and Racial Overtones: The Trial of Joan Little," *Law and Contemporary Problems* 41 (1977): 206, 212; and "JoAnne Little Case. Editorial," *The Black Panther* 13 (1975): 2.

38. Jerrold K. Footlick, "Defending Joan Little," *Newsweek*, July 28, 1975, 34.

39. "Joan Little's Story," *Time*, August 25, 1975.

40. After her acquittal, Little was returned to prison to finish her seven-to-ten-year sentence for breaking and entering. She was released in 1979 on the condition that she stay out of North Carolina.

41. Marlene Schmitz, "Georgia: Dessie Woods and Cheryl Todd Convicted," *off our backs* 6:1 (March 1976): 25.

42. Kai Lumumba Barrow, telephone interview with author, July 12, 2007.

43. Julie Alibrando, "Interview with Kathie Gottesman of the SF Bay Area Dessie Woods's Support Coalition," *Aegis: Magazine on Ending Violence Against Women* (March/April 1979): 14–15.

44. "'Sweet Honey in the Rock': Concert Slated for Dessie Woods," *Sun Reporter* 35 (1978): 4.

45. Marcy Rein, "Women Unite: Reclaim the Night," *off our backs* 8:6 (June 1978): 8.

46. Mary Klein, "Activist Harassed," *off our backs* 9:9 (October 1979): 8; Laureen France, "Help Free Dessie Woods," *Aegis* (September/October 1979): 46. In addition to publicizing her case and demanding her freedom, committee members also cared for Woods's two children during her incarceration.

47. Alice Walker, "Trying to See My Sister," in *Living by the Word* (Orlando: Harcourt Brace Jovanovich Publishers, 1981), 21.

48. Janis Kelly, "Dessie Woods Beaten, Denied Parole," *off our backs* 11:1 (January 1981): 18.

49. Nancy Fithian, "Dessie Woods Speaks Out," *off our backs* 11:10 (November 1981): 11.

50. Kai Lumumba Barrow, telephone interview with author, July 12, 2007.

51. Kai Lumumba Barrow, interview with author, June 29, 2007.

52. Diana Block, telephone interview with author, January 19, 2009.

53. Lois Ahrens, letter to author, January 8, 2009.

54. "Study of Female Killers Finds 40% Were Abused," *New York Times*, December 20, 1977, 20.

55. Susan Schechter, *Women and Male Violence: The Visions and Struggles of the Battered Women's Movement* (Boston: South End Press, 1982), 171.

56. *off our backs*, for example, devoted six articles to Dessie Woods, seven to Yvonne Wanrow, six to Inez Garcia, and five to Joan Little. During that same period, women who killed their abusers never merited a full article about their cases. There were only six articles about incarcerated battered women in this period, and women who killed their abusers were mentioned only three times.

57. Liz Stanford, "Up Against the Prison Blocks," *off our backs* 9:3 (March 1979): 7.

58. "Men Kill Lightly but Women Pay in Full," *off our backs* 8:8 (September 1978): 8. In October 1978, Barbara Jean Gilbert's sentence was reduced to a five-year probationary period on the condition that she see a psychiatrist. Ellen Frye, "Abused Women: Two Freed, Three Murdered, Wife-Killer Walked," *off our backs* 8:10 (November 1978): 2.

59. Madden, "Fighting Back with Deadly Force: Women Who Kill in Self-Defense," in *Fight Back!*, 146–147.

60. Ann Jones, *Women Who Kill* (New York: Holt, Rinehart and Winston, 1980), 290–291.

61. Frye, "Abused Women," 2. The judge also found that the jury had been inadequately informed about the "law of justification" or degree of physical force permissible.

62. Jerrold K. Footlick, "Wives Who Batter Back," *Newsweek*, January 30, 1978, 54.

63. Until recently, the reasonableness standard (or "reasonable man" standard) asked jurors to determine whether what the defendant did was what a "reasonable man" would have done faced with the same circumstances. There was no acknowledgment of gender or cultural differences in this standard.

64. Schechter, *Women and Male Violence*, 62–63.

65. Patricia Gagne, *Battered Women's Justice: The Movement for Clemency and the Politics of Self-Defense* (New York: Twayne Publishers, 1998), 12.

66. For more about these first feminist shelters and their structures, see Schechter, *Women and Male Violence*; and Anne Enke, "Taking Over Domestic Space: The Battered Women's Movement and Public Protest," in *The World the Sixties Made: Politics and Culture in Recent America*, ed. Van Gosse and Richard Moser (Philadelphia: Temple University Press, 2003), 162–190.

67. Angela Browne and Kirk R. Williams, "Exploring the Effect of Resource Availability and the Likelihood of Female-Perpetrated Homicides," *Law and Society Review* 23:1 (1989): 79.

68. Ibid., 80.

69. Lois Ahrens, "Battered Women's Refuges: Feminist Cooperatives vs. Social Service Institutions," *Aegis* (Summer/Autumn 1980): 13–14.

70. John M. Johnson, "Program Enterprise and Official Cooptation in the Battered Women's Shelter Movement," *American Behavioral Scientist* 24:6 (July/August 1981): 831.

71. Marie Gottschalk, *The Prison and the Gallows: The Politics of Mass Incarceration in America* (New York: Cambridge University Press, 2006), 145. The LEAA is a coalition of law enforcement professionals, crime victims, and others pushing a law-and-order agenda.

72. Georgia Wralstad Ulmschneider, "Rape and Battered Women's Self-Defense Trials as 'Political Trials': New Perspectives on Feminists' Legal Reform Efforts and Traditional 'Political Trials' Concepts," *Suffolk Law Review* 29 (1995): 115.

73. Elizabeth Schneider, "Describing and Changing: Women's Self-Defense Work and the Problem of Expert Testimony on Battering," *Women's Rights Law Reporter* 9:3, 4 (Fall 1986): 211.

74. See Angela Mae Kupenda, "Law, Life, and Literature: A Critical Reflection of Life and Literature to Illuminate How Laws of Domestic Violence, Race, and Class Bind Black Women," *Howard Law Journal* 42:1 (1998) for a discussion on how the law views certain women, particularly women of color, as "hardened by harsh treatment" and thus less deserving of freedom from further abuse.

75. Gagne, *Battered Women's Justice*, 79. In *State v. Koss* (1990), the court overturned a battered woman's conviction for voluntary manslaughter against her batterer due to the exclusion of testimony concerning Battered Woman's Syndrome.

76. Lorraine Sorrel, "Neglecting Abused Women," *off our backs* 11:6 (June 1981): 23.

77. Lois Ahrens, letter to author, January 22, 2009.

78. Susan Schechter, "Speaking to the Battered Women's Movement," *Aegis* (Spring 1982): 43.

79. Gail Sullivan, "Funny Things Happen on our Way to Revolution," *Aegis* (Spring 1982): 14.

80. Only six women had been killed when the pamphlet was written. Less than three months later, six other black women and one white woman had been murdered.

81. Duchess Harris, "'All of Who I am in the Same Place': The Combahee River Collective," *Womanist Theory and Research: A Journal of Womanist and Feminist of Color Scholarship and Art* 3:1 (1999). Available at http://www.uga.edu/~womanist/harris3.1.htm (accessed May 28, 2009).

82. Although some may feel that the word "racism" is too harsh a term to apply to many of the white feminist (and white left) movements, I chose to use this word rather than a less charged term, such as "racial chauvinism" or "racial prejudice," because it was the terminology that women of color used at the time to critique liberal white feminist organizations. Further, I believe this word more accurately highlights the severity of the concerns, indignations and frustrations that many women of color experienced (and continue to experience) in predominantly white organizations and movements. For prominent critiques of racism within the women's movement at the time, see Cherríe Moraga and Gloria Anzaldúa, eds., *This Bridge Called My Back: Writings by Radical Women of Color* (New York: Kitchen Table Press, 1981); bell hooks, *Ain't I a Woman? Black Women and Feminism* (Boston: South End Press, 1981); Angela Y. Davis, *Women, Culture, and Politics* (New York: Vintage Books, 1990) and *Women, Race, and Class* (New York: Vintage Books, 1981); Audre Lorde, *Sister Outsider: Essays and Speeches* (1984; rpt. Berkeley: Crossing Press,

2007); and Beth E. Richie, "A Black Feminist Reflection on the Antiviolence Movement," in *Domestic Violence at the Margins: Readings on Race, Class, Gender, and Culture*, ed. Natalie J. Sokoloff (New Brunswick, NJ: Rutgers University Press, 2005), 50–55.

83. For example, radical feminists left Austin's Center for Battered Women as the center moved more towards a social service orientation that focused on courts and policing to solve battering. Phyllis B. Frank, now the director of the VSC Community Change Project, recalled, "Women of Color rightfully argued how this [emphasis on arrest and imprisonment] would differentially harm Communities of Color. Some women left, feeling estranged and defeated in relation to the mainstream movement—to begin organizing within their communities and to develop effective strategies"; Phyllis B. Frank, e-mail interview with the author, May 3, 2008. Some women of color created shelters focusing on their communities: South Asian women, influenced not only by the U.S. civil rights and women's movements but also their family's participation in the Indian independence movement, recognized the limitations of the larger (white) battered women's movement and began their own organizations. On the Rosebud Reservation in South Dakota, women created the White Buffalo Calf Shelter; see Enke, "Taking Over Domestic Space," 185.

3

"The Struggle Is for Land!"

Race, Territory, and National Liberation

DAN BERGER, WITH ROXANNE DUNBAR-ORTIZ

> My lands are where my dead lie buried.
>
> —Crazy Horse

> Revolution is based on land. Land is the basis of all independence. Land is the basis of freedom, justice and equality. . . . A revolutionary wants land so he can set up his own nation, an independent nation.
>
> —Malcolm X

National liberation, the dominant response of the Third World to colonialism by the First World, became an increasingly salient political framework for radical people of color in the United States in the 1970s. To a large number of these activists, and even an expanding coterie of academics and other observers, this call for decolonization seemed a necessary response to the political, economic, cultural, and geographic oppression faced by black, indigenous, Mexican, and Puerto Rican people in the United States. This perspective was not original to the 1970s. Its roots were, in fact, both ancient and recent, present since the first European settlement of the Americas and manifesting in various campaigns and projects throughout the twentieth century.[1] Like its counterparts in Africa, Asia, and Latin America, national liberation politics in the United States often, but not always, conceded the logic of the nation-state system that gave rise to colonialism in the first place.

Beginning in the late 1960s, this territorial struggle for self-determination achieved new coherence in various experiments with sovereignty. This turn to land and independence owed, in part, to the non-aligned movement and the various national liberation struggles whose apparent success in overthrowing colonial rule seemed to point toward revolutionary changes worldwide.[2] The war in Vietnam, both against U.S. invasion and for national liberation, amplified this

approach within the United States. American power and policies overseas inculcated a belief among many radicals that American imperialism was the biggest
enemy, and that it could be defeated through the combined efforts of national liberation struggles domestically and abroad. At the same time, processes of urbanization and displacement found an increasing number of black and Indian
working-class people moving from the country, reservations, and the rural South,
to the urban North. This postwar population density of black and indigenous
people in urban areas coincided with the growing power of suburban elites in the
South and Southwest.[3] In the mid-1960s, these same cities witnessed organizing
efforts against police brutality and poverty—struggles that sometimes spilled into
full-fledged riots. All told, such conflagrations led to dozens of deaths, thousands
of arrests, millions of dollars in damage, and a National Guard presence in numerous American cities. For many of those who witnessed or participated in these
events, the city was a battleground—the place where large numbers of people of
color lived and therefore a strategically valuable place to build a base of support.
Black communist autoworker and theorist James Boggs described urban areas as
"the black man's land."[4] Some emerged from those city battles with renewed
efforts to take control of urban politics, through both formal political power and
grassroots mobilization: The election of black mayors, the growth of the welfare
rights movement, and the organizing of groups such as the Black Panthers and the
Committee for a Unified Newark all testify to this urban focus.[5] But others, citing
ancestral connection and a belief that the city was too easily repressed to prove a
long-term base for radical advancement, looked for alternate bases of power.
These activists turned from the cityscape to the countryside as a more appropriate
space in which to wield power.[6]

An evangelical preacher and farmer in New Mexico experimented with the
politics of assuming sovereignty in 1967. In a departure from familiar 1960s political models, longtime land-rights activist Reies López Tijerina led an armed
takeover of the Rio Arriba County courthouse in Tierra Amarilla, New Mexico. The
raid was an attempt to free imprisoned members of Tijerina's group, La Alianza de
Pueblos y Pobladores, to execute a "citizen's arrest" of the district attorney, and to
serve notice to the U.S. government that the area rightfully belonged to the heirs
of Mexican farmers given land grants by the Spanish. The group had exerted its
self-proclaimed judicial authority the previous year when it arrested and tried two
forest rangers for trespassing.[7]

Tijerina's audacious actions eventually landed him two years in prison. Yet
elsewhere within the "internal colonies" of "occupied America,"[8] his example was
evidence that political power grew out of sovereign-held land. Less than a year
after Tijerina attempted to abrogate the sanctity of American legal terrestrial
authority, two organizations that adopted a land-based strategy formed in the
urban Midwest. The year of the barricades, 1968, saw the birth of the American
Indian Movement (AIM) in St. Paul, Minnesota, and the Republic of New Afrika
(RNA) in Detroit.[9] While both groups began in urban contexts, they quickly moved

to establish land bases in non-urban settings nationwide. They looked mostly to the South, Southwest, Great Plains, and Northwest, all areas that did not otherwise appear to be bastions of radicalism. For these militants, land was not a retreat from revolutionary organizing but a consolidation of it. Both groups emerged from the swelling radicalism of that moment, yet their focus on land, rather than cities, served to distinguish them from similar groups—particularly the Black Panthers, whose approach informed AIM and received more sustained national attention than the RNA in discussions of black radicalism at the time. By turning away from organizing for control of urban areas, AIM and the RNA rejected formal U.S. political structures as venues for social change and rejected U.S. citizenship as a framework for proclaiming rights. Rather, their political and strategic orientation called for the development of alternative structures of governance on land to be "liberated" from U.S. control. Such an approach sought to break up U.S. authority by calling into question the legitimacy of its power and the stability of its borders. Even for those similarly focused on building a radical mass movement that challenged the government, these were bold—and not necessarily enticing—ideas.

Both groups described their struggle as continuing the legacy of their ancestral leaders: AIM fought "in the spirit of Crazy Horse" and the RNA staked its claims "by the grace of Malcolm."[10] AIM and RNA saw Native American and black peoples as nations standing off against settler colonialism. The United States had systematically violated hundreds of treaties it had made with Native Americans, the acknowledged first inhabitants of these lands, and AIM attempted to revive those treaties and retake control of Indian Country, both those recognized areas of it (i.e., reservations) and those yet to be recognized (the rest of the United States). The RNA, meanwhile, argued that black people in the United States constituted a new political subject: the New Afrikan, an identity born within the confines of the United States as a result of the trans-Atlantic slave trade and the ensuing centuries of white supremacy. Born in the United States, the New Afrikan could only achieve independence here through claiming the territory that slaves had built and that therefore had been historically home to large populations of black people. Both AIM and the RNA were at the forefront of a 1970s radicalism that viewed land reclamation as essential to dismantling the U.S. empire from within its domestic colonial boundaries. Both groups reflect and helped shape core tenets of 1970s radicalism. They emerged alongside the new visibility achieved by other political communities: feminists, gay radicals, Chicanos, Puerto Rican independentistas, and others. In that sense, AIM and the RNA contributed to the 1970s radical ethos of rejecting the traditional boundaries of American dissent. They expressed the concerns of the 1970s Left: seeking a power base under the assumption of impending revolution, developing politics through ideology as much as popular support, and modeling their strategies on Third World struggles—all done in a spirit that prized audacious confrontation with the U.S. government.

At the center of these projects was the effort to decolonize the United States by stripping from it the wealth it extracted from black and indigenous (as well as

Chicano and Puerto Rican) people and *their* land. Using the political logic of national liberation, these groups combined direct action and international law in what Nikhil Singh, extrapolating from Eldridge Cleaver, has called a "'projection of sovereignty'—a set of oppositional discourses and practices that exposed the hegemony of Americanism as incomplete, challenged its universality, and imagined carving up its spaces differently."[11] That is, *they attempted to secure self-determination by acting with the autonomy they sought.* They established as many of the elements of freely governing societies that they could in the course of working to achieve independence. It was a two-pronged approach, based on defending what they saw as national territory while simultaneously pursuing international support through an appeal to the global move toward decolonization. Such a militant stance earned both groups the enmity of U.S. law enforcement at multiple levels, while in some cases, particularly with the RNA, also generating schisms within the larger political formations from which they emerged. This chapter briefly examines AIM and the RNA as two experiments in claiming sovereignty in the 1970s, each one having long-range impacts on the experience of race, nation, and empire in the United States. To be sure, both groups emerged from complex and multifaceted dynamics particular to their specific circumstances and the tenor of Native American and black radicalism, respectively. However, their simultaneous emergence and political development point to a broader attempt in the 1970s to decolonize the United States through land-based struggles for national liberation.

In the Spirit of Crazy Horse

AIM was born in 1968, and although largely demoralized by the 1980s, it had forged a new direction and new dimension for indigenous resistance—from victim to victor, in a collective assertion of the right to land and self-determination and freedom. The strategy, tactics, and goals of indigenous resistance in the 1970s have not been ignored in accounts of the period, but the key component, the land question, was and remains the elephant in the living room. In the 1970s, a period when leftists were trying to find or form a revolutionary "vanguard" organization, indigenous militants looked to the land as the source of their vanguard practice.

The expropriation of the lands and resources of indigenous peoples by the United States, through its military, corporations, and settlers, was accomplished by the annihilation and dispersal of indigenous populations through direct military attacks, settler attacks, and refugee conditions, with their resultant diseases and demoralization. The expropriation of indigenous territories provided the land base necessary for the development of the U.S. economy. Although less dramatic than under the genocidal practices of the U.S. government in the nineteenth century, the situation of indigenous people at the time of AIM's founding in 1968 was dire: forced birth control and sterilization, various kinds of forced assimilation, removal of Indian children from their homes and communities, destruction of the environment, and theft of water and natural resources under various national and reservation "development" schemes. Of all populations in the United States, indigenous communities had among the lowest wages, highest unemployment (up to 80 percent in the reservations), lowest life expectancy, and highest infant mortality rates. There were widespread malnutrition and related diseases, particularly diabetes; high alcoholism rates and suicide; and shocking conditions of health, education, and housing.[12]

In the late 1960s, reservations comprised 50 million acres of noncontiguous and often arid lands across the United States. Disarmed, confined to reservations requiring permits to leave—with the children removed at six years old and sent far away to government boarding schools for a decade or more, not allowed to speak their languages, prepared for nothing except service work—several generations were stuck in deep colonization, isolated, hungry, and hopeless. Nevertheless, reservations, born of colonial conquest, constitute an existing land base and thus served as a point of departure for indigenous radicalism. Even though urban Indians started AIM, they grew to respond to the conditions of and strategies emerging from rural Indians—especially in the Midwest and Northwest, the largest territory of federal Indian trust lands. For American Indians, land was an economic issue of production and livelihood as well as a social issue of human rights. Indigenous ceremonial practices, religious beliefs, and cultural integrity are deeply rooted in their homelands, even when the present homeland is not the original or traditional land base. Fighting for land, liberty, and self-determination is passed on through indigenous oral traditions and historical memory.[13]

Following the "New Deal" for Indians in the 1930s, which implemented the Indian Reorganization Act to establish "tribal governments" on most reservations, as well as provisions for acquiring additional lost lands, the 1950s cold war administrations reversed the commitment to permanent, land-based indigenous communities and passed legislation to terminate Indian status and land base. The Indian Relocation Program was created to entice indigenous people to move to designated urban areas: Los Angeles, the San Francisco Bay Area, Phoenix, Dallas, Denver, Chicago, and Cleveland. Indians joined African Americans, Chicanos, and poor rural whites who had already left the land and moved into impoverished sections of cities looking for jobs.[14]

The National Indian Youth Movement in New Mexico and the American Indian Movement in Minneapolis were founded by these new urban Indians and quickly spread across the country. From the beginning, the sit-in tactic common to the early civil rights movement (and the labor movement before that) was reinterpreted by indigenous people as land retrieval. The strategy of occupying, reclaiming, or defending land began in the late 1960s and continued into the 1980s, creating militant encampment communities that sometimes became semi-permanent—for instance, Alcatraz (1969–1971), Akwesasne in New York State (1974–1977, with flare-ups continuing for the next two decades), and Deganawidah-Quetzalcoatl, or D-Q, University, a free Indian-Chicano educational institution near Davis, California (1971–2005). There were dozens, if not hundreds, of such actions by indigenous

people all over North America during this period, even leading Richard Nixon, as
early as July 1970, to speak of Indian self-determination.[15]

The elder traditional leaders whom the young indigenous militants respected
and revered taught them that land and self-determination were necessary for
Indian survival. The elders took in a motley crew of returning Indian Vietnam vets,
ex-cons, students, workers, alcoholics, and even "hippie wannabes." The new
indigenous resistance emerged in this period because of attempts to terminate
both the indigenous land base itself and the juridical ability to lay claim to said
territory. The 1971 Alaska Native Claims Settlement Act (ANCSA) was the forerun-
ner of this federal policy. The act extinguished all indigenous Alaskan land claims.
It created twelve regional corporations and roughly two hundred indigenous village corporations—the largest land-claims settlement in United States history,
leaving indigenous Alaskans with one-ninth of their original land base. The corporations are organized on the corporate business model, with the indigenous
people as shareholders, not citizens, receiving shares of stock in oil production.[16]

In 1972, indigenous activists and allies walked from San Francisco to Washington, DC, in the Trail of Broken Treaties. They seized the Bureau of Indian Affairs
building for a week, renamed it the Native American Embassy, and emitted a "20
Point Program," stressing land, resources, and self-determination, as well as federal
government responsibility. The program largely concerned treaties between indigenous nations and the U.S. government, and it became the chief statement of the
activist Indian movement. Specifically addressing the land question, the militants
demanded "land reform and restoration of a 110-million acre native land base":

> The next Congress and Administration should commit themselves and effect
> a national commitment implemented by statutes or executive and adminis-
> trative actions, to restore a permanent non-diminishing Native American
> land base of not less than 110-million acres by July 4, 1976. This land base and
> its separate parts, should be vested with the recognized rights and conditions
> of being perpetually non-taxable except by autonomous and sovereign
> Indian authority, and should never again be permitted to be alienated from
> Native American or Indian ownership and control.[17]

Following the march on Washington, indigenous organizers returned to their
communities filled with ideas and projects to present to an ever-growing indigenous mass base. Russell Means, one of the AIM founders, was from the Pine Ridge
Sioux reservation in South Dakota, but his family had relocated to the San Francisco
Bay Area for defense-plant work during World War II.[18] He went from Washington
to Pine Ridge in February 1973 in response to the traditional elders' plea that AIM
assist them in ousting the corrupt and violent tribal chairman, Richard Wilson, and
his band of vigilantes known as the Guardians of the Oglala Nation (GOONs). The
71-day resistance inside Wounded Knee to massive federal assault, including the FBI
and National Guard, garnered publicity, mostly sympathetic to AIM, around the
world. Viewing the subsequent legal proceedings as an opportunity to further

engage the sovereignty issues, the support campaign for those arrested in the stand-off called itself the Wounded Knee Legal Defense/Offense Committee.[19]

Often described as the swan song of indigenous militancy, Wounded Knee marked a transition rather than a declension. The standoff catapulted AIM into the leadership of an Indian nationalist movement concerned primarily with the land. Before this point, AIM had primarily been a local, urban group, much like the Chicano Brown Berets in Los Angeles or the Black Panthers in Oakland before 1968. AIM's militancy appealed to the local Pine Ridge Sioux Oglala Civil Rights Organization, which invited AIM to help in its campaign against Wilson. The meeting of urban nationalist indigenous youth and traditional reservation groups at Wounded Knee galvanized indigenous people from all over the United States. The alliance of elders—the militants of the 1930s and 1940s who refused to recognize the authority of the U.S. government or the tribal governments—with the nationalist, urban youth became the pattern of the indigenous struggle. Indians, traditional and urban, old and young, traveled to Wounded Knee, and then returned home to organize support for those under siege. AIM chapters, as well as Wounded Knee solidarity groups, sprang up everywhere—even as various law enforcement agencies and vigilantes initiated a reign of terror against those who had participated in or supported the action.[20]

Following the negotiated end of the siege of Wounded Knee, the Lakota (Sioux) movement brought their stolen-lands demands to the forefront, focusing on the Fort Laramie Treaty of 1868 between the United States and the Sioux nation, which guaranteed a contiguous land base for all Sioux that included the Black Hills (Paha Sapa, sacred territory to the Sioux); after gold had been discovered in the Black Hills, they were illegally appropriated. As settlers were urged to develop ranching and farming, more and more land was taken from the Sioux nation–guaranteed land base, until noncontiguous islands were all that remained in indigenous hands. The United States Court of Claims awarded the Sioux monetary compensation for the illegal taking of the Black Hills, but the Sioux have refused to take the money and continue to demand the return of the territory.[21]

In 1974, just over a year after Wounded Knee, AIM sponsored the founding of the International Indian Treaty Council (see chapter 7 by Roxanne Dunbar-Ortiz), which applied for and gained consultative nongovernmental status in the United Nations division related to human rights, including the right to self-determination. Its founding document, the Declaration of Continuing Independence, pledged solidarity with national liberation movements throughout the Third World, specifically highlighting the "colonized Puerto Rican People in their struggle for Independence from the same United States of America."[22] This initiative launched what would become a hemispheric, then global pan-indigenous movement with a strong presence in the United Nations, inscribed by the UN in 2007 by the UN Declaration on the Rights of Indigenous Peoples.

By 1980, AIM was not as big or as visible as it once had been. External repression and internal dissension had significantly weakened the organization, as with most groups of the era. Yet the political perspective and strategic approach it helped usher in persisted. Navajos at Big Mountain in the western Arizona part of the Navajo reservation filed a complaint against the U.S. government at the Fourth Russell Tribunal on the Rights of the Indians of the Americas, held in Rotterdam, Holland, in November 1980. On the reservation, meanwhile, the Navajo and Hopi Indians continued to protect their land and livelihood from a 1974 congressional act to relocate the reservation and confiscate its territory. Big Mountain remains an ongoing battle over land rights between indigenous peoples and the U.S. government.

By the Grace of Malcolm

The RNA formed out of the 1968 Black Government Conference held at Detroit's Shrine of the Black Madonna, church of the stalwart black nationalist Reverend Albert Cleage. About five hundred people—frustrated youth, insurgent workers, fiery Marxists, old Garveyites—attended the conference, which concluded with one hundred of the attendees signing a declaration of independence from the United States. As one of the organizers said at a press conference accompanying the declaration, "We want out."[23] While defining all black people in the United States as colonized by white supremacy, the statement identified five states of the Black Belt South—Alabama, Georgia, Louisiana, Mississippi, and South Carolina—as New Afrika's national territory. The RNA was one of several black radical organizations to declare itself dedicated to national liberation, yet the RNA moved quickly and boldly to establish the apparatus of an independent nation. New Afrika was to be the North American outpost of the unfolding struggle for a united, socialist Africa. For better and worse, such an approach called on many of the models put forward by other Third World movements, which inherited imperialist frameworks of national boundaries and capitalist logics of development that, even when used in countering colonialism, still replicated some of its forms.[24]

From Tanzania, RNA president-elect Robert F. Williams issued a statement calling the Republic "one of self-determination for an oppressed people" rooted in black nationalism, grassroots democracy, and a socialist economics.[25] Williams's presidency was more symbolic than material, but he was not the only high-profile black militant attracted to the RNA; other early RNA officials included Muhammad Ahmad and Herman Ferguson of the Revolutionary Action Movement; Maulana Karenga of the organization US (before he was expelled from the RNA after members of US killed two Black Panthers at UCLA in 1969); Amiri Baraka, then of the Committee for a Unified Newark; H. Rap Brown of the Student Nonviolent Coordinating Committee (SNCC); and Malcolm X's widow, Betty Shabazz. The goal of an independent Republic also appealed to many in the Black Panther Party: Los Angeles Panther (and Vietnam veteran) Geronimo ji Jaga helped the RNA build its ministry of defense, and by 1971, many people within the New York Panther chapter announced their citizenship in the Republic.[26] Avowed revolutionaries were not the only ones who offered their support. After police fired on and arrested almost 150 attendees of the 1969 RNA meeting at the New Bethel Baptist Church in Detroit, the Reverend C. L. Franklin (father of singer Aretha Franklin and head of the church) said he shared the RNA's goals, if not its methods. Southern Christian Leadership Conference director Ralph Abernathy came to Detroit to investigate the melee and sharply criticized the police.[27]

Despite the RNA's emphasis on the U.S. South, Detroit remained its home base until 1970. The group's co-founders, Imari and Gaidi Obadele, formerly Richard and Milton Henry, each had long and impressive organizing histories in the motor city.[28] The group spread east and west before going south. Immediately after its founding conference, the RNA "established consulates in New York, Philadelphia, Chicago, Pittsburgh, San Francisco, Los Angeles, Baltimore, Cleveland, and Washington, D.C." and began meeting with foreign governments, including the Soviet Union, Tanzania, Sudan, and China.[29] This attempt to develop a presence nationally and internationally emerged from the RNA's commitment to the political strategies advanced by Malcolm X toward the end of his life. Malcolm was, in fact, the guiding influence for the RNA. What became the RNA's founding conference was organized by a group, started by the Henry brothers, called the Malcolm X Society. Imari Obadele dedicated his 1966 pamphlet, *War in America: The Malcolm X Doctrine* to "the Malcolmites."[30] From Malcolm, who had been their friend as well as their inspiration, the Obadele brothers identified the key constituents of revolutionary struggle as land, self-defense, and internationalism.

To this strategy, RNA advisor Queen Mother Audley Moore, a veteran of both the Communist Party and the Garvey movement, as well as the first person to sign the New Afrikan Declaration of Independence, emphasized the need to look south, build a nation-state, and fight for reparations.[31] The call for reparations, in fact, was one of the RNA's central demands from its beginning. Initially, the RNA argued that reparations were essential to building the black nation. Its stalwart demand for reparations extended beyond the 1970s, as witnessed in the RNA's role, with the New Afrikan People's Organization and the National Conference of Black Lawyers, in helping found the National Coalition of Blacks for Reparations in America (N'COBRA) in 1987, an alliance of groups working for slavery reparations.[32]

While organizing for reparations, the RNA continued to establish its national policy. The Obadele brothers, however, disagreed over the correct strategy to pursue and whether the group should build a broader black united front throughout the United States or focus on developing the New Afrikan national infrastructure in the South. This disagreement led to a rancorous falling out between the two of them, and Gaidi left the group. In 1970, Imari Obadele led a small, disciplined cadre of RNA activists in a move to Jackson, Mississippi, to establish the Republic's national headquarters. The group hoped that Jackson would be the base of the developing black revolution. Other black groups also looked south at the time, more for cultural sustenance than political mobilization. The same year the RNA moved to Jackson, a separate, unaffiliated group of black cultural nationalists established the Oyotunji African Village near Charleston, South Carolina, as a "Yoruba Empire" in the United States.[33]

A year after their move south, however, much of the RNA leadership found itself incarcerated following an August 1971 shootout, when the FBI and Jackson police raided an RNA house; they also arrested RNA activists without incident at a second house nearby.[34] But the Republic continued. In 1972, the RNA unveiled its "Anti-Depression Program," with legislative actions for securing independence. The program made three basic demands of the U.S. government: ceding land and sovereignty to the RNA "in areas where blacks vote for independence" via plebiscite; paying $300 billion in reparations "for slavery and unjust war against the black nation"; and establishing a negotiations procedure to determine reparations payment. This program, it was hoped, would help "end poverty, dependence, and crime," "raise self-esteem, achievement, and creativity, and . . . promote interracial peace." The plebiscite demand was especially critical for the RNA—as well as the Black Panthers, who made a similar call—for it would enable black people to decide if they *wanted* the citizenship that had been bestowed upon them by the Fourteenth Amendment.[35] Within months of its release, the program was presented to the first National Black Political Convention, in Gary, Indiana; submitted to the U.S. Congress; supported by comedian Dick Gregory; and approved by the NAACP-headed Mississippi Loyalist Democrats. In addition to supporting the Anti-Depression Program, the National Black Political Assembly held public hearings on the incarceration of the eleven RNA members after the 1971 shootout.[36]

The Anti-Depression plan called for the development of New Communities throughout RNA territory, especially Mississippi. These communities were to model Ujamaa, Tanzanian socialism, and make real the RNA's territorial claims through development and emigration. To the RNA, these communities were a demonstration of New Afrikan sovereignty by providing a rear base and free state for the embattled black masses. Together with reparations, the plan argued, New Communities would provide the infrastructure for black people displaced by economic necessity or political terror to move back south.[37] These communities were part of the RNA's organizing for reparations. In March 1974, the RNA held an election in thirty counties across Mississippi, where nearly five thousand black people over the age of fifteen voted for reparations and elected Imari Obadele president of the Mississippi Black Assembly. The election was monitored by the Election Commission of the Black Political Scientists. That fall, the National Black Political Convention unanimously approved a resolution calling for the National Black Political Assembly to join the RNA and the Mississippi Black Assembly in demanding $300 billion in reparations.[38]

The RNA maintained its presence in Mississippi throughout the 1970s. In September 1975, the RNA-sponsored National Black Elections established the officiating body as the Provisional Government of the Republic of New Afrika (PG-RNA). This election, drawing in supporters of New Afrikan independence in Mississippi, Detroit, and Washington, DC, distinguished between the *idea* of New Afrika and its *governmental apparatus*. With revolutionary black nationalism no longer commanding as significant a base as it once did, some self-described New Afrikans did not want the mechanisms of governing to get in the way of the social-movement organizing they deemed necessary to improve people's lives and rebuild this nationalist consciousness.[39] These activists, echoing early Black Panther critiques of the RNA, as well as Gaidi Obadele's earlier disagreements with his brother, argued that running a government was premature, given the organizing demands of the moment. While defining themselves as New Afrikans loyal to the Provisional Government, these dissidents committed themselves to bringing other black people into the New Afrikan fold and organizing campaigns against the U.S. government—rather than focusing their efforts primarily on building the nascent New Afrikan governmental apparatus. In particular, this grouping included radical black prisoners and their supporters. While many black prisoners supported the PG-RNA, their lack of physical mobility helped feed their interest in intellectual production and political mobilization as a first priority over state-building. The prison movement of the middle to late 1970s, weakened from its height in the early part of the decade, was perhaps the site where New Afrikan politics blossomed the most.

Prisoners occupied a central place in the New Afrikan political imagination. Prisoner leadership and visibility within RNA groupings, as well as their role as theorists of black radicalism, owed not only to the increasing number of black people being incarcerated. It was, rather, a vital part of the group's analysis, which defined blackness as a site of incarceration, and black bodies as always already confined and colonized within the United States. That position spread RNA ideology throughout the prison system nationally and kept radical black prisoners at the forefront of an admittedly weakened black nationalist organizing in the 1970s, even after the prison movement itself had significantly contracted.[40]

RNA politics spread throughout the prison system partly due to the organizing done inside prisons by RNA activists and sympathizers. Imari Obadele, for instance, participated in the formation of a multiracial coalition of radical prisoners at the Marion control-unit prison and wrote for a black nationalist prisoner magazine based there, *Black Pride*.[41] Formed in 1972, *Black Pride* was one of several prison-based or -focused publications to adopt a New Afrikan political perspective throughout the decade. In California, deemed the epicenter of prison activism in the early 1970s, New Afrikan prisoners started a quarterly newspaper in 1978 called *Arm the Spirit*.[42] As with *Black Pride*, *Arm the Spirit* was written and edited by a group of prisoners—in this case, a coalition of former Black Panthers and people whose political activism began only after their incarceration. Though the editorial decisions were made inside, the paper was produced and distributed by outside supporters, first by the Prairie Fire Organizing Committee, a white anti-imperialist organization, and then briefly by the African People's Socialist Party. The paper lasted until the early 1980s, covering prison rebellions, political prisoners, armed struggle and the state of black politics in the United States, and anti-colonial battles overseas (especially in Africa).[43]

One of the most prolific New Afrikan theorists was incarcerated at Stateville Prison in Illinois. Atiba Shanna formed the Stateville Prisoners Organization and began producing the journal *Notes from a New Afrikan P.O.W.* in 1977 (renamed *Vita Wa Watu: A New Afrikan Theoretical Journal* in the 1980s). From his cell at Stateville, Shanna publicized and helped organize support for the Pontiac Brothers, seventeen black prisoners charged with murder stemming from a deadly 1978 revolt at the central Illinois prison.[44] (Pontiac was the biggest collective death-penalty case involving blacks since the Scottsboro Boys.) Shanna also formed the New Afrikan Prisoners Organization (NAPO), which drafted a petition to the United Nations in 1977. This petition anticipated one submitted to the United Nations Sub-Commission on the Prevention of Discrimination and Protection of Minorities on December 11, 1978, by the National Conference of Black Lawyers, the National Alliance Against Racist and Political Repression, and the Commission on Racial Justice for the United Church of Christ.[45] The NAPO petition proudly resurrected the famous 1951 petition by black radicals at the United Nations, "We Charge Genocide." NAPO expanded its rationale for the petition into a pamphlet titled *We Still Charge Genocide*. The pamphlet and petition both originated out of a prisoner study group focused on the Thirteenth Amendment. As a result of this research, and clearly in line with the RNA's plebiscite demand, the prisoners determined that the amendment widely seen as abolishing slavery actually legalized it by explicitly legitimating its use "as a punishment for crimes."[46] To New Afrikan activists, the U.S. Constitution proved that black people were destined for slavery, imprisonment, or death within the U.S. borders. Even reform efforts, such as the Thirteenth, Fourteenth, and Fifteenth amendments only served to extend black subjection, as far as they surmised. From behind prison walls, New Afrikan activists organized based on Malcolm X's dictum—"If you're black, you were born in jail."[47]

Believing themselves the target of genocide, New Afrikans argued that they needed to, as poet-singer-activist Gil Scott-Heron put it, "take it to the United Nations."[48] This international demand characterized New Afrikan activism throughout the decade. The National Black Human Rights Coalition organized a march of five thousand people on November 5, 1979, at the UN under the banner "Black People Charge Genocide" and "Human Rights is the Right to Self-Determination." Organizers also called for a one-day strike by black prisoners in solidarity with the march. The march, organized as the tenth annual Black Solidarity Day, came three days after Black Liberation Army (BLA) prisoner Assata Shakur escaped from prison in New Jersey.[49] A communiqué from the BLA taking responsibility for helping Shakur escape was read at the rally. A statement from Shakur, herself a proponent of New Afrikan politics, was also circulated among the participants, as signs celebrating her freedom could be seen among the crowd. Speakers included Dara Abubakari, Queen Mother Moore, and Chokwe Lumumba, all of whom had been active in the RNA (although Moore, by this point, was not). The march demands included "freedom for all Black political prisoners and prisoners of war" as well as land, self-determination, and an end to police violence.[50]

Into the 1980s, in both the urban North and rural South, New Afrikan activists continued to press for reparations, an end to police brutality, and freedom for imprisoned radicals. Such campaigns endured amidst a new round of court cases that beset New Afrikans and their supporters following a failed armored car robbery in 1981 outside New York City by the BLA that left one security guard and two police officers dead. Subsequent arrests in the following days and months targeted other RNA activists, including Mtyari Sundiata, a charter member of the New York branch who was shot and killed following a high-speed chase by police, and Fulani Sunni-Ali, who was arrested in a large-scale police raid on the RNA farm in Mississippi.[51] During the ensuing rounds of trials prosecuting the robbery and Shakur's escape, RNA adherents and supporters protested the proceedings, as several defendants adopted the position that they were prisoners of war—armed combatants in the struggle for national liberation and therefore not subject to U.S. criminal law. In a series of trials that lasted until the late 1980s, a dozen people were convicted and sentenced to lengthy terms in prison, and dozens more served time for refusing to cooperate with grand-jury investigations.[52]

Terra Incognita

Neither AIM nor the RNA ever commanded a majority of people, even among the population it claimed as its own. Both groups were weakened by a combination of factors internal and external to their work. By the start of the next decade, their respective programs seemed out of step to most people. The 1980s witnessed an incredible backlash against the gains made by radical social movements of the previous twenty years, particularly those of indigenous and black activists. President Ronald Reagan's celebration of resurgent American hegemony at all costs was the polar opposite of the critique leveraged by national liberation groups such as AIM and the RNA. Both groups, and their allied organizations, articulated a strategy of defeating U.S. imperialism through the coordinated efforts of internal colonies withdrawing their material resources and political loyalty from the United States.

Besides AIM and the RNA, organizations in the 1970s and 1980s that also saw land as the fulcrum of freedom and advocated for the dissolution of the U.S. nation-state included the Crusade for Justice (Chicano), the Movimiento de Liberación Nacional (which included Puerto Rican and Chicano groups), and the Prairie Fire Organizing Committee (white), among others.[53] These groups, independently and sometimes in coalition, argued that radicalism in the United States must contend with and ultimately overturn the country's settler-colonial roots.[54] Rather than influencing or trying to seize power within the existing structures of the country, these groups opted for the far more controversial position of working to dissolve the United States as such. The groups pursued this program through directly challenging the U.S. government and by building institutions to counter and prefigure replacements to its power. These organizations routinely confronted the government, voluntarily through particular campaigns or demonstrations, but as often involuntarily, as a result of numerous arrests and trials that thinned their already small numbers.

There were, of course, many differences between the two groups studied here, including their relationship to the state as a concept and their historic claims to the land in question. The RNA conceived of itself as a state-building project, whereas AIM did not.[55] The groups themselves were burdened by competing land claims, given that New Afrika is located firmly within Indian Country. By the early 1980s, the RNA had acknowledged indigenous land claims and sought to craft a land-based strategy that accommodated their different historical positions. Others, however, remained dissatisfied with any attempt by non-Indians to claim land or indigenous status. In 2001, for instance, Cherokee activist Pamela Kingfisher told RNA activists that "You can have the mule; but the forty acres are ours."[56] Kingfisher's quip highlights some of the difficulty embedded within projects aiming to remake long-imposed boundaries.

But their shared strategy disarticulated nation from state by assuming, affirming, and appealing to a presumed national consciousness within their respective populations. Both projects, then, attempted to operationalize the assertion LeRoi Jones (later Amiri Baraka) made in 1962: "'Black' [or Red] is a country." Moving beyond the rhetoric of national identities, these groups made concrete the political logic embedded in the claims of racial solidarity leveraged throughout the 1960s and 1970s.[57] These organizations called for redrawing the political boundaries of the modern world. Or, as a popular AIM slogan put it, "U.S. Out of North America."

These and related groups contribute to an understanding of the spatial politics of race and radicalism in the post-sixties, post–civil rights United States. Their collective emphasis on land and independence, rather than concessions within the existing political framework, posited race as a material concept embedded in the formation of the United States—its very geography—and the demarcation of its boundaries and its citizenship. Their organizing, admittedly small but decidedly ambitious, tried to apply international law to the most disenfranchised populations, such as people living in prison or on reservations. They often operated within Leninist notions of vanguard political programs and fought to bolster imagined national communities[58] by emphasizing racial unity as its own national identity against an American national unity. As a result, it is tempting, perhaps, to see them as part of the 1970s defense of ethnic particularity. But their emphasis on land and international law as mechanisms to empower disenfranchised populations applied tactics and strategies of the 1960s social movements to the increasingly globalized world of the 1970s. Their struggles center questions of land and identity as fundamental to addressing the vexing history and shifting future of the United States.

ACKNOWLEDGMENTS

Thanks to Ed Onaci, Dylan Rodriguez, and Akinyele Umoja for their comments on drafts of this essay. Conversations with Abdul Shanna, as well as several others over the years, helped clarify some of the conceptual terrain.

NOTES

1. See, for instance, Daniel M. Cobb and Loretta Fowler, eds., *Beyond Red Power: American Indian Politics and Activism Since 1900* (Santa Fe: School for Advanced Research Press, 2007); and Robin D. G. Kelley, *Freedom Dreams: The Black Radical Imagination* (New Boston: Beacon Press, 2002). Theories of "internal colonialism" could be found among both academics and activists at the time. For one overview, see Cynthia A. Young, *Soul Power: Culture, Radicalism, and the Making of a U.S. Third World Left* (Durham, NC: Duke University Press, 2006).

2. See Vijay Prashad, *The Darker Nations: A People's History of the Third World* (New York: The New Press, 2007); Robert J.C. Young, *Postcolonialism: An Historical Introduction* (Malden, MA: Blackwell Publishing, 2001).

3. Bruce J. Schulman, *The Seventies: The Great Shift in American Culture, Society, and Politics* (New York: De Capo Press, 2001); Thomas J. Sugrue, *The Origins of the Urban Crisis: Race and Inequality in Postwar Detroit* (Princeton, NJ: Princeton University Press, 1996).

4. James Boggs, *Racism and the Class Struggle: Further Pages from a Black Worker's Notebook* (New York: Monthly Review Press, 1970), 39–50.

5. Cf. Cedric Johnson, *Revolutionaries to Race Leaders: Black Power and the Making of African American Politics* (Minneapolis: University of Minnesota Press, 2007); Felicia Kornbluh, *The Battle for Welfare Rights: Politics and Poverty in Modern America* (Philadelphia: University of Pennsylvania Press, 2007); Robert Self, *American Babylon: Race and the Struggle for Postwar Oakland* (Princeton, NJ: Princeton University Press, 2003); and Komozi Woodard, *A Nation Within a Nation: Amiri Baraka (LeRoi Jones) and Black Power Politics* (Chapel Hill: University of North Carolina Press, 1999).

6. This turn to the countryside mirrored Mao Zedong's emphasis on the revolutionary potential of the peasantry. While some in AIM and the RNA may have been sympathetic to Mao or the Chinese Revolution, they did not articulate their emphasis on land in a specifically Maoist framework.

7. Lorena Oropeza, "The Heart of Chicano History: Reies López Tijerina as a Memory Entrepreneur," *The Sixties* 1:1 (2008): 49–67; Patricia Bell Blawis, *Tijerina and the Land Grants: Mexican Americans in Struggle for their Heritage* (New York: International Publishers, 1971).

8. Rodolfo Acuña, *Occupied America: The Chicano's Struggle Toward Liberation* (San Francisco: Canfield Press, 1972).

9. At the convention and for several years after, the group spelled Africa with a "c," as is traditionally done in English. It ultimately switched to spelling it with a "k," as is done here. Former Black Panther and current political prisoner Sundiata Acoli explained the difference in an essay: "We of the New Afrikan Independence Movement spell 'Afrikan' with a 'k' as an indicator of our cultural identification with the Afrikan continent and because Afrikan linguists originally used 'k' to indicate the [hard] 'c' sound in the English language." See Sundiata Acoli, "An Updated History of the New Afrikan Prison Struggle," in *Imprisoned Intellectuals: America's Political Prisoners Write on Life, Liberation, and Rebellion*, ed. Joy James (Lanham, MD: Rowman & Littlefield, 2003), 138. Because this chapter discusses the RNA and the New Afrikan Independence Movement it helped launch, including some political formations that still exist, the current spelling is used throughout, unless direct quotations use an alternate spelling.

10. Peter Matthiessen titled his best-selling book about AIM's struggle for sovereignty and against government repression *In the Spirit of Crazy Horse*. Chaat Smith and Warrior write that AIM leader Russell Means had a charismatic style that "made many people think of Crazy Horse," among other well-known indigenous militants. See Paul Chaat Smith and

Robert Allen Warrior, *Like a Hurricane: The Indian Movement from Alcatraz to Wounded Knee* (New York: The New Press, 1996), 134. The "New African Creed" printed in Imari Abubakari Obadele's *Foundations of the Black Nation* (Detroit: House of Songhay, 1975), 153, lists fifteen principles, including a belief in the "community as a family," "the constant struggle for freedom," and "that the fundamental way to gain that power [to control our lives], and end oppression, is to build a sovereign black nation." The creed concludes with a statement of affirmation: "Now, freely and of my own will, i [sic] pledge this creed, for the sake of freedom for my people and a better world, on pain of disgrace and banishment if i prove false. For, i am no longer deaf, dumb or blind. I am—by the grace of Malcolm—a New African." The lower-case "i" was typical of RNA discourse, alongside its corollary, a capitalized "We." Both nontraditional spellings were a part of the efforts within the RNA and others in the New Afrikan independence movement to challenge individualism and celebrate collectivity.

11. Nikhil Pal Singh, *Black Is a Country: Race and the Unfinished Struggle for Democracy* (Cambridge, MA: Harvard University Press, 2004), 205.

12. American Indian Policy Review Commission, *Final Report*, submitted to Congress May 17, 1977 (Washington, DC: U.S. Government Printing Office, 1978). Other Native Americans were publicizing the histories and contemporary conditions indigenous people faced. Perhaps the most famous were Dee Brown, *Bury My Heart at Wounded Knee* (New York: Holt, Rinehart, and Winston, 1971); and Vine Deloria, *Custer Died for Your Sins* (New York: Macmillan, 1969). For more recent accounts, see, for example, Luana Ross, *Inventing the Savage: The Social Construction of Native American Criminality* (Austin: University of Texas Press, 1998); and Andrea Smith, *Conquest: Sexual Violence and American Indian Genocide* (Cambridge, MA: South End Press, 2005).

13. Roxanne Dunbar-Ortiz, "Land Reform and Indian Survival in the United States," in *Land Reform, American Style*, ed. Charles C. Geisler and Frank J. Popper (Totowa, NJ: Rowman & Allanheld, 1984), 155–156.

14. Donald L. Fixico, *Termination and Relocation: Federal Indian Policy, 1945–1960* (Albuquerque: University of New Mexico Press, 1986).

15. Dunbar-Ortiz, "Land Reform and Indian Survival," 158–159; Douglas M. George-Kanentiio, *Iroquois on Fire: A Voice from the Mohawk Nation* (Westport, CT: Praeger, 2006), 11–38; and James M. Naughton, "President Urges Wider Indian Role in Aid for Tribes," *New York Times*, July 9, 1970, 1.

16. Gary C. Anders, "Social and Economic Consequences of Federal Indian Policy: A Case Study of the Alaska Natives," *Economic Development and Cultural Change* 37:2 (1989): 285–303.

17. The entire document is available at http://www.aimovement.org/ggc/trailofbroken treaties.html (accessed July 23, 2009). More generally on the BIA takeover, see Chaat Smith and Warrior, *Like a Hurricane*, 87–168.

18. Russell Means, *Where White Men Fear to Tread: The Autobiography of Russell Means* (New York: St. Martin's Press, 1995).

19. For more on Wounded Knee, see Matthiessen, *In the Spirit of Crazy Horse*; see also Bruce D'Arcus, "Protest, Scale and Publicity: The FBI and the H. Rap Brown Act," *Antipode* 35:4 (2003): 718–741.

20. Dunbar-Ortiz, "Land Reform and Indian Survival," 159–160.

21. Edward Lazarus, *Black Hills, White Justice: The Sioux Nation versus the United States, 1775 to the Present* (Lincoln: University of Nebraska Press, 1999).

22. Quoted in Dunbar-Ortiz, "Land Reform and Indian Survival," 160.

23. Anthony Ripley, "Negro Group Asks End of Ties to U.S.," *New York Times*, March 31, 1968, 32.

24. María Josefina Saldaña-Portillo, *The Revolutionary Imagination in the Americas and the Age of Development* (Durham, NC: Duke University Press, 2003).

25. Robert Williams was the head of the Monroe, North Carolina, chapter of the NAACP and a well-known advocate of armed self-defense for black people. His efforts to train and defend black people in Monroe made him a target of the white establishment and vigilantes, ultimately forcing him out of the country for many years. He became an early symbol of Black Power and black militancy. His statement is printed as a sidebar to Robert Sherrill, "Birth of a (Black) Nation," *Esquire*, January 1969, 73. The RNA helped make possible Williams's return to the United States in September 1969, after an almost decade-long absence. He resigned his post as president two months later. See Timothy Tyson, *Radio Free Dixie: Robert F. Williams and the Roots of Black Power* (Chapel Hill: University of North Carolina Press, 1999), 297–298, 302–305.

26. Chokwe Lumumba, *The Roots of the New Afrikan Independence Movement* (Jackson, MS: New Afrikan Productions, 1991), 10; Geronimo ji Jaga, "Every Nation Struggling to Be Free Has a Right to Struggle, a Duty to Struggle," in *Liberation, Imagination, and the Black Panther Party: A New Look at the Panthers and Their Legacy*, ed. Kathleen Cleaver and George Katsiaficas (New York: Routledge, 2001), 75.

27. As the RNA's meeting was ending, two police officers approached the church after seeing men with guns, possibly armed guards for Gaidi Obadele, who feared assassination attempts on revolutionary black leaders. Shooting erupted between police and the RNA; both sides accuse the other of firing first. One officer died, and police swarmed the church, shooting four and arresting everyone inside. Well-known Detroit black radical judge George Crockett released most of those arrested, saying their rights had been violated, and held the district attorney in contempt for questioning his judgment. Crockett was widely criticized by the Detroit police and politicians for his action. See Dan Georgakas and Marvin Surkin, *Detroit: I Do Mind Dying: A Study in Urban Revolution* (Cambridge, MA: South End Press, 1998), 55; "Nab 135 As Cop is Killed," *Chicago Defender*, March 31, 1969, 1; "Police Storm into Detroit Church as Officer Is Killed," *Los Angeles Times*, March 31, 1969, 1; "Policeman Killed in Detroit Battle," *New York Times*, March 31, 1969, 1; "Judge Draws Criticism for Releasing Suspects," *Los Angeles Times*, April 1, 1969, 4; and Anthony Ripley, "Detroit's Mayor Defends Police," *New York Times*, April 2, 1969, 24.

28. Lumumba, *The Roots of the New Afrikan Independence Movement*, 9; Peniel E. Joseph, *Waiting 'Til the Midnight Hour: A Narrative History of Black Power in America* (New York: Henry Holt, 2006), 51–57.

29. Donald Cunnigen, "The Republic of New Africa in Mississippi," in *Black Power in the Belly of the Beast*, ed. Judson L. Jeffries (Urbana: University of Illinois Press, 2006), 98.

30. Brother Imari, *War in America: The Malcolm X Doctrine* (Chicago: Ujamaa Distributors, 1968), iii. See also the "New Afrikan Creed," reprinted in Imari Abubakari Obadele, *Foundations of the Black Nation* (Detroit: House of Songhay, 1975), 153.

31. Lumumba, *The Roots of the New Afrikan Independence Movement*, 11–13. For more on Moore, see Muhammad Ahmad, *We Will Return in the Whirlwind: Black Radical Organizations 1960–1975* (Chicago: Charles H. Kerr Publishers, 2007), 7–13; Thomas J. Sugrue, *Sweet Land of Liberty: The Forgotten Struggle for Civil Rights in the North* (New York: Random House, 2008), 272–273, 434–435.

32. Sherrill, "Birth of a (Black) Nation"; Adjoa A. Aiyetoro, "The National Coalition of Blacks for Reparations in America (N'COBRA): Its Creation and Contribution to the Reparations Movement," in *Should America Pay? Slavery and the Raging Debate on Reparations*, ed. Raymond A. Winbush (New York: Amistad, 2003), 209–225.

33. Kamari Maxine Clarke, *Mapping Yoruba Networks: Power and Agency in the Making of Transnational Communities* (Durham, NC: Duke University Press, 2004).

34. On August 18, 1971, Jackson police and FBI approached RNA headquarters at 6 A.M. with a warrant to arrest a person who was not there. After giving the occupants 75 seconds to exit, police opened fire with tear gas and almost 300 bullets. Inside the house, RNA activists returned fire, killing one officer and wounding two. Police ultimately arrested seven people inside and moved six blocks down to an affiliated RNA residence, arresting four people without violence. The group, which included RNA president Imari Obadele, became known in radical circles as the RNA 11. Seven were convicted of murder, and three were sentenced to life, although a campaign on their behalf, along with some legal technicalities that played in their favor, resulted in all eleven being released by 1981. Imari Obadele's perspective on the shootout can be found in Obadele, *Foundations of the Black Nation* and Imari Abubakari Obadele, *Free the Land! The True Story of the Trials of the RNA-11 in Mississippi and the Continuing Struggle to Establish an Independent Black Nation in Five States in the Deep South* (Washington, DC: House of Songhay, 1984). See also Christian Davenport, "Understanding Covert Repressive Action: The Case of the U.S. Government Against the Republic of New Africa," *Journal of Conflict Resolution* 49:1 (2005): 120–140; Associated Press, "FBI Agent, 2 Officers Wounded in Shootout with Miss. Blacks," *Los Angeles Times*, August 18, 1971, 2; Andrew Reese Jr., "3 Wounded in RNA Gun Battle," *Chicago Defender*, August, 19, 1971, 4; and Roy Reed, "Black Separatist Guilty in Slaying," *New York Times*, September 15, 1972, 11.

35. For the Panthers plebiscite demand, see G. Louis Heath, ed., *Off the Pigs: The History and Literature of the Black Panther Party* (Metuchen, NJ: Scarecrow Press, 1976), 377–382.

36. National Black Political Assembly press release, August 17, 1973, National Alliance Against Racist and Political Repression papers, box 1, folder 1, Schomburg Center for Research on Black Culture, New York Public Library. The program is reprinted in Obadele, *Foundations of the Black Nation*, 73–106.

37. "Launch New Organization," *Chicago Defender*, August 9, 1973, 11; "New Africa Opens 1st New Site," *Chicago Defender*, March 27, 1971, 15.

38. Obadele, *Foundations of the Black Nation*, 132; "Reparations Plan Supported," *Chicago Defender*, March 26, 1974, 9.

39. Lumumba, *The Roots of the New Afrikan Independence Movement*; Imari Obadele, "A People's Revolt for Power and an Up-Turn in the Black Condition: An Appeal and a Challenge," in *The New Abolitionists: (Neo)Slave Narratives and Contemporary Prison Writings*, ed. Joy James (Albany: State University of New York Press, 2005), 153–160.

40. In addition to the RNA, black nationalist groups such as the Afrikan People's Party and collectives of former Black Panthers continued emphasizing prisoners in their work. Antiracist white solidarity activists in groups such as the Prairie Fire Organizing Committee (PFOC) and the Sojourner Truth Organization supported their efforts through media and funding. Much of this organizing is reflected in publications produced by PFOC (*Breakthrough*) and a newspaper produced by an autonomous collective of former Black Panthers (*Seize the Time*), among others. See, for instance, *Breakthrough* vertical file and *Seize the Time* vertical file, Freedom Archives.

41. *Black Pride*, Jessica Mitford Papers, Harry T. Ransom Center, University of Texas at Austin, box 56, folder 3. See also Alan Eladio Gómez, "Resisting Living Death at Marion Federal Penitentiary, 1972," *Radical History Review* 96 (Fall 2006): 58–86. Obadele also describes his prison organizing in *Free the Land!*, 246–282.

42. Eric Cummins, *The Rise and Fall of California's Radical Prison Movement* (Stanford, CA: Stanford University Press, 1994).

43. *Arm the Spirit* vertical file, Freedom Archives; Kalima Aswad, interview with Dan Berger, October 24, 2008. Diana Block, one of the PFOC activists to work on the newspaper, describes the process briefly in her memoir, *Arm the Spirit: A Woman's Journey Underground and Back* (Oakland, CA: AK Press, 2009), 148–150.

44. Shanna also went by the name Yaki Yakuba. See Nancy Kurshan and Steve Whitman, "A Yaki-Sized Hole in the Universe," April 18, 2008, available at http://boricuahuman rights.org/2008/04/18/a-yaki-sized-hole-in-the-universe/ (accessed July 23, 2009). *Notes from an Afrikan P.O.W.* and *Vita Wa Watu* were distributed by supporters in the Chicago area and elsewhere. Several issues have since been made available online; see http:// www.prairiefire.org/Crossroad.shtml (accessed July 23, 2009).

45. The petition and some supporting documents were published in Lennox S. Hinds, *Illusions of Justice: Human Rights Violations in the United States* (Iowa City: School of Social Work, 1978). Shortly before the petition was submitted, the U.S. ambassador to the United Nations, former civil rights activist Andrew Young, told a French newspaper during an interview that there were "hundreds, maybe even thousands of people I would call political prisoners" incarcerated in the United States. The Carter administration chastised Young for his remarks, as did several other politicians. See, for instance, Associated Press, "Political Prisoners in U.S., Young Says," *New York Times*, July 13, 1978, A3.

46. New Afrikan Prisoners Organization, *We Still Charge Genocide* (n.p., 1977). NAPO vertical file, Freedom Archives.

47. Malcolm X, "The Ballot or the Bullet," speech delivered April 3, 1964, available at http://teachingamericanhistory.org/library/index.asp?document=1147 (accessed July 23, 2009).

48. Gil Scott-Heron, "Who Will Pay Reparations on my Soul?" *Small Talk at 125th and Lenox* (Flying Dutchman Records, 1970).

49. Black Solidarity Day began in 1969 and was sparked by Douglas Turner Ward's 1965 play "The Day of Absence." The play attempted to highlight the centrality of black labor to the U.S. economy by imagining what would happen if black people suddenly disappeared. Black Solidarity Day was organized to fall near election day and encourages people to stay home from school or work.

50. Information about the march, including a promotional flyer featuring these slogans, is reprinted in *Arm the Spirit* 5 (November 1979): 1. See also Sheila Rule, "On Solidarity Day, Blacks Say 'We Are Still Slaves,'" *New York Times*, November 6, 1979, B3; "Black Liberation Movement Re-emerging," *Arm the Spirit* 6 (February–April 1980): 1. Akinyele Umoja, telephone conversation with Dan Berger, June 16, 2009. More generally, see Assata Shakur, *Assata: An Autobiography* (Chicago: Lawrence Hill Books, 1987); Evelyn A. Williams, *Inadmissible Evidence: The Story of the African-American Trial Lawyer who Defended the Black Liberation Army* (Chicago: Lawrence Hill Books, 1993); and Robert Hanley, "Miss Chesimard Flees Jersey Prison, Helped by 3 Armed 'Visitors,'" *New York Times*, November 3, 1979, 1.

51. Diane C. Fujino, *Heartbeat of Struggle: The Revolutionary Life of Yuri Kochiyama* (Minneapolis: University of Minnesota Press, 2005), 178. Sundiata was a longtime RNA citizen and the one who brought Yuri Kochiyama, the only nonblack person to become a citizen of the Republic, into the RNA.

52. Dan Berger, *Outlaws of America: The Weather Underground and the Politics of Solidarity* (Oakland, CA: AK Press, 2006), 245–264.

53. For more on these groups, see Ernesto B. Vigil, *The Crusade for Justice: Chicano Militancy and the Government's War on Dissent* (Madison: University of Wisconsin Press, 1999); Block, *Arm the Spirit*, 148–150; Movimiento de Liberación Nacional (MLN), "Program and Ideology of the MLN: First Congress of the Movimiento de Liberación Nacional

Puertorriqueño," in author Dan Berger's files, courtesy of Matt Meyer. Besides the organizations mentioned in the text, white solidarity organizations include the May 19th Communist Organization, which split off from the PFOC, and the Sojourner Truth Organization.

54. These groups cooperated on publications, conferences, and campaigns—especially dealing with political repression and incarceration. For instance, New Afrikan, Puerto Rican, and white solidarity activists organized the National Conference Against Repression in Denver in May 1982, sponsored by the National Committee to Free Puerto Rican Prisoners of War, the National Committee to Defend New Afrikan Freedom Fighters, the National Committee Against Repression, and the New Movement in Solidarity with Puerto Rican Independence and Socialism. A similar coalition organized a conference against repression in New York City in September 1979. See *War in America* pamphlet, Ruth Reynolds Papers, series IV, reel 3, box 4, folder 1, Centro de Estudios Puertorriqueños, Hunter College; and José López, interview with Dan Berger, May 24, 2009.

55. For more on this point in relation to contemporary Indian activism, see Andrea Smith, *Native Americans and the Christian Right: The Gendered Politics of Unlikely Alliances* (Durham, NC: Duke University Press, 2008).

56. Quoted in Andrea Smith, "Reparations and the Question of Land," *Union Seminary Quarterly*, available at www.aclu.org/hrc/NativeRights_AndreaSmith.pdf (accessed July 23, 2009).

57. LeRoi Jones (Amiri Baraka), *Home: Social Essays* (1966; rpt. New York: Akashic Books, 2009), 101–106.

58. Benedict Anderson, *Imagined Communities: Reflections on the Origins and Spread of Nationalism* (London: Verso Books, 1991).

4

Canada's Other Red Scare

The Anicinabe Park Occupation and Indigenous Decolonization

SCOTT RUTHERFORD

In October 1967, the Parliament of Canada came alive after Robert Thompson, a representative of the right-wing Social Credit Party, accused Cuba of sending revolutionary messages to First Nations people[1] in western Canada by way of Radio Havana.[2] The governing Liberal Party took the accusation seriously by promising to investigate the charge; the country's media intelligentsia, however, could not contain its sarcasm. Though the government's official investigation was just beginning, readers in western Canada were assured that "the White man doesn't have anything to worry about."[3] As the nationally read *Globe and Mail* put it: "There is no Ché in Canada: there is just an alleged Indian in Havana. . . . If Cuban based insurrection comes it will play for only a summer season: the Cubans will prefer the heat and sultry eyes of the Latin quarter to the cold reality of our northern winter."[4]

Neither Ché nor Fidel rode across the chilly western plains to lead a First Nations "Red Power" rebellion in 1967. Despite this, we should avoid quickly dismissing how local actions in opposition to colonialism and racism in Canada during the late 1960s and 1970s related to similar global movements. Montrealers, for example, rang in the 1970s by wrestling through the question of their own unique relationship with colonialism and the many different paths toward decolonization.[5] Meanwhile, new immigrants to Canada, including many young Caribbean and West Indian students, envisioned "the Great White North," especially Montreal and Toronto, as centers of imperial power. Accordingly, they developed their own form of Black Power to undo racism and capitalism in Canada while simultaneously shaping the politics of liberation in their homelands of Jamaica, Martinique, and Haiti.[6] Debates raged among "Old" and "New" leftists and a smattering of New Democrats, liberals, and conservatives as to how American economic and cultural imperialism interfered with Canadian sovereignty.[7]

The sociologist Howard Ramos argues that in Canada, during the period between 1973 and 1976, twice as many indigenous protest actions and legal challenges took place per year as compared to any year between 1960 and 1969.[8] Yet, perhaps because Red Power in Canada reached its zenith some time after 1968, the global imagination of indigenous activists is often forgotten. Historian Ken Coates suggests that this internationalism resulted in the emergence of "a dramatic new rhetoric . . . immersed in the language of decolonization and antiracism."[9] The forty-day armed occupation of Anicinabe Park in Kenora, Ontario, during the summer of 1974 by the Ojibway Warriors Society was one such moment, demonstrating intersections between the global and the local. In this event, we can observe links between indigenous engagement with colonialism and capitalism in Canada and the global forces of international decolonization that were dominant in the post–World War II period. The nearly six-week occupation illuminates the intersections of identity politics and the culture of anticolonialism in the 1970s. Commentators on all sides of the conflict explained the drama in a language that extended beyond the nation.

From Marches to Occupations

The Anicinabe Park occupation in 1974 was not the first sign of public resistance in Kenora during the 1960s and 1970s. In the summer of 1965, a widely read magazine article exposed Canadians to the poor living conditions, lack of economic opportunities, and racism faced by First Nations men and women in the Kenora area. Journalist Ian Adams described the world of First Nations people in Kenora as reminiscent of the injustices endured by African American men and women in the southern United States.[10] That November, Kenora became the site of what was described at the time as Canada's first "civil rights" march. Five hundred people, from seven different reserves, marched hand-in-hand down Main Street, only stopping upon arrival at a meeting of town council to have a list of grievances read aloud by those leading the procession.[11] Town council members attempted to downplay the situation. Media from all over Canada, though, immediately jumped to claim Kenora as the country's own Little Rock or Selma.[12]

Beyond sensational headlines, the march generated responses from a variety of reform-minded organizations. The Ontario Human Rights Commission, in conjunction with local indigenous leaders and a hesitant town council, formed a committee to oversee the implementation of programs and the documentation of further abuses.[13] The human rights workers assigned to Kenora remained busy throughout the period, documenting the everyday discrimination endured by First Nations members. Other well-meaning people, including student and church-based activists, converged to conduct studies and carry out various projects that they hoped would improve the lives of First Nations in the Kenora area. These efforts, in addition to the increased media attention, helped keep racism and segregation exposed. However, as the 1960s gave way to the 1970s, indigenous people saw little improvement. Across the country, on rural reserves and in urban ghettos, First Nations and Métis continued to face debilitating effects of social and cultural oppression. Yet, like so many other marginalized people did during this time, young indigenous women and men publicly challenged the powers they believed impeded their opportunity to live freely. They did so by developing new languages to theorize their oppression and new methods by which to reshape their daily lives. In the words of Howard Adams, a radical Métis intellectual, they replaced "the civil rights movements of the 1960s" with movements for liberation and self-determination. The era of Red Power had arrived.[14]

This is the climate within which the Ojibway Warriors Society (OWS) emerged. Formed in 1972 by a group of Ojibway men and women from northwestern Ontario, the group first drew significant attention in November 1973, with a thirty-six-hour occupation of a federal Department of Indian Affairs office in Kenora. Once inside the offices, they told those who would listen that the "pow-wow at Indian Affairs" was to bring attention to a number of grievances, including greater economic autonomy for First Nations, compensation for the mercury contamination of a river near the Grassy Narrows reserve, and an end to the overtly racist actions and physical brutality against First Nations in Kenora.[15] Officials agreed to consider the grievances and did not charge the OWS for the occupation. Though this moment of rebellion passed somewhat unnoticed outside of Kenora, the ground had been broken for a new type of resistance to take shape the following year.

1974: Anicinabe Park

The OWS helped organize a major gathering in Kenora in late July 1974, in an effort to bring together indigenous people from across North America. They promoted the conference as an opportunity to "unify our Indian people" for "drastic changes," and plans were made to accommodate close to five thousand people at Anicinabe Park, a fourteen-acre parcel of land on the southeast edge of Kenora.[16] While not declaring so publicly, town officials were worried "that the rally was going to be a mere cloak for subversive activities."[17] The presence of Dennis Banks and other members of the American Indian Movement (AIM), the memory of the Warriors' occupation of Kenora's Department of Indian Affairs office less than a year earlier, and rumors that white vigilantes were prowling the area had the town officials questioning whether they could effectively police such an event. In response to the privately expressed concerns of Mayor Jim Davidson, Grand Council Treaty #3 President Peter Kelly wrote that the OWS would conduct their own security patrol.[18] He recommended, however, that the town would be wise to "police their own people, particularly their own police," some of whom were known for their "hostile and prejudicial attitudes."[19]

As the weekend conference got underway, hundreds of people drummed, danced, and talked with each other. While attendance was lower than expected, the estimated five hundred who came to the park finished the weekend by listening to the conference's keynote speaker, Dennis Banks, the national director of

AIM. On trial that summer along with Russell Means for their roles in the Wounded Knee standoff, Banks was given special permission to cross the U.S.-Canadian border to speak in Kenora.[20] Banks argued that colonial oppression had inflicted shame on indigenous people across North America. Yet he did not limit his remarks to simply providing examples of oppression, because, in his opinion, the colonized did not need much evidence that they were colonized. Instead, Banks argued that First Nations people could work together for their own protection. "When society initiates and creates laws detrimental to our members, then we must disobey those laws. We must disobey the laws of the crooks. We must disobey the laws of people who have forgotten about mother earth and human rights."[21] The time to resist, according to Banks, was now, "for no matter where they have been born, Indian people are standing up in lonely towns and on lonely reservations to be heard. We have been silent about these injustices for too long, and we have been silent as a group."[22] Once he finished, those who remained watched a taekwondo exhibition—martial arts for self-protection.[23]

On the morning of July 23, a day after the conference ended, news spread that the one hundred and fifty members of the OWS would not vacate the park until the land was "liberated Indian territory."[24] Town officials quickly tried to downplay the development, suggesting that those left in the park were staging "nothing more than a sit-in."[25] "Let them have the park," Mayor Jim Davidson told the *Toronto Star*, "After a week or so they will drift away and there will be no problem."[26] Louis Cameron, the OWS's twenty-four-year-old spokesperson, from Whitedog Reserve, who would become the focus of much media attention, responded to the prognosis of a short-lived sit-in with his own forecast: "We'll live here . . . we may even get married here."[27]

The OWS listed twenty-five points of contention that were organized as local, provincial, and national concerns. At the top of the list was a demand that propelled the early days of negotiations: a claim to Anicinabe Park, a parcel of land with disputed legal entitlement.[28] Yet there were twenty-four other issues, many of which received scant media attention. Most expanded on the grievances first laid out during the 1973 Indian Affairs office sit-in and again in press releases prior to the Ojibway Nation Conference. The OWS requested attention in the form of an "investigation into the violent deaths of Indian people in the Kenora area," increased availability of jobs, more cooperation from town police, and "better and fairer coverage of Indian issues in the local press." Most of the provincial and national issues demanded reforms to the justice system in order to better reflect First Nations values, as well as a "speedy and just settlement of land claims,"[29] and compensation for the people devastated by mercury pollution, an act that the OWS called "an outright crime against two communities."[30]

Away from Kenora, AIM organized solidarity rallies in Toronto toward the end of the occupation's first week, with Vernon Bellecourt speaking to an audience of between fifty and one hundred people.[31] By the second week, the first signs of serious negotiations appeared, as did media reports of a tentative deal. Such reports, however, were premature.[32] In fact, the OWS believed that negotiations were bypassing or not taking seriously most of their demands. In part, this frustration resulted from the Department of Indian Affairs sending an official who, admittedly, had little power to make decisions for the federal government.[33] "We came honestly to talk," Cameron exclaimed, "but we have to return to the park and tell our people there is no hope in these talks."[34] Furthermore, some in the OWS were growing skeptical of their own negotiating committee (made up of representatives from Grand Council Treaty #3), so much so that the militants took negotiations with government and municipal officials into their own hands. Some townspeople and media outlets portrayed this split as evidence that the park occupiers had lost support of First Nations around the Kenora area. A press release from Treaty #3 refuted this argument: "The Grand Council Treaty #3, the organization of Chiefs in the Kenora–Fort Frances area, wish to reiterate their solidarity with the desire for immediate changes as expressed by the Ojibway Warrior Society now occupying Anicinabe Park. The fact that some Indian people are turning away from peaceful approaches to change is a direct result of years of exploitation and persecution of Indian people by those with power."[35] Internal disagreements clearly existed, as did distrust among some militants toward the chiefs, but the message to the public remained clear: the divide and conquer tactics of colonialism were not going to work this time.

With the OWS members representing themselves at the bargaining table, talks continued to focus mainly on the land question and on getting the park occupiers to relinquish their weapons. While government negotiators focused on the peaceful resolution of the occupation, a different form of militancy began to rise outside of the park. Some white citizens began to advocate a new, more aggressive, strategy to end the standoff, one that abandoned negotiation.[36] One "concerned citizen" wrote into the local newspaper, rhetorically asking, "in this country, in this province, in this town, is there no one with authority who has guts enough to say, 'The Law is the Law, it will be upheld'?"[37] The first meeting of the Committee of Concerned Citizens (CCC) reportedly drew seven hundred residents. They discussed a number of strategies for ending the occupation. These included storming the park to "evict" the OWS if a ten-day truce, established in early August, passed without a resolution.[38] One person in attendance, reflecting the concern that the CCC would be perceived by non-Kenorans as a white vigilante group, told reporters that "they don't want to act like a bunch of red necks or the Ku Klux Klan, *but it will be necessary* if something doesn't happen soon" (emphasis added).[39]

Amid rumors that some police were eager to storm the park, and in the face of growing militancy from white townspeople, negotiations took on a more desperate tone. Various attempts at having human-rights committees and government arbitrators oversee the talks could not break the impasse. Finally, an unlikely arbitrator arrived on the scene. After much consternation from elected officials, all sides agreed to let Dennis Banks take on the role of mediator.[40] Shortly thereafter, the OWS agreed to lay down their weapons on August 19 as an act of "good faith"—not, however, as an act of surrender. "The Ojibwa Warriors Society has spoken," Cameron announced. "We will now see if the government listened."[41] Ten days later, on August 29, 1974, the OWS, in conjunction with Dennis Banks and representatives from Grand Council Treaty #3, agreed to a tentative deal with the town, the provincial government, and the federal government, with further promises to study and implement several of the OWS recommendations. Grand Council Treaty #3 would file a land claim on behalf of the OWS for Anicinabe Park, which, in the meantime, would reopen and remain a free camping and recreation space for all visitors. Town council noted that if the land claim was not settled by May 1, 1975, "the matter of charges for use of Park facilities will be reviewed."[42] As well, it was agreed that, for the most part, the park occupiers would be granted amnesty, save for a variety of minor theft- and vandalism-related charges. Moreover, no trials would "take place until the land claim concerning Anicinabe Park" was resolved.[43]

Understanding the Park Occupation and Red Power in the 1970s

The six-week occupation brought indigenous protest, armed struggle, and the town of Kenora back into the national and international spotlight. One might call it a moment of struggle between the colonized and the colonizer. In the broadest sense, this is true. The Anicinabe Park occupation pitted colonized First Nations against white settlers who had actively oppressed First Nations for centuries. While these binaries make the occupation understandable, unquestioned adherence to them is problematic. Media coverage, public protests, and the state response show that in an increasingly globalized world, indigenous militancy could elicit a wide spectrum of meaning.

Throughout the 1960s and 1970s, indigenous critiques of Canada were shaped by a worldview that integrated their actions within a wider sphere of global rebellion. One of the enduring legacies of Red Power is that it attempted to stretch the definition of who was colonized, seeking links among indigenous peoples, other racialized minorities, and the working poor. In doing so, groups such as the OWS demonstrated a social imaginary that simultaneously looked to the global, national, and local as sources of knowledge and as spaces in which their political activism could have importance. Such recognition is important because, in the words of historian Ken Coates, a global view "provided broad explanations which helped make sense of the nuances and complexities of local historical circumstances."[44] Yet helping make sense of one's circumstances should not be confused with providing a recipe for change. The historian Anthony Hall illustrates this point through his work on George Manuel, a Shuswap activist whose book *The Fourth World: An Indian Reality* became an influential text for the growth of pan-indigeniety in the 1970s. Before becoming the first president of the National Indian Brotherhood, Manuel traveled extensively outside of Canada, attending, for example, Tanzanian independence celebrations. Though he drew inspiration from such liberation struggles, Manuel's work also critiques Third World decolonization for, in the words of Hall, leaving "little room for the recognition of the value, worth, and contemporary applicability of indigenous knowledge and philosophy."[45] Howard Adams, a Métis activist and intellectual from Saskatchewan, approached Third World decolonization in a similar fashion. In *Prisons of Grass*, published at the height of Red Power in Canada, Adams wrote at length about how Malcolm X and Frantz Fanon shaped his approach to decolonization, especially the need to liberate the mind and body from the effects of racism and colonization. Yet when it came time to discuss tactics for decolonization, Adams advocated abandoning the idea of "revolutionary nationalism" exemplified by "Cuba and Vietnam" for an approach he termed "radical nationalism"—essentially meaning local struggles for indigenous sovereignty.[46]

The OWS spoke of locating Red Power within a global moment, but one that was contextualized within an indigenous historical framework. Cameron emphasized the place of spiritual and medicinal traditions—specifically Midewiwin—in the long history of anticolonial struggle. Midewiwin, prohibited by the federal government for much of the twentieth century, provided what some scholars have called the institutional setting for the teaching of an Ojibway worldview; Cameron said it reflected "a full and material understanding of the ways of the Anicinabe people."[47] A ceremony in which healing, drumming, and knowledge of the natural world occupied central roles, Midewiwin's central concept, according to scholars, is that not only are human beings, animals, and plants alive, "but so were *some* natural and created objects such as specific stones, locations, dolls, etc. All such being or creatures, not just humans, were considered to have what in English is termed a soul, and thus to be alive, and have power."[48]

As scholar Michael Angel notes, Midewiwin was also a tool of resistance, employed by Ojibway communities in the eighteenth and nineteenth centuries as a way to adapt to the spread of Christian missionaries across central Canada.[49] Some chose to incorporate aspects of Christianity into the practice, while others used it as a tool to protect themselves from Christianity. In 1974, with the conference and subsequent occupation, Midewiwin once again became part of opposition to colonialism. "The Indian movement, spiritually and in every way," Cameron believed, "is part of human revolution." Midewiwin was "not something you pray for, you just do it. It's a search for justice; and practice, not talk about God, is the key."[50] It meant "going through the deep ceremonies, learning about your families and the traditions or history, for the purpose of going forward—not going backward but forward."[51]

Organizing under the title of "Ojibway Warriors Society" also used the past to move forward. OWS literature, along with articles published by the Toronto Warrior Society, informed readers that the Warriors Society was a response "to the specific conditions and needs of the people," that sought "justice and the return of the rights of our people." The Toronto Warriors Society implicitly created a sense of global consciousness by including a wide variety of international stories in its newspaper, *Native Peoples Struggle*. This included a story that documented a trip to China made by a group of indigenous men and women, "a message from an Amazon Indian to his North American relatives," and a comparative study of the health of indigenous children in Canada with that of children in Vietnam. The newspaper also published the stirring "Apolitical Intellectuals," a poem by Guatemalan poet Otto Rene Castillo and noted that "Castillo was one of the leading poets of Guatemala. In the year 1967, in a show of guerilla strength, he died fighting for his people."[52] In pamphlets and interviews, the OWS portrayed itself as not simply an incarnation of the 1960s and 1970s, but as a contemporary materialization of a longstanding Ojibway tradition. As a result, besides being in solidarity with contemporary global struggles, the warriors who fought in Kenora were the heirs of warriors who "fought the invaders, the British troops, the French troops and the Spanish troops throughout North America."[53] Such a narrative located the Anicinabe Park occupation within a pan-indigenous anticolonial struggle. Moreover, it explicitly depicted the summer of 1974 as one moment in a centuries-long resistance.

Indigenous anticolonial movements attempted to use representations of the past as ways to move forward in the 1970s. Yet the present provided a variety of political challenges. As within many movements, gender was a site of struggle within Red Power. One way to understand this is to situate Red Power within a global framework. Kristin Ross is one of many to argue that the recovery of manhood shaped Fanon's anticolonial philosophies, an insight Laura Pulido argues was "one of the main impulses" of "Third World left" activism of the 1960s and 1970s in Los Angeles.[54] According to historian John Sayer, AIM leader Russell Means used similar language at the Wounded Knee trials in 1974, characterizing activism as an avenue to reclaim and express "Indian manhood."[55] Similar themes emerged in the Anicinabe Park occupation. Louis Cameron spoke often about the role of Ojibway men as the protector of indigenous communities, an analysis seemingly echoed by some women, as well. OWS activist Lyle Ironstand recalled how his wife spurred him into action by challenging him to act like the men who took over Wounded Knee.[56] Accounts from various Red Power activists however demonstrate that attempts to recover manhood often failed to challenge contemporary forms of patriarchy and consequentially blunted political success. On his experience during the Native Peoples' Caravan, which crossed Canada just after the occupation ended, Vern Harper described the limitations of the campaign. "Some of the younger brothers," he writes, "didn't want to do kitchen detail, and they tried to use tradition—so-called tradition—to get out of it. When they were asked to pick up the mop they would say 'oh no, warriors don't do that.' "[57]

Women from diverse indigenous nations responded in various ways to the masculinity of anticolonial struggle in the late 1960s and early 1970s. I have found only a small number of public commentaries from indigenous women located in Canada, none of which came directly from the Anicinabe Park occupation. In an account of her years spent as a Red Power activist, Lee Maracle relates the difficulty faced by women who wanted to be involved in radical anticolonial activism while at the same time having to attend—usually without help—to the needs of young children.[58] Vern Harper suggests that indigenous men involved in the Native Peoples' Caravan took seriously the challenges by women to deal with sexist, and sometimes homophobic, behaviors. In his words, "a lot of us were just opening our eyes and ears for the first time."[59] However, for indigenous women, the patriarchy and sexism they encountered in everyday life, and for some, in radical political movements, were deeply connected to their tenuous racial and national status, as defined by the Indian Act. Challenges to the most significant clauses, those that at their essence stripped indigenous women—but not men—of their "Indian" identity if they chose to marry non-indigenous Canadians, were the most public anticolonial (and feminist) struggles led by indigenous women in the 1970s.[60] Ironically, though the challenge to the Indian Act can be thought of as an act of anticolonial persuasion, in the mid-1970s, at the time of the Anicinabe Park occupation, prominent indigenous nationalists vehemently rallied against such measures. Bonita Lawrence suggests that since 1968, when the federal government attempted to replace the entire Indian Act in favor of assimilation, many official indigenous leaders and representatives viewed changing any part of the Indian Act as way for the federal government to erode indigenous nationhood through step-by-step assimilation.[61]

Anticolonial actions in the 1970s, such as the Anicinabe Park occupation, need to be understood through both culture and politics. The same holds true for how the public made sense of dramatic moments such as that in Kenora. Throughout the six weeks, the occupation drew intense interest from local, national, international, and alternative media. In the mainstream, the tone of the coverage varied, from condemnation and cynicism to sympathy and pity for indigenous people in the Kenora area. The narrative told to readers was one that undoubtedly represented men as the central actors in the drama. Though the mainstream press noted the presence of "mothers and children" in the park, the views of indigenous women, either as militants or otherwise, remained unknown to those following the occupation. Stereotypes that conceived indigenous women as either "squaws" or "princesses" pervaded media representations. Even the new stereotype of the revolutionary woman—baby in one hand, rifle in the other—did not appear in the media coverage of the occupation, save a single photograph in one radical leftist publication in Canada.

Representations of indigenous men, however, were far more present. In *The Imaginary Indian*, Daniel Francis asks readers to test their stereotyping of indigenous people by closing their eyes and describing the first image that comes to mind. "When I did," writes Francis, "the first image that occurred to me was a photograph . . . of a young Ojibway man taking part in a roadblock at [Anicinabe Park] sitting on the hood of a car cradling a rifle."[62] For Francis, this illustrated that only two representations of masculinity were available for indigenous men: warrior or elder. His memory was not betraying him; indeed for many Canadians the only knowledge, or at least the first representation they saw, of the occupation was often a photograph of a young indigenous man holding a gun with a small caption—such as the one used by the *Montreal Gazette*: "Armed Pow-wow."[63]

The widely circulating photographs and television images of brown-skinned men holding guns in Anicinabe Park portrayed the militants as a late-twentieth-century return of the romantic warrior figure that had simultaneously fascinated and scared white people for centuries. During the occupation, the press seemed to stretch the binary of warrior versus elder to mean male militant versus male elected official. Though, as noted earlier, Grand Council Treaty #3 publicly attempted to create distance from this divisive discourse, I suggest that much of negative characterization of the OWS was a way to control who was allowed to speak, and in what form. This is made clear in a lengthy editorial in northern Ontario's largest newspaper, the *Chronicle Journal* of Thunder Bay. Instead of issues, the editorial suggested, the OWS were simply publicity seekers, martyrs, and naïve "young Indians" believing that they could change the world "with a wave of the magic wand."[64] Recalling his night in the park, *Globe and Mail* reporter Derik Hodgson characterized the militants as "thugs," "madmen," and "crazies" who "talked tough" and giggled when pointing guns at people's faces. He described a park inhabited by giddy revolutionaries who spent the night "sere-nading policemen" with beating drums and talking revolution, which, reportedly, was a philosophy adopted from Algerians and Angolans. Hodgson painted a pic-ture of a mystical and frightening space, yet he afforded virtually no space to griev-ances, even the land claim.[65] Historians Mark Anderson and Carmen Robertson note that in Kenora's newspaper, indigenous people were regularly described as having, as a race, a predilection to violence and a lack of self-control.[66] Nationally, as commentators demonstrated, such characterizations, based in colonial-racist stereotypes, were a political tool that could discredit the voice of Ojibway mili-tants. Such representations suggested that indigenous people were expected to have only one voice—and one that required the legitimation of white people.

Alongside reports that Third World philosophies inspired the OWS, AIM became a target for commentators who tried to characterize the six-week occupa-tion as the work of foreign agents. AIM's presence at, or at least inspiration to, the Anicinabe Park occupation cannot be denied. Dennis Banks and oft-quoted vet-eran AIM member Harvey Major were sizeable presences during the occupation. Even the reported cheers emanating from the park the day that President Richard Nixon resigned point to some degree of AIM influence. Yet blaming outsiders was another strategy to delegitimize the voice and claims made by the OWS. The dis-course of "bad Indians" storming across the forty-ninth parallel to corrupt and destroy the harmonious relations that docile "good Indians" had with their white Canadian neighbors is not unique to Canada, or the 1970s, as several historians have demonstrated.[67] This dichotomy of good or bad Indians in the 1970s, coded through references to AIM and outside interference, can also be seen as a commentary on the symbolic status of race and nation in Canada. AIM was not only provoking otherwise "good Indians" but also in the words of one journalist they were doing so with American methods rather than Canadian.[68] Not only could the OWS be ridiculed for fitting the stereotype of the "bad Indian," they were also betraying the code of peaceful coexistence that supposedly characterized indigenous-white relations in Canada. This alleged racial harmony was a marker of Canadianness itself. The OWS acknowledged its intellectual and political debts to AIM as well as other decolonization struggles, as indicated by Cameron's references to Algeria and Angola. At the same time as the Anicinabe Park occupation, opposition was also circulating in Canada to the increased immigration from Africa and the Caribbean. The bodies that moved from South to North during the global migration of the 1970s brought with them more than just cheap labor and visual representations of multiculturalism. For those who opposed non-white immigration, perhaps nothing was more frightening than the radical ideas brought by Third World immigrants. Concerned readers demanded the government stop "importing" black and brown immigrants who "refused" to assimilate and who brought with them "Third World propaganda" of racial equality. "Colored immigration to Canada on such a massive scale spells only one thing," Basil Flood wrote in the *Toronto Star*: "Trouble."[69]

The meanings of transnational associations, however, were not uncontested. Indigenous militants used their global language to foster a sense of power and history that located struggle outside local boundaries. During the mid-seventies, imagining intersections between indigenous resistance in Canada and global consciousness was a way for sympathetic journalists and allies to positively portray the occupation. During the occupation, author and journalist Les Whittington suggested, in an article sympathetic to the indigenous militants, that the stance of the OWS "echoes the posture of their ancestors who fought the white man." Moreover, returning to armed resistance was "nothing less than the renewal of the wars of the last century."[70] Scattered references both to AIM and Dee Brown's *Bury My Heart at Wounded Knee* suggest that the wars to which Whittington referred took place in the contemporary United States, not in nineteenth-century Canada. Was this simply a slip of the pen? Or, was he attempting to link indigenous struggles across national boundaries, creating a sense of a transnational struggle uncontrolled by colonial and imperial boundaries? The two possibilities are not mutually exclusive. A smattering of radical leftist groups in Canada were not shy in making sense of local indigenous movements through a transnational framework. Through public protests and literature, Maoists—whose involvement in Red Power activism sparked controversy[71]—along with various Trotskyist groups, supported and helped shape the idea that actions such as the park occupation were not unlike anticolonial uprisings in Africa, the Caribbean, and Latin America. Other leftists, such as those involved with the social democratic publication *Canadian Dimension*, tended to make more subtle reference to the transnational aspect of

Red Power. In a multi-article feature that appeared in the fall of 1974, the authors argued that the occupation grew out of problems "inherited" from nineteenth-century colonial polices. Moreover, the OWS were "good leaders" who "seized the initiative in Kenora, took risks they felt necessary and demonstrated themselves to be skilled tacticians during the negotiations."[72] The significance of Kenora for activists, however, was that it served as an example of "the ones who will get fed up enough to trade in their copies of Robert's Rules of Order for a volume of Frantz Fanon."[73] They had turned away from North American parliamentary procedure for Third World–inspired armed resistance.

Conclusion

During the late 1960s, some commentators scoffed at the idea that national liberation movements would find a home among First Nations in Canada. Rumors of Cuban-inspired insurrection, for example, were imagined as the paranoid fantasies of the far Right or the deluded Left. Yet by the mid-1970s, ignoring the influence of global decolonization on local struggles proved impossible. During the Anicinabe Park occupation, the OWS partially attributed the spirit and substance of their actions to movements outside of Canada. Such statements of global solidarity were not simply superficial bravado. While the occupation faded into memory in the last months of 1974, the connections—either imagined or real—between Red Power activists and other radicalized minorities grew stronger. In 1975, protests in Canadian cities demanded a halt to the deportation orders of Caribbean radical Rosie Douglas and 1,500 Haitian immigrants.[74] The protesters also demanded that charges against OWS activist Lyle Ironstand be dropped. In the minds of protesters, the marginalization of Third World peoples was not that distinct from the marginalization of First Nations activists (and their homelands).

After vacating Anicinabe Park, "going forward" meant a number of different things. Some joined up with other Red Power activists to form the Native Peoples' Caravan, which traveled across Canada in the fall of 1974. The caravan attempted to further bring national and international attention to the situation on First Nations reserves and urban ghettos. The hundred-or-so activists ended up on the doorsteps of Parliament Hill, only to be met by a contingent of officers from the Royal Canadian Mounted Police. Much blood was spilled, most of it the result of police billy clubs.[75] Others returned to their communities, where they continued to push for change. In Kenora, racial division did not become any less prevalent. Some used the occupation to advocate for stricter laws, a sentiment that found success when Mayor Davidson lost the municipal election to a candidate running on a "law and order" platform.[76] In spring 1975, the land claim to Anicinabe Park was denied. Yet the space continues to derive symbolic importance. Thirty-two years later, in late June 2007, the park hosted celebrations marking the first annual Aboriginal Day of Action, a day in which thousands across Canada protested continued injustice. Louis Cameron was one of the guest speakers at the Kenora event.[77]

The Anicinabe Park occupation represented many different things to many different people. This chapter has tried to make sense of some of those narratives, most notably those that tie the occupation into broader global histories of radical politics and culture of the 1970s. As indigenous movements inch closer to the center of our understanding of the 1960s and 1970s, many questions need to be considered. Of great importance is a better understanding of the relationship between global and local interactions. It is not enough to demonstrate how anti-colonial and anti-racist movements in Canada adapted a global political imaginary to local campaigns for justice. We should also move to understand how the spirit and substance of these movements across Canada shaped the actions of others who imagined the possibility of new worlds in the 1970s. Doing so promises not only to open up new windows to our understanding of the past, but also, perhaps, to help create new spaces to imagine future movements for justice and dignity that reach across personal, local, national, and international borders.

NOTES

1. A note on terminology: I use *First Nations* to refer to the Aboriginal peoples of Canada. *Indigenous* is used here to refer collectively to First Nations, Inuit, and Métis peoples.

2. "Seditious Cuban Broadcasts Charged," *Montreal Gazette*, October 18, 1967, 1; Lewis Seale, "SC Charge: Cubans Inciting Quebec," *Globe and Mail*, October 18, 1967, 1; Tom Hazlitt, "Is Cuban Radio Inciting Separatists, Indians? MP asks," *Toronto Star*, October 18, 1967, 4; Robert Wright, *Three Nights in Havana: Pierre Trudeau, Fidel Castro and the Cold War World* (Toronto: Harper Collins Publishers, 2007), 106. The numerous biographies, memoirs, and autobiographies of both Lester Pearson (Canada's prime minister in October 1967) and Fidel Castro do not mention this incident.

3. Gary Lautens, "Fidel! Our Indians Are Pretty with It—I Mean, Those Beads," *Toronto Star*, November 1, 1967, 4.

4. "New Empires," *Winnipeg Free Press*, October 19, 1967, 33.

5. On Quebec and decolonization in the 1960s and 1970s, see Sean Mills, "The Empire Within: Montreal, the Sixties, and the Forging of a Radical Imagination" (Ph.D. diss., Queen's University, 2007).

6. See David Austin, "All Roads Lead to Montreal: Black Power, the Caribbean, and the Black Radical Tradition in Canada," *Journal of African-American History* 92:4 (Fall 2007): 513–536.

7. For a broad overview of the Left in Canada during the 1960s and 1970s, see Ian McKay, *Rebels, Reds, Radicals: Rethinking Canada's Left History* (Toronto: Between the Lines, 2005), 183–210.

8. Howard Ramos, "Divergent Paths: Aboriginal Mobilization in Canada, 1951–2000" (Ph.D. diss., McGill University, 2004), 53.

9. Ken Coates, *A Global History of Indigenous Peoples: Struggle and Survival* (New York: Palgrave Macmillan, 2004), 239.

10. Ian Adams, "The Indians: An Abandoned and Dispossessed People," *Weekend Magazine*, July 31, 1965, 2–6.

11. A. Alan Borovoy, *Uncivil Obedience: The Tactics and Tales of a Democratic Agitator* (Toronto: Lester Publishing Ltd., 1991), 33.

12. Ian Adams, "The Indians: An Abandoned and Dispossessed People," *Weekend Magazine*, July 31, 1965, 2–6; Perry Anglin, "100 Kenora Indians Plan 'Selma' March," *Toronto Star*, November 17, 1965, 1, 4; "The Shame of Our 'Mississippi' Indians," *Toronto Star*, November 22, 1965, 6; Tim Traynor, "Kenora: Racial Hotspot That Rivals Little Rock," *Winnipeg Free Press*, November 27, 1965, 10.

13. The Ontario Human Rights Commission maintained extensive documentation of the day-to-day discrimination and racism endured by First Nations people in the Kenora area.

14. Howard Adams, *Tortured People: The Politics of Colonization,* rev. ed. (Penticton, B.C.: Theytus Books, 1999).

15. Ojibway Warriors Society, "Statement to Indian Affairs," November 27, 1973. Ojibway Warriors Society, "Statement to the Press," November 27, 1973.

16. Ojibway Nation Conference, promotional poster, July 1974.

17. E. C. Burton, *Journal of a Country Lawyer: Crime, Sin and Damn Good Fun* (Blaine, WA: Hancock House Publishers, 1995), 199.

18. In 1873, the Canadian government and First Nations (mainly Ojibwa) people around the Lake of the Woods (Kenora) area entered into Treaty #3. Significant debate continues over the treaty's terms. Grand Council Treaty #3 is the official territorial political organization for the twenty-eight nations (twenty-six in Ontario, two in Manitoba) that are represented by Treaty #3.

19. Peter Kelly, correspondence to Jim Davidson, July 16, 1974.

20. The memoirs of Kenora crown attorney E. C. Burton provide the most detailed explanation that I have been able to find on Banks's ability to cross the U.S.-Canadian border in July and August 1974 though he was on trial. Burton claims that "the district attorney and the judge [in St. Paul, Minnesota] both held Banks in high esteem" and agreed to let him travel to Kenora. Burton claims that Canadian officials, not American officials, were leery about Banks's presence during the conference and subsequently during the park negotiations. See Burton, *Journal of a Country Lawyer*, 215–217.

21. Dennis Banks quoted in April Holland, "Native People Urged to Work Together," *Kenora Daily Miner and News*, July 22, 1974, 1.

22. Ibid.

23. "Conference Orderly on the Weekend," *Kenora Daily Miner and News*, July 22, 1974, 14.

24. David Lee, "100 Armed Indians Seize Kenora Park," *Winnipeg Free Press*, July 23, 1974, 1.

25. Clarence Dusang, "Sessions Held over Protest," *Kenora Daily Miner and News*, July 24, 1974, 1; David Lee, "Little Reaction to Takeover; Park Indians More Militant," *Winnipeg Free Press*, July 24, 1974, 1.

26. Pat Brennan, " 'Let Indians Have the Park,' Kenora Mayor Opposes Force," *Toronto Star*, July 24, 1974, 2.

27. Ken Nelson, "Leader Vows He Won't Leave the Park," *Kenora Daily Miner and News*, July 25, 1974, 1.

28. At issue was the legality of the town's 1959 purchase of the land from the federal government, who had held it as "Indian land" since the signing of Treaty #3. The state claimed that the purchase was legal; the OWS, with the support of Grand Council Treaty #3, argued that not only was it illegal for the federal government to sell the land in 1959, but that the land should not have been the federal government's to sell in the first place.

29. Louis Cameron interviewed in James Burke, *Paper Tomahawks: From Red Tape to Red Power* (Winnipeg: Queenston House Publishing, 1976), 378–396.

30. Louis Cameron, *Ojibway Warriors Society in Occupied Anicinabe Park, Kenora, Ontario, August, 1974* (Toronto: Better Read Graphics, 1974), 9. By 1969, the federal and provincial governments both had knowledge of the mercury poisoning. The extent of their action was to appoint an executive from the Thompson Company, the group that owned the mill, to do an environmental impact assessment. In 1971, the World Health Organization released a report warning people in Whitedog and Grassy Narrows reserves that the mercury level of the Wabigoon River was above the level deemed safe for human consumption. The mercury, which had been dumped into the river system for more than twenty years, was traced back to a pulp and paper mill in Dryden, Ontario, a town one hundred miles east of Kenora. See "The Slow Death of Mercury Poisoning," *Akwesasne Notes* 7:3 (1975): 16; Anastasia M. Shkilnyk, *A Poison Stronger Than Love: The Destruction of an Ojibwa Community* (New Haven: Yale University Press, 1985).

31. The rally took place at Queen's Park in Toronto on Friday, July 26, 1974. Reports claim that fifty supporters showed up to see Vernon Bellecourt, an AIM director, speak about the occupation. See "Toronto Demonstrators Support Kenora Indians," *Chronicle-Journal* (Thunder Bay, Ontario), July 27, 1974, 11; a copy of Bellecourt's speech can be found in Trent University Archives, CASNP fonds, Box 3, File 50.

32. "Agreement Likely on Indian Dispute: Mayor to Release Details Later Today," *Kenora Daily Miner and News*, August 2, 1974, 1. David Lee, "Mayor Is Contradicted: No Pact, Say Kenora Indians," *Winnipeg Free Press*, August 3, 1974, 1.

33. "Little Progress Seen at Joint Meeting," *Kenora Daily Miner and News*, August 1, 1974, 1; "Only Limited Success in Kenora Discussions," *Chronicle-Journal*, August 1, 1974, 17.

34. Louis Cameron quoted in "Little Progress Seen at Joint Meeting," 1, and "Only Limited Success in Kenora Discussion," 17.

35. Grand Council Treaty #3, "Press Release," August 4, 1974, 2.

36. "500 Kenora Citizens Hold Meeting, Demand Indians Drop Weapons," *Chronicle-Journal*, August 7, 1974, 3.

37. Concerned Citizen, "Where's All the Law and Order?" *Kenora Daily Miner and News*, August 16, 1974, 4.

38. David Lee, "Kenora Residents Ask End to Park Takeover," *Winnipeg Free Press*, August 7, 1974, 1, 5; Bruce Kirkland, "The Indian Occupation: Backlash Brewing by Kenora's Whites," *Toronto Star*, August 24, 1974, B7; "Citizens' Committee Outlines Meeting," *Kenora Daily Miner and News*, August 26, 1974, 1; and Ross Porter, "Group Says No Law and Order Exists," *Kenora Daily Miner and News*, August 26, 1974, 1.

39. Marion Fawcett quoted in David Lee, "Kenora Residents Ask End to Park Takeover," *Winnipeg Free Press*, August 7, 1974, 5; Dennis Braithwaite, "Obey the Law? Who's Going to Make Us?" *Toronto Star*, September 4, 1974, B6.

40. "Local Crown Attorney Wants Banks on Scene," *Kenora Daily Miner and News*, August 15, 1974, 1. In his memoirs, Burton recalls, in extensive and sometimes sensationalistic detail, the series of events that resulted in Banks leaving the Wounded Knee trial and being allowed into Canada to act as a mediator in Kenora. See Burton, *Journal of a Country Lawyer*, 215–223. Banks was accompanied by his personal pilot, Douglas Durham. In 1975, after being confronted by AIM, Durham admitted to being an agent provocateur. For more on Durham and his involvement in First Nations protest in Canada, see Johanna Brand, *The Life and Death of Anna Mae Aquash* (Toronto: James Lorimer & Company, 1978), 100–101, 105.

41. Louis Cameron quoted in "Militants Lay Down Arms," *Kenora Daily Miner and News*, August 19, 1974, 1; "Indians Lay Down Their Arms As Talks Resolve Park Siege," *Montreal Gazette*, August 19, 1974, 1.

42. James N. Davidson, mayor's office, August 28, 1974.

43. Letter co-signed by Douglas T. Wright, deputy provincial secretary for social development, and E. C. Burton, crown attorney, Ministry of the Attorney General, August 29, 1974, 2.

44. Coates, *A Global History of Indigenous Peoples*, 243.

45. Anthony J. Hall, *The American Empire and the Fourth World: The Bowl with One Spoon* (Montreal & Kingston: McGill-Queen's University Press, 2003), 240.

46. Howard Adams, *Prison of Grass: Canada from a Native Point of View* (1975; rpt. Calgary: Fifth House Publishers, 1989), 167–170.

47. Basil Johnston, *Ojibway Heritage: The Ceremonies, Rituals, Songs, Dances, Prayers, and Legends of the Ojibway* (Toronto: McClelland & Stewart, 1976), 83. Johnston, an influential Ojibway scholar, was on a lecture tour about Midewiwin (and the book referenced above) during the summer and fall of 1974. Michael Angel, *Preserving the Sacred: Historical Perspectives on the Ojibwa Midewiwin* (Winnipeg: University of Manitoba Press, 2002), 48.

48. Angel, *Preserving the Sacred*, 20.

49. Ibid., 122–123.

50. Louis Cameron quoted in Tom Harpur, "Kenora Indian Leader Says Rebellion Is Religious," *Toronto Star*, September 7, 1974, C04.

51. Cameron in Burke, *Paper Tomahawks*, 394.

52. *Native Peoples Struggle: An Organ of the Toronto Warrior Society* 1:1 (July 1975), McMaster University Archives, Canadian Liberation Movement fonds, Box 19, File 23.

53. "Caravan 1974: Correspondence re Caravan from West to Ottawa, 1974," Trent University, CASNP, Box 2, File 16.

54. Kristin Ross, *Fast Cars, Clean Bodies: Decolonization and the Reordering of French Culture* (Cambridge, MA: The MIT Press, 1996), 158–159; Laura Pulido, *Black, Brown, Yellow, and Left: Radical Activism in Los Angeles* (Berkeley: University of California Press, 2006), 184.

55. John William Sayer, *Ghost Dancing the Law: The Wounded Knee Trials* (Cambridge, MA: Harvard University Press, 1997), 91.

56. Lyle Ironstand in Burke, *Paper Tomahawks*, 365–366; Timothy Tyson notes something similar in his study of early civil rights organizing in the United States, arguing that black women "deployed gender stereotypes in assertive ways—demanding of black men, in effect, 'Why aren't you protecting us?'" See Timothy B. Tyson, *Radio Free Dixie: Robert F. Williams and the Roots of Black Power* (Chapel Hill: University of North Carolina Press, 1999), 141.

57. Vern Harper, *Following the Red Path: The Native Peoples Caravan 1974* (Toronto: NC Press Limited, 1979), 27.

58. For one of the most extensive memoirs of Red Power activism in Canada, see Lee Maracle, *Bobbi Lee: Indian Rebel* (Toronto: Women's Press, 1990).

59. Harper, *Following the Red Path*, 27.

60. In 1971, Jeannette Corbiere Lavell, a Native woman who lost her status through marriage, challenged sections of the Indian Act that disempowered Native women. "Status" is the term used to refer to those who are recognized by the federal (national) government as "Indian" for the purposes of the Indian Act. Prior to 1985, the act's membership provisions stripped status from any Indian woman who married anyone other than a status Indian man. Their children were not recognized as Indian, and nonstatus Indians could not reside on reserves or participate in the political life of reserve communities. Status Indian men, however, retained their status upon marriage and conferred it upon

their wives; thus, non-Indian women acquired status upon marriage to status Indian men, and the children of these marriages were recognized as "Indian." See Joyce Green, "Balancing Strategies: Aboriginal Women and Constitutional Rights in Canada," in *Making Space for Indigenous Feminism*, ed. Joyce Green (Centralia, WA: Fernwood Press, 2007), 155.

61. See Colleen Glenn with Joyce Green, "Colleen Glenn: A Métis Feminist in Indian Rights for Indian Women, 1973–1979," in *Making Space for Indigenous Feminism*, ed. Joyce Green, 235; for the most comprehensive examination of Indian Act regulations on gender and its centrality to colonialism in Canada, see Bonita Lawrence, *"Real" Indians and Others: Mixed Blood Urban Native Peoples and Indigenous Nationhood* (Vancouver: UBC Press, 2004).

62. Daniel Francis, *The Imaginary Indian: The Image of the Indian in Canadian Culture* (Vancouver: Arsenal Pulp Press, 1992), 220.

63. "Armed Powwow," *Montreal Gazette*, July 25, 1974, 1.

64. "An Unnecessary Occupation," *Chronicle Journal*, August 16, 1974, 4.

65. Derik Hodgson, "Revolutionary Rhetoric, Indian Phrases Mix Tom-Toms and Tough Talk at Kenora Campsite," *Globe and Mail*, August 6, 1974, 2.

66. Mark Anderson and Carmen Robertson, "The 'Bended Elbow' News, Kenora 1974: How a Small-Town Newspaper Promoted Colonization," *American Indian Quarterly* 31:3 (2007): 428.

67. Francis, *The Imaginary Indian*, 167; Ward Churchill, *The Ward Churchill Reader* (New York: Routledge, 2003), 194–198.

68. "Trouble at Anicinabe," *Chronicle-Journal*, July 25, 1974, 4.

69. John MacGregor, "Racism Exists in Canada and I Say It's Natural," *Toronto Star*, July 30, 1974, B05; Basil Flood, "Citizenship Is a Privilege, Not a Right," *Toronto Star*, August 7, 1974, B05.

70. Les Whittington, "Ojibway Nation Rebelled against Injustices Steeped in Time," *Gazette*, August 20, 1974, 7.

71. The controversy over Maoist involvement derives primarily from participation of members of the Communist Party of Canada (Marxist-Leninist) (CPC-ML) in the Native Peoples' Caravan in 1974. Members of AIM, the Ojibway Warriors Society, and other indigenous radicals from British Columbia and Toronto organized the caravan in September 1974 to raise attention about indigenous issues in Canada. They started out in Vancouver, ending in Ottawa the day Parliament reopened for the fall session. At the ensuing gathering on Parliament Hill, riot police clashed with indigenous protesters and their allies. Mainstream media largely blamed CPC-ML for the violence. The CPC-ML presence within the caravan also provoked controversy. They helped organize and fund a speaking tour by Louis Cameron to raise attention about the caravan and its purpose. Yet, according to journalists who participated in the caravan, CPC-ML participation led to a split in the caravan, with those who left accusing the CPC-MLers of having too significant a role in the group's political direction. See David Ticoll and Stan Persky, "Welcome to Ottawa: the Native People's Caravan," *Canadian Dimension*, 10:6 (1975): 14–31. Vern Harper helped organize the caravan. He also ran in the August 1974 federal election as a CPC-ML candidate in Toronto but left the party not long afterward. He agrees that tension existed between the CPC-ML and the caravan leadership. Yet he also suggests that leadership may have been, in his words, "paranoid, seeing Communists under every tree." See Harper, *Following the Red Path*, 27, 43–44, 49.

72. John Gallagher and Cy Gonick, "The Occupation of Anicinabe Park," *Canadian Dimension*, 10:5 (1974): 22, 35.

73. Wayne Edmonstone, "A Cure for Which There Is No Disease," *Canadian Dimension*, 10:5 (1974): 33. Edmonstone originally wrote his comments for the *Toronto Sun*, after which they were reprinted in *Canadian Dimension*'s feature on Anicinabe Park.

74. "Racism, 1974–1976," McMaster University, Revolutionary Marxist Group fonds, 1947–1980, Box 3, File 33.

75. Harper, *Following the Red Path*, 55–65; Hall, *The American Empire and the Fourth World*, 273–274.

76. Burton, *Journal of a Country Lawyer*, 206.

77. Mike Aiken, "Candidate Speaks Out: Solidarity Day Festivities Include Political Message," *Kenora Daily Miner and News*, June 25, 2007.

PART TWO

Solidarity

5

"A Line of Steel"

The Organization of the Sixth Pan-African Congress and the Struggle for International Black Power, 1969–1974

FANON CHE WILKINS

The struggle being waged in Guinea-Bissau, in Mozambique, in Angola, in Guinea, demonstrates that today Africans are not seeking mere political independence. Those who are fighting today make no distinction between political independence and complete economic control. Upon this policy, which Africans are carrying out with arms in hand, the SIXTH PAN AFRICAN CONGRESS must draw a line of steel against those, Africans included, who hide behind the slogan and paraphernalia of national independence while allowing finance capital to dominate and direct their economic and social life. This is for Africans everywhere an unalterable principle.

–*The Call to the Sixth Pan-African Congress*, 1973

Following in the wake of the great pageant of the regaining of political independence, there has come the recognition on the part of many that the struggle of the African people has intensified rather than abated, and that it is being expressed not merely as a contradiction between African producers and European capitalists, but also as a conflict between the majority of the Black working masses and a small African possessing class. This admittedly, is to state the contentious; but the Sixth Pan-African Congress will surely have to walk the tightrope of this point of contention.

–Walter Rodney, 1974

Following the heady days of 1968, when the talk of global revolt was at a fever pitch throughout the Third World, Europe, and the United States, no single organized international event captured the optimism, challenges, and dilemmas of the black world more vividly than the Sixth Pan-African Congress (Sixth PAC) held in Dar es Salaam, Tanzania, in 1974.[1] Initiated by political activists residing largely in the United States and the Caribbean, the Sixth PAC was the first Pan-African Congress to be held on the African continent and serves as a critical marker for understanding the development and contradictions of Pan-Africanism and black internationalist insurgency in the post–World War II period.[2] The Sixth PAC followed a long history of Pan-African congresses begun in 1900 under the leadership and direction of Trinidadian barrister Henry Sylvester Williams. W.E.B. Du Bois, the towering African American scholar and activist who devoted his adult life to African emancipation on a world scale, organized succeeding congresses in Europe and the United States up to the Fifth PAC in 1945.[3]

Whereas the Fifth PAC, held in Manchester, England, was principally concerned with how and when African societies would achieve political independence from European colonial powers, the Sixth PAC, convened three decades later, turned inward and set the task of examining the shortcomings of decolonization in the newly independent nation-states of Africa and the Caribbean. This focus on the challenges facing the postcolonial African world included the United States, where African American radical activists and intellectuals were engaged in organizing efforts and contentious debates around the meaning of Black Power.[4] Emerging in the wake of the incomplete decolonization process referred to by Walter Rodney in the chapter epigraph, the Sixth PAC reflected the dual persistence of colonial domination in the Portuguese colonies and the settler colonial-states of southern Africa, and the dogged reality of neocolonialism in the newly decolonized states on the continent and the Caribbean. Moreover, participants raised sharp questions about socioeconomic class antagonisms, the role of elites, the problems of state power, the persistence of poverty among the great mass of African working peoples, and the Third World's general place in a world economy dominated by the industrialized nations of the North.

The Sixth PAC brought together an older generation of leftist activists who had come of age politically during World War II with a younger group of organizers and intellectuals who emerged out of the New Left. The mobilization efforts that went into the development of the congress provide a critical lens for understanding how black internationalist initiatives developed, sputtered, and fragmented along political lines as African and African-descended radical activists attempted to theorize, negotiate, and engage in a direct challenge to the colonial and post-colonial state through formal and informal organizational channels.

With the exception of a brief analysis of the ideological debates revolving around the political primacy of race and class during the Sixth PAC, scholars concerned with the black freedom movement and the history of Pan-Africanism have not yet examined the Sixth Pan-African Congress's significance for understanding the development of black internationalism in the context of decolonization.[5] Scholars examining the black freedom movement in the United States have neglected to study the critical role of former Student Nonviolent Coordinating

Committee (SNCC) activists in organizing the congress, their vast political networks beyond the U.S. South, and their far-reaching international contacts.[6] But
the Sixth PAC is a critical turning point in the development of black internationalism. The conference organizing, as well as the conference itself, exposed points
of tension and unity between African Americans and the African diaspora. It also
served as a bridge connecting late 1960s Black Power militancy to 1980s struggles
against apartheid, showing that 1970s radicalism does not have a clear ten-year
boundary. To explore these issues, this chapter is divided into four sections: The
first briefly covers the emergence of Black Power as a concept that reverberated
beyond the U.S. nation-state and captured the cultural and political imagination
of people of color around the world; the second engages the political disjuncture
and difference in the black world that was reflected in the early organizing efforts
for the congress; the third examines the central role that C.L.R. James played in
creating *The Call to the Sixth Pan-African Congress* and in providing mentorship for
a handful of budding Pan-Africanists who had been members of SNCC; and the
fourth discerns the race, class, and power debate that became a critical ideological impasse dividing the congress and illuminating the internal tensions and challenges of post-independent African and Caribbean statecraft.

Global Black Power

By the initial planning stages of the Sixth PAC in 1969, more than three dozen
African countries had achieved juridical independence. Similar transformations
took place in the Caribbean, while the black freedom movement in the United
States placed civil rights, urban poverty, and U.S. imperialism firmly at the center
of North American politics.[7] From the mid-1950s to 1965, the black freedom movement succeeded in ending legal segregation and securing voting rights for black
southerners marginalized by Jim Crow. Yet as a critical mass of African and
Caribbean working people, peasants, and students began to shift the political discourse in their respective locales and demand that national governments and
political parties deliver on the promises of independence, African American
activists began to amplify questions about the limits of civil-rights reforms and
the capacity of the movement for Black Power to meet the basic socioeconomic
and political needs of the most oppressed sectors of black America.[8]

As Black Power came to be loosely associated with a militant call for self-
determination, a cultural renaissance in black self-reclamation, and the growth of
autonomous black institutions and organizations, it quickly gained a large following outside the African world and was embraced by an array of Third World
peoples within and outside the United States. From Asia and the South Pacific, to
Europe and South America, the cry for Black Power captured the imaginations of
people of color around the world.[9] However, Black Power, both culturally and
politically, was of utmost importance on the African continent.[10] The anticolonial
struggles that raged in the Portuguese colonies and the settler-states of southern

Africa reminded African Americans and the larger black world that formal colonial domination had not been fully defeated on the continent. The experience,
political practice, and ideas that emerged from these movements animated black
internationalist activity everywhere and served as a driving force behind the Sixth
PAC that was organized to develop strategies for ameliorating the shared challenges of the African world in particular, and the larger Third World in general.[11]

Difference and Disjuncture in the African World

According to James Garrett, a Washington, DC–based SNCC worker and one of the
founding organizers of the congress, the initial idea for a Sixth PAC grew out of the
1969 International Conference on Black Power held in Bermuda. During the Black
Power gathering, a letter written by former Ghanaian president Kwame Nkrumah
was read to delegates, suggesting that "a meeting of Black people take place on the
African continent."[12] Nkrumah's idea for a continental conference echoed the sentiments of activists within radical Black Power circles in the United States and the
Caribbean who saw national liberation movements in Africa as being at the forefront of the black liberation movement globally. Roosevelt Browne, a member of
the Bermuda Parliament and host of the International Conference on Black Power,
initiated the first planning meeting for the congress in response to Nkrumah's
suggestion. According to Garrett, early speculation for a site "center[ed] on four
states—Guinea, Nigeria, Algeria, and Tanzania," with the latter gaining Nkrumah's
ringing endorsement.[13] Tanzania was especially coveted because of its professed
practice of Ujamaa socialism, commitment to self-reliance, and the progressive
role it played as the head of the Organization of African Unity's Liberation Committee, the primary base of continental support for liberation movements
engaged in armed struggle in southern Africa and the Portuguese colonies.[14]

The first phase of organizing ebbed and flowed between April and December
1971. In addition to establishing Tanzania as the site for the congress, organizers
devoted their early efforts to creating an organizational structure that eventually
evolved into the Secretariat, broadening the base of support for the congress
within the United States, developing a short list of programmatic and institutional
initiatives (e.g., the Pan-African Center of Science and Technology) that would
endure beyond the congress, and writing a draft of *The Call to the Sixth Pan-African
Congress* that was to summarize the broad objectives of the congress and circulate
around the world for feedback and amendments.[15]

Garrett recalled that international mobilization for the congress did not
begin in earnest until January 1972, when he, Roosevelt Browne, writer Liz Gant,
and Tanzania High Commissioner to Canada Abbas Sykes traveled to Europe "to
make direct contact with Black communities" and organize support for the congress. Browne was expected to provide background to the congress, while Garrett
would familiarize potential supporters of the efforts to organize the Sixth PAC.
Sykes provided credibility from the Tanzanian side, and Gant served as a French

translator during the group's visit to France and other parts of the francophone world.[16]

The Garrett group began their organizing effort in England and met with a range of Black Power–oriented organizations. These groups included the West Indian Afro-Brotherhood (Yorkshire), the Afro-Caribbean Self-Help Organization (Birmingham), the Black People's Liberation Party (Yorkshire), the Afro-Caribbean Circle (Wolver Hampton), the Black People's Liberation Party (Leicester), and the Black Panther Movement (London).[17] Though enthusiastic to meet the Garrett group and mildly supportive of a congress, these organizations proved difficult to mobilize because of a general skepticism for Pan-Africanism as an ideology and an organizing strategy. According to Garrett, the English Black Power organizers believed that Pan-Africanism "meant Marcus Garvey, and Marcus Garvey meant 'Back to Africa,' and 'Back to Africa' meant reactionary nationalism." Moreover, the Sixth PAC organizers' interest in trying to harness Africa's scientific and technical capacity raised eyebrows, because many of the British Black Power activists believed that "technically skilled people had 'bourgeois' mentalities and could not be trusted" to work in the best interests of African peasants and workers. To properly serve Africa, the Sixth PAC had to be "decidedly anti-imperialist, anti-colonialist, and anti-racist" in orientation. The latter meant involving people of non-African descent (particularly East Indians in the British context) in organizing the congress, which would vault beyond a narrow racialism that included only people of African origin.[18]

The Garrett contingent's exchanges with the British Black Power militants offered some of the first international glimpses into the difficult challenges for organizers attempting to mobilize support and participation in the congress. The British racial context, where all former colonials, including people of Asian descent, self-identified as "black," produced a particular kind of radical politics with deep investments in a transracial nationalism, based on common colonial experience in the colonies and in the metropolitan center. Though U.S.-based Black Power advocates provided certain radical texts, a performative language, and militant energy for organizers based in England, these did not produce the same kind of ideological results on the ground.[19]

While in London, Garrett and company met several representatives of the national liberation movements from Rhodesia/Zimbabwe, South Africa, Southwest Africa, and Mozambique at the Tanzania High Commission. The national liberation leaders were supportive of an initiative to hold a Sixth PAC; however, they believed that an open Pan-African forum was unlikely to take place in the near future. They were also concerned about the "progressive nature" of the congress and wanted to know what general outcome the organizers expected. In addition to having no reasonable answer for the liberation groups, the Garrett contingent "caught glimpses of the internal antagonisms between liberation movements from the same states, as the meeting broke down several times in verbal attacks."[20]

The Garrett group encountered additional challenges in France, when Caribbean student groups and worker organizations representing Guadalupe and Martinique purportedly "laughed" at the idea of a Sixth Pan-African Congress. Garrett reasoned that much of the skepticism for the congress emanated from a "well-financed anti-[Sekou] Toure group based in Paris," who vehemently opposed any political platform that smelled of support from the Guinean president, an avid Pan-Africanist and supporter of the Sixth PAC. Additionally, Garrett and company met with Alioune Diop of *Présence Africaine*, one of the leading journals of the African diaspora devoted to arts and politics, and obtained a fair number of contacts in Paris. Among them was Carlos Moore, a well-known Afro-Cuban journalist who endorsed the Sixth PAC yet stridently opposed Fidel Castro, all forms of Marxism and communism, and Arabs of any nationality. Moore's journalism and political ideas had circulated in activist periodicals in the United States, and he was known to espouse a rigid and acutely narrow form of black nationalism that was generally opposed to all political projects which involved anyone of non-African descent. Still, Moore's political ideas resonated with other supporters of the Sixth PAC and would be at the center of the ideological debates that influenced the organization and the execution of the congress.[21]

Once the group departed Europe, Garrett declared that "three things were clear: the Congress needed a clear focus and direction; it would be very difficult to organize; and though having traveled a great deal, [they] were still amateurs in the international arena." The latter problem was symptomatic of the political disjuncture in the African world that greeted a fairly ambitious group of organizers who expected greater unanimity for a congress that promised to speak broadly to the African world's political needs and aspirations. Garrett's recollection and representation of the early organizational efforts in Europe encapsulated the principal ideological divide that would drive the development and execution of the congress—the political and tactical primacy of race versus class. Thus, when the Garrett group set out to write a draft of the call upon their return from Europe, they did so recognizing full well that such a political statement had to be broad, yet politically and ideologically sharp on questions of class and the ubiquity of neocolonialism in the African world. Within this context, the seasoned ideas and experiences of an elder statesmen of the Pan-African movement came to play a key role in setting the tone and the political trajectory for a congress that promised to advance the fight for African self-determination beyond the acquisition of flag independence in the colonies and electoral political power in the United States.

The Call to the Congress

Once the Garrett group returned to the United States, the small organizing committee that spearheaded the congress was expanded, and plans were made to create a Secretariat. Several planning-committee meetings were held in the early months of 1972 in the United States and the Caribbean, with mixed results.

The call was drafted and opened forcefully with the declaration that "The 20th century is the century of Black Power." For organizers, the Black Power century was driven by two important global dynamics: the decline of European empire and formal colonial domination on the one hand, and the emergence of the Third World as a dynamic geopolitical force on the other. The call argued that the "most significant members of the Third World [were] those who strive for power to the people." The call emphasized the importance of self-reliance in the African world and called for the development of a Pan-African Center of Science and Technology that was to "be a locus for organizing scientific and technological expertise to assist, advise, and develop various projects touching on the human and technical development of African societies." In addition to being fully financed by Africans the world over, the center was to also serve as a "human, technical and scientific resource" in developing "a viable and self-supporting agricultural system in Africa."[22] For organizers, a self-sustaining Africa translated into a stronger Third World. Though the Sixth PAC was principally organized to address the issues, concerns, and problems of Africa and its diaspora, congress organizers recognized the inextricable interconnectedness of the Third World and argued that the politics of Pan-Africanism had to revolve around an unflinching commitment to "people's power" beyond the African world. These developments were by no means unique to the Sixth PAC. Preceding congresses, particularly the Fifth PAC, recognized the vital importance of the larger colonial world and extended overtures of political solidarity and support for anticolonial struggles outside the African context.[23]

The call employed Black Power as a political signifier that served to underscore the centrality of people's power from below. Black Power was cast in class terms as a way to invigorate debates about its meaning and link the political challenges of the 1960s and early 1970s to a much longer global history of black resistance. The call's authors were largely members of SNCC who were residing in Washington, DC, just as SNCC's political activity began to slow and cease altogether between 1967 and 1971. Although the group had declined by 1970, many SNCC workers continued their political work through new and old organizational channels across the United States, and Washington, DC, became a critical base for a handful of SNCC workers in the late 1960s. In addition to being the birthplace of a number of former field secretaries, DC was also the home of Howard University, where many SNCC workers, largely through their work with the Nonviolent Action Group (NAG), had attended college and became formally involved in the black freedom movement. Moreover, DC was both familiar territory and a majority-black city that had no congressional representation because of its nonstate status. SNCC worker Stokely Carmichael quipped that his desire to return to full-time organizing in DC during SNCC's organizational decline rested on the idea that DC was "a classic internal colony" where black people had been "effectively disenfranchised" as they were "in Mississippi."[24] For Carmichael and others, the task after 1966 was to organize northern ghettoes and tackle the problems of de facto segregation, political disempowerment, substandard housing, poor education, police brutality, and unemployment, among a host of other concerns.[25]

In many ways, DC became a temporary retreat and place of return for a battle-tested, beleaguered band of SNCC workers attempting to regroup and refocus their activist efforts in the urban North. Within this context, SNCC workers established Drum and Spear bookstore in 1967, in an attempt to build an independent black institution that met the growing interest and demand for black nationalist, Marxist, and Third World political writing. Shortly after its founding, Drum and Spear established a press under the same name and a community school called the Center for Black Education (CBE).[26]

The CBE sponsored regular forums and talks by activists from around the black world, developed broad-ranging political-education classes for aspiring organizers, and served as a general base of operations for a host of black activists within and beyond SNCC, oscillating between a range of black nationalist and Marxist political circles within the greater Washington, DC, area. The CBE's early credibility rested on the veteran leadership of SNCC workers who had survived the U.S. South. Yet the presence of several elder statesmen, which included historian Chancellor Williams and veteran activist-scholar C.L.R. James, bolstered the center's reputation as a major node of the black liberation movement globally.[27]

C.L.R. James, one of the key architects of the call, came to advise and work closely with members of the CBE after a chance meeting at the Congress of Black Writers held in Montreal, Canada, in October 1968.[28] James Garrett, who was the founding director of the CBE, recalled that Stokely Carmichael was "on the outs" with SNCC leadership after his "unauthorized" derby around the Third World (among other things) in 1967. Thus, when CBE organizers journeyed to Montreal, their primary objective was "to support Stokely," with whom they were politically aligned within SNCC. In addition to reuniting with Carmichael, however, the SNCC group met C.L.R. James and was "blown away" by how effortlessly he melded Pan-Africanist sentiments with Marxist-Leninist theory. Although this appeared novel and refreshing to some in the SNCC group, for James, it was consistent with what he had been arguing for decades, to the consternation of his comrades on the Left.[29] According to James, "Black people ha[d] a right to struggle in their own way, by their own principles, and their own organizations." As a Marxist, James upheld that "there had been a lot of Marxists who [had] tried to keep Blacks down and make the movements subject to the Marxist movement, but that [was] not Marxism." Indeed, Marxism was fundamentally concerned with the material circumstances that undergirded revolutionary change in a society and was "not bound to be the doctrine of the people" engaged in making the actual change.[30]

James's presence and advisory role became the nucleus for a small group of SNCC workers looking more acutely at African liberation movements for guidance and political direction. Activists within the Pan-Africanist/nationalist/Marxist community in DC and across the United States coveted James's presence as an elder statesmen and historic figure. James, however, was just as impressed with political developments in the United States and took a particular interest in the movement for Black Power, despite some of its adherents' tendency to promote a narrow racialism and parochial black nationalism.[31]

Without question, the call reflected James's political insights and progressive Pan-Africanist vision, engaging the postcolonial challenges anticipated by Frantz Fanon in his seminal work, *The Wretched of the Earth*. For Fanon, the African elite, or what he termed the national bourgeoisie, who had inherited the "political kingdom" of the colonial state, served merely as intermediaries between European finance capital and the great mass of African producers.[32]

As a political strategist and theoretician, James, in agreement with Fanon, was quite concerned with the responsibility and historic mission of the national middle class (throughout the African world) in playing either a revolutionary or a reactionary role in the process of decolonization and national reconstruction. Although many looked to Africa as the embodiment of hope and possibility for unbridled political freedom, James insisted that comprador elites be exposed, the limits and challenges of state power be critically engaged, and the self-activity and ideas of ordinary African workers and peasants be unapologetically supported.[33] These ideas were not just idle pronouncements, but grew from more than forty years of sustained engagement with anticolonial politics throughout the African world. James's ideas and currency as a major international figure proved invaluable to the Sixth PAC's early mobilization efforts.

Race, Class, and African Liberation

By 1972, a permanent Secretariat for the congress was established, with Courtland Cox, a former SNCC worker and secretary general of the CBE. Initially, the Secretariat was housed at the CBE, before moving to Dar es Salaam, Tanzania, in the early months of 1974. Though the bulk of the work revolved around a handful of CBE organizers, the division of labor began to widen and involve a handful of seasoned activists and intellectuals based largely in black studies programs across the country. Most notably, James Turner of the Africana Studies and Research Center at Cornell University and Sylvia Hill of Macalester College came to play a key role in organizing the North American delegation. Hill was named North American regional secretary general and was responsible for developing local working meetings and ensuring that the composition of the delegation was evenly represented in terms of "youth, women, men, and the elderly as well as a cross section of representatives from the scientific and technical communities, labor groups, institutions of higher education, community-based institutions, political organizations and the church."[34]

In the Caribbean, regional organizing meetings were held in Jamaica and Guyana—and were divided from the very beginning. According to the call, the Sixth PAC would be an open meeting of nongovernmental individuals and organizations in agreement with the basic principles of the call. In nearly every

Caribbean state there was a social movement or party opposed to the current regime. Between 1967 and the months leading up to the Sixth PAC, there had been numerous rebellions, riots, and strikes in the Caribbean and South America, including Belize, Guyana, Jamaica, Trinidad, Antigua, Grenada, Suriname, St. Croix, Dominica, and other locations.[35] The majority of the Caribbean regional planners for the congress were participants in these movements and were generally opposed to their respective regimes. The Sixth PAC promised to be an open political forum that drew "a line of steel against those, Africans included, which [hid] behind the slogan and paraphernalia of national independence while allowing finance capital to dominate and direct their economic and social life." This, however, did not prove to be the case.

Weeks before the congress, the Tanzanian government announced that the Sixth PAC was no longer a nongovernmental affair and that participants were required to be delegates of their respective countries. Because neither the U.S. nor Canadian governments were officially involved in the congress, none of the delegates from North America were required to adhere to the protocol imposed upon the Caribbean participants. According to James Garrett,

> The criteria for delegations from Black states were changed and now consisted of: government delegations; delegations from ruling parties; Liberation Movements; and delegates and guests found not objectionable to the governments or ruling parties or states from which they came. This decision totally changed the framework in which the SIX-PAC began. From a non-governmental Congress with governmental participation, the Congress had become a governmental Congress with open participation for Blacks from Black states and qualified participation by progressive leaders from Black states. It also meant that [Caribbean radicals] would have to seek permission to attend the Congress from governments that they opposed.[36]

This policy effectively barred most members of the Caribbean delegation; as a result, C.L.R. James, a founding member of the congress, along with other leading Caribbean militants, boycotted the Sixth PAC on principle.

One of the leading Caribbean militants that stood alongside James was Eusi Kwayana of Guyana. Kwayana, a member of the African Society for Cultural Relations with Independent Africa (ASCRIA), took a conspiratorial stance and argued that the barring of Caribbean delegates was "the greatest act of betrayal of Black people in the Caribbean that could have been committed." Kwayana charged that the United States had "instigated" the affair because of U.S. imperial interests in the region and a longstanding desire to control and suppress progressive political activity.[37] However, James Garrett, who was a close political ally of Kwayana, suggests that the move was largely rooted in the foreign-policy objectives of Tanzania, which was seeking to mitigate its political isolation as a socialist state and desired to develop diplomatic ties with independent black governments in the Caribbean.

One leading theoretician who anticipated the challenges experienced by the Caribbean delegation was none other than Guyanese political economist and Marxist Walter Rodney. In terms of Pan-Africanism, Rodney argued that "any 'Pan' concept was an exercise in self definition by a people, aimed at establishing a broader redefinition of themselves." Utilizing the experience of the Pan-Slavic nationalist movement in Eastern Europe during the late nineteenth century as an example, Rodney suggested that all nationalist formations had to confront the question of which "specific social group or class . . . speaks on behalf of the population as a whole." Thus, the central task of the Sixth PAC, in keeping with the call during the postcolonial/neocolonial era of African independence, was to answer the following questions: "Which class leads the national movement? How capable is this class of carrying out the historical tasks of national liberation? Which are the silent classes on whose behalf 'national' claims are being articulated?"[38]

These questions were at the heart of the debates between Pan-Africanists of the Marxist variety and their nationalist detractors, who argued that race was the most fundamental determinate of African people's socioeconomic status in the world.[39] Rodney, however, sought to prove that with the coming of independence in the Third World and civil rights reforms in the United States, questions of class in Africa and the diaspora had ascended to new levels of importance, as Africans and their descendants held new positions of political power around the globe. Yet the global persistence of white supremacy insured that race remained critically important, as different geographical contexts unevenly shaped the socioeconomic landscape that governed black life.

Marxist-oriented militants throughout the Caribbean and the United States who were directly engaged in challenging their respective governments to deliver on the promises of independence echoed Rodney's sentiments in condemning the congress. Following the example of James and Kwayana in this regard, many did not attend the gathering.[40] Though these sentiments were relatively widespread throughout North America and the Caribbean, organizers in the United States assembled the largest nongovernmental delegation to the congress, and these debates intensified in Dar es Salaam. Garrett, like Cox and others who had invested nearly four years in the congress's organizational planning, decided that the Sixth PAC had to go on, "for better or for worse."[41]

Held at the University of Dar es Salaam from June 19 to 27, the congress attracted more than six hundred participants from around the black world. The North American delegation was by far the largest group, with approximately two hundred attendees; nearly half were designated as delegates, while the rest "were alternates, observers, press and various types of tourists."[42] *Black World* editor Hoyt Fuller observed that "the grounds around the conference center seemed to be dominated by Afro-Americans, who outnumbered all the other conferees combined."[43] In the early hours of the congress, Fuller quipped that there did not appear to be much camaraderie among participants. However, things improved after attendees got adjusted to their new surroundings. Many in the

North American delegation, visiting Africa for the first time, appeared smug when they were subjected to rigid security checks upon arriving at the airport. Weeks before their arrival, several African American expatriates in Dar es Salaam were jailed after a cache of guns was discovered in their possession, and they were suspected of being a part of some undisclosed plot that rattled the Tanzanian government. Throughout the congress, the incident was shrouded in mystery, and the African Americans remained in jail, with very little explanation from the Tanzanians.[44]

The ideological debates that preceded the actual convening of the congress took on new life in and around the conference grounds. Individuals and groups who proffered a range of political persuasions argued and debated in the halls, bathrooms, and plenary sessions of the congress. Within the North American delegation, the Marxist-versus-nationalist tension reignited, and their differences were amplified in the meetings and speeches of some of the leading male personalities, such as Imamu Amiri Baraka, Bill Chaka, Ed Vaughn, and Owusu Sadauki. All of these figures and their respective organizations had been part of the African Liberation Support Committee's initiatives in the United States, especially the development of African Liberation Day, and had been squabbling over which political ideas would lead that coalition. Baraka, the head of the Congress of African People, and Sadauki, the founder of Malcolm X Liberation University, had attracted a great deal of attention for the increasingly Marxist tenor of their ideological positions, to the consternation of their nationalist comrades.[45] Dar es Salaam proved more than ideal for the budding Marxists, who found tremendous support from many of the continental African participants, especially representatives of the Portuguese colonies' liberation movements. However, in a closed meeting between several members of the North American delegation and Tanzanian President Julius Nyerere, the esteemed president made the point "that he was not a Marxist" but could be aptly described as a socialist and Christian humanist who was "not a racialist." Nyerere also defended the idea that his ruling party, the Tanzanian African National Union, should remain a party of black Africans because, in the context of a multiracial, postcolonial, but majority-black state, "Africans needed to build up their concept of themselves so they could deal effectively with whites and Asians."[46] Nyerere's intervention resonated with both sides of the warring factions within the North American delegation. He also suggested, according to Owusu Sadauki, that although there was class struggle in the United States, white Americans' investment in whiteness put all of them in direct conflict with African Americans. Ever attentive to space and place, Nyerere suggested that it was important for Tanzanians to pay more visits to the United States in an effort to better understand the specificity of race and class in North America as a whole.

Perhaps one of the most important legacies of the Sixth PAC was the way in which it amplified the importance of participants' recognizing how local circumstances demanded that activists be politically flexible and ideologically dexterous.

This point hit home when a member of the Popular Movement for the Liberation of Angola (MPLA) "held up his fist and shouted, 'You Black Americans shout Black Power, but our situation is not the same as yours. We're not against people because they are not Black.'" According to Hoyt Fuller, "efforts to explain to him that 'Black' in America included people he would call 'mullatoes' proved unavailing."[47] Activists often held rigid ideological positions despite dynamic political circumstances that demanded more nuance and specificity, and the Sixth PAC was no exception. In the case of the relationship of African Americans to the liberation movements struggling against Portuguese colonialism, this was not a one-way street. The liberation movements in the Portuguese colonies tended to be, Walter Rodney observed, "hyper-sensitive to language of racial overturn which [was] used by Afro-Americans, since it bared some similarity to counter-revolutionary positions in their own midst" that used race as a chasm to denounce the mixed-race *assimilados*, who often held positions of leadership within their respective organizations.[48] Meeting and arguing these issues at the Sixth PAC went a long way in unveiling and clarifying the complicated ways in which local conditions determined different outcomes and demanded greater specificity from self-avowed Pan-Africanists, whose broad visions of global unity were generally shattered when they were forced to grapple with varying political circumstances on the ground.

Sixth PAC—Lessons and Legacies

Opinions about the merits and successes of the Sixth PAC varied from deeming it a rousing success to calling it a dismal failure. This was the first visit to Africa for many of the African Americans. Just being there meant a great deal to them, so the trip took on a personal importance despite the ideological and political differences that animated the congress.[49] Many of the ideological and political debates within the North American delegation continued to rage within the African Liberation Support Committee, the Congress of African People, the Pan African People's Organization, Malcolm X Liberation University, and the plethora of periodicals and newspapers devoted to the black liberation movement as a whole. Some congress participants deepened their commitment to their respective organizations, while others retreated and devoted their energy to other matters. Tanzania continued to be a place of refuge for expatriates from the United States and beyond, and the anti-apartheid movement that picked up steam in the 1980s involved veteran activists who had cut their teeth in Dar es Salaam and remained steadfast in their pursuit of freedom and justice, no matter how arduous and daunting.

In many respects, the ideological conflicts that were amplified during the organization and convening of the Sixth PAC reflected larger tensions that had been reverberating throughout the black liberation movement as a whole.[50] Yet despite the complex challenges, Africa remained a key locus of interest and a starting point for building global solidarity within the black world. Prior to the

Sixth PAC, a growing movement had explicitly opposed Portuguese colonialism and white settler domination in southern Africa. Moreover, black liberation movement activists, many of whom had participated in the Sixth PAC, began to challenge U.S. corporate complicity in its economic support of South African apartheid.[51] Across the country, thousands of students began to amp up demands for corporate and university divestment, while organizations as diverse as the American Committee on Africa, the Africa Information Service, the Center for Black Education, the Polaroid Revolutionary Workers Union, the Student Organization for Black Unity, the Congress of African People, the Patrice Lumumba Coalition, and TransAfrica began to sow the seeds of the anti-apartheid movement that would reach its zenith in the 1980s and play a critical role in the ending of apartheid in 1994.

Sixth PAC organizer Sylvia Hill, who played a critical role in every aspect of the organization and coordination of the North American delegation, returned to the United States and relocated from Minneapolis to Washington, DC. She became an active member in the Southern Africa Support Project, the Free South Africa Movement, and TransAfrica. According to Hill, "a core of activists," because of their experience at the Sixth PAC, returned to the United States with renewed interest in continuing to organize, support, and agitate on behalf of the southern Africa liberation movements. For Hill, the international experience gained through working with the Sixth PAC was invaluable, because it was foundational to her later work that involved lobbying in the nation's capital to influence U.S. foreign policy toward Africa. More importantly, however, Hill believed that the Sixth PAC provided activists with an invaluable opportunity to "have a connection with Africa" and to be exposed to the complexity of global African experience.[52] Though many of its lessons were bitter and sobering, the opportunities and experiences of those involved helped to refuel a movement that brought apartheid to it knees and continued to raise critical questions that confronted the African world then, yet have no easy answers today.

NOTES

1. In terms of the international contours of 1968, see Carole Fink, Philipp Gassert, and Detlef Junker, eds., *1968: The World Transformed* (New York: Cambridge University Press, 1998); and George Katsiaficas, *The Imagination of the New Left: A Global Analysis of 1968* (Boston: South End Press, 1987).

2. Although they are similar and sometimes overlapping, I want to distinguish between Pan-Africanism and black internationalism, because the former refers to a general desire to restore freedom and dignity to Africans on the continent and in the diaspora through a process of building global unity, while black internationalism bespeaks a notion of international solidarity that extends beyond the African world and advocates for the right of self-determination for all peoples struggling globally against oppression and exploitation. Although Pan-Africanism is inherently internationalist, black internationalism enables scholars to make sense of solidarity efforts within and outside the African world. The literary critic Brent Hayes Edwards has suggested that the term

intercolonial internationalism is useful in explaining the circuits of collaboration and solidarity between colonial subjects in the metropoles, and in some instances the colonies. For a useful analysis of the distinction between Pan-Africanism, black internationalism, and intercolonial internationalism, see Brent Hayes Edwards, "The Uses of Diaspora," *Social Text* 19:1 (Spring 2001): 52–55; and "The Shadow of Shadows," *Positions* 11:1 (2003): 12–16. For a larger discussion on black internationalism between the First and Second World Wars, see Brent Hayes Edwards, *The Practice of Diaspora: Literature, Translation, and the Rise of Black Internationalism* (Cambridge, MA: Harvard University Press, 2003). For a more comprehensive look at black internationalism in general see Michael O. West, William G. Martin, and Fanon Che Wilkins, eds., *From Toussaint to Tupac: Black Internationalism Since the Age of Revolution* (Chapel Hill: University of North Carolina Press, 2009).

3. Pan-African congresses were held in Paris in 1919, simultaneously in London, Brussels, and Paris in 1921, and in 1927 in New York. For a brief overview of the formal evolution of the Pan-African Congress movement, see James Turner, "Sixth Pan African Congress 1974: Historical Perspective," *Black World*, March 1974, 11–19. For more comprehensive studies, see Vincent Thompson, *Africa and Unity: The Evolution of Pan-Africanism* (New York: Longmans, 1969); and Imanuel Geiss, *The Pan-African Movement: A History of Pan-Africanism in America, Europe, and Africa* (London: Holmes & Meier, 1974).

4. The historian William Van Deburg argued that Black Power militants could be divided into two main ideological camps, pluralists and nationalists. Pluralists "hoped to generate Black Power within the economic, educational, and political institutions of their communities. Then, using the local constituencies as their support base, they would promote black empowerment and participation at the state and national levels." The nationalists were essentially made up of territorial separatists, revolutionary nationalists, and cultural nationalists. Though ideologically different, they shared the idea that there was no "immediate prospect of blacks gaining significant decision making power within white American institutions." Each of these groups "vied for supremacy" within the Black Power movement and was engaged in a dynamic ideological discourse that overlapped with resurgent Pan-Africanist sentiments during the period. See William L. Van De Burg, *New Day in Babylon: The Black Power Movement and American Culture, 1965–1975* (Chicago: University of Chicago Press, 1992), 112.

5. Manning Marable, *Blackwater: Historical Studies in Race, Class Consciousness, and Revolution* (Dayton, OH: Black Praxis Press, 1981), 111.

6. The most comprehensive examination of SNCC's organizational life remains Clayborne Carson, *In Struggle: SNCC and the Black Awakening of the 1960s* (Cambridge, MA: Harvard University Press, 1981). Carson does not, however, explore SNCC activity beyond 1969 and fails to explore how SNCC activists and their ideas circulated nationally and globally in other political circles. For a more detailed history of SNCC's early internationalist efforts, particularly as they pertained to Africa, see Fanon Che Wilkins, "The Making of Black Internationalists: SNCC and Africa before the Launching of Black Power, 1960–1965," *Journal of African American History* 92:4 (2007): 467–488.

7. As a result of the temporal and ideological overlap of the civil rights struggle with the movement for Black Power during the long 1960s, Clayborne Carson suggests that the formulation "black freedom struggle" best defines the period. See Clayborne Carson, "Civil Rights Reform and the Black Freedom Struggle," in *The Civil Rights Movement in America*, ed. Charles W. Eagles (Jackson: University Press of Mississippi, 1986), 19–29.

8. For a sampling of the activities of African workers, students, and peasants, see Aquino de Braganca and Immanuel Wallerstein, eds., *The African Liberation Reader: Documents of*

the National Liberation Movements, vol. I (London: Zed Press, 1982). For a fairly comprehensive assessment of radical activity in the Caribbean, see Liz Gant's interview with Willy Look Lai, a Trinidadian lawyer, journalist, and then-active member of the New Beginnings Movement. On a visit to the United States to "make contact" with those "seriously concerned about the fate of the Afro-Caribbean revolutionary movement," Look Lai provides a report and analysis of the revolts, rebellions, protests, and strikes that were ubiquitous in the Caribbean from roughly 1967 to 1974. See "New Directions? Trinidad and the Caribbean: Interview with Willy Look Lai," *Black World*, May 1974, 60–74. Also, see Rupert Charles Lewis, *Walter Rodney's Intellectual and Political Thought* (Detroit: Wayne State University Press, 1998); Brian Meeks, *Radical Caribbean: From Black Power to Abu Bakr* (Barbados: University Press of the West Indies, 1996); and Perry Mars, *Ideology and Change: The Transformation of the Caribbean Left* (Detroit: Wayne State University Press, 1998).

9. In terms of the U.S. domestic influence of Black Power on the emergence of nationalism among Latinos, Native Americans, Asian Americans, and white radicals, see Jeffrey O. G. Ogbar, *Black Power: Radical Politics and African American Identity* (Baltimore: Johns Hopkins University Press, 2004). For the South Pacific, see Gayleatha B. Cobb, "Black Nationalism in the South Pacific: An Interview with Roosevelt Browne," *Black World*, March 1976, 32–40; and Bobbi Sykes, "Towards Pan-Africanism: Word from Down Under," *Black World*, June 1973, 46–48. According to Browne, he first made contact with Australian Aboriginal organizers in England in 1969, during the mobilization trip for the Sixth PAC, when he developed ties with Bob Maza of the Aborigines Advancement League (AAL). He hosted them in the United States during the Congress of African People in 1970. After the congress, the AAL visited the National Black Theater in New York and then returned to Australia, where it developed a National Black Theater and performed plays that highlighted the atrocities of whites towards the Kooria people of Australia. According to Browne, the AAL likened their position to those of African Americans and Native Americans in the United States and were always curious about Muhammad Ali and basketball star Kareem Abdul-Jabbar.

10. George M. Fredrickson, *Black Liberation: A Comparative History of Black Ideologies in the United States and South Africa* (Oxford: Oxford University Press, 1995).

11. One of the most politically and ideologically influential national liberation movements on the African continent was that of the African Party for the Independence of Guinea and Cape Verde (PAIGC). The international face of the PAIGC was Amilcar Cabral, whose creative and philosophically complex writings on culture, Marxism, armed struggle, and leadership were widely circulated in left periodicals around the world. In terms of Cabral's direct influence on African Americans, see "Connecting the Struggles. An Informal Talk with Black Americans," in *Return to the Source: Selected Speeches of Amilcar Cabral*, ed. Africa Information Service Staff (New York: Monthly Review Press, 1973), 75–92.

12. James Garrett, "A Historical Sketch: The Sixth Pan African Congress," *Black World*, March 1975, 5.

13. Ibid., 6–7; also see C.L.R. James, "The Sixth Pan African Congress: An Overview," *Black World*, March 1974, 21–24.

14. For a larger discussion of Tanzania and the Liberation Committee within the Organization of African Unity, see Toine Huysmans, *The Liberation Committee of the Organization of African Unity* (n.p., 1978); and Michael Wolfers, *Politics in the OAU* (London: Methuen, 1976).

15. Garrett, "A Historical Sketch," 12.

16. Ibid.

17. Ibid., 11. Also, for a brief exploration of the Black Power upsurge in Britain, see Robert G. Weisbord, "Black Power with a British Accent," *Black World*, May 1969, 22–33.

18. Garrett, "A Historical Sketch," 12.

19. By the early 1970s, the term "Black Power" retained a currency in England that it did not maintain in the United States, where black radicals began to amplify overtures of solidarity towards Africa and reinvigorate Pan-Africanist initiatives in their search for radical ideological alternatives on the continent and throughout the world. Hence by 1970, the slogan "We Are an African People" replaced "Black Power" in most black radical political circles in the United States and became the catchphrase of choice for a grassroots movement principally concerned with support and solidarity for African liberation movements engaged in armed struggle on the continent. Further, the Nixon administration co-opted the term "Black Power" to be a stand-in for U.S. state-sponsored "Black Capitalism." For further exploration, see Manning Marable, *Blackwater*, 102.

20. Garrett, "A Historical Sketch," 12–13.

21. Ibid., 13.

22. *The Call*, 221.

23. For a detailed examination of the Fifth Pan-African Congress, see Imanuel Geiss, *The Pan-African Movement*, 385–411.

24. Stokely Carmichael with Ekwueme Michael Thelwell, *Ready for Revolution: The Life and Struggles of Stokely Carmichael (Kwame Toure)* (New York: Scribner, 2003).

25. In terms of the black freedom struggle's impact in the urban North, see Jeanne F. Theoharis and Komozi Woodard, eds., *Freedom North: Black Freedom Struggles Outside the South, 1940–1980* (New York: Palgrave, 2003).

26. James Garrett, interview with author, 1999. Also see Robin D. G. Kelley's introduction to C.L.R. James, *A History of Pan African Revolt* (1969; rpt. Chicago: Charles H. Kerr Publishing, 1995), 18–23.

27. Garrett, interview with author.

28. Fanon Che Wilkins, " 'In the Belly of the Beast': Black Power, Anti-Imperialism, and the African Liberation Solidarity Movement" (Ph.D. diss., New York University, 2001), 15–53.

29. For a sampling of James's examination of the centrality of African American movements for self-determination within the larger movement for socialist transformation within the United States, see his articles in the *New International* under the pseudonym J. P. Johnson and James Johnson. J. P. Johnson, "Native Son and Revolution," *New International*, May 1940, 92–93; and James Johnson, "The Revolution and the Negro," *New International*, December 1939, 339–343.

30. Patrick Griffith, "An Interview: C.L.R. James and Pan-Africanism," *Black World*, November 1971, 9.

31. C.L.R. James, "Black Power," speech delivered in London, 1967, available at http://www.marxists.org/archive/james-clr/works/1967/black-power.htm (accessed July 24, 2009).

32. Frantz Fanon, *The Wretched of the Earth* (1961; rpt. New York: Grove Press, 2005), 123–126.

33. Milton Coleman, "Session with C.L.R. James—Pan-Africanism—Past, Present and Future," *The African World*, August 21, 1971, 6–7.

34. Sylvia Hill, "Sixth Pan African Congress: Progress Report on Organizing," *Black Scholar* 5:7 (April 1974): 36.

35. See "New Directions?," 60–74.

36. Garrett, "A Historical Sketch," 20.

37. "Interview with Eusi Kwayana on WHUR: Howard University," *The Pan Afrikan World* (n.d., in author's files); and Eusi Kwayana, interview with author, 1998.

38. Walter Rodney, "Towards the Sixth Pan-African Congress: Aspects of the International Class Struggle in Africa, the Caribbean and America," in *Pan Africanism: The Struggle against Imperialism and Neocolonialism, Documents of the Sixth Pan-African Congress*, ed. Horace Campbell (Toronto: Afro Carib Publications, 1975), 19.

39. In terms of how these debates played themselves out in the U.S. context, see Marable, *Blackwater*, 106–120.

40. Shabaka Bayano, "Why I Did Not Attend the 6th PAC," *The Pan Afrikan World* (n.d., in author's files).

41. Garrett, "A Historical Sketch," 20.

42. Owusu Sadauki, "General Comments" on the Sixth PAC (n.d., in author's files).

43. Hoyt W. Fuller, "Notes from a Sixth Pan-African Journal," *Black World*, October 1974, 73.

44. Owusu Sadauki, "Basic Points Covered in the Meeting with Nyerere" (n.d., in author's files).

45. For an assessment of the debates, see Haki Madhubuti, *Enemies: The Clash of Races* (Chicago: Third World Press, 1978), 41–73.

46. Sadauki, "Basic Points." Although the comment quoted above may sound racialist, Nyerere was trying to negotiate how one governs a multiracial society where the majority population has been brutalized by colonialism and is struggling to develop a since of confidence in the face of other groups who do not carry the same scars and psychological wounds.

47. Fuller, "Notes From A Sixth Pan-African Journal," 75–76.

48. Walter Rodney, "Southern Africa and Liberation Support in Afro-America and the West Indies," March 1976, 5, in author's files.

49. La TaSha Levy, "Remembering Sixth-PAC: Interviews with Sylvia Hill and Judy Claude, Organizers of the Sixth Pan-African Congress," *The Black Scholar*, Winter 2008, 43–44.

50. In assessing the larger context of the African liberation solidarity movement in the United States during the early 1970s, activist William Minter recalled that after returning to the United States from Tanzania in 1969, "the antiwar movement, the civil rights movement, and the U.S. Left were fracturing along multiple ideological and strategic lines. The debates pitted violent against non-violent tactics, black nationalist against multi-racial strategies, and various Marxist ideologies against each other." See William Minter, Gail Hovey, and Charles Cobb, Jr., eds., *No Easy Victories: African Liberation and American Activists over a Half Century, 1950–2000* (Trenton, NJ: Africa World Press, 2008), 27.

51. Ibid., 28–37.

52. La TaSha Levy, "Remembering Sixth-PAC," 45–46.

6

How Indigenous Peoples Wound Up at the United Nations

ROXANNE DUNBAR-ORTIZ

The period bookended between the U.S. constitutional crisis generated by Richard Nixon's reelection in 1972 and Ronald Reagan's accession to office in 1981 was historic for indigenous peoples in the United States and throughout the Americas. The 1960s had ushered in a new direction in the indigenous struggles for land and self-determination throughout the country and the continent. Following decades of bare survival, of petitioning Congress, filing court cases, and attempting to work with federal government programs, a focus on indigenous sovereignty went from aspiration to formulation. Then came harsh repression under the infamous FBI Counterintelligence Program (COINTELPRO) operation that nearly crushed the indigenous movement in the United States. The movement was saved largely by its decision to embrace, insist on, and apply international human rights law. The story of how that came about is the subject of this contribution, which is based on my own participation in the UN work and my position as an historian of Native American history.

Groundwork

Emerging prior to the Johnson administration's "Great Society" and "War on Poverty," a renewed sense of indigenous nationalism gave birth to the National Indian Youth Council (NIYC), based in Albuquerque, New Mexico. NIYC became both a vehicle for action and a center for the development of strategy. When the Johnson administration transferred priorities from the War on Poverty to the war in Vietnam, the nascent pan-Indian movement took more radical directions than it had before. The mode of action, which began in the mid-1960s and continued into the 1980s, was the occupation of land and symbolic sites, producing militant encampment communities. NIYC was founded in 1961, initially to gain support for the indigenous struggle in the Pacific Northwest for the preservation of treaty rights to fishing. Survival of American Indians (SAIA) formed in 1964 in the indigenous fishing villages and began widely publicized civil disobedience with "fish-ins," an extended social movement that ended in victory for indigenous fishing rights. Hank Adams, Ramona Bennett, Janet McCloud, and other Pacific Northwest indigenous activists who participated in the fish-ins established the standard for indigenous activism in the U.S. and became important leaders in the pan-indigenous movement.

A great deal of activity that advanced the indigenous movement was organized in the San Francisco Bay Area in the 1960s, where one of the largest and most diverse indigenous urban populations existed by then. Three currents of indigenous migrations to the San Francisco Bay Area created this pan-Indian vortex, beginning with the pre–World War II development of Pueblo Indian and Navajo communities due to their work on the Santa Fe Railroad that terminated in Richmond, California. The booming shipbuilding industry in the Bay Area during World War II brought indigenous workers. Among them was a large, extended Pine Ridge Sioux family that included many future American Indian Movement (AIM) figures—Russell Means being the best known, but also his parents, uncles and aunts, brothers and cousins, and, at the forefront, Lakota women—all of whom were active in formulating the indigenous treaty movement. Then, with the U.S. Congress Termination Act of 1954, which had the goal of dismantling the existing Indian land base by terminating tribal status, the Bureau of Indian Affairs devised a program to relocate Indians to designated industrialized urban centers for job training and jobs. The San Francisco Bay Area was one of the designated sites. Indian centers were established in San Francisco, Oakland, and San Jose.[1]

The first public manifestation of Red Power in the Bay Area occurred in March 1964, when five Sioux Indians landed at Alcatraz and claimed possession under the 1868 Fort Laramie Sioux Treaty, which enabled Sioux Indians to take possession of surplus federal land. They called for the establishment of an Indian cultural center and a university. The action lasted only a few days, but the idea germinated over the following five years, leading to a more auspicious Alcatraz occupation that endured for nineteen months (November 1969–June 1971), long enough to create a pilgrimage of Indians from all over the United States to the site, some visiting for hours or days, others to stay for the duration.

Already existing pan-Indian activities that had been apolitical, such as pow-wows, fancy dancing contests, and basketball tournaments, also became politicized. The National Congress of American Indians (NCAI), founded by tribal leaders in 1944, became more dynamic with the influx of militant young activists, such as Vine Deloria, Jr., whose 1969 bestselling book, *Custer Died for Your Sins: An Indian Manifesto*, followed the next year by his *We Talk, You Listen: New Tribes, New Turf*, electrified the indigenous surge and garnered widespread and international solidarity for indigenous demands.[2]

The birth of two important organizations in 1968 coalesced activists and made the occupation possible: United Native Americans (UNA), a pan-Indian organization launched in the Bay Area to promote self-determination; and AIM, founded in Minneapolis to protect the city's indigenous community from police and to develop community programs, influenced by the success of the Black Panthers in Oakland, California (see chapter 3). During the same period, Mohawk Indians formed a blockade at the Cornwall International Bridge between the United States and Canada to challenge U.S. government restriction on indigenous peoples' movement over the border that cut through their communities. They, too, based their highly publicized action on a treaty, in this case the Jay Treaty between the United States and Great Britain.

In the midst of such uprisings and occupations all over North America, in mid-1970 the Nixon administration nullified the federal termination policy. He established and proclaimed a new Indian policy of "self-determination without termination," introducing twenty-two pieces of legislation supporting Indian self-rule,[3] as well as establishing the National Tribal Chairmen's Association (NTCA). Soon after, and with Alcatraz still occupied, even conservative Republican California governor Ronald Reagan announced a fifty-thousand-dollar planning grant to the Bay Area Native American Council to create programs to meet the needs of urban Indians in the San Francisco Bay Area. It was clear that the Nixon and Reagan administrations intended to pacify indigenous protests and destroy militancy, and their bold actions temporarily succeeded in taking the wind out of indigenous radicalism.[4]

But not for long; in November 1972, AIM organized the historic "Trail of Broken Treaties." Thousands of Indians from all over the United States walked from the West Coast to Washington, DC, on the eve of the presidential election and attempted to present a twenty-point program to the White House.[5] Frustrated in soliciting a response, they entered the building that serves as headquarters for the Bureau of Indian Affairs (BIA), which brought the DC and federal police in great numbers, forcing the protesters to lock themselves inside, where they remained for a week. Many of the veterans of earlier occupations were there, along with many indigenous students who were recipients of the new and improved Indian higher-education grants that paralleled affirmative-action programs on campuses. They organized themselves and formed a cooperative community while rifling through, reading, and copying government documents that revealed the corruption of the BIA—and downright fraudulent relations with indigenous governments.

The BIA occupants dispersed to their homes, schools, and reservations, newly energized and with solid connections all over the country. Those from the Pine Ridge Sioux reservation in South Dakota returned determined to confront the tribal government, on which they now had concrete evidence of criminal actions in cheating the Lakota residents, particularly the traditional full-bloods. This political confrontation turned violent on February 27, 1973, when AIM, by that time having deep roots among the most traditional and poor in the Sioux communities, led a protest at the iconic site of the 1890 Wounded Knee massacre.[6] The corrupt tribal chairman, Richard Wilson, called in armed federal police—along with armed Indian paramilitaries who called themselves "Guardians of the Oglala Nation" (GOONs)—to attack the protesters, then called it an occupation. The hamlet of Wounded Knee and a large perimeter around it were under siege for seventy-one days, ending on May 8, 1973. Police and vigilantes fired more than five hundred thousand rounds of ammunition into the resisters' camp. Two Indians and one FBI agent were killed, with some twelve hundred people arrested. Although the Nixon administration guaranteed that grievances would be dealt with, nothing was forthcoming, in light of Nixon's imminent impeachment and subsequent resignation.

The rest of the decade saw a "reign of terror," as the AIM-affiliated people of Pine Ridge called and experienced it, directed by Chairman Wilson but with a fully cooperative FBI, resulting in sixty-one homicides among AIM supporters. The terror continued with little notice by the media and public until June 26, 1975, when two FBI agents were killed at Oglala on the Pine Ridge reservation after they burst into an AIM camp firing. One of the many AIM defenders who escaped, Leonard Peltier, was later convicted of murder by an all-white jury and sentenced to two consecutive ninety-nine-year terms in federal prison.

The reign of terror and attempt to wipe out indigenous militancy was accompanied by draconian legislation, with nearly a hundred congressional bills that would have effectively terminated indigenous status and territorial rights. In addition, the Carter administration established the Department of Energy and developed an energy resource policy that declared much of the West, home to the majority of Indians, a "national sacrifice area" that would be thoroughly exploited for sources of energy, with plans for coal strip-mining and coal gasification plants. This led to the five-month (February to July 1978) indigenous protest march from Alcatraz to Washington, DC, called "The Longest Walk."

One of AIM's central demands—the return of the Black Hills (the site of Mount Rushmore National Memorial), which were illegally taken, counter to the Fort Laramie Treaty of 1868—came from a strong part of its base among the Sioux and Cheyenne communities. In 1980, the U.S. Supreme Court ruled that the Black Hills were illegally seized and ordered the federal government to compensate the Indians hundreds of millions of dollars. But the Indians refused payment, demanding return of their sacred Paha Sapa. It was a great tribute to a decade of remarkable organizing, which had, in the meantime, gone international.

Going International

In July 1974, AIM called a weeklong intertribal meeting with other Native organizations and communities from North and Latin America to hammer out a common strategy. More than five thousand indigenous representatives from ninety-eight distinctive indigenous communities participated. Parallel indigenous struggles in Latin America had been increasing under old dictatorships and military regimes as well as emerging ones. In particular, the Mapuches of southern Chile were targeted by the Pinochet military dictatorship, which had brought about the U.S.-supported coup that overthrew the socialist government of Salvador Allende. The Mapuches had found most of their demands being met by the Allende administration, only to see them reversed and their leaders killed in the aftermath of the coup. Many went into exile, some in the United States, many more in Europe. Their participation in the 1974 gathering garnered deep solidarity with North American indigenous activists. Also, representatives of African liberation and Puerto Rican independence movements were present. Out of the deliberations, the International Indian Treaty Council was born, with a mandate to establish an office at the United Nations (UN) and to explore the avenues for linking up with the international human rights agenda that had been activated by the issuance in 1972 of the International Covenants on Human Rights.

In 1972, the United Nations Sub-Commission on the Prevention of Discrimination and Protection of Minorities (later called Sub-Commission on the Promotion and Protection of Human Rights) commissioned the "Study of the Problem of Discrimination against Indigenous Populations." A member of the sub-commission, Ambassador José R. Martínez Cobo of Ecuador, was selected as rapporteur. The study was completed a decade later, in 1982, having taken longer than any other study in the history of the UN.[7] Particularly during the last five years of that decade, indigenous representatives took control of the new item on the UN human rights agenda.

This was not an auspicious beginning. The sub-commission was composed of twenty-six "independent experts" who served, technically, in their own capacity but are elected by the UN Commission on Human Rights from nominations made by UN member states.[8] The Commission on Human Rights, the parent body of the sub-commission, was composed of UN member states, as is the commission's parent, the Economic and Social Council of the United Nations (ECOSOC), a parallel body to the UN General Assembly that focuses on human rights and social issues. (In a 2006 reorganization of the UN human rights mechanisms, the United Nations Commission on Human Rights was replaced with the Human Rights Committee, and the Sub-Commission on Human Rights, as well as the Working Group on Indigenous Peoples, were abolished; subsequently, the new Human Rights Committee established an Expert Group on Indigenous Rights.)

Although the sub-commission's original mandate was to prepare comprehensive reports in the areas of discrimination and minorities, it actually did much more, making dozens of resolutions to the commission regarding all aspects of human rights. For that reason, the name of the sub-commission was changed, without changing its structure and status. All the sub-commission members are close to, or work within, the foreign ministries of their respective governments. Several members also serve as their nations' representatives to the UN Commission on Human Rights. Despite this reality, the sub-commission is the only official body of the UN in which non-governmental organizations (NGOs) are able to enjoy full access and participation. However, NGOs are required to have official recognition and consultative status under ECOSOC, which requires an arduous process of application and approval by consensus. Also, human rights issues, as well as development and disarmament, are centered at UN headquarters in Geneva, Switzerland, an expensive and inaccessible site for indigenous peoples.

During the first stages of the study on indigenous peoples, governments were sent lengthy questionnaires, which formed the basis of monographs on state practices. The rapporteur also had the authority to solicit or receive information from experts and ECOSOC-recognized NGOs. During each annual session of the sub-commission, convening in Geneva for the month of August, interim reports on the study were submitted in the form of chapters. Between the 1975 and 1978 sessions, no reports were submitted, and it seemed that the study—whose reports the sub-commission members had not received with any great enthusiasm—would simply be discontinued. Martínez Cobo was no longer a member of the sub-commission, and none of the members appeared interested in reviving the study. However, the 1977 International Conference on Indigenous Peoples of the Americas asked, among other things, that the sub-commission establish a working group on indigenous populations. Thus, the conference and direct participation of indigenous representatives revived the study. Martínez Cobo, as an outside expert, was appointed to complete it.

The definition used by the sub-commission for the study, and the definition that persists, is the following:

> Indigenous populations are composed of the existing descendants of the peoples who inhabited the present territory of a country wholly or partially at the time when persons of a different culture or ethnic origin arrived there from other parts of the world, overcame them, and, by conquest, settlement or other means, reduced them to a non-dominant or colonial condition; who today live more in conformity with their particular social, economic and cultural customs and traditions than with the institutions of the country of which they now form part, under a State structure which incorporates mainly the national, social and cultural characteristics of other segments of the population which are predominant.

In its elaboration of the definition, the sub-commission made it clear that the subordinate position of such groups is unrelated to population figures; equally, it is irrelevant whether the groups live in more than one country or are scattered throughout a particular country. On the other hand, the study took into account the factor of circumstance that established the particular relationship between the state in question and the indigenous group under study, as well as the national and cultural characteristics that form the basis of the state structure.

The definition's fundamental consideration was the existence of certain groups prior to the establishment of the state, as well as whether the original inhabitants and their descendants are regarded as indigenous in relation to the colonizers and their descendants. As long as the group remains so identified, the degree of racial intermixing with the colonizers or any other group is not relevant, removing the possibility of racial identification per se.

The definition of *indigenous* also assumed that the original groups or their descendants were forced within the new state structure when it was established, and had no voice in creating it. In general, although not in all cases, the definition would apply to groups who are rural and whose land-ownership systems are based on the clan or community, not on private ownership, and whose land base is not recognized as a nation.

The time-scale relates to whether the group was present at the time the colonizers arrived, not whether they had always been there or had migrated there from other regions in precolonial periods: "This study is not concerned with the question of establishing who may have been the original inhabitants of a country or region . . . in most countries at least substantial groups of the present inhabitants are descendants of people who arrived there from other parts of the world at one time or another."[9] The definition uses the terminology, "present territory of a country," rather than "country," explaining that it is doubtful whether, at the time of first contact, the country existed as a state or had the same territory as today. In explaining the terminology, the phrase, "by conquest, settlement or other means, reduced them to a non-dominant or colonial condition," clarifies this as meaning simply "by colonization."

In reference to the phrase, "who today live more in conformity with their particular social, economic and cultural customs and traditions than with the institutions of the country of which they now form part," the elaboration is worth reproducing in full:

> No existing indigenous population can validly be said to conform to institutions it has maintained, unchanged, since the time of the conquest, settlement or other form of reduction to a non-dominant or colonial condition. What are now known as 'indigenous institutions' are a mixture, in varying degrees, of colonial and precolonial institutions as adapted by the indigenous populations to their new condition. Nevertheless, it is necessary to indicate that indigenous populations 'today live more in conformity with their particular social, economic and cultural customs and traditions than with the institutions of the country of which they now form part.' This wording seeks to avoid any characterizations of the customs and traditions beyond the fact that they are 'particular' to such groups, not whether they were originally their own or not.[10]

The analysis makes clear that the definition is not intended to attack the very existence of state structures when it characterizes them as mainly reflecting the national, social, and cultural characteristics of the dominant segments of the population, but rather that the reference is to the reality of the "non-neutral State structure." The study identifies this as the crux of the problem and calls for protective measures favoring the indigenous populations.

Due to its long and unusual history, the study is more like two separate studies. The reports from its first three years, 1973–1975, are dry and legalistic, as well
as being paternalistic—indigenous peoples were not involved. They nevertheless
contain important material and constitute an archive on state policies and claims.
The second part of the study is more dynamic and balanced, with the inclusion of
material from indigenous organizations and experts and other non-governmental
sources.

The first interim report, submitted to the sub-commission's 1973 session,
contains all measures adopted by the UN that are applicable to indigenous
peoples, including the UN Charter.[11] The International Labor Organization (ILO)
1953 Convention on Tribal and Indigenous Populations is analyzed in detail. More
importantly, three other international treaties are taken up: the 1948 Convention
on the Prevention and Punishment for Genocide; the Convention on the Abolition
of Slavery, the Slave Trade, and Institutions and Practices Similar to Slavery; and
the International Convention on the Elimination of All Forms of Racial Discrimination. In addition, actions and initiatives by all organs of the UN are reviewed,
together with actions taken by its specialized agencies.

The 1974 report outlines actions taken by the Organization of American States
(OAS), the Inter-American Commission on Human Rights, and the Inter-American
Indian Institute.[12] Finally, it begins preliminary consideration of certain substan-
tive aspects of the problem of discrimination against indigenous peoples in the
areas of housing, political rights, religious rights and practices, protection of
sacred places and objects, and protection of places and objects of archaeological
interest.

The 1975 report is structured around the governments' questionnaire responses
as well as information from experts.[13] It addresses the issue of definition first. The
definition of *indigenous populations* is analyzed in terms of ancestry, culture, religion, the fact of living under a tribal system, membership of an indigenous
community, dress, livelihood, language, group consciousness, acceptance by the
indigenous community, residence in certain parts of the country, legal definitions,
change in status from indigenous to non-indigenous and vice versa, registration
and certification, and the authority to decide who is and who is not indigenous.
The report also deals with population—both composition and statistical trends—
although the analysis is superficial and incomplete.

After two years with no reports, the study resumed in 1978, and the reports
from the following years, up to the final report in 1982, reflect the participation of
indigenous representatives.

Two important individuals behind the scenes in Geneva played key roles in
incorporating indigenous peoples into the UN human rights agenda. One was
Augusto Willemsen-Diaz, a Guatemalan international law specialist and longtime
staff member of the UN human rights secretariat, now retired. Although not
Mayan himself, Willemsen-Diaz was preoccupied with the situation of the Mayan
people, who comprised the majority of the Guatemalan population—a situation

that would soon turn into state genocide against them. He befriended Martínez Cobo and persuaded him to propose the sub-commission study of indigenous peoples. Willemsen-Diaz also made certain that "indigenous peoples" was a category in the UN Decade to Combat Racism, Racial Discrimination, and Apartheid, which began in 1974.[14] The decade focused on apartheid in South Africa but also dealt with peoples living under military occupation and migrant workers. His goal was to build a base of documentation upon which indigenous peoples could construct infrastructure within the UN system. Willemsen-Diaz, the actual architect of the sub-commission study and its definition of indigenous peoples, was a mentor to the indigenous lobbyists, myself included, at the UN.

The other essential figure was Jimmie Durham, a successful Cherokee sculptor and artist. Durham lived in Geneva during the late 1960s and early 1970s, during a time that his wife worked for the Geneva-based World Council of Churches. This was a time of national liberation movements for decolonization, particularly in Africa, inspired and emboldened by Vietnamese resistance to U.S. aggression. Durham befriended a number of the African liberation leaders who came there to present their cases at the UN, including Amílcar Cabral of the Partido Africano da Independência da Guiné e Cabo Verde (PAIGC), the liberation front in Guinea Bissau; the African National Congress (ANC) and South West Africa People's Organization (SWAPO) of southern Africa; and movement leaders from Angola, Mozambique, and Zimbabwe. From afar, Durham followed the birth of AIM in the United States, from the 1969 occupation of Alcatraz to the 1972 seizure of the Bureau of Indian Affairs building in Washington, DC, and, most importantly, the more than two-month siege at Wounded Knee on the Pine Ridge Sioux reservation. He returned to the United States, met with AIM leaders, and proposed an international project that was realized in the June 1974 founding of the International Indian Treaty Council (IITC), which Durham headed for the following six years, gaining ECOSOC non-governmental organization status for it in 1977. Even before that, Durham had persuaded some of the most important international NGOs to sponsor a conference on Indians of the Americas at UN offices in Geneva. These organizations included the World Council of Churches (WCC), the World Peace Council (WPC), the Women's International League for Peace and Freedom (WILPF), the International Commission of Jurists (ICJ), and others.

At the same time, the National Indian Brotherhood of Canada, headed by George Manuel, the National Congress of American Indians in the United States, headed by Joe de la Cruz and Phillip (Sam) Deloria, and the Nordic Sami ("Lapland") Council had founded an international NGO, the World Council of Indigenous Peoples (WCIP), which gained ECOSOC status in 1977.

The key event, then, that marked the beginning of indigenous peoples' direct activity in the international context was the 1977 International Non-Governmental Organizations Conference on Indians of the Americas, held at UN offices in Geneva. The more than one hundred indigenous representatives from all over the Western Hemisphere reflected organized forces of inestimable dimensions.

The conference was initiated by the IITC and was organized by the NGO Sub-Committee on Racism, Racial Discrimination, Apartheid, and Colonialism, of the Special Committee of NGOs on Human Rights, based in Geneva and made up of an influential and broad-based group of international NGOs.[15] More than fifty international NGOs with consultative status in ECOSOC registered for the conference, and thirty-eight UN member nations officially participated. The conference formulated a program of action for NGOs,[16] with recommendations to submit all documents to divisions of the UN.[17] The twelfth of October ("Columbus Day") was declared International Day of Solidarity and Mourning with Indigenous Peoples of the Americas, with a view to establishing a permanent United Nations' day honoring indigenous peoples.[18]

The recommendations included a call for respect for traditional law and customs, and for unrestricted rights of landownership and control by indigenous peoples over natural resources in their territories. The conference found that indigenous peoples in the Americas have the right to own land communally and manage it according to their traditions, and that such ownership must be recognized and protected in international as well as national laws. Governments of all the states of the Western Hemisphere were called upon to ratify the Declaration of Human Rights and the United Nations' human rights conventions. A recommendation was made for the Sub-Commission on the Prevention of Discrimination and Protection of Minorities to establish a working group on indigenous peoples. This recommendation was taken up in the 1981 session of the sub-commission and was approved by the Commission on Human Rights and ECOSOC in their 1982 sessions. The newly established Working Group on Indigenous Populations met for the first time in August 1982.

The indigenous representatives participating in the 1977 conference spent all-night sessions hammering out a document that they submitted collectively. This document, entitled "Draft Declaration of Principles for the Defense of the Indigenous Nations and Peoples of the Western Hemisphere,"[19] represents the dominant theme of the conference and set the basis for subsequent UN negotiations regarding the question of indigenous peoples. The declaration contains thirteen brief and unequivocal statements of indigenous rights:

1. *Recognition of Indigenous nations*: Indigenous people shall be accorded recognition as nations, and proper subjects of international law, provided the people concerned desire to be recognized as a nation and meet the fundamental requirement of nationhood, namely: (a) having a permanent population; (b) having a defined territory; (c) having a government; (d) having the ability to enter into relations with other states.
2. *Subjects of International Law*: Indigenous groups not meeting the requirements of nationhood are hereby declared to be subjects of international law and are entitled to the protection of this Declaration, provided they are identifiable groups having bonds of language, heritage, tradition, or other common identity.

3. *Guarantee of Rights*: No indigenous nation or group shall be deemed to have fewer rights or lesser status for the sole reason that the nation or group has not entered into recorded treaties or agreements with any state.

4. *Accordance of Independence*: Indigenous nations or groups shall be accorded such degree of independence as they may desire in accordance with international law.

5. *Treaties and Agreements*: Treaties and other agreements entered into by indigenous nations or groups with other states, whether denominated as treaties or otherwise, shall be recognized and applied in the same manner and according to the same international laws and principles as the treaties and agreements entered into by their states.

6. *Abrogation of Treaties and other Rights*: Treaties and agreements made with indigenous nations or groups shall not be subject to unilateral abrogation. In no event may the municipal laws of any state serve as a defense to the failure to adhere to and perform the terms of treaties and agreements made with indigenous nations or groups. Nor shall any state refuse to recognize and adhere to treaties or other agreements due to changed circumstances where the change in circumstances has been substantially caused by the state asserting that such change has occurred.

7. *Jurisdiction*: No state shall assert or claim to exercise any right of jurisdiction over any indigenous nation or group unless pursuant to a valid treaty or other agreement freely made with the lawful representatives of indigenous nation or group concerned. All actions on the part of any state which derogate from the indigenous nations' or groups' right to exercise self-determination shall be the proper concern of existing international bodies.

8. *Claims to Territory*: No state shall claim or retain, by right of discovery or otherwise, the territories of an indigenous nation or group, except such lands as may have been lawfully acquired by valid treaty or other cessation freely made.

9. *Settlement of Disputes*: All states in the Western hemisphere shall establish through negotiations or other appropriate means a procedure for the binding settlement of disputes, claims, or other matters relating to indigenous nations or groups. Such procedures shall be mutually acceptable to the parties, fundamentally fair, and consistent with international law. All procedures presently in existence that do not have the endorsement of the indigenous nations or groups concerned, shall be ended, and new procedures shall be instituted consistent with this Declaration.

10. *National and Cultural Integrity*: It shall be unlawful for any state to take or permit any action or course of conduct with respect to an indigenous nation or group which will directly or indirectly result in the destruction or disintegration of such indigenous nation or group or otherwise threaten the national or cultural integrity of such nation or group, including, but not limited to, the imposition and support of illegitimate governments and the

introduction of non-indigenous religions to indigenous peoples by non-indigenous missionaries.

11. *Environmental Protection*: It shall be unlawful for any state to make or permit any action or course of conduct with respect to the territories of an indigenous nation or group which will directly or indirectly result in the destruction or deterioration of an indigenous nation or group through the effects of pollution of earth, air, water, or which in any way depletes, displaces or destroys any natural resources or other resources under the dominion of, or vital livelihood of an indigenous nation or group.

12. *Indigenous Membership*: No state, through legislation, regulation, or other means, shall take actions that interfere with the sovereign power of an indigenous nation or group to determine its own membership.

13. *Conclusion*: All of the rights and obligations declared herein shall be in addition to all rights and obligations existing under international law.

The declaration could be characterized as the fundamental political document of the international indigenous movement.[20]

Another recommendation made by the 1977 conference was to its own constituency to organize a conference that would focus on the land and its relationship to indigenous rights, broadening the geographical scope to global. The NGO sub-committee on racism followed through with this directive and organized the International NGO Conference on Indigenous Peoples and the Land, which was held September 15–18, 1981, at the UN in Geneva.

The 1981 conference was organized into four commissions, whose individual reports made up the final report, covering the following areas: land rights, international treaties and agreements; land reform and systems of tenure; indigenous philosophy; and the impact of nuclear arms build-up. The following indigenous international and regional groups were invited to solicit and submit documentation for the conference and to organize delegations: the IITC, the World Council of Indigenous Peoples, the South American Indian Council (CISA), the Australian National Conference of Aborigines, the Indian Law Resource Center (ILRC), and the Inuit Circumpolar Conference.[21]

Participants in the 1981 conference included one hundred fifty indigenous representatives from the Americas, as well as aboriginal representatives from Australia and Sami delegates from Norway. Fewer governments participated officially than in 1977, due at least in part to the Reagan administration's call for a government boycott of the conference. Among Western countries, only the government of Norway registered, although other governments were present unofficially, and dozens of African, Asian, and Latin American governments registered and attended. Nearly fifty international NGOs with consultative ECOSOC status registered. Dozens of scholars and experts participated as individuals.

A striking aspect of both the 1977 and the 1981 conferences was the active participation of several national liberation organizations that held official UN

Observer status, including the Palestine Liberation Organization (PLO), the ANC, the Pan-African Congress (PAC), and SWAPO, with the latter representative chairing the Commission on Transnationals.[22] They were joined at the 1981 conference by the Farabundo Martí National Liberation Front/Revolutionary Democratic Front of El Salvador (FMLN/FDR), and special sessions were held on El Salvador, Angola, Namibia, and Nicaragua. The government of Nicaragua, where the Frente Sandinista de Liberación Nacional (FSLN) had taken power in 1979, sent a special delegation headed by Comandante Lumberto Campbell, a native of the eastern, indigenous region of the country, who was vice-minister for that zone; also attending were representatives of the Nicaraguan Miskitu and Sumu indigenous communities, some of whom supported the FSLN, some of whom opposed.

The participants unanimously supported the conference's final declaration and resolutions, which manifested solidarity with indigenous peoples in their "just struggle for self-determination and for the right to determine the development and use of their land and resources, and to live in accordance with their values and philosophy."

One of the excuses for the Reagan administration boycott was the presence of Romesh Chandra of WPC as president of both the 1977 and 1981 conferences, and of Edith Ballantyne, secretary general of WILPF, as the secretary. The Reagan administration accused Chandra and the WPC of being a Soviet front, and Ballantyne and WILPF of being Soviet dupes. These were the days of the cold war and binary politics in the UN. This had not been an issue in 1977 with the Carter administration, which claimed to champion international human rights. President Carter's UN representative, Dr. Andrew Young, a high-profile African American civil rights leader, cooperated to some extent with the IITC in organizing the 1977 conference, although he expressed his displeasure with the initiative. The Carter administration sent two activist Native Americans, Kirk Kickingbird and Shirley Hill Witt, as members of its delegation. At the time, IITC people were suspicious of the cooperation and kept the administration at arm's length to remain independent.[23]

Jimmie Durham had set the stage for the IITC to be linked with the Non-Aligned Movement (NAM), the organization of African, Asian, Latin American, and Caribbean states and national liberation organizations. NAM had been founded by Jawaharlal Nehru of India, Gamal Abdel-Nasser of Egypt, and Josip Broz Tito of Yugoslavia in the 1950s, in order to avoid the cold-war binary and stake out an autonomous path for decolonization, nation building, and economic development. United States administrations consistently charged that NAM was a tool of the Soviet Union. However, the Soviet Union and the Soviet bloc always voted in the UN on the side of NAM, not the reverse. The NAM states were a varied lot with many different systems of governance—only a few, such as Cuba, being actual Soviet allies.[24] The other international indigenous NGOs eschewed the NAM linkage and instead sought allies in the North Atlantic states.

Despite harassment by the Reagan administration, in 1981 the sub-commission discussed the next step toward completion of its study on indigenous peoples, and the Working Group on Indigenous Populations (WGIP) met for the first time in 1982. Tribute for UN support of the working group must be paid to the UN's director of human rights, Dr. Theo van Boven, whom the Reagan administration promptly pushed out of his post due to his advocacy for the working group and for other human rights initiatives.

The mandate of the WGIP is spelled out in the UN resolution that established it.[25] The WGIP would meet annually for up to five working days—this soon increased to ten working days—before the annual sessions of the sub-commission. Its task would be to review developments concerning the promotion and protection of the human rights and fundamental freedoms of indigenous populations, and "especially" information from indigenous peoples. The conclusions from such reviews were to be submitted to the sub-commission. The terms of the resolution were open and broad, despite various governments' attempts to narrow the task to establishing legal standards and writing a convention, both of which could be taken up within the broader mandate. Importantly, the resolution called for open attendance by indigenous representatives regardless of ECOSOC consultative status. The WGIP was, and is, made up of five members of the sub-commission, chosen by the sub-commission and appointed by its chair.[26]

At its first meeting in 1982, the WGIP discussed its mandate and reiterated its broad nature. The problem of definition was discussed, as were standards. Several areas of concern were identified and discussed, and these were summarized in the final report under seven categories: "a) the right to life, to physical integrity and to security of the indigenous communities; b) the right to self-determination, the right to develop their own culture, traditions, language and way of life; c) the right to freedom of religion and traditional religious practices; d) the right to land and to natural resources; e) civil and political rights; f) the right to education; and g) other rights."[27]

Observers at the first meeting of the WGIP included the governments of Argentina, Australia, Brazil, Canada, India, Morocco, New Zealand, Nicaragua, Panama, Sweden, the United States, and North Yemen, as well as the PLO. Also represented in the session were several UN specialized agencies, including the ILO and the UN High Commissioner for Refugees (UNHCR). The three indigenous organizations holding UN consultative status were present, as well as ten indigenous organizations without such status, eight of them from North America. CISA was represented by its director. The ECOSOC NGOs that had organized the 1977 and 1981 conferences sent representatives, as did numerous NGOs that had not in the past shown an interest in issues concerning indigenous peoples. Soon, they would take up indigenous issues within their own organizations.

Despite the explosive and sensitive issues involved, a remarkable unanimity pervaded the establishment of the WGIP and its first meeting, certainly due in part to the excellent leadership of its elected chairman, Asbjørn Eide, a Norwegian expert-member of the sub-commission. Some observers pointed out that the presence and participation of representatives of indigenous groups was the key factor that did not allow the WGIP to become politicized along East-West cold-war lines. However, it was the presence and testimony of Rigoberta Menchú Tum, a Mayan leader in exile from Guatemala, that galvanized the first meeting and set the tone of urgency that has remained inherent to WGIP meetings. The Guatemalan military had murdered Menchú's parents and brother in 1980, driving her and her other siblings into exile. She became the most important spokesperson for the Mayan people in their struggle to survive the genocidal project of the Guatemalan military government. There had been little interest or knowledge of Guatemala in international and human rights movement circles until Rigoberta Menchú arrived.[28]

Results and Lessons

The 1980s brought increased counterattack against the gains the indigenous movement had made in the previous two decades. In the fall of 1982, a decade before the looming quincentennial of Columbus's voyage, the Spanish government and the Holy See (the Vatican, which holds a nonvoting seat in the UN) proposed to the UN General Assembly that the year 1992 be celebrated in the UN as the five hundredth anniversary of an "encounter" between Europe and the peoples of the Western Hemisphere, with Europeans bearing the gifts of civilization and Christianity to indigenous peoples. To the surprise of the North Atlantic states that supported Spain's resolution (including the United States), the entire African delegation walked out of the meeting and returned with an impassioned statement condemning this proposal to celebrate colonialism at the UN.[29] That killed the resolution, but it was not the end of the story.

The Indians of the Americas conference at the UN in 1977 had proposed that 1992 be made a UN "year of mourning" for the onset of colonialism, African slavery, and genocide against the indigenous peoples of the Americas, and that October 12 be designated as the UN's International Day of the World's Indigenous Peoples. As the time drew near to the quincentenary, Spain took the lead in fighting the indigenous proposals for the year of mourning and for October 12. Spain and the Vatican also spent years and huge sums of money preparing for their own celebration of Columbus, enlisting the help of all the countries of Latin America—except Cuba, which refused.[30] The United States cooperated with the Spanish-Vatican project and produced its own series of events. In the end, compromise won at the UN: Indigenous peoples won a Decade for the World's Indigenous Peoples, which began in 1994 but was inaugurated at UN headquarters in New York in December 1992. August 9, not October 12, was designated as the UN's International Day for the World's Indigenous Peoples, to be commemorated annually.[31] In 1992, the Nobel Foundation cast its lot with the side of indigenous people by giving the Nobel Peace Prize to Guatemalan Mayan leader Rigoberta

Menchú on October 12, a decision that angered the Spanish government and the Vatican.[32]

The quincentenary debate and activities mobilized indigenous peoples of the Americas as nothing else had and garnered solidarity from other social justice movements in the United States and elsewhere. This was soon followed by the January 1, 1994, uprising of the little-known Tzeltal-, Tzotzil-, Chol-, and Tojolabal-speaking Mayans of Chiapas, Mexico, who called themselves "Zapatistas."[33] They declared: "We have nothing to lose, absolutely nothing, no decent roof over our heads, no land, no work, poor health, no food, no education, no right to freely and democratically choose our leaders, no independence from foreign interests, and no justice for ourselves or our children. But we say enough is enough! We are the descendants of those who truly built this nation, we are the millions of dispossessed, and we call upon all of our brethren to join our crusade, the only option to avoid dying of starvation!"[34] Although indigenous peoples in Mexico had been organizing within the international indigenous movement for nearly two decades before the Zapatista uprising, they had made little impact on the deep and abiding discrimination and lack of recognition of the country's indigenous peoples, who make up 30 percent of the population and a much greater percentage of the rural population. The Zapatista uprising and subsequent statements in favor of indigenous rights put the issue at the forefront of Mexican politics, and the cultural changes there have been deep and dramatic. The Zapatista uprising and subsequent program reverberated worldwide, particularly among the indigenous peoples of North, Central, and South America.

One of the mandates of the sub-commission working group was to draft a Declaration of the Rights of Indigenous Peoples, which was completed in 1994. The UN Commission on Human Rights then established a working group to debate the text and forward a completed draft for consideration and adoption by the UN General Assembly, which approved it in 2007. A UN declaration is a prelude to the drawing-up of substantial international law, as was the 1948 UN Declaration on Human Rights, which was finally codified in the 1970s.[35]

By the early twenty-first century, over a period of three decades, indigenous peoples' representatives from the Western Hemisphere, the Arctic Circle, and the Pacific, along with a few groups from Africa and Asia, have participated in the above process, both surviving as peoples and strengthening their movements by internationalizing their issues. Significantly, for the first time since the onset of colonialism in the Western Hemisphere, a true indigenous representative, who emerged from local indigenous struggles with links to the international process, was elected president of an American state: Evo Morales, of the Aymara people, in Bolivia, in November 2005. One can actually speak of an authentic international indigenous movement that has deep roots in many indigenous communities.

Indigenous activism, because of its aspiration to vindicate stolen land, is often understood as a parochial issue; it engages our national mythologies, but its practice is presumably located in local fights over land rights and resources.

However, the reality of indigenous peoples' engagement internationally calls for reconsideration of that story, complicating it by examining the ways indigenous activists utilized the international arena and developed an internationally recognized presence among the hall of nations. Indigenous peoples' reliance on the international law of self-determination is a further argument that indigenous resistance challenges the United States by rejecting its claims of unified, singular nationhood. Research and study of indigenous social movements need to account for the international dimension, to read indigenous activism as a challenge to national myths through global bodies and policies of governance.

NOTES

1. The other relocation centers were in Chicago, Denver, Los Angeles, St. Louis, Cincinnati, Cleveland, and Dallas. Seven hundred fifty thousand Indians migrated to the cities between 1950 and 1980, most through the relocation program, but others on their own. The urban Indian population increased from 8 percent in 1940 to 64 percent in 2000. For an excellent survey of the history of U.S. Indian policy, see Sharon O'Brien, *American Indian Tribal Governments* (Norman: University of Oklahoma Press, 1993).

2. Deloria, trained both in theology and law, remained a bestselling author, publishing more than two dozen substantial books, until his death in 2005. No institution or sacred cow in the United States was spared Deloria's brilliant debunking, particularly in his *Red Earth, White Lies: Native Americans and the Myth of Scientific Fact* (Golden, CO: Fulcrum Publishing, 1997); and *God Is Red: A Native View of Religion*, 3rd ed. (Golden, CO: Fulcrum Publishing, 2003), first published in 1972.

3. In 1975, the "Indian Self-Determination and Education Assistance Act" gave Native Americans more control in administering federal programs and services to their communities.

4. For a brilliant analysis of Nixon's neocolonial strategy to control indigenous organizing, see Jack Forbes, *Native Americans and Nixon: Presidential Politics and Minority Self-Determination, 1969–1972*, with a foreword by Roxanne Dunbar-Ortiz (Los Angeles: UCLA American Indian Studies Center, 1981).

5. Read the twenty-point program at http://www.aimovement.org/archives/index.html (accessed May 22, 2009). The principles contained in the document form the basis of the United Nations Declaration on the Rights of Indigenous Peoples, which was formalized by the UN General Assembly in September 2007.

6. Dee Brown's *Bury My Heart at Wounded Knee: An Indian History of the American West*, 4th ed. (New York: Macmillan, 2007) was published in 1970 and familiarized nearly everyone in the world with the 1890 winter massacre of unarmed Lakota refugees, mostly old people, women, and children, attempting to surrender to the U.S. authorities.

7. United Nations Document No. E/CN.4/Sub.2/1982/33. August 25, 1982.

8. For the history and functions of the sub-commission, see Tom Gardeniers, Hurst Hannum, and Janice Kruger, "The U.N. Sub-Commission on Prevention of Discrimination and Protection of Minorities: Recent Developments," *Human Rights Quarterly* 4:3 (1982): 353–370; and Peter Haver, "The United Nations Sub-Commission on the Prevention of Discrimination and the Protection of Minorities," *Columbia Journal of Transnational Law* 21 (1982): 103–134. In a 2006 reorganization of the UN human rights mechanisms, the United Nations Commission on Human Rights was replaced with the Human Rights Committee, and the Sub-Commission on Human Rights, as well as the

Working Group on Indigenous Peoples, were abolished; subsequently, the new Human Rights Committee established an Expert Group on Indigenous Rights.

9. United Nations Document No. E/CN.4/Sub.2/L566. June 29, 1972.

10. Ibid.

11. United Nations Document No. E/CN.4/Sub.2/L84. June 25, 1973.

12. United Nations Document No. E/CN.4/Sub.2/L596. June 19, 1974.

13. United Nations Document No. E/CN.4/Sub.2/L707. July 17, 1975.

14. U.S. administrations from those of Jimmy Carter to George W. Bush and Barack Obama have boycotted the UN initiatives on racism, including the activities of the two official decades—1974–1983, 1984–1993—ostensibly because of the inclusion of the Palestinian question on the agenda. However, although Zionism as racism was removed from that agenda after the 1993 Oslo accords, the United States continued to be unsupportive of antiracist initiatives. The George W. Bush administration registered for, then walked out of, the 2001 World Conference against Racism in Durban, South Africa. Many U.S. NGO representatives of color, including Native Americans, believe that the U.S. rebuff to the issue of racism internationally is due to the institutionalized racism inherent in the U.S. government itself.

15. I was a member of the IITC staff organizing and directing the conference. Delegates to the conference were elected at the annual meeting of the IITC in June 1977 at the Standing Rock Sioux reservation. The IITC also invited Latin American indigenous organizations to send delegates of their choice.

16. United Nations Document No. E/CN.4/Sub.2/L.684 Annex IV, p. 3. July 21, 1978. United Nations Sub-Commission, 31st Session, Item 16. See also: *Official report from the NGO Sub-Committee on Racism, Geneva, 1978*, and *Report from the International Indian Treaty Council*, New York, November, 1978. These and other documents are available from doCip—the Indigenous Peoples' Center for Documentation, Research and Information, located at 14, av. de Trembley, CH-1209 Genève, online at http://www.docip.org (accessed May 22, 2009). doCip was founded at the 1977 Geneva conference, with the mandate to collect and house all documents relevant to the international indigenous peoples' movement.

17. The conference documentation was formally submitted to the UN secretary-general and the president of the UN General Assembly in November 1977.

18. See *Fact Sheet No. 9 (Rev. 1), The Rights of Indigenous Peoples: Programme of Activities for the International Decade of the World's Indigenous People (1995–2004)*, para. 4, General Assembly resolution 50/157 of 21 December 1995, annex, available online at: http://www.ohchr.org/Documents/Publications/FactSheet9rev.1en.pdf (accessed May 22, 2009). August 9 was selected as the day (General Assembly resolution 49/214 of 23 December 1994 para. 8), and 1993 as the year, for indigenous peoples (resolution 45/164 of 18 December 1990), while the UN Decade for the World's Indigenous People spanned 1995–2004 (General Assembly resolution 50/157 of 21 December 1995, annex). These dates were compromises after a long attempt by the governments of Spain, Italy, the Vatican, and the United States to acknowledge the five-hundred-year anniversary of the "encounter" of Europe and the Americas with the landing of Columbus on October 12, 1492, by celebrating that event in the United Nations in 1992, calling for a day, a year (1992), and a decade (1993–2002). I was present in the General Assembly meeting in October 1982 when Spain presented the proposal. I was shocked, then disgusted, when the Irish and Norwegian ambassadors teased the Spanish that their countries had been first to "discover America." After a half-hour of general hilarity, suddenly one of the African delegates stood up and walked out of the room, followed by every other African representative. A recess was called, and the Western European and North American

delegates appeared dazed and confused. I heard one say, "Why on earth would Africans even be interested in the issue?" I was amazed at their ignorance. When the African bloc returned an hour later, its elected spokesperson read a statement that condemned the call to celebrate the onset of "colonialism, the trans-Atlantic slave trade, and genocide" in the halls of the United Nations. That killed the proposal but did not faze its supporters. The Vatican even wanted to expand the concept of "encounter" to include a phrase about the "gift" of bringing Christianity to the heathens. During the decade that followed, Spain, the Vatican, Italy, the United States, and all the Latin American countries they could bribe brought full pressure on the African states to agree, but they never budged. Meanwhile, the international indigenous movement and local indigenous groups of the Western Hemisphere opposed it and insisted on those dates to honor indigenous peoples, a battle they won in the end. To pacify Spain and the Vatican for their total defeat, August 9 was designated as the day, and 1993 rather than 1992 was named the "UN Year for the World's Indigenous Peoples," followed by a UN decade (1995–2004) by the same name.

19. United Nations Document No. E/CN.4/Sub.2/L.684 Annex IV, p. 3. July 21, 1978.

20. It would provide the basis for the elaboration of the Draft Declaration of Principles for the Rights of Indigenous Peoples in the Working Group on Indigenous Populations, which became the subject of a decade of negotiations in the UN Commission on Human Rights, and which was approved by the United Nations General Assembly in September 2007, with only the United States, Canada, New Zealand, and Australia voting against the declaration (Australia rescinded its opposition with the election of a new government).

21. United Nations Document No. E/CN.4/Sub.2/476/Add.5, 198a: 56. The ICC did not respond to the invitation. The invited indigenous NGOs were selected due to their status as consultative NGOs with ECOSOC. During the 1980s and 1990s, numerous other indigenous NGOs gained consultative status.

22. When SWAPO took power in Namibia and the African National Congress (ANC) in South Africa in the early 1990s, they developed a cooperative relationship with the international indigenous movement, developing initiatives for the San people ("Bushmen"), who are the indigenous people of Southern Africa.

23. The Reagan administration made any progress on human rights at the UN nearly impossible, and it was tough during those eight years. Yet, indigenous representatives did not give up and kept the working group alive.

24. In 1978, following the 1977 Geneva conference, I became a representative of the Afro-Asian Peoples Solidarity Organization (AAPSO), a nongovernmental organization with ECOSOC consultative status based in Cairo, which was associated with NAM, in order to develop stronger links with NAM.

25. United Nations Document No. E/CN.4/ Sub.2/L.772. September 1, 1981: 3. Only two representatives for indigenous issues, including myself, were present at the sub-commission to lobby for the WGIP.

26. Five is the minimum number of members allowed on UN working groups, as it is required that an equal number of representatives from the five UN regions be members of any UN body. These regions are the Western states, including Western Europe, North America, Australia, and New Zealand; the Eastern European states; Asia; Africa; and Latin America and the Caribbean.

27. United Nations Document No. E/CN.4/ Sub.2/1982/33. August 25, 1982.

28. Menchú went on to receive the Nobel Peace Prize in 1992 and was appointed UN special ambassador for the UN decade for indigenous peoples, 1995–2004.

29. I observed the debate.

30. A formidable Spaniard, Federico Mayor, led the campaign, first as Spain's cultural minister, and after 1987, as director-general of UNESCO. Mayor was a hero of anti-Franco resistance.

31. August 9, 1982, was the date of the first meeting of the WGIP.

32. Read an account of the quincentenary and the work of the international indigenous movement in Roxanne Dunbar-Ortiz, *Blood on the Border: A Memoir of the Contra War* (Cambridge, MA: South End Press, 2005).

33. EZLN is the Spanish acronym for Zapatista National Liberation Army, named in honor of Emiliano Zapata, who led Indian farmers in the Mexican state of Morelos during the 1910–1920 Mexican Revolution that established the contemporary Mexican state.

34. EZLN First Declaration of the Lácandon Jungle, 1993. For EZLN history, statements, and documents, see John Holloway and Eloina Pelaez, eds., *Zapatista! Reinventing Revolution in Mexico* (London: Pluto Press, 1998); John Ross, *The War against Oblivion: The Zapatista Chronicles* (Monroe, ME: Common Courage Press, 2002); Tom Hayden, ed., *The Zapatista Reader* (New York: Thunder's Mouth Press/Nation Books, 2002); and Subcomandante Insurgente Marcos and Ziga Vodovnik, eds., *Ya Basta! Ten Years of the Zapatista Uprising* (London, Oakland, CA: AK Press, 2004). See also Subcomandante Insurgente Marcos, "The Zapatistas and the Other: The Pedestrians of History," Part One, August–September 2006, available at http://www.elkilombo.org/documents/peatonesI.html (accessed May 22, 2009).

35. Pressure on the UN to approve the declaration led to the establishment of the Permanent Forum on Indigenous Issues (PFII) in 2000, the first institution dealing with indigenous peoples at UN headquarters in New York. In 2001, Dr. Rodolfo Stavenhagen was appointed as the special rapporteur on the situation of the human rights and fundamental freedoms of indigenous peoples. The work of the PFII and that of the special rapporteur advanced the process.

7

"Hit Them Harder"

Leadership, Solidarity, and the Puerto Rican Independence Movement

MEG STARR

Several of the largest and most radical mobilizations of the 1970s were called by the Puerto Rican independence movement. "A Day in Solidarity with Puerto Rico" brought twenty thousand people to New York City's Madison Square Garden in October 1974, and the headcount for the "Bicentennial without Colonies" protests in Philadelphia and San Francisco was approximately fifty thousand.[1] In addition to these mass demonstrations, notable independence activities of the decade included the ten-day takeover of Sydenham Hospital in New York (September 1980),[2] the occupation of the Statue of Liberty (October 25, 1977), and bombings by the Armed Forces of National Liberation (Fuerzas Armadas de Liberación Nacional, FALN; 1974–1983) and other clandestine groups. These and other actions consistently drew the media's attention to the Puerto Rican movement in its many and varied forms, as advocates for Puerto Rican independence continued to pressure the United States and the United Nations for a resolution to the island's status.

If we consider the Puerto Rican movement on the mainland U.S. as one wing of a larger, island-based independence movement, then the scale of Puerto Rican radicalism in the 1970s increases exponentially. Thousands of university students confronted the police at the University of Puerto Rico in San Juan in 1976, after years of militant campus demonstrations there and elsewhere on the island protesting the Reserve Officer Training Corps (ROTC), the war in Vietnam, and the conscription of Puerto Ricans into the U.S. military. A united labor movement broke free from U.S. union control, with Puerto Rican strikers supported by a front of six armed, underground organizations. The antimilitarist direct actions on Vieques saw fishermen in creaky wooden boats with slingshots stopping U.S. Navy warships from using the island as a munitions training ground.[3]

Whether or not the Puerto Rican movement on the U.S. mainland can be seen both as part of a national liberation struggle with a land base in the Caribbean and as a revolutionary struggle of an ostensibly "American" minority has long been a topic of debate for the Puerto Rican Left and its allies, as well as for scholars.[4] Puerto Rican activists told me in the 1980s that, during the height of the U.S. war in Southeast Asia, cadre from the National Liberation Front of Vietnam referred enviously to the number of Puerto Ricans living in the United States. If they had had such a numerous "rear guard" within U.S. borders, the Vietnamese said, the war would be over.[5] The United States has maintained a colonial presence in Puerto Rico since 1898. By the 1970s, at least one-third of Puerto Ricans lived in the diaspora, mostly in big cities such as New York, Chicago, and Philadelphia. The large number of Puerto Ricans living in the United States made the 1970s a time of peril and possibility for those who believed in independence.

This chapter focuses on the New York base of the Puerto Rican movement during the tumultuous 1970s. Some of this history might be familiar to those well-versed in Latino radicalism of the era—the Young Lords, the Puerto Rican Socialist Party (PSP), the so-called "new communist movement," and the grassroots campaigns of that time. Woven into the text, however, through both archival sources and oral histories, is a significant strand of history not well represented in current research or memoir: those whose belief in "people's war" led them to create the FALN, the most active of the clandestine militant organizations of the period. In addition, this chapter discusses the various organizations of their supporters, from the National Liberation Movement (Movimiento de Liberación Nacional, MLN) to the white, anti-imperialist New Movement in Solidarity with Puerto Rico, and others. The militant sectors of the independence movement, along with the solidarity activists who supported them, provoked similar debates and proceeded through similar schisms as befell the Black Power movement and the mostly white New Left. In the Puerto Rican example, the high point of this organizing, including both public and clandestine activities, occurred after many had marked the death of Black Power and New Left militancy. It succeeded in reviving a notion of Puerto Rican nationalism, rearticulated through a Marxist framework. This organizing was manifested both in campaigns for community control as well as in international appeals targeted at the United Nations and relying on political unity across the diaspora. Bringing together committed pacifists, guerilla insurgents, and many in between, the Puerto Rican independence movement of the mid- to late 1970s challenged U.S. colonial control and a growing conservative movement on the island. It also marked the potent rise of a militant Latino politics in an America newly conscious of its "multiethnic" status.

As the mass radicalism in the Puerto Rican communities of the 1960s crystallized, new organizational models and strategies for the independence movement emerged. In the 1970s, the independence movement began to recover from the widespread repression of the 1950s. U.S. and Puerto Rican forces put down an island-wide insurrection that began on October 30, 1950, and included the November 1 attack on President Truman in Washington, DC, by two nationalists living in New York City. Four years later, four U.S.-based members of the Nationalist Party attacked the U.S. Congress. The response to these actions included the arrests of thousands of nationalists, causing major fragmentation within Puerto Rico's Left and functionally destroying the Puerto Rican Nationalist Party, which had led these insurrections.[6] The Cuban and Vietnamese revolutions, the black liberation movement, and antidraft and antimilitarist movements on the island, which had raised consciousness throughout the 1960s, served as examples in the 1970s, bringing new energy to Puerto Rican radicals and their allies.[7]

My own first exposure to the Puerto Rican independence movement came in 1981, as the dramas of the 1970s were beginning to give way to a new wave of repression and struggle. The site was the crowded Ukrainian Labor Hall on the Lower East Side of Manhattan in New York City. The working-class and bohemian Puerto Rican community had turned out in record numbers to see and hear for themselves the legendary, recently released political prisoner Lolita Lebrón. She was a young woman when she first became involved with the Nationalist Party in the late 1940s. Now, despite twenty-five years in jail, Lebrón was as militant and defiant as the day she was first arrested in 1954. She described in detail the times that U.S. attorneys had offered her a quick release if only she would sign a paper apologizing for her actions.[8] She had led a small unit of Puerto Rican nationalists—one of the first women of any national liberation struggle to hold such a key position within a military structure—and shot up at the ceiling of the U.S. Congress to protest persecution of the Puerto Rican Nationalist Party and the ongoing colonization of Puerto Rico.[9] "I said, 'I'm not sorry, and I'd do it again!'" she proclaimed. When the crowd yelled, in a united voice, "Lolita, seguro, a los Yanquis dale duro!" ("Lolita, hit the yankees harder!"), the room seemed to shake.[10]

Since the 1898 U.S. military invasion of Puerto Rico, resistance had been a consistent feature of life on the island. After years of direct military rule, by the 1950s an unprecedented level of outrage characterized people's feelings about their colonial condition. Puerto Ricans had been drafted into the U.S. Armed Forces since 1917 and fought in record numbers during World War II, yet they were not able to vote in U.S. presidential or congressional elections. One-third of all the arable farmland was occupied by U.S. military bases. Children of this Spanish-speaking island were forced to attend English-only schools until 1915, and imposed usage of the English language has continued, off and on, to be a source of contention within Puerto Rican society. English is still, in the twenty-first century, required in all federal matters (including federal court) conducted in Puerto Rico.[11] Pedro Albizu Campos, a Harvard-educated lawyer and leader of the Nationalist Party, had attracted a large following by the 1930s, and he became a scourge of U.S. authorities. He was imprisoned multiple times in his tenure as head of the Puerto Rican Nationalist Party: in 1936 after two nationalists killed Colonel Francis Riggs, the police chief appointed to Puerto Rico and who had repressed nationalist protests; after the October 1950 revolt, during which time, many allege, he was subject to radiation poison; and after the 1954 attack on Congress.[12] He died in 1965, not long after being released from prison following his 1954 arrest, but his

image, especially as an uncompromising revolutionary, continued to inspire independence activists in the 1970s and beyond.[13]

Although the Nationalist Party had been almost destroyed in the 1950s, the
1960s were a period of recovery for independence activism.[14] These groups were
joined by the rise of Puerto Rican activism within the United States. Many nationalists in this country supported community struggles as individuals, cautious of
formal organizational affiliation. And most new groups were greatly influenced by
the civil rights and Black Power movements of the era.[15] One such Lower East
Side–based educator, Luis Fuentes, who would go on to become New York City's
first Puerto Rican community school district superintendent, noted that "it was
the Black Movement who did everything first . . . then we all followed."[16] The issues
around which black neighborhoods mobilized—economic and welfare rights,
school conditions and curricular reform, housing issues and tenant rights—
affected the Puerto Rican barrio groups with similar intensity.

Many of the Puerto Rican community leaders of this period were not *independentistas* or radicals, but rather belonged to neighborhood clubs based on social
networks carried over to the United States from various regions of the island.
From these clubs came some of the first initiatives for bilingual education and
other human rights issues. "The struggle integrated as many people as possible;
there was no consciousness of separation," noted Julio Rosado, a journalist and
organizer on the Lower East Side.[17] Rosado was a young independentista who grew
up in the United States and went to college in Puerto Rico. He participated in the
grassroots movements of the time, and years later served in the PSP, went to jail for
refusing to testify before a grand jury investigating clandestine Puerto Rican
groups, and was a founding member of the MLN. Some of the earliest forms of solidarity in the 1970s were organic to the situations in which people found themselves. The New York City coalition "Por Los Niños" (For the Children) brought
together parents—Puerto Rican, black, Asian, and white—who wanted to reform
the school system. Though the Board of Education and the United Federation of
Teachers fought against community control, many white parents and progressive
white teachers who wanted to see improvement in the schools joined the community organizing campaigns. During a series of bitter teacher strikes in 1968 and
1969, they helped to keep community-based schools open. For instance, Lynne
Stewart, who at the time was a school librarian on the Lower East Side and later
became a high-profile criminal attorney specializing in human rights cases, stood
on a toilet to hide when the night security guards came by, so that she could open
the doors of her school the next morning.[18]

Another significant New York–based struggle—for open admissions and the
development of ethnic studies courses and departments within the City University
of New York (CUNY), as well as for an end to the war in Vietnam—brought together
large numbers of white, black, and Puerto Rican activists. In addition to serving as
a training ground for grassroots activists of the 1970s, the CUNY struggle brought
together many key leaders who were to become central to the struggles of the

following decade. At one CUNY campus, only two students—Assata Shakur and Luis Rosado—showed up on time for a planned occupation in 1969. Not ones to get discouraged, the pair went off to a hardware store, where they bought chains to bolt the building shut. By the time they returned, their comrades were there, and the blockade had begun. (Shakur went on to become a leader of the clandestine Black Liberation Army and is now living in exile in Cuba after escaping from a New Jersey prison in 1979; Rosado, still a fugitive in the early twenty-first century, is accused of membership in the FALN.) When the police began to arrest CUNY blockaders at campuses across the city, community members marched out of their neighborhoods and brought food to the protesters. They also placed themselves between the students and the police force.[19]

The late 1960s and early 1970s also saw the development of the Young Lords. Begun in Chicago as a street organization, they soon spread to New York and other major Puerto Rican centers up and down the East Coast with a more revolutionary political agenda. Modeled in some ways on the Black Panther Party, the Young Lords centered their work on a combination of community-based empowerment and national liberation through human rights. As they developed, the Lords gained increasing awareness of developments in Puerto Rico itself, and committed themselves to the cause of Puerto Rican independence.[20]

In 1970, the same year they staged a high-profile takeover of the decrepit Bronx-based Lincoln Hospital, with supportive staff continuing to treat patients, the Young Lords attempted to establish themselves on Puerto Rico as leaders of the independence movement.[21] The island-based organizations responded with outrage and declared that Puerto Rican independence movement organizations must lead campaigns from Puerto Rico.[22] This debacle, in combination with FBI-initiated repression, infiltration, and open harassment led many people to leave the Young Lords. By 1972, a small group of remaining Young Lords declared themselves the Puerto Rican Revolutionary Workers Organization (PRRWO). In 1973, the PRRWO joined with a predominantly white Maoist organization, the Revolutionary Union (RU), and the Black Workers Congress and the Chinese American radical group I Wor Kuen (IWK) in a merger process exploring the possibility of creating a new communist party. After a few years, the PRRWO, the Black Workers, and IWK intensified their criticism of the RU for "trying to submerge people of color groups" in a process "destined to produce a white dominated party."[23] By 1974, the PRRWO had broken off from the other groups.[24] Some influential former Lords remained involved in this formation until the organization's formal disbanding in 1976.

The Young Lords were not the only Puerto Rican group to experience this shift. Another barrio group, El Comité, also transitioned from community group to communist party in the mid-1970s. Developed out of the housing campaigns in the barrios, El Comité emphasized community-building and helped to develop the Latin Women's Collective. The group also called the first conference, in 1971, dedicated to developing shared campaigns for the release of Puerto Rican political prisoners. The conference helped build efforts in support of Carlos Feliciano, a nationalist whom the government put on trial for planting more than forty bombs in New York City as part of the clandestine group Movimiento Independentista Revolucionario Armado (the Armed Revolutionary Independence Movement, MIRA).[25] But as it moved toward building a communist party, Comité leader Esperanza Martell recalls, the group's approach grew more abstract and theoretical, less grounded in barrio realities.[26] By 1981, these weaknesses led to a split within and the ultimate dissolution of the group (which had changed its name to El Comité-MINP, Movimiento Izqueirda Nacional Puertorriqueña, the Puerto Rican National Left Movement), primarily over the issue of whether emphasis on a "federalized" Puerto Rican component of the overall multinational working class was correct and strategic.[27]

The mass unrest within Puerto Rican communities made young Puerto Ricans an appealing population for leftist groups looking to recruit new members. Artist and student activist Elizam Escobar, who later would be arrested and accused of membership in the FALN, described his brief membership in the Progressive Labor Party by saying that the group mixed good intentions with the "naiveté and the typical arrogance of Yankee culture."[28] Community organizer Sandra Trujillo commented, "In general most Left organizations, in chauvinist fashion, sought to incorporate us into their formations, rather than to offer to help us in our own development."[29]

A vibrant organization based in Puerto Rico looked as if it might change this dynamic in the 1970s. The PSP, formed in 1959 as the Movimiento Pro Independencia (MPI—Movement for Independence), had become the largest island-based group of the decade. In 1973, the PSP held its founding conference in New York, with three thousand activists in attendance. Chapters soon sprung up wherever the Puerto Rican diaspora had settled: Chicago, Hartford, and Philadelphia, among other cities. Many young people who were originally mobilized by student activism or by the Young Lords now joined the PSP. The U.S. branch of the PSP attempted to combine support for independence and socialism on the island with work around the human rights demands of the Puerto Rican communities in the United States. One of its main rallying cries was the demand for the release of the five Nationalist Party prisoners: Oscar Collazo (the surviving member of the pair who attacked Truman), Lolita Lebrón, Rafael Cancel Miranda, Irving Flores, and Andrés Figueroa Cordero. Though the PSP called for organized solidarity from the white Left, it was clear that they would only accept this support on their own terms. They set up a Committee for Puerto Rican Decolonization, which included non–Puerto Rican activists who wanted to organize in direct support.[30] The committee put out a newsletter called *Puerto Rico Libre!*, which was targeted at potential white "North American" allies. It was an auspicious time to put out a call for solidarity. As the war in Southeast Asia wound down, activists who had been supporting the Vietnamese National Liberation Front focused greater attention on other liberation movements.[31]

Dana Biberman, for example, was a veteran of the Columbia Students for a Democratic Society (SDS) and the 1968 student strike there whose passion for social change had not diminished since graduation. She was involved with the Vietnam Moratorium and later helped organize antiwar soldiers at Fort Dix through the National Lawyers Guild. She first learned about Puerto Rico from Young Lord activist Mickey Melendez, who had much contact with the white Left in the early 1970s in part due to his personal relationship with Jennifer Dohrn, a radical organizer and the younger sister of Weather Underground leader Bernardine Dohrn. Melendez recruited Biberman and several other white activists of her generation to join the PSP's Committee for Puerto Rican Decolonization in 1973.[32]

The PSP asked Biberman to join the staff to organize the 1974 Madison Square Garden rally. "At first I was not comfortable with one organization proclaiming itself the leadership of the movement," Biberman noted; "however, the majority of the independence organizations eventually joined together to organize for the Garden." Called "A Day in Solidarity with Puerto Rico," the rally at Madison Square Garden was impressive. More than twenty thousand people filled the complex. While the majority attending were Puerto Rican, radicals from many movements participated as well. Afterward, the Committee for Puerto Rican Decolonization transformed into the Puerto Rican Solidarity Committee (PRSC), and chapters spread across the country. By 1976, *Puerto Rico Libre!* reported that there were nineteen active chapters of the PRSC. Their masthead listed an advisory board that included significant leaders of all ethnicities, including Yuri Kochiyama of the Japanese and New Afrikan Left, Clyde Bellecourt of the American Indian Movement, Ella Baker of the civil rights movement, and radical white nonviolent activist Dave Dellinger.[33]

Puerto Rico Libre! contained vivid and detailed stories about Puerto Rican conditions—on the island and in the United States. One issue reported that the Puerto Rican commonwealth government was "shipping" fifty thousand migrant farm laborers to the East Coast of the United States to work for two and a half cents an hour while living in old army barracks.[34] The PRSC arranged speaking tours for island activists working against such obvious abuses. It worked on campaigns against the sterilization of Puerto Rican women, a widespread practice among U.S.-trained doctors on the island, and solicited support from the burgeoning feminist movement. The PRSC supported the efforts to free the five nationalists and on behalf of the Vieques fishermen fighting against the U.S. Navy.[35] "Our best work was when we were really connecting people to the conditions of colonialism in Puerto Rico," Biberman said, and the PRSC newsletter was a vivid way in which such connections were made.[36]

After the Garden event, the New York–based leadership of the PSP invited Biberman and other solidarity staff members on a special delegation. Up in the hills of Puerto Rico, the visitors witnessed thousands of activists in Lares—site of a famous 1868 rebellion against Spanish colonial rule—rallying for independence.

"It was incredible," Biberman remembers. "People from all over the island came together to celebrate." The festive nature of their trip was marred, however, by the January 11, 1975, bombing by an unidentified reactionary group in the town of Mayagüez, at a restaurant known for hosting independence movement gatherings; many independence activists charged that the bombing was organized by right-wing Cubans with CIA connections. It resulted in the deaths of two independen-tistas and the maiming of six others, including one six-year-old girl. Two and a half months later, the eldest son of PSP Secretary General Juan Mari Brás was "mysteri-ously assassinated."[37] Despite the excitement of the growing independence efforts, it was, in Biberman's words, "a very scary time."[38]

Shortly after this trip, a coalition of Puerto Rican groups, including the PSP and El Comité, asked Biberman to chair a new Committee to Free the Five, a cam-paign for the release of the imprisoned nationalists. As this was a coalition of independence organizations, it was an honor for a "North American" (white per-son) to serve as the chair. Biberman was seen as a "neutral" solidarity activist with a history of good practice, important at a moment when the Puerto Rican groups were experiencing an increasingly volatile partisanship. But the divisions proved too severe, and Biberman resigned the post after a "disastrous few months."

Turning Points

Many different radical movements in the United States experienced significant splits and sectarianism during the second half of the decade. While blame is often attributed to a variety of issues specific to each group's own politics, one must assume that there were common trends at work as well. The new-communist his-torian Max Elbaum admits that "in hindsight it is clear that the obstacles to the consolidation of a mass revolutionary current were much greater—and the favor-able factors much weaker—than virtually the entire Left believed."[39] The PSP itself, and the dedicated coalitions of Puerto Rican organizations working to free the five nationalists, had greater numbers and momentum than many other sectors of the United States Left. Yet they experienced bitter splits and dealt with constant pres-sure from the FBI and other police forces, as well as from unknown forces. From June 1976 to November 1977, nine activists in Chicago and New York were jailed for refusing to cooperate with grand juries investigating the FALN. Several more would be jailed for the same reason during the next five years, and hundreds of other activists and community residents were questioned in this period. On the island, the offices of the PSP newspaper, *Claridad*, were bombed, and two young independence activists were set up and murdered by police agents on the moun-tain Cerro Maravilla in 1978.[40] On November 11, 1979, LSP activist Angel Rodríguez Cristóbal was found hanged in a Tallahassee prison cell. He was serving a six-month sentence for a nonviolent civil disobedience action in which he partici-pated with twenty others in Vieques. As anthropologist Katherine McCaffrey writes of the incident, "Prison officials declared the death a suicide, but an independent autopsy the family had performed concluded that he was beaten to death. Photos of the cadaver showed that the face was heavily bruised, inconsistent with charges of suicide by strangulation." A month later, several clandestine groups collaborated to attack a busload of Navy personnel in Sabana Seca, killing two sailors and wounding ten others in an act of retaliation.[41]

Despite a climate of suppression—felt in the United States through grand juries and in the island through the rise to power of a new conservative party, the Partido Nuevo Progresista (New Progressive Party, PNP), and violent attacks on the independence movement—the PSP moved into 1976 with its campaign to organize a massive protest against the nation's July 4 bicentennial celebrations.[42] The anti–July 4 demonstration, to be based in Philadelphia alongside the official celebrations, brought together tens of thousands of activists from many parts of the Left in the call for a Bicentennial Without Colonies. In a challenge to the PSP's leadership, the Revolutionary Union called its own rally in Philadelphia (not focused on colonialism or national liberation), which brought out another several thousand participants. While many attendees thought that the PSP-initiated rally was a tremendous success, debates were brewing within the organization. The event sapped the energy and finances of the PSP, which ended up not receiving the kind of significant support from the white Left that it had expected. More than that, however, many in the rank and file of the PSP chapters in the United States were disturbed and confused by the organization's decision—contrary to its previous anti-electoral politics and rhetoric—to run a candidate in the 1976 election for governor of Puerto Rico. Focusing on the election campaign removed PSP organizers from the human rights campaigns of Puerto Rican barrios in the United States. The party's poor showing at the polls further demoralized many PSP partisans.[43]

In addition to these debates within the PSP, Puerto Rican independence activists and supporters found themselves in contentious discussions over strategy and tactics. The use of violence by independentistas, especially in the United States, was the most controversial issue within the movement, sparked by the rise of clandestine guerilla actions in the mid-1970s. The FALN emerged with a series of unclaimed bombings in 1973. In 1974, the group initiated its campaign of "armed propaganda" with public communiqués providing the political context to their work. The night before the Madison Square Garden rally, the FALN announced its presence in the United States with the bombing of four banks in Midtown Manhattan, each with holdings in Puerto Rico, and a proclamation: "We are not pure militarists. Therefore we do not oppose those parties or people who believe in mass organization. However, to be truly revolutionary, a party must educate and organize the masses for the seizure of power by way of an organized and disciplined vehicle." The October 26, 1974, statement ended with a message of support for the Garden event, suggesting that it would be "a significant step in the formation of an anti-imperialist front in the United States, which will support the fight for the national liberation of Puerto Rico, and educate the American people to the murderous and genocidal policies of the Yanki capitalists throughout the world."[44]

Largely influenced by the Cuban Revolution, armed actions against colonialism had been taking place in Puerto Rico since the early 1960s. By the late 1970s, four underground organizations joined forces to carry out armed struggle.[45] These organizations carried out a consistent campaign of armed assaults, in both Puerto Rico and the United States, to support workers' strikes, to attack military targets, and to avenge violence against the independence movement. This turn to violent underground actions was highly controversial within the independence movement, especially regarding the FALN, the group whose actions were almost entirely on U.S. soil, rather than, as with the other groups, in Puerto Rico. Many activists rejected violent action as strategically misguided and politically dangerous. The FALN, meanwhile, saw itself as akin to the Algerian National Liberation Front (FLN) because it operated inside the colonial center. To those in the aboveground movements who supported them, these freedom fighters were described as working toward initiating an armed "people's war" in Puerto Rico. FALN leader William Guillermo Morales said in 1991 that the group had hoped its bombings would win over other people of color and disaffected whites as allies against the U.S. government.[46] Borrowing the phrase and the strategy successfully used by both the Vietnamese and Chinese communist armies, the Puerto Rican clandestine movement emphasized popular education and propaganda through its targets and statements.[47] Even though violence continued to be hotly debated, the statements emerging from the Puerto Rican underground in the 1970s (and 1980s) articulated a vision of people's war that included both armed struggle and nonviolent mass action components.

The debates over the FALN became more personal and more fraught after the group claimed its first, and only intentional, casualties in one of its first attacks. The lunchtime bombing of the Fraunces Tavern's executive dining room on January 24, 1975, killed four people. The communiqué accompanying the attack said it was meant as retaliation for the bombing in Mayagüez, operating under the incorrect assumption that only ruling-class diners would be found at the famous Wall Street establishment. Most sectors of the independence movement condemned the action. But a visible and vocal element of the movement supported it. In a statement signed by several top leaders of the Liga Socialista Puertorriqueña (Puerto Rican Socialist League, LSP), including Puerto Rican national poet and LSP Secretary General Juan Antonio Corretjer, the independentistas stated that "the action inspires greater respect for Puerto Ricans living in the U.S. In no way does it hurt them. The hatred the Yankees have for Puerto Ricans could not be greater, nor the discrimination. They hate us from before we arrive in this world; from before the time we leave the womb of a Puerto Rican woman we are hated."[48]

The FALN was responsible for another death, when a bomb it placed in the Mobil Oil building in Midtown Manhattan in August 1977 killed an executive. With one hundred thousand people evacuated from busy Midtown offices, headlines screamed that Puerto Rican terrorists were lurking everywhere.[49] The group continued into the early 1980s, ultimately claiming responsibility for more than 100 bombings and also participating in other actions, such as the simultaneous armed takeover of Carter and Bush campaign offices in Chicago and New York City in March 1980 during the presidential election campaigns.[50] After the Fraunces Tavern bombing, the PSP withdrew its initial support for the FALN.[51] Some from the Puerto Rican and white Left suggested that the FALN was an FBI-led disruption; others believed they were an "ultra-Left" development that was detrimental to the overall movement. For FALN supporters, people's war was seen as the only means of achieving real change in the battle against the U.S. empire. They believed that such a war must be led by a political-military front with a developed clandestine capacity.[52] The basic theory of people's war posits that armed propaganda actions should be used to help break a fear of the state, especially in a time of repression. In addition, this theory holds that those with armed training should work to protect the mass movement. For the sector that followed this view, the FALN was a logical and necessary development: the rear-guard of the one internal U.S. colony that also had a classic "external" colony in the Caribbean.[53] (It is worth noting that the terms of this debate—accusations of FBI-led disruptions or "ultra-Left adventurists," refuted by those who upheld people's war—were, by this time, familiar within much of the Left after years of debates around organizations such as the Weather Underground, the Black Liberation Army, the George Jackson Brigade, the Symbionese Liberation Army, and the New World Liberation Front, among others. Yet with the FALN, the debate took on an added urgency due to the significantly greater number of actions the group carried out relative to other clandestine forces of the time.)

Within the PSP, some young activists were disappointed about the debates and vacillation over support for the newly emerged armed clandestine movement. Several young Latino activists, some of them members of PSP chapters, especially in Chicago and New York, were called to testify before grand juries investigating the FALN. Most of those subpoenaed refused to cooperate with the grand jury, in the spirit of non-collaboration laid out by Pedro Albizu Campos, Juan Antonio Corretjer, and the Nationalist Party of the 1930s and 1940s.[54] A number of these grand-jury resisters ended up serving time in jail, and the debate around non-collaboration and support for the armed movement led to the formation of the MLN (National Liberation Movement), a new, U.S.-based Puerto Rican group.[55]

The MLN began in 1977 as an organization with both Puerto Rican and Mexican members. The Mexican members were from Colorado and the U.S. Southwest and called for the "socialist reunification" of Mexico, which would merge the current nation-state with the northern lands incorporated into the United States after the Mexican-American war of 1845–1848 (Texas, California, Nevada, Utah, and parts of Colorado, Arizona, New Mexico, and Wyoming). The MLN Puerto Rican members were largely based in New York and Chicago. In addition to publishing theoretical and practical journals, they worked to defend both the grand-jury resisters—many of whom were MLN members—and, in the late 1970s and afterward, the captured FALN members. The connections between the imprisoned combatants and the MLN community leaders were more than simply political—political prisoner Oscar López Rivera, whom the government described as a leader of the FALN, is the older brother of Puerto Rican Cultural Center Executive Director José E. López, an MLN founder and Chicago community activist who went to jail in 1977 for refusing to testify before a grand jury. MLN organizers in Chicago testified to the UN on several occasions and played a leading role in organizing to free the five nationalists, in addition to running the Rafael Cancel Miranda High School (now the Pedro Albizu Campos High School, an award-winning charter school in Humboldt Park). By the 1980s, the Mexican and Puerto Rican sections of the MLN decided to go their separate ways, in order to focus upon their own national constituents.[56]

During the second half of the 1970s, human rights struggles regarding the plight of Puerto Ricans were increasingly linked to the overall question of independence and colonialism. The PRSC had provided the initial groundwork for these struggles, and reformist campaigns now seemed possible (the major fragmentation on the Left notwithstanding). Journalists such as Juan Gonzáles, Pablo Guzman, and Geraldo Rivera, all of whom got their start with the Young Lords, helped spotlight key issues of this period, most notably the mass sterilization of Puerto Rican women. In a policy referred to as *l'operación* (the operation), women were encouraged to have a procedure that would leave them sterile, often without being well informed about what the procedure entailed or that it was irreversible. By 1976, a report commissioned by the governor of Puerto Rico estimated that 35 percent of all Puerto Rican women on the island had undergone *l'operación*. In 1977, the New York City Council was pressured to respond, and it approved comprehensive guidelines to protect women from sterilization abuse.[57]

Another issue that gained broad attention during the late 1970s was the island of Vieques. The U.S. Navy had appropriated two-thirds of the small island off the coast of Puerto Rico for target practice. Vieques was not the only part of the Puerto Rican archipelago that the U.S. military was using for target practice. Protests had, in fact, succeeded in removing the U.S. Navy from Culebra, another island that is part of Puerto Rico, by 1975. But this victory only enhanced the navy's reliance on Vieques. Already by the 1960s, many villagers had been relocated to the barren center of the island with minimal remuneration for their homes. Periodic bombing of the western and eastern thirds of Vieques devastated a once-thriving fishing industry. Cancer rates on Vieques skyrocketed, as depleted uranium was dropped from warplanes high above. Throughout the late 1970s, the Vieques fishermen and their supporters organized blockades of the various navy maneuvers. Chaining their tiny boats together to lengthen the waterway blockades, they used slingshots against navy battleships, like David confronting Goliath on the high seas. In the United States, the issue fostered broad coalitions of Puerto Rican organizations and (mostly white) pacifist groups, among others. In Washington, DC, Jean Zwickel—a radical pacifist who had befriended Albizu Campos and been supporting the independence movement since the early

1950s—led an ad-hoc church-based support committee that helped raise awareness about and money for the people of Vieques.[58]

On October 25, 1977—a date chosen to mark the anniversary of the 1950 uprising in Puerto Rico—independence activists staged a bold action in New York that helped bridge the divide between mainstream work and clandestine struggles and included both Puerto Ricans and white solidarity activists. A small group of Puerto Ricans and their supporters occupied the Statue of Liberty and hung a giant Puerto Rican flag across her face: Lady Liberty blinded by Puerto Rico's ongoing colonization. All the major media outlets on the island and throughout the United States carried the image and covered the story. The main demand of the action was to free the five nationalists. Dr. Barbara Zeller, a graduate of Columbia University's medical school and a longtime anti-imperialist activist, was part of the takeover. "We were not recruited for the action by an organization but by personal connections," Zeller recalled. "None of the white leftists knew what the action was going to be [in advance]. It was based on trust, and on following leadership." On the day of the takeover, several "official-looking" people asked the tourists to leave the tower, which they did obediently. The action went smoothly and without significant repression; in Zeller's words, "It felt great!" Panama Alba, a former Young Lord who had gone on to be involved in the campaign to free the five nationalists in New York, was the main public spokesperson for the action.[59]

Less than a year later—on July 12, 1978—FALN leader William Guillermo Morales was arrested after a bomb he was working on exploded in his hands, severing most of his fingers. Morales had been a leader of the 1969 CUNY student strike. After four years and dozens of FALN bombings, police had their first high-profile arrest of an alleged underground leader. In a desperate search for the identities and whereabouts of other possible FALN members, police beat Morales's wife, Dylcia Pagán. Guillermo's severed fingers were taken by the FBI for fingerprinting, as Morales was moved to a prison hospital under heavily armed guard. After several grand juries attempting to locate FALN members, and despite the arrests of Alba and three others around this time on suspicion of FALN involvement (a charge later disproven in court), the FBI had made its first FALN arrest.[60]

In court, Morales proclaimed that he was a prisoner of war in his people's decades-long fight to be free. He invoked the Puerto Rican Nationalist Party's position of *retraimiento*, non-collaboration, in denying the legitimacy of the U.S. courts to prosecute a colonial subject, that is, a Puerto Rican radical. The atmosphere of confrontation and repression intensified in response to his bold move. Despite this climate of hostility, a year of intensive campaigning succeeded in moving Morales to a regular hospital for treatment of the injuries he sustained from the blast. With stumps that had barely healed, and bed sheets tied together to form a rope, Morales climbed out of the hospital window on May 21, 1979, and escaped—first to Mexico, then to Cuba, where he remains in exile.[61] Juan Antonio Corretjer, writing from San Juan for the PSP-sponsored newspaper,

Claridad, jubilantly called Morales "the handless hero who has slapped the face of God."[62] The FALN claimed responsibility for helping coordinate the escape.[63]

The Legacy

Despite these dramatic events—the antisterilization and pro-Vieques campaigns, the Statue of Liberty takeover and the Morales escape—the end of the 1970s saw the decline of many of the independence organizations whose numbers had swelled earlier in the decade. Some of the demands of the time, however, had successfully been met, with at least minor victories won. Bilingualism had come "out of the closet" and was, by 1979, a significant part of the education systems of most major cities. Puerto Rican Studies courses or departments were available at many colleges, and many cities began celebrating a Puerto Rico Day Parade.

The decade closed with one of the central demands of the movement having been met. On October 6, 1977, Andres Figueroa Cordero, one of the five jailed nationalists, who had become seriously ill, was released from prison. His release was celebrated across Puerto Rican civil society, although it was a bittersweet victory, as he died of cancer eighteen months later. Finally, after years of work on all political fronts, involving an outpouring of support from the villages of Puerto Rico to the major cities of the United States, President Jimmy Carter granted clemency to the remaining Nationalist Party political prisoners—Lolita Lebrón, Rafael Cancel Miranda, Irvin Flores, and Oscar Collazo—on September 10, 1979. They greeted thousands of supporters in Chicago and New York upon their release and returned to Puerto Rico in triumph to crowds of ecstatic supporters, ready to continue their uncompromising struggle for the freedom of their land.[64] They returned to the United States for a bigger speaking tour months later and remained active proponents of Puerto Rican independence.

The sense of victory at winning the freedom of the nationalists was, for some, short-lived. On April 4, 1980, police arrested eleven suspected FALN members in Evanston, Illinois. Ten of the eleven adopted the *retraimiento* position that Morales had used upon his arrest; they refused to recognize the court system, deeming it a colonial entity unfit to try captured revolutionaries. As a result, they received lengthy sentences, stretching from thirty to one hundred years. Six more people were arrested in 1981 and 1983 on suspicion of being part of the FALN. Although some of those arrested later mounted a more traditional legal defense than the activists arrested in 1980 had, all of them denounced U.S. colonialism in open court. The four who maintained their prisoner-of-war status received lengthy sentences.[65] The charges in these cases, however, were not connected to specific acts of violence. Rather, these women and men were charged with seditious conspiracy—organizing to overthrow the U.S. government by force. Clandestine actions continued to occur in the United States, most notably the Macheteros' 1985 robbery of $7.5 million from Wells Fargo in Hartford, Connecticut. The FBI raided Puerto Rico to capture those it thought responsible, leading to the prosecution of sixteen people in the late 1980s and early 1990s. In response to these arrests, organizers launched a new effort to free another batch of Puerto Rican revolutionaries held in U.S. prisons—a campaign that succeeded in President Bill Clinton's granting clemency to eleven of them (and reduced sentences for another five) in September 1999, twenty years to the day after the four nationalists were released.[66]

Though the fight for a free Puerto Rico continues in the twenty-first century, the transformative and tumultuous events and organizations of the 1970s indelibly shaped contemporary efforts. Pedro Albizu Campos declared that Puerto Rican nationalism comprised courage and sacrifice, and the efforts of the 1970s applied such temerity as part of a global anticolonial upsurge. In a 1978 speech celebrating Grito de Lares, a Puerto Rican national holiday marking the 1868 revolt in Lares against Spanish rule, Juan Antonio Corretjer discussed these revolutionary efforts as proof that Puerto Rican independence was lived as much as won. "I have already seen it," he said, repeating the answer he would give to any who asked if Puerto Rico would be free in his lifetime. "Whoever fights with all [they] have for the independence of Puerto Rico lives independence, is free, is sovereign, is independent, as all our people will be on the day of victory."[67] The strategic and tactical differences gripping the Puerto Rican independence movement of the 1970s were indeed severe, reflecting alternate ideas of leadership and solidarity. Yet this notion of independence as both a demand and an ongoing practice characterized a wide variety of campaigns and initiatives throughout the decade. It was this commitment to both *achieving* and *living* independence that made the Puerto Rican movement one of the most active and audacious sectors of the Left in the 1970s.

NOTES

1. José E. Velázquez, "Coming Full Circle: The Puerto Rican Socialist Party, U.S. Branch," in *The Puerto Rican Movement: Voices from the Diaspora*, ed. Andrés Torres and José E. Velázquez (Philadelphia: Temple University Press, 1998), 56.

2. Joanne R. Reitano, *The Restless City* (New York: Routledge, 2006), 194.

3. César J. Ayala and Rafael Bernabe, *Puerto Rico in the American Century: A History Since 1898* (Chapel Hill: University of North Carolina Press, 2007); Katherine T. McCaffrey, *Military Power and Popular Protest: The U.S. Navy in Vieques, Puerto Rico* (New Brunswick, NJ: Rutgers University Press, 2002).

4. See, for instance, Andrés Torres, "Introduction: Political Radicalism in the Diaspora—The Puerto Rican Experience," in *The Puerto Rican Movement*, ed. Torres and Velázquez, 1–22.

5. The March 1 Bloc's 1976 critique of the Puerto Rico Solidarity Committee makes a similar argument. See March 1 Bloc, *Arguments and Proposals for the PRSC Conference*, pamphlet, in author's files (n.p., c. 1977), 3. The March 1 Bloc, by 1977, became the Movimiento de Liberación Nacional (MLN).

6. Ivonne Acosta-Lespier, "The Smith Act Goes to San Juan: La Mordaza, 1948–1957," in *Puerto Rico Under Colonial Rule: Political Persecution and the Quest for Human Rights*,

ed. Ramón Bosque-Pérez and José Javier Colón Morera (Albany: State University of New York Press, 2006), 59–66.

7. Esperanza Martell, Rosemari Mealy, and Julio Rosado, among others, have elucidated over the years of our friendship the central role these phenomena played in shaping their activism in the 1970s.

8. While she remains proud of her actions in 1954, in more recent years Lebrón has committed to nonviolence.

9. Although Lebrón fired at the ceiling, at least some of her comrades fired down at the Congress members. Five were wounded in the attack; none was killed. See Clayton Knowles, "Five Congressmen Shot in House by 3 Puerto Rican Nationalists," *New York Times*, March 2, 1954, 1.

10. Despite her being a potent symbol of Puerto Rican independence, there is little biographical writing about Lebrón, at least in English. Fragments of it appear in Manuel Roig-Franzia, "When Terror Wore Lipstick," *Washington Post Magazine*, February 22, 2004.

11. English is not the only language heard in Puerto Rico that signifies colonialism. Spanish as an official language is obviously a direct result of Spanish colonial rule. Yet Puerto Rican nationalists and independence activists have traditionally upheld Spanish as a symbol of national pride against English as a sign of foreign dominance.

12. Michael González-Cruz, "The U.S. Invasion of Puerto Rico: Occupation and Resistance to the Colonial State," *Latin American Perspectives* 25:5 (1998): 7–26; Michael Staudenmaier, "The Puerto Rican Independence Movement, 1898–Present," in *International Encyclopedia of Revolution and Protest*, ed. Immanuel Ness (New York: Blackwell Publishing, 2009), 2766–2774. On Albizu Campos, see Federico Ribes Tovar, *Albizu Campos, Puerto Rican Revolutionary* (New York: Plus Ultra, 1971). A valuable study of Puerto Rican society and activism under U.S. colonialism can be found in Ayala and Bernabe, *Puerto Rico in the American Century*.

13. For a recent analysis of Albizu's symbolic power, see Ana Y. Ramos-Zayas, *National Performances: The Politics of Class, Race, and Space in Puerto Rican Chicago* (Chicago: University of Chicago Press, 2003), 168–205.

14. On the island, new groups formed to fight U.S. militarism, to work for the release of nationalist fighters imprisoned since the 1950 uprising, and to join longstanding demands for independence with emergent struggles for socialism.

15. Andrés Torres, "Political Radicalism in the Diaspora—The Puerto Rican Experience," in *The Puerto Rican Movement*, ed. Torres and Velázquez, 7–8.

16. James Jennings and Francisco Chapman, "Puerto Ricans and the Community Control Movement: An Interview with Luis Fuentes," in *The Puerto Rican Movement*, ed. Torres and Velázquez, 293.

17. Julio Rosado, interview with author, May 17, 2008.

18. Lynne Stewart, interview with author, April 11, 2008.

19. Rosado, interview.

20. See the Young Lords newspaper, *Palante*, "A La Izquierda: The Puerto Rican Movement" collection, Centro de Estudios Puertorriqueños, Hunter College. See also Miguel "Mickey" Melendez, *We Took the Streets: Fighting for Latino Rights with the Young Lords* (New York: St. Martin's Press, 2003).

21. Pablo Guzman, "*La Vida Pura*: A Lord of the Barrio," in *The Puerto Rican Movement*, ed. Torres and Velázquez, 165–167.

22. Iris Morales, "°Palante, Siempre Palante! The Young Lords," in *The Puerto Rican Movement*, ed. Torres and Velázquez, 221–222.

23. Max Elbaum, *Revolution in the Air: Sixties Radicals Turn to Lenin, Mao, and Che* (New York: Verso, 2002), 187.

24. For one take on the mergers and splits that took place within the PRRWO, see "The Degeneration of the PRRWO: From Revolutionary Organization to Neo-Trotskyite Sect," written by "former PRRWO cadres," available at http://www.mltranslations.org/US/degenprrwo.htm (accessed July 16, 2009).

25. The Committee to Defend Carlos Feliciano, *Carlos Feliciano: History and Repression* (New York: Committee to Defend Carlos Feliciano, 1972). After five years and multiple trials, Feliciano was acquitted of most charges and released from jail in 1975. The name of the group Feliciano was accused of belonging to, MIRA, was fitting to its purpose: in Spanish "mira" means "look," and the bombs were meant to focus attention on the colonialism of Puerto Rico.

26. Esperanza Martell, "'In the Belly of the Beast': Beyond Survival," in *The Puerto Rican Movement*, ed. Torres and Velázquez, 183–186.

27. El Comité-MINP, *Revolutionary Left Movement: A Summation of the Development and Split of MINP-El Comité* (New York: RLM, 1982), 48–49.

28. Carlos Gil, "Artist, Writer, and Political Prisoner: An Interview with Elizam Escobar," in *The Puerto Rican Movement*, ed. Torres and Velázquez, 235.

29. José E. Velázquez, "Another West Side Story: An Interview with Members of El Comité-MINP," in *The Puerto Rican Movement*, ed. Torres and Velázquez, 94.

30. José E. Velázquez, "Coming Full Circle: The Puerto Rican Socialist Party, U.S. Branch," in *The Puerto Rican Movement*, ed. Torres and Velázquez, 48–54.

31. A careful review of leadership, solidarity, and national liberation within the United States remains an urgent task, and the Puerto Rican example is critical. Organizations in the (post–) New Left disagreed on the primacy and shape of solidarity and national liberation. These debates and differences played out in work around Puerto Rico and whether revolution would be led by a vanguard, multinational, political party of workers or by the movements of black, Puerto Rican, Chicano, and Native peoples, with whites acting as allies working to destroy the "oppressor nation" from within. Two dramatic events changed the landscape for the New Left of the early 1970s. The end of the draft meant an end to a tremendous radicalizing force in young people's lives. And the end of U.S. military involvement in Vietnam meant that Vietnam's communist leaders, so often looked to as the center of the global revolution, were no longer viewed as at "center stage." Instead of working with a National Liberation Front formed on the periphery of empire in Southeast Asia, young white activists found themselves working with revolutionaries more or less their own age, who were forming new organizations of national liberation inside the United States. These new groups could never be at the same stage of ideological development as the Vietnamese formations, but their efforts at maintaining a revolutionary space within the United States were far from the common portrayals of them as crazy, chaotic actions.

32. Dana Biberman, interview with author, May 11, 2008.

33. *Puerto Rico Libre!*, 8:11 (November 1976), "A La Izquierda: The Puerto Rican Movement" collection, Centro de Estudios Puertorriqueños, Hunter College. For more on Kochiyama as an activist in both Asian American and New Afrikan communities, see Diane C. Fujino, *The Heartbeat of Struggle: The Revolutionary Life of Yuri Kochiyama* (Minneapolis: University of Minnesota Press, 2005).

34. *Puerto Rico Libre!* 1:1 (August 1973), "A La Izquierda: The Puerto Rican Movement" collection, Centro de Estudios Puertorriqueños, Hunter College; See also People's Press Puerto Rico Project, *Puerto Rico: The Flame of Resistance* (San Francisco: People's Press, 1977), 165–166.

35. See *Puerto Rico Libre!*, in author's files; an incomplete collection of the newsletter and other materials of the PRSC can be found in A La Izquierda: The Puerto Rican Movement, 1923–2002, reels 12–13, Centro de Estudios Puertorriqueño, Hunter College.

36. Biberman, interview with author, May 11, 2008.

37. Ramón Bosque-Pérez, "Political Persecution against Puerto Rican Anti-Colonial Activists in the Twentieth Century," in *Puerto Rico Under Colonial Rule*, ed. Bosque-Pérez and Colón Morera, 13–48. In 2009, Puerto Rico's Commission for Truth and Justice released declassified FBI documents showing that the bureau knew in 1975 of plots to assassinate Mari Brás or members of his family but failed to inform him. See, for instance, "FBI Skirts Discussing Cover-Up of Assassination Plot," http://www.verdadyjusticia.net/index.php?option=com_content&view=article&id=118&Itemid=154 (accessed December 12, 2009); and Xavira Neggers Crescioni, "Papers: FBI Failed to Act on Plot to Kill Mari Brás," *Puerto Rico Daily Sun*, December 3, 2009, available at http://www.prdailysun.com/news/Papers-FBI-failed-to-act-on-plot-to-kill-Mari-Brs (accessed December 12, 2009).

38. Biberman, interview with author, June 25, 2009.

39. Elbaum, *Revolution in the Air*, 320.

40. See flyer, "Grand Jury Chronology" (ca. November 1977), in author's files. See also John Brown Anti-Klan Committee, May 19th Communist Organization, Movimiento de Liberación National, New Movement in Solidarity with the Puerto Rican and Mexican Revolutions, and Prairie Fire Organizing Committee, *Repression/Resistance* (Chicago: Rebeldia Publications, ca. 1985), in author's files; Manuel Suarez, *Requiem on Cerro Maravilla: The Police Murders in Puerto Rico and the U.S. Government Cover-Up* (Washington, DC: WaterFront Press, 1987).

41. McCaffrey, *Military Power and Popular Protest*, 90.

42. The official organizing for the bicentennial was itself fraught with tensions and controversy, ultimately leading the celebration to be focused locally rather than nationally. See Christopher Capozzola, "'It Makes You Want to Believe in the Country': Celebrating the Bicentennial in an Age of Limits," in *America in the 70s*, ed. Beth Bailey and David Farber (Lawrence: University Press of Kansas, 2004), 29–49. For more on the PNP's formation and rise, as well as the violence against independence movement activists in that time period, see Ayala and Bernabe, *Puerto Rico in the American Century*, 223–290.

43. People's Press Puerto Rico Project, *Puerto Rico*; Alfredo Lopez, *The Puerto Rican Papers* (New York: Monthly Review Press, 1973); Velázquez, "Coming Full Circle," in *The Puerto Rican Movement*, ed. Torres and Velázquez, 48–68.

44. This communiqué, along with several others by the FALN and island-based armed-struggle groups, was in a booklet printed by several organizations working in solidarity with Puerto Rican independence. See Committee in Solidarity with Puerto Rican Independence, May 19th Communist Organization, October 30th Committee, Prairie Fire Organizing Committee, and the Sojourner Truth Organization, eds., *Toward People's War for Independence and Socialism in Puerto Rico: In Defense of Armed Struggle. Documents and Communiqués from the Revolutionary Public Independence Movement and the Armed Clandestine Movement* (New York: Interim Committee, 1979), 58. Several communiqués and documents related to the FALN are also available at http://www.latinamericanstudies.org/faln.htm (accessed July 17, 2009).

45. The organizations were the FALN, the Fuerzas Armadas de Resistencia Popular (FARP; Armed Forces of Popular Resistance), the Organización de Voluntarios Para la Revolución Puertorriqueña (OVRP; Volunteers Organization for the Puerto Rican Revolution), the Partido Revolucionario de Los Trabajadores Puertorriqueños—Ejercito Popular Boricua (PRTP-EPB; Revolutionary Party of Puerto Rican Workers—Boricua Popular Army,

also known as the Macheteros or Machete Wielders, a reference to the island's sugar-cane workers). The MLN released its collaborative communiqué, along with a brief introductory essay, as a pamphlet in 1979 under the title *First Joint Message From the Clandestine Organizations to the People*. Pamphlet in author's files.

46. William Guillermo Morales, interview with author and Matt Meyer, Havana, Cuba, July 24, 1991.

47. Vo Nguyen Giap, *How We Won the War* (New York: Recon Publishers, 1976).

48. La Liga Socialista Puertorriqueña, "Act of War of the FALN in New York," in *Towards People's War for Independence and Socialism in Puerto Rico*, 24.

49. Mary Breasted, "100,000 Leave New York Offices as Bomb Threats Disrupt City; Blasts Kill One, Hurt Seven," *New York Times*, August 4, 1977, 39; "Clinton Pardons Terror," *New York Post*, August 13, 1999, available at http://www.latinamericanstudies.org/puertorico/sep4.htm (accessed July 16, 2009); Murray Weiss and Deborah Orin, "FALN Crew No Innocents: Report," *New York Post*, August 31, 1999, available at http://www.latinamericanstudies.org/puertorico/sep2.htm (accessed July 16, 2009).

50. FALN members tied up campaign workers and painted slogans on the walls of both offices. See "Puerto Ricans Strike Two Cities," *TIME*, March 24, 1980, available at http://www.time.com/time/magazine/article/0,9171,921860,00.html (accessed November 11, 2009).

51. Daniel James, "Puerto Rican Terrorists also Threaten Reagan Assassination," *Human Events*, December 19, 1981. See also Candida Cotto, "1959–2009: CLARIDAD y la lucha de independencia," available at http://claridadpuertorico.com/content.html?news=7EFBA5E3304856266FA0BA8A9008697C&page=1 (accessed July 30, 2009).

52. See, for instance, *Towards People's War and Independence for Puerto Rico*.

53. Those who adhered to this view included those sectors of the Left who saw themselves as part of (or supporting) national liberation movements within the United States. Parallel to the anticolonial movements abroad, these movements considered the black nation, occupied northern Mexico, Native American nations, and Puerto Ricans inside the United States as "internal" colonies. Groups such as the LSP, the American Indian Movement, the Black Liberation Army, and the Republic of New Afrika all adhered to this view, as did white supporters in groups like the Weather Underground Organization, Prairie Fire Organizing Committee, Sojourner Truth Organization, May 19th Communist Organization, and others. There are many texts that reflect these basic politics; for a recent and reasoned personal account, see Diana Block, *Arm the Spirit: A Woman's Journey Underground and Back* (Oakland, CA: AK Press, 2009).

54. In the 1930s, the Nationalist Party developed a stance of *retraimiento*, or non-collaboration. While initially developed to refer to nonparticipation in colonial elections, it grew to include refusal to participate in grand juries or similar investigations. See Staudenmaier, "The Puerto Rican Independence Movement." In the early twenty-first century, a new round of grand-jury investigations has led to a rearticulation of *retraimiento*.

55. See, for example, Jose E. Lopez, ed., *Puerto Rican Nationalism: A Reader* (Chicago: Editorial El Coqui, 1977).

56. See MLN, *Program and Ideology of the MLN* (Chicago: MLN, 1987), pamphlet, in author's files.

57. See Ana Maria Garcia (director), *La Operación*, Latin American Film Project, 1982. The New York City–based Committee for Puerto Rican Decolonization released portions of a 1973 report commissioned by the governor of Puerto Rico, "Opportunities for Employment, Education and Training," which implied that the policy was a means of reducing high unemployment percentages. See the Chicago Women's Liberation Union Herstory

Project, www.cwluherstory.com/CWLUArchive/puertorico.html (accessed July 17, 2009). This number was confirmed by numerous reports, including by community physician and researcher Dr. Helen Rodriguez-Trias. See Our Bodies, Ourselves Health Resource Center, www.ourbodiesourselves.org/book/companion.asp?id=18&compID=55&page=2 (accessed July 17, 2009).

58. See Jean Zwickel, *Voices for Independence: In the Spirit of Valor and Sacrifice* (Pittsburg, CA: White Star Press, 1988). The book is now available at http://home.earthlink.net/~truebadour/voic-index.html (accessed July 17, 2009). More generally on the Vieques struggle, see McCaffrey, *Military Power and Popular Protest.*

59. Barbara Zeller, interview with author, June 22, 2008. See also Melendez, *We Took the Streets*, 199–212; Mary Breasted, "30 in Puerto Rican Group Held in Liberty I. Protest," *New York Times*, October 26, 1977, 30.

60. See, for instance, the flyer "The Frame-Up Continues," about the arrest of four Puerto Rican activists in New York, Ruth Reynolds Papers, series IV, Centro de Estudios Puertorriqueños, Hunter College. See also MLN, "Guillermo Morales: Prisoner of War," *De Pie y En Lucha* special edition (ca. March 1977), 9, 12.

61. The U.S. government, under Ronald Reagan, recalled its ambassador to Mexico to protest Mexico's decision to let Morales escape to Cuba after he was released from a Mexican prison. See Elaine Sciolino, "U.S. Recalls Mexico Envoy Over Militant's Release," *New York Times*, June 29, 1988, A3.

62. Hector Morales Jaime Martell, "The Completed: Tales of Juan Antonio Corretjer," *Claridad*, February 22–28, 1980, 6–7. As with subsequent arrests of alleged FALN members, Morales was supported in court by the MLN and a coalition of white solidarity activists that included members of Prairie Fire Organizing Committee, the Sojourner Truth Organization, and the newly formed Committee in Solidarity with Puerto Rican Independence (CISPRI), which became the Free Puerto Rico Committee. Eventually, activists in this solidarity coalition ran literature tables to distribute information about Morales's health, the situation in Vieques, and other aspects of the independence movement. I remember from personal experience in white neighborhoods that including Morales's situation as part of our work often led to confrontations or confusion from passersby.

63. Both FALN claims and commentary from U.S. law enforcement suggest FALN and possibly Black Liberation Army support for the Morales escape. See, for example, "Statement of Special Agent (Retired) Donald R. Wofford," U.S. Senate Committee of the Judiciary, hearing on FALN clemency, September 15, 1999, available at http://www.latinamericanstudies.org/puertorico/wofford.htm (accessed July 16, 2009).

64. Francisco Ortiz Santini, "The National Security Council during the Carter Administration and the Liberation of the Puerto Rican Nationalists in 1979," *Centro Journal* 19:2 (2007): 150–181.

65. For more on the cases, see Ronald Fernandez, *Prisoners of Colonialism: The Struggles for Justice in Puerto Rico* (Monroe, ME: Common Courage, 1998); Jan Susler, "Unreconstructed Revolutionaries: Today's Puerto Rican Political Prisoners/Prisoners of War," in *The Puerto Rican Movement*, ed. Torres and Velázquez, 144–152; National Committee to Free Puerto Rican Prisoners of War, *The Puerto Rican Prisoners of War and Violations of Their Human Rights* (Chicago: n.p., ca. 1985).

66. Many materials prepared as part of the campaign for the release of these prisoners have been collected in Matt Meyer, ed., *Let Freedom Ring: A Collection of Documents from the Movements to Free U.S. Political Prisoners* (Oakland, CA: PM Press, 2008), 311–361.

67. CISPRI et al., eds., *Toward People's War for Independence and Socialism in Puerto Rico*, 18.

8

Unorthodox Leninism

Workplace Organizing and Anti-Imperialist Solidarity in the Sojourner Truth Organization

MICHAEL STAUDENMAIER

The North American revolutionary Left during the 1970s can generally be split into two camps: those who emphasized questions of class and devoted themselves to workplace organizing, and those who prioritized anti-imperialist struggles both within the United States and around the world.[1] But this division was not necessarily hard and fast, since a range of radicals attempted at different points to map the intersection between these areas. One such outfit, notable both for its theoretical contributions and its practical work, was the Sojourner Truth Organization (STO). STO was a small group—rarely exceeding even fifty members—that emphasized participation in mass struggles, opposed Stalinism as both politic and method, and helped develop the theory of white-skin privilege, which it identified as the central impediment to successful movements for revolution within the United States. This set of commitments ensured that STO's take on both workplace and anti-imperialist struggles was unorthodox for its time, and as a result its efforts looked rather different from the dominant expressions of the two camps.

The organization was founded in late 1969 and carried on until the mid-1980s, paralleling the historical trajectory of many larger and better-known radical groups that developed in the aftermath of the New Left. Its origins lay in a small coterie in Chicago—veterans of Students for a Democratic Society, the Black Panthers, the women's movement, labor struggles, and Old Left parties—who began intervening in popular struggles in both community and workplace contexts as the 1960s ended, just as various Trotskyist and new communist movement organizations were doing in other parts of the country.

Two theoretical innovations marked STO's contribution to the revolutionary Left. First, the group rearticulated the Italian Marxist Antonio Gramsci's understanding of hegemony as an analysis of "dual consciousness," arguing that the working class displayed both a broad acceptance of the status quo and an embryonic awareness of its own revolutionary potential as a class.[2] An early pamphlet produced by STO suggested that "what is in the worker's head is a source of power insofar as it reflects the worldview of the working class—and a source of weakness—insofar as it reflects the world view of the capitalist class."[3] The task of revolutionaries was to help expand the level of proletarian consciousness through participation in mass struggle, while challenging the acquiescence to bourgeois consciousness. STO believed that this process required the creation of a revolutionary party, but it rejected what it called the "Stalin model" of party-building in favor of an eclectic mix of organizational ideas drawn from Lenin and, as the 1970s progressed, from the Trinidadian Marxist C.L.R. James.[4]

This conception of consciousness, the potential of the working class, and the role of revolutionaries was unusual, to say the least, within the developing new communist movement of the early 1970s. Most other groups organizing at the "point of production" maintained the traditional position associated with Lenin's well-known tract *What Is to Be Done?*: workers themselves can only obtain the sort of "trade union consciousness" that leads them to accept partial concessions from management in a permanently reformist cycle. Thus, the class will remain divided and ineffectual until the guiding leadership of organized, conscious revolutionaries transforms the perspective of the workers from the outside, creating the "revolutionary consciousness" that is necessary for the overthrow of capitalism.[5] This line of thinking led to the creation of multiple self-appointed vanguard parties throughout the 1970s, such as the Revolutionary Communist Party (previously the Revolutionary Union, or RU) and the Communist Party Marxist-Leninist (initially the October League, or OL). Both of these organizations at their respective heights were far larger than STO, each including hundreds of members spread across the country. Depending upon one's perspective, they could also be viewed as having been more "successful" in their workplace interventions. Despite the group's smaller size, however, the ingenuity of STO's unusual approach makes the organization worth careful study. STO was largely uninterested in its own organizational growth, preferring instead to advance its politics directly within broader movements. This strategy allowed a relatively small number of committed revolutionaries to make a significant impact on a wide range of industrial workplaces. Similarly, STO's theoretical contributions emerged from within a context of continued engagement with working class struggles. The group's major thinkers were not professional academics, and despite some university background they fell largely into the category of organic intellectuals.[6] Partly as a result, STO's intellectual and strategic contributions were always disproportionate to the group's small size. In a context where a new generation of radicals is considering historical models for political action, STO's unique experiences offer important lessons on topics such as dealing with union bureaucracies, engaging in labor struggles outside of unions, and combining antiracism with working-class militancy.

The second quintessential aspect of STO's revolutionary theory was its analysis of white-skin privilege as a bulwark of white supremacy. A founding member of the group, Noel Ignatin (now Ignatiev), helped pioneer the concept by reframing ideas initially advanced by W.E.B. Du Bois, especially in his classic work *Black*

Reconstruction.[7] According to the theory, people identified as "white" benefit from material and psychological advantages that people of color are denied. STO argued that white workers must "actively and militantly reject their partial, selfish and counterfeit interests as part of a group which is favored in relation to blacks, on behalf of their total, broad and true interests as part of a class which is coming alive."[8] As a largely white group, STO saw its role as spurring the white working class in this direction and supporting organizing efforts emerging from black, Puerto Rican, and other nonwhite communities.

The white-skin privilege theory was in many ways the theoretical pivot that allowed STO to shift from its early workplace organizing orientation to its later emphasis on anti-imperialist solidarity efforts. As with the question of dual consciousness, the white-skin privilege analysis sharply differentiated STO's politics from those of many other leftists during the 1970s. Most Trotskyists and the bulk of the new communist movement rejected the theory altogether as a counterproductive manifestation of white guilt in the service of reactionary forms of nationalism among blacks and other oppressed communities. On the other hand, the white anti-imperialist Left, including the Weather Underground (WUO) and its supporters, embraced a variation on the theory, and former members of STO remember being criticized for having a supposedly naïve attachment to the possibility of class-based organizing among white workers.[9] Even as STO's self-understanding changed during the mid-1970s, away from the new communist movement and toward the anti-imperialist milieu, it retained its own distinctive analysis of white-skin privilege. Partly as a result, its subsequent relations with other groups active in the anti-imperialist Left, such as the Prairie Fire Organizing Committee (PFOC), were somewhat strained.

Within this intellectual framework, STO spent the decade of the 1970s engaged in a striking array of practical work. These efforts can be categorized roughly into two periods: a workplace organizing period lasting approximately from 1970 through 1975, and an anti-imperialist solidarity period running more or less from 1976 through the end of the decade. These demarcations are not exact, as both sorts of organizing continued at some level during both periods. They also neglect a range of other essential components of STO's work, including a continuing commitment to autonomous organizing by working-class women and an intense focus on theoretical development and internal education. Nonetheless, an assessment of these two periods can shed significant light on STO's unique place within the movements of the 1970s.

Workplace Organizing

STO's early emphasis was on organizing at the point of production, especially in large factories in the steel, auto, and manufacturing sectors. In contrast to many groups of the period also engaged in workplace organizing, STO rejected mainstream labor unions as a venue for struggle, calling instead for "independent mass workers' organizations."[10] Group members participated in the creation of many such organizations, in both unionized and non-union factories, always agitating for demands that challenged what STO, following Antonio Gramsci, described as the compromise of "industrial legality."[11] This compromise doomed traditional labor unions, which necessarily negotiated workable relationships between workers and management. STO's activities within several dozen factories in and around Chicago resulted in hundreds of job actions during the early 1970s, ranging from short-term work stoppages to longer wildcat strikes and sabotage at the workplace.

STO's approach to workplace struggles was heavily influenced by radical workers' movements in Italy and the United States. In 1969, the Italian industrial working class rose up in a widespread rebellion known as the Autunno Caldo (Hot Autumn).[12] When a number of major union contracts came up for renewal simultaneously, the collaboration between the company bosses and the union bureaucrats was plain to see. At the same time, the Italian government was in the beginning stages of a lengthy campaign to foment fascist paramilitary violence against leftists and working-class militants. Major Italian factories like Fiat and Pirelli were staffed, in large part, by internal migrants from southern Italy, whose agrarian backgrounds included extensive experience with direct action and sometimes violent confrontation but only limited previous interaction with trade unions. As a result, maneuvering by union officials failed to impress the rank and file, while incidents of fascist terror largely reinforced the militancy of the working class.

The Hot Autumn featured a number of factory occupations and, in the end, resulted in enormous concessions from management, including an average wage increase of almost 25 percent. More importantly, however, the Italian events highlighted the potential for a type of permanent organization of workers outside the trade-union model, which generated new theories of revolution grouped under the general heading of *operaismo*, or "workerism."[13] The key theoretical innovation to come out of the Italian context was "autonomy," meaning the independence of the working class not only from capital, but also from its "official" representatives in the unions and from its would-be vanguards in the Leninist Left. In the North American context, most of the new communist movement took inspiration from the Hot Autumn's factory occupations while ignoring or rejecting its organizational and theoretical innovations.[14] For STO, however, these elements were to prove decisive in the creation of a novel approach to workplace organizing.

Closer to home, the trajectory of the League of Revolutionary Black Workers (LRBW) in Detroit was perhaps more inspiring than the Italian events, even though it was much smaller in its impact and more fragile in its outcomes. The inspiring aspect of the Detroit experience was precisely in its location. Detroit was a largely black city in a country where all recent radical movements had emerged either from, or in response to movements within, the black community. It was also closer to Chicago than was Turin. The league had in fact established direct contact with many of the Italian radicals in the winter before the Hot Autumn, when LRBW member John Watson traveled to Rome for a conference on anti-imperialism.[15] Detroit was hardly unique in producing militant rank-and-file labor struggles, but the sophistication of the LRBW gave the city enough national prominence on the Left that, decades later, Noel Ignatiev could still speak metaphorically of the "Petrograd-Detroit industrial proletariat" as the context for STO's initial forays into workplace organizing.[16]

The guiding principle of STO's attempts at workplace organizing was the rejection of trade unions as the vehicle for their efforts. Following the strategy outlined in *What Is to Be Done?*, most other Left groups of the era (including both the RU and the OL, as well as several Trotskyist organizations) emphasized the creation of opposition caucuses that could eventually take over the unions and turn them into fighting organizations of the working class. But for STO the very concept of "trade union consciousness," combined with the experiences of the LRBW, as well as the overall arc of organized labor's increasingly corrupt history in the twentieth century, implied profound limits to the unions' radical potential.[17] In this context, the experiences of the original Industrial Workers of the World (IWW, or the Wobblies), from its inception in 1905 to its decline in the mid-1920s, provided an example of an alternative to the AFL-CIO. STO referred to this alternative as "independent mass workers' organizations," which largely paralleled the Wobbly concept of "one big union." In its prime, the IWW had organized thousands of workplaces, led hundreds of strike actions, and throughout had shown complete disregard for bourgeois niceties like legality, reasonableness, and respectability.[18] The Wobblies reflected and crystallized the revolutionary aspirations of a vast cross-section of semi-skilled and unskilled industrial workers all across the United States. Beginning from Chicago more than half a century later, STO optimistically hoped to accomplish something similar.

For the most part, STO's strategy took one of two approaches: either the group provided support to independent organizations as they developed in a range of workplaces, or members of STO took jobs in specifically targeted factories and attempted to organize independent groupings directly, with and alongside other militant coworkers. The flagship factory for this sort of industrial concentration was the Stewart-Warner facility on the North Side of Chicago, although similar efforts were made at Motorola, at the International Harvester Plant in Melrose Park, and in the steel mills of South Chicago and northwestern Indiana. In the early years, the organization was structured into multiple branches, and for a time each branch was associated with a major factory concentration, although in no case did every member of a branch work in the target plant.[19] In each instance, however, several STO members obtained work in each factory and set about organizing rank-and-file groups that always included nonmembers as well. Many of these workplaces featured female majorities among the workers, and women in STO were just as likely to take factory jobs as the men. In fact, the first periodical published by STO, a single issue of a tabloid named *Bread and Roses*, was aimed directly at working-class women, especially those employed in factories and hospitals.

The first part of building an industrial concentration was obtaining employment in the chosen factories. This was not always easy, especially for middle-class radicals with years of university experience in their recent past. Lies had to be told, job applications had to be fudged, and eyebrow-raising aspects of personal histories had to be rewritten for the benefit of hiring agents. When John Strucker, for example, applied for work at the Stewart-Warner factory, he needed to explain away the seven years he had spent pursuing his undergraduate and graduate degrees full-time. He concocted an elaborate tale, wherein he had completed high school but then had been obligated to take over the family hardware store in New Jersey when his father became ill. Being good with his hands but not much of a manager, the store struggled for several years and eventually went under, after which he had headed to Chicago in search of a factory job. This story was good enough to get him work as a lathe operator, a position he held for more than a decade. Early on, however, he was identified as a troublemaker, and the company eventually researched his back-story. Once they determined that no such hardware store had ever existed, management attempted to fire him. With help from STO's contingent of lawyers, Strucker appealed his case to the National Labor Relations Board (NLRB). Upon consideration, the NLRB ruled in his favor, noting that although he had in fact lied on his job application, he had lied "down," underplaying his credentials rather than overstating them.[20]

In the early 1970s, the Stewart-Warner factory employed several thousand people, more or less evenly split among black, white, and Latino (largely Puerto Rican) workers, of whom perhaps one-half were women.[21] The plant manufactured a variety of electrical components for use in cars, boats, and other vehicles. It had a range of military contracts that were lost in the aftermath of the Vietnam War.[22] As many as a dozen STO members had jobs in a variety of departments and were thus able to slowly build a factory-wide presence for the group's politics. The first step in this regard was the initiation of a shop newsletter called *Talk Back*, which was published irregularly for close to a decade. Initially, *Talk Back* was published and distributed anonymously to prevent the company from punishing those responsible. As time went on, however, the members began to distribute the newsletter publicly as a way to build solidarity within the factory. In addition, STO members also produced and distributed a range of stickers in and around the factory, which were used as propaganda and as morale-boosters.

The distribution of shop sheets and agitational newspapers was a common tactic for leftists involved in workplace organizing in the 1970s, and there is no evidence that STO was any more successful than competing groups like the RU or OL at integrating workers into their preparation or at tying their production to specific struggles. The distinctiveness of STO's approach to the workplace became clearer when, building upon the initial work of producing shop sheets, in-plant efforts graduated to supporting and even initiating organizing efforts within the factory.[23] These campaigns ran the gamut from small-scale attempts to remove particularly mean-spirited or racist foremen to plant-wide struggles around improving working conditions and health and safety precautions.

Three elements helped clarify the differences between STO's efforts and those of other groups involved in factory work. First, unlike other Left groups organizing in factories, STO did not attempt to change the union leadership. Rather than develop oppositional caucuses that could challenge corrupt union bureaucrats, STO argued that the institution of the trade union was itself the problem, and that changing the names on the leadership slate would, at best, have no effect, or, at worst, make workers even more complacent than they had previously been. At Stewart-Warner, for example, *Talk Back* mocked union caucus efforts by promoting a garbage can, "Filthy Billy" Trash, as a "CANdidate" for president of the local.[24] Criticized by skeptics both inside and outside STO, this abstention from fights over union leadership extended even to the level of departmental steward, which represented to many leftists both a winnable and a meaningful position in the union hierarchy. Stewards have responsibility for pursuing worker grievances, and the choice between a responsive steward and a corrupt one can make the difference between success and failure in, for example, a worker's compensation claim. Nonetheless, STO's critical perspective on trade unions led the group to decide that no STO member could run for steward, although members did sometimes support, and shop sheets periodically reported on, the candidacies of militant coworkers.[25]

Of course, not all workplaces were unionized. In non-union plants, a different set of problems presented themselves, but the contrast between STO and other Left groups attempting to organize workers remained. At the Motorola factory on the West Side of Chicago, for example, STO members were involved in creating the Motorola Organizing Committee and publishing the newsletter *Breakout!* But this was not a campaign to win union recognition and a first contract. Even after several years of organizing at the plant, the editors of *Breakout!* could write: "We do not work for any union. We are not against unions, but mostly we are for people fighting the company."[26] Just as in unionized factories, the STO members at Motorola thought unions were not a productive way to fight the company, so they never attempted to bring one in.

Another major difference between STO's approach and that of other Left groups committed to industrial concentration related to the kinds of demands that were put forward in organizing projects. Many Left groups pushed campaigns that promised to improve working conditions for all workers in a supposedly equal fashion, such as across-the-board pay raises. STO members, by contrast, involved themselves first and foremost in struggles to improve the situations of those they saw as the most oppressed workers, typically people of color and women. For example, the *Talk Back* group helped coordinate an eventually successful campaign at Stewart-Warner to eliminate a particular pay grade that was being used by the management as an excuse to pay black and Puerto Rican women significantly less than white women for similar work.[27] Organizing workers around this issue meant persuading the majority of the workers—men and white women—to back a demand that had no immediate effect on their personal working conditions. The arguments advanced by STO members and their allies in campaigns like this were both moral and strategic, and, win or lose, they helped define the approach taken by STO to workplace organizing.

The third key difference between STO's work in factories and that of other Left groups concerned recruitment. All Leninist organizations agreed on the need to create a new and truly revolutionary party that could serve as the vanguard of all struggles against capitalism, and STO had made party-building a part of its self-conception from its 1969 founding. Further, all these groups recognized that any such party needed to be demographically representative of the working class it claimed to represent. For the OL, the RU, and most other new communist groups, this implied a significant emphasis on recruiting workers, and especially non-white workers, to their organizations. For STO, however, defending workers' autonomy (implied in the critical view of the trade unions) meant that the involvement of workers in independent organizations in the workplace was *not* normally a first step toward recruitment into the group, but primarily a way to build the workers' experience and self-confidence.[28] Further, the analysis of white supremacy and white-skin privilege led STO to be even more leery of attempts to recruit workers of color (or "third-world workers" as they were commonly known in the 1970s), for fear that such efforts would undermine the autonomy of people of color to determine the course of their own struggles.[29] In the end, few people joined STO directly from the shop floor, and of those who did, almost none maintained their membership for longer than a year or two.[30] On the whole, STO was less interested in recruitment than in supporting the autonomy of the working class. Thus, the group attempted to intervene in struggles that it believed might eventually result in the creation of a revolutionary party in the United States, but it generally did not consider itself the organizational kernel around which that party would develop.

STO's workplace efforts produced, at best, mixed results. By defining the terms of success so narrowly—excluding union reform, for example—the recipe for failure was perhaps self-imposed. Other leftist groups faced their own problems as the independent labor upsurge of the early 1970s waned dramatically by 1975, and the revolutionary momentum remaining from the late 1960s slowed at about the same time.[31] In this context, the particulars of STO's near-demise in 1974 seem predictable: a faction of the group left, disgruntled with the majority's refusal to embrace a more orthodox approach to Leninism; another segment withdrew because it viewed STO as too orthodox and unwilling to fully integrate with workers' struggles.[32] In the aftermath of these two splits, much of the remaining membership abandoned STO out of simple demoralization, leaving a tiny core of perhaps a half-dozen committed members. This core, in attempting to regenerate the group, decided to deemphasize (but not abandon totally) workplace organizing. Following the momentum of broader movements, STO reconstituted itself largely on the terrain of anti-imperialist solidarity with national liberation struggles.

Anti-Imperialist Solidarity

STO's rebuilding process preserved the core ideological commitments of the organization, but some strategic shifts manifested. First, the group extended its reach geographically, merging in 1976 with like-minded groups in Iowa and Missouri to become a regional organization and eventually growing to include perhaps sixty active members in nearly a dozen states coast to coast.[33] Second, STO began to emphasize the importance of national liberation struggles. Solidarity with, most prominently, the Puerto Rican independence movement and the Iranian student movement in the United States became central components of the group's practical work. The group's shift from workplace organizing to anti-imperialist solidarity was partly reflective of the overall strength of various movements at different times: The surge in labor radicalism during the early 1970s receded around the time that several revolutionary nationalist movements were gaining momentum. Other factors included the practical reality of deindustrialization, which progressively limited the ability of STO to pursue a workplace-organizing strategy, and accidents of history, such as key encounters between STO members and activists involved in the Puerto Rican and Iranian revolutionary movements around 1975.[34]

With the focus on factory work decentered, concrete solidarity with national liberation movements was one important way to maintain an active membership without getting sucked into a purely scholastic focus on internal theoretical development. During this period, STO developed particularly strong ties with the Puerto Rican independence movement and organized in solidarity with the Iranian student movement (in exile) against the Shah, with the Republic of New Afrika and other black nationalist groupings, and with the struggles for liberation in southern Africa, especially in Rhodesia/Zimbabwe and South Africa/Azania. The relationship STO developed with the Puerto Rican movement was in many ways exemplary of the group's theory and practice during the second half of the 1970s, especially in Chicago.

By the mid-1970s, the Puerto Rican independence movement was one of the largest and most vibrant radical movements in the Western Hemisphere. It responded militantly to a broad range of issues: the military occupation and environmental devastation of the island of Puerto Rico; the extreme economic exploitation and racist discrimination faced by the working class, both on the island and in the diaspora; and the forced sterilization imposed on huge numbers of Puerto Rican women. Among national liberation struggles, the Puerto Rican movement had one of the largest communities of adherents and supporters in the United States, as a result of massive working-class migration from the island during the 1950s. Because of the booming industrial economy of the 1960s, a significant segment of this diaspora eventually arrived in Chicago, and STO members early on were acquainted with various radical trends within the Puerto Rican community.

As early as 1966, the Puerto Rican community in Chicago rioted against police brutality and discrimination in housing and employment.[35] The aftermath of this melee helped radicalize the Young Lords street gang, which later became the Young Lords Organization and eventually the Young Lords Party, with members in New York City and on the island itself.[36] The influence of the Black Panther Party on the Young Lords was clear, and innovative forms of militant community organizing became the primary form of political engagement for a whole generation of Puerto Rican radicals in Chicago. Protests against police brutality continued, but they were joined with actions against slumlords and demonstrations against racism in the public schools. During the early 1970s, many of the core organizers in Chicago were linked to (but often not members of) the Partido Socialista Puertorriqueño (PSP), which was probably the largest of the new communist groups, and as a result they developed ties with like-minded activists in New York, Puerto Rico, and elsewhere.[37]

By the mid-1970s, sections of the PSP had distanced themselves from the idea of armed struggle, and a new group based heavily in Chicago, the Movimiento de Liberación Nacional (MLN), became STO's primary point of contact with the independence movement. Around the same time, a clandestine group of Puerto Rican militants, the Fuerzas Armadas de Liberación Nacional (FALN), began an armed campaign within the United States on behalf of Puerto Rican independence. From 1974 until 1984, the FALN carried out more than one hundred bombings against U.S. control of Puerto Rico, primarily in New York and Chicago.[38] From its beginning, the MLN was vocally supportive of the FALN and other clandestine Puerto Rican groups, and STO acted in solidarity with both groups as leading organizations of the Puerto Rican independence movement.

STO's role in this situation was to provide material support and organizing assistance to the Puerto Rican movement. Thus, the group regularly sponsored speaking and fundraising tours for Puerto Rican radicals, from the island or from Chicago, through places like Kansas City, Denver, or Portland, which had no Puerto Rican communities but did have STO branches. STO also utilized its in-house printing press to help produce agitational material supporting Puerto Rican independence, including leaflets and pamphlets edited by the MLN or other similar groups. Emergency support was also a regular feature of STO's solidarity efforts: When Puerto Rican militants were arrested or harassed, STO members were always on hand for support rallies. And with a large number of lawyers in the group's membership, STO was often able to provide immediate legal assistance to those in need.

Most importantly, STO participated for several years in a coalition of solidarity groups operating in support of independence, alongside other anti-imperialist groups like the Prairie Fire Organizing Committee (PFOC) and the May 19th Communist Organization.[39] Despite many political disagreements, these groups were united in their support for armed struggle as a legitimate strategy for the independence movement. In this, they were opposed by most of the new communist movement, including much of the leadership of the PSP, which supported independence for Puerto Rico but considered armed struggle to be adventurist and premature.[40] STO's shift from workplace organizing to anti-imperialist solidarity was only cemented by the dismissive attitudes emerging from its former milieu.

Apart from the armed struggle issue, the other main dividing line within the solidarity movement was the knotty topic known as the "national question." In the Puerto Rican context, the question was whether the diaspora population constituted part of the Puerto Rican nation, or whether it was instead a "national minority" in the United States. This latter perspective, common to much of the new communist movement as the 1970s progressed, derived from Josef Stalin's famous analysis of nations and nationalism: "A nation is a historically constituted, stable community of people, formed on the basis of a common language, territory, economic life, and psychological makeup manifested in a common culture." This conception, which gained prominence when Stalin came to power, was exceptionally rigid: "it is sufficient for a single one of these characteristics to be lacking and the nation ceases to be a nation."[41]

One unifying factor among almost all the groups participating in these debates, whether from within the new communist movement or from within the anti-imperialist Left, was the continued, largely unthinking reliance upon Stalin's definition of the nation. For the Puerto Rican diaspora, the "territory" clause in particular was used to exclude this population from the nation. STO began its analysis of the national question, in typically anti-Stalinist fashion, by rejecting Stalin's framework altogether. In its place, the group substituted the analysis developed by Lenin during the period immediately prior to the revolution of 1917. In a classic example of the caricature of Leninist theory as Talmudic scholarship, STO engaged in a seemingly endless series of written debates with its opponents, each of which featured numerous lengthy quotations from obscure sections of Lenin's *Collected Works*.[42] While most of the disputes focused on the question of black nationhood, the Puerto Rican example was more prominent in STO's practical work.

The group's increased focus on the national question during the mid-1970s represented a shift in its implementation of the white-skin privilege analysis, de-emphasizing "race" and highlighting "nation" as a key category. STO was one of many groups to develop a Marxist theoretical analysis to justify its emphasis on anti-imperialist solidarity. Updating Lenin's famous dictum that imperialism was the highest stage of capitalist development, members of the group argued that anti-imperialism was a more productive framework for all the organization's efforts than "anticapitalism" could hope to be. What STO meant by "anti-imperialism" was somewhat more complicated than simply opposing U.S.

intervention in the Third World. This was a result of what the group perceived as the objective reality of capitalism's global development, including the heightened possibility of an impending "secular" crisis in the functioning of the law of value. According to this analysis, the anti-imperialist struggles then playing out worldwide seemed likely to grow in the coming era, but to be torn between revolutionary and reformist poles.[43] The practical implication was an attempt to initiate an "anti-imperialist tendency" within the North American Left that could lend support to the most radical elements of the impending global upsurge in anti-imperialism.[44]

In this context, STO's efforts in support of the Iranian student movement in the United States represented another example of the group's focus on anti-imperialist organizing, as well as its contradictions. By the middle of the 1970s, the struggle against the U.S.-backed dictatorship of the Shah had reached critical mass within Iran. In the United States, support for the coming revolution was strongest within the large Iranian student movement, which represented something of a throwback to the generalized student militancy of the late 1960s.[45] STO developed a range of ties with various Iranian student organizations, each espousing a different variation on Marxist-Leninist ideology and strategy. From STO's perspective, the value of this work lay as much in the potential to radicalize broader sections of the student Left in the United States as it did in the prospects for a revolution halfway around the world in Iran. As with its work around Puerto Rico, the main tasks STO took on in support of the Iranian student movement were related to propaganda: supporting speaking tours and printing leaflets and articles. By 1979, however, with the revolution imminent in Iran, a significant portion of the most active students returned to their home country to participate more directly in the struggle. STO's work after this point was limited largely to publishing translated documents sent abroad by various Marxist-Leninist groups in Iran.[46]

Meanwhile, the ongoing organizing in solidarity with the Puerto Rican independence movement eventually took a toll on STO as a group. The intense state repression visited upon both the above-ground and clandestine wings of the Puerto Rican movement resulted in permanent crisis, where there were always more responsibilities and work to be done than there were people or resources to draw on. Similarly, many tasks were considered so urgent that an emergency-response model came to characterize a wide cross-section of all the activities undertaken by the solidarity coalition within which STO operated. This approach left less time for STO or the other groups involved to plan and execute other vital work, whether theoretical or practical. As the 1970s came to a close, STO began to reconsider the possibilities of expanding its workplace organizing efforts again, and it became more involved in a variety of new social movements, especially the anti-nuclear and anti-fascist and anti-Klan struggles then gaining momentum on the Left. These movements, among many others, shared a high level of militancy, a commitment to novel forms of direct action, and a cross-class character that differentiated them from previous generations of radical movements more clearly focused on traditional organizing within either the working-class or university settings.[47] While the anti-Klan struggle emerged largely from within the same antiracist wing of the revolutionary Left inhabited by STO, it quickly expanded to include a wide variety of participants with little in common politically, apart from a fierce opposition to white supremacist paramilitary terror.[48] Over time, however, STO's ability to focus on these areas of work was compromised by its commitment to the ongoing responsibilities of solidarity work.

As the 1970s progressed, STO also became increasingly aware of the ideological differences that separated it from both the other solidarity organizations and the Puerto Rican movement itself. During this period, STO's outlook had become more fervently anti-Stalinist. This political analysis led STO to insist on greater democracy within its organization—unlike groups such as the MLN, whose interpretation of democratic centralism was heavily centralist and light on the democracy. In principle, at least, STO's internal structure was a more balanced mix of these two elements, insofar as political disagreement was highly prized, and the final authority for all strategic and ideological decisions rested with the annual general membership meeting. At the same time, this approach did not always translate easily into effective democratic practice. One former member, for instance, argues that among the leading members of STO, "there was a profound impact of the CP [Communist Party USA] on the organization, that wasn't completely recognized, even by the people themselves. They had definitely made a break from Stalinism in a very profound way, but they were all kind of raised in a political culture, however, where certain things were very controlled, and they never completely let go of it. . . . There was a tendency of the informal leadership to circle the wagons and direct things."[49] Nonetheless, most former members agree that this same informal leadership also led the group's effort to democratize the intellectual culture of the organization, often through formal classes on topics like political economy and dialectics.[50]

At the same time, STO's internal difficulties in dealing with the issue of democracy seem only to have enhanced its frustration with similar (or worse) behavior in other organizations. STO was loathe to publicly criticize the politics of the MLN or other national liberation groups with which it acted in solidarity, but the underlying disagreements are clear in a number of published documents aimed more directly at STO's coalition partners. In 1979, for example, STO criticized

the confusion of unconditional support for national liberation with an uncritical identification with positions taken by the national liberation leadership or elements of it. Unconditional support involves a conscious subordination of political differences for definite political reasons. The political leadership of national liberation movements must be followed on questions concerning the form and content of the movements they head, not because this leadership is always right, but because it is the social force whose correct and incorrect positions "matter." This has nothing to do with any attribution of infallibility and omniscience. We do liberation movements no favor by disguising disagreements, or, still worse, by evading questions which must be of concern to all revolutionaries.[51]

This represented a not-so-subtle attack on the solidarity politics of PFOC and May 19th, which STO considered overly subservient to the dictates of particular revolutionary nationalist organizations. In practice, however, STO would challenge liberation movements only within the internal structures of the coalitions within which it operated, and the group's public stance was for the most part functionally identical to the one criticized above.

This contradiction within STO's approach to solidarity work only compounded the growing sense of political divergence between the group and its allied organizations in the anti-imperialist Left. Eventually, the intense focus on anti-imperialist solidarity became untenable for STO, just as the workplace orientation had been several years previously. This time, the membership was not sharply divided over the question, although there were disagreements about which areas of work deserved increased emphasis afterwards. (A faction had left the group in 1978, partly due to disagreement with the prioritization of anti-imperialist work over workplace efforts, but even this splinter grouping continued to participate actively in the solidarity coalition with STO, PFOC, and other groups.) And again, anti-imperialist politics were never fully jettisoned, as until its demise STO continued, however periodically, to collaborate with the MLN. The framework, however, was fundamentally different by the 1980s.

The Legacy of STO

At the beginning of the 1980s, STO altered its strategy again, focusing on the new social movements: especially the antinuclear movement, antifascist and anti-Klan organizing, youth and student efforts, and reproductive-rights struggles. Within this context, the group consistently emphasized the importance of both anti-imperialism and an orientation toward the working class. The group also encouraged a strategic orientation toward what it called, following the Italian autonomists, "mass illegality." For example, the group led an attempt to blockade the military base at Rock Island, Illinois, in 1985 to protest U.S. intervention in Central America.[52] This was not a traditional civil disobedience action where arrests were expected and encouraged, but rather a militant effort to disrupt the functioning of a major symbol of U.S. imperialism, and get away with it. But these efforts proved to be too little, too late in terms of resuscitating the radical milieu within which STO had developed and, for a time, had thrived. Disillusionment caused by the Reagan Revolution quickened the decline of the 1970s movements, and within STO a new series of splits over strategic direction undermined the group's organizational viability. By the late 1980s, almost two decades after its founding, the group was defunct.

The STO was never very large, but its legacy has been both outsized and underappreciated. The group consistently attempted to create theoretical frameworks within which it could contextualize its work, while remaining engaged in a range of practical endeavors that could never become perfect reflections of some pure theoretical outlook. This dialectical tension, between the purity of theory and the messiness of action, paralleled STO's conflicted relationship with the sometimes contradictory worlds of class-struggle workplace organizing and anti-imperialist solidarity with national liberation struggles. STO was never completely comfortable within either of the two main trends that defined much of 1970s radicalism, partly because its unorthodox brand of Leninism integrated significant insights from a wide variety of revolutionary traditions.

Its idiosyncrasies notwithstanding, STO's experience was exemplary of the broader radical movements of the 1970s. The issues it confronted—from labor militancy to national liberation—were seen as pressing by a wide range of progressives, radicals, and revolutionaries as the 1960s faded from view. Additionally, in spite of its small size, STO was deeply engaged in an ongoing series of broader left campaigns, so that its perspectives and its work were widely known within radical circles across the United States. But this involvement was itself distinctive, given STO's unorthodox approach to most questions of politics and strategy. This uniqueness has also carried over into the work done by former members in the years since the group's demise: The journal *Race Traitor*, for instance, was co-founded by former member Noel Ignatiev and carried on STO's analysis of white-skin privilege in a controversial (and less organizationally driven) fashion. Similarly, the writings and organizing around the issues of fascism, antifascism, and far-right movements in the United States and elsewhere by former members such as Don Hamerquist and Leonard Zeskind have contributed greatly to contemporary understandings of the far right.[53] As a result, a comprehensive understanding of left politics since the 1970s requires an assessment of STO's historical trajectory as part of understanding race- and class-based organizing. Unfortunately, previous scholarship on the group has been extremely sparse, effectively limited to brief references in a handful of books about broader topics.[54] Expanding this scholarship is needed to flesh out the record of post-1960s U.S. radicalism.

STO's relevance for the present and future persists. In positioning itself as a small cadre organization committed to participation in mass struggles, rather than a vanguard party or a collective of isolated individuals, STO defined the terms of its own existence. Even as it was pulled in multiple directions by the broader social movements of its era, the group managed to influence the trajectories of these very same movements, albeit in subtle ways. The hope that animated the Sojourner Truth Organization—the promise of autonomy; militant, mass direct action; and a society rid of white supremacy, patriarchy, and capitalism—still inspires radical movements today.

NOTES

1. For an overview of the class/workplace tendency during this period, see Max Elbaum, *Revolution in the Air: Sixties Radicals Turn to Lenin, Mao and Che* (London: Verso, 2002); A. Belden Fields, *Trotskyism and Maoism: Theory and Practice in France and the United States* (Brooklyn: Autonomedia, 1988); and Jim O'Brien, "American Leninism in the 1970s," *Radical America* 11:6 and 12:1 (November 1977 and February 1978): 27–63. For discussion of the anti-imperialist tendency, see Dan Berger, *Outlaws of America: The Weather Underground and the Politics of Solidarity* (Oakland, CA: AK Press, 2006); and E. Tani and Kae Sera, *False Nationalism, False Internationalism: Class Contradictions in the Armed Struggle* (Chicago: Seeds Beneath the Snow, 1985).

2. The source of this term, in its usage by STO, is somewhat murky. W.E.B. Du Bois used the phrase "double consciousness" in his classic work *The Souls of Black Folk* (1903: rpt. New York: Signet Classic, 1995), 45, to describe the experience of black people living in a white supremacist society. Despite the group's obvious debt to Du Bois, there is no clear evidence that his work represented the source of STO's usage. Don Hamerquist, who first introduced the term within STO, recalls Lenin's critique of trade-union consciousness as an important influence in how the organization used the term "dual consciousness" in its work. Hamerquist, e-mail to the author, October 26, 2009.

3. Sojourner Truth Organization (STO), *Towards a Revolutionary Party: Ideas on Strategy & Organization* (1971; rpt. Chicago: STO, 1976), available at www.sojournertruth.net/tarp.html (accessed February 18, 2009).

4. For a concise explanation of STO's anti-Stalinism, see Don Hamerquist, "Discussion Points on the Party and Revolutionary Strategy," in *Collective Works* 3 (June 1975): 8–10, in author's possession. Thanks to Traci Harris for providing me a copy of this publication from the archive. (This document can also be viewed in the Max Elbaum Papers, New Communist Movement Collection, at the Southern California Library.) "The Leninist conception of the party must be recaptured from Stalinist distortion. . . . Party life must emphasize clear, sharp and critical debate over points of principle. . . . Fear of public differences and 'factions' is no part of Leninist theory or practice on the question of the party. . . . The so-called 'party principle' must be cleared of any implication that runs contrary to the central Marxist thesis that the emancipation of the working class is the task of the working class itself."

5. See Vladimir Ilyich Lenin, *What Is to Be Done?: Burning Questions of Our Movement* (1902; rpt. Peking: Progress Publishers, 1980).

6. The phrase "organic intellectuals," usually associated with Antonio Gramsci and referring to the development and spread of knowledge by nonprofessionals and the working class, seems appropriate in describing STO in light of the ways in which many of the group's leading members personally distanced themselves from the academy. None of STO's three major theorists (Don Hamerquist, Noel Ignatiev, and Ken Lawrence) held college degrees while members of the group, although Ignatiev did receive a Ph.D. after leaving the group. It is true that the "second tier" of intellectuals (the range of members who contributed in varying ways to developing theory within the group but were not major theorists) in STO featured a number of attorneys and some people who obtained advanced degrees before joining the group, as well as a number who, like Ignatiev, returned to school and obtained advanced degrees after leaving STO. Author interviews with Hamerquist, Ignatiev, Lawrence, David Ranney, and Carole Travis, as well as Lawrence, e-mail to the author, November 13, 2009, support this assessment.

7. See especially W.E.B. Du Bois, *Black Reconstruction in America, 1860–1880* (1935; rpt. New York: Free Press, 1998), 700–701, where he describes the "public and psychological wage"

that white workers received in compensation for reinforcing white supremacy during the period after reconstruction.

8. STO, *The United Front Against Imperialism?* (Chicago: STO, 1972), available at www .sojournertruth.net/unitedfront.html (accessed February 18, 2009).

9. For examples of criticisms of STO's approach emerging from the new communist movement, see the summary, including quotations, in Don Hamerquist, *White Supremacy and the Afro-American National Question* (Chicago: STO, 1978), especially in Part V, "A Response to Criticisms." Available at http://www.sojournertruth.net/natlquestion.html (accessed February 18, 2009). Author's interviews, conducted between 2005 and 2008, with former STO members Ira and Lee Churgin, Noel Ignatiev, Don Hamerquist, and Janeen Porter all indicate a perception on STO's part that PFOC was critical of its approach to white supremacy and working-class organizing.

10. See, for example, STO, *Mass Organization at the Workplace* (Chicago: STO, 1972), available at http://www.sojournertruth.net/massorganization.html (accessed February 18, 2009).

11. Don Hamerquist, "Trade Unions/Independent Organizations" in *Workplace Papers* (Chicago: STO, 1980), 37, where Gramsci is quoted. Available at http://www.sojournertruth .net/unionsorganizations.html (accessed February 18, 2009).

12. See Steve Wright, *Storming Heaven: Class Composition and Struggle in Italian Autonomist Marxism* (London: Pluto Press, 2002); and Dan Georgakas, ed., "Italy: New Tactics and Organization," *Radical America* 5:5 (September/October 1971): 3–40.

13. This use of "workerism" must be distinguished from the term's usage as (more or less) a synonym for syndicalism, a usage that was common within the new communist movement and STO in the early 1970s.

14. On the positive response of U.S. radicals to the Italian Hot Autumn, see Elbaum, *Revolution in the Air*, 88.

15. Dan Georgakas and Marvin Surkin, *Detroit, I Do Mind Dying: A Study in Urban Revolution* (1975; rpt. Boston: South End Press, 1998), 49–51.

16. Noel Ignatiev, telephone interview with the author, July 16, 2005.

17. For an analysis of the conservative and corrupt character of the North American labor movement at the end of the 1960s, see Stanley Aronowitz, *False Promises: The Shaping of American Working Class Consciousness* (New York: McGraw-Hill, 1973). For a broader historical overview of union corruption, see Robert Fitch, *Solidarity for Sale: How Corruption Destroyed the Labor Movement and Undermined America's Promise* (New York: Public Affairs, 2006).

18. For more on the history of the IWW, see Joyce Kornbluh, ed., *Rebel Voices: An IWW Anthology* (Chicago: Charles H. Kerr, 1998); and Paul Buhle and Nicole Schulman, eds., *Wobblies! A Graphic History of the Industrial Workers of the World* (New York: Verso, 2005).

19. See the unsigned *Outline History of Sojourner Truth*, September 1972, in Detroit Revolutionary Movements Collection, Subseries F, box 15, Reuther Library, Wayne State University.

20. John Strucker, telephone interview with the author, February 5, 2006.

21. Kathy and Lynn, "Organizing in an Electrical Plant in Chicago," *Collective Works* 1:1 (October 1974): 11–20. This piece pseudonymously refers to the "AC" plant and changes the names of STO members and ex-members then working there, in order to protect the then-ongoing organizing efforts. However, the description of the plant and STO's efforts there clearly match the descriptions offered in my interviews in 2006 with several former STO members, especially John Strucker (February 5, 2006).

22. This information comes largely from my interviews in 2006 with John Strucker, Don Hamerquist (who worked there for a time), and Noel Ignatiev (who never worked there).

23. In some cases, both for STO and more broadly among radicals active in workplace organizing, the progression was in the opposite direction: campaigns first, publications second, although in most of STO's major points of concentration, and certainly at Stewart-Warner, the publications came first. See Kathy and Lynn, "Organizing in an Electrical Plant in Chicago."

24. In *Talk Back* 2:5 (February 25, 1974), in author's possession. Sections of this issue, including documents from the "Filthy Billy" union election campaign, as well as other leaflets STO distributed on the shop floor are available through the digital archive of the Sojourner Truth Organization: http://www.sojournertruth.net/shopleaflets.pdf.

25. In at least one case, an STO member at Stewart-Warner helped initiate a campaign to unseat a particularly corrupt steward, only to be forced to abandon the effort when no other candidate was forthcoming from the department, despite his coworkers' attempts to persuade him to run himself. See Kathy and Lynn, "Organizing in an Electrical Plant in Chicago."

26. "Who We Are," *Breakout!* 1:4 (December 11, 1973): 2, in author's possession.

27. Strucker, telephone interview with author, February 5, 2006.

28. Ibid.

29. Kingsley Clarke, interview with author, July 6, 2005.

30. This information comes from my interviews with Noel Ignatiev, January 22, 2006; Don Hamerquist, September 14, 2006; and Carole Travis, June 6, 2006.

31. On the independent labor upsurge, see Kim Moody, *An Injury to All: The Decline of American Unionism* (London: Verso, 1988), especially 71–94 and 249–270.

32. STO described these splits in the second version of its *Outline History of Sojourner Truth*, circa 1980, in author's possession. Additional information comes from my interviews with Mel and Marcia Rothenberg (who left in the first split), October 12, 2006; Elias Zwierzynski, January 1, 2007; and Guillermo Brzostowski, October 10, 2008 (both of whom departed in the second split). Neither faction produced a lasting organizational alternative to STO, though several participants later ended up elsewhere in the new communist movement or in the mainstream labor movement.

33. By the turn of the decade, STO had an active presence in Chicago, Kansas City, Iowa City, Denver, Portland, Seattle, San Francisco, New Orleans, Jackson, Philadelphia, and New York City. This expansion was a result of at least three factors: the increasing popularity of anti-imperialist politics within the Left during the late 1970s, the broad distribution during the same period of *Urgent Tasks*, STO's regularly published political journal, and, perhaps most importantly, strategic decisions by STO members (made autonomously, but in consultation with the organization's leadership) to move from core cities like Chicago and Kansas City to new outposts like Denver, Portland, and others.

34. On deindustrialization, see David C. Ranney, *Global Decisions, Local Collisions: Urban Life in the New World Order* (Philadelphia: Temple University Press, 2003). Ranney was a member of STO for several years in the mid-1970s.

35. See Mervin Méndez, "A Community Fights Back: Recollections of the 1966 Division Street Riot," *Dialogo Magazine* 2 (Winter/Spring 1998).

36. For more on the 1970s trajectory of the Puerto Rican Left in the mainland United States, see Andrés Torres and José Velázquez, eds., *The Puerto Rican Movement: Voices from the Diaspora* (Philadelphia: Temple University Press, 1998).

37. Jose Lopez, interview with author, October 18, 2008.

38. For a partisan overview and chronology of the Puerto Rican armed-struggle movement during the 1970s, see the pamphlet co-published by STO, PFOC, and others, entitled *Toward People's War for Independence and Socialism in Puerto Rico: In Defense of Armed Struggle. Documents and Communiqués from the Revolutionary Public Independence Movement and the Armed Clandestine Movement* (Chicago: STO, et. al., 1978).

39. Both Prairie Fire and May 19th emerged from aboveground efforts supporting the Weather Underground during the mid-1970s. May 19th resulted from a split within Prairie Fire, and Chicago was one of few cities in the United States to house active branches of both organizations. See Berger, *Outlaws of America*, 225–243, for an overview of the activities and perspectives of PFOC and May 19th during this period.

40. See *Urgent Tasks* 1 (May 1977), in author's possession, which contains a "pull-out" section focused on the battles within the Puerto Rican solidarity movement, which included much of the new communist movement as well as the anti-imperialist Left, over the legitimacy of armed struggle in the Puerto Rican context.

41. Josef Stalin, *Marxism and the National Question* (1913), quoted in Jasper Collins, "Who's Being Dogmatic?" *Urgent Tasks* 2 (October 1977): 4, in author's possession. Stalin's text is available online at http://www.marxists.org/reference/archive/stalin/works/1913/03.htm (accessed February 18, 2009).

42. See Collins, "Who's Being Dogmatic?"; and Hamerquist, *White Supremacy and the Afro-American National Question* (Chicago: STO, 1978), among others. The various Puerto Rican revolutionary organizations also developed their own analysis of the national question in the particular context of Puerto Rico and its diaspora population. Part of the reason STO developed strong ties with the MLN was their shared analysis of Puerto Ricans as a single, unified nation regardless of location. Jose Lopez, interview with author, October 18, 2008.

43. In Don Hamerquist, "Anti-Capitalism or Anti-Imperialism," *Internal Discussion Bulletin* 18 (January 1980), in author's possession.

44. A later attempt to reflect on the problems of this analysis can be found in the organizationally signed editorial "A Revolutionary Left," *Urgent Tasks* 13 (Spring 1982), available at http://www.sojournertruth.net/revleft.html (accessed February 18, 2009).

45. See Afshin Matin-Asgari, *Iranian Student Opposition to the Shah* (Costa Mesa, CA: Mazda Publishers, 2002) for an overview of the movement in Europe and the United States during the 1960s and 1970s.

46. See, for example, Ashraf Dehghani, "Documents of the Iranian Revolutionary Movement," *Urgent Tasks* 8 (Spring 1980), available online at http://www.sojournertruth.net/irandocs8.html (accessed March 20, 2009).

47. For background on the concept of "new social movements," see Marcy Darnovsky, Barbara Epstein, and Richard Flacks, eds., *Cultural Politics and Social Movements* (Philadelphia: Temple University Press, 1995). For a critical analysis of the direct-action aspect of these movements, see Barbara Epstein, *Political Protest and Cultural Revolution: Nonviolent Direct Action in the 1970s and 1980s* (Berkeley: University of California Press, 1991).

48. Ken Lawrence, interview with author, August 24, 2006.

49. David Ranney, interview with author, December 20, 2005.

50. The dialectics classes in particular became widely known within the Left in the late 1970s and early 1980s, and on numerous occasions the course was offered by STO members to nonmembers active in antinuclear and environmental movements, among others. A sample curriculum was published as "How to Think: A Guide to the Study of Dialectical Materialism," *Urgent Tasks* 7 (Winter 1980), available online at

http://www.sojournertruth.net/htt.html (accessed February 18, 2009). Versions of this curriculum are used to this day by various radical groups in the United States. The small revolutionary organization Bring the Ruckus, for example, has developed an updated course modeled on the original STO version and has offered it to both members and non-members in several cities since 2008.

51. "'Unconditional Support' and 'Follow Third World Leadership': An Editorial," *Urgent Tasks* 6 (Fall 1979), available online at http://www.sojournertruth.net/ut6editorial.html (accessed February 18, 2009).

52. Author interviews with Kingsley Clarke, April 2, 2006; and Janeen Porter, September 18, 2006.

53. See Noel Ignatiev and John Garvey, eds., *Race Traitor* (New York: Routledge, 1996). Additional content from the journal *Race Traitor* is available on the internet at http://racetraitor.org/. Ignatiev's analysis of whiteness is also reflected in his historical monograph, *How the Irish Became White* (New York: Routledge, 1995). Relevant writings on fascism and antifascism produced by former members of STO include Don Hamerquist et al., *Confronting Fascism: Discussion Documents for a Militant Movement*, (Chicago and Montreal: Arsenal, Anti-Racist Action and Kersplebedeb, 2002); and Leonard Zeskind, *Blood and Politics: The History of the White Nationalist Movement from the Margins to the Mainstream* (New York: Farrar, Straus and Giroux, 2009). More recent writings by Hamerquist on a range of topics can be found on the blog "Three Way Fight" at http://threewayfight.blogspot.com/.

54. Brief mentions of the group appear in Paul Buhle, ed., *CLR James: His Life and Work* (London: Allison & Busby, 1986); Elbaum, *Revolution in the Air*; and Martin Glaberman, ed., *Marxism for Our Times: CLR James on Revolutionary Organization* (Jackson: University Press of Mississippi, 1999).

PART THREE

Community

9

Play as World-making

From the Cockettes to the Germs, Gay Liberation to DIY Community Building

BENJAMIN SHEPARD

Years before gay liberation, sex was recognized as "play"—especially when practiced for connection and pleasure rather than procreation or productivity.[1] Yet it was queer organizers who turned the struggle for a place to play into a living and breathing work of art. The modern gay liberation movement has its roots in mid-1960s disruptions at Compton's Cafeteria in San Francisco, the Black Cat Bar in Los Angeles, and the 1969 riots at the Stonewall Inn in New York. These watershed moments were followed by challenges to sodomy laws, psychiatric classifications, and public mores around pleasure. By the 1970s, the gay liberation movement was dynamic and vast.[2] It embraced an organizing ethos that, while patently militant, eschewed physical confrontation with the state in favor of creative and colorful, visionary and vibrant expressions of an alternative political reality. Tactics ranging from drag performances to underground dance parties and musical gatherings were enlisted to build community while challenging society's gender norms, sexual rigidity, and penchant for monoculture. The politics of play would propel the gay liberation movement and other cultural practices including radical street performance, performance art, do-it-yourself (DIY) culture, and punk.[3] A spirit of liberatory play coursed through these movements, infusing pleasure and fun into world-making practices supporting social and sexual freedom as well as cultural resistance.

This chapter considers the historic trajectory of play and its manifestations within gay liberation organizing as well as cultural activism and politics. Explorations of play in DIY performance groups the Cockettes and the Germs, as well as early gay liberation organizing, serve as exemplars. While the politics of play has roots dating back to the Dada, Surrealist, Situationist, and Beat movements, play found a distinct social and cultural manifestation in the early days of gay liberation and DIY politics throughout the 1970s.[4] Here, play's contrast with work and drudgery manifested itself in cultural and political projects organized around community building and the possibility of creating cultural space outside

177

of a capitalist bottom line.[5] And for a short while, play subverted a system rather than supported it.

From Riots to Rhinestones

Notions of play interact magnetically with efforts focused on emancipation, pleasure, social protest, and pluralistic democracy. In the months after the riots outside the Democratic National Convention in 1968, many questioned the tenor of the protests. In a 1969 interview for *Playboy* magazine on the counterculture, the poet Allen Ginsberg addressed the limitations of militant confrontation.[6] He ruminated about the possibility of a different outcome in Chicago in 1968, had collective energies focused on creating an orgy of activism rather than on a riot. For Ginsberg, dance and play, yoga and street theater, chanting and singing could serve as alternatives to the street violence of 1968. In the face of massive police repression, Ginsberg regretted that there was less of an effort to speak to a generative spirit. "Now, nobody got naked in Chicago, but the few times there was communal chanting of mantras, that proved helpful."[7] Rather than a "morbid" uniformity, Ginsberg called for a reinvigorating "theatricality of disorder" and pleasure capable of cultivating a truly pluralistic democracy built on a respect for both difference and pleasure. In part, he was talking about a form of community building that focused on affect rather than rational ends, with an aim toward a new democracy of pleasure. Herein, democratic ideals, including pursuit of happiness, found their expression in a movement built on respect for queer difference, rather than the bland same.

In the months and years to come, the nation would increasingly come to know what Ginsberg was talking about. His flights of fancy offer a narrative trajectory for what gay liberation activism would look like. His musings reflected a growing movement at the time, involving a new cohort of social actors looking to the politics of play as an alternative to violent confrontation. For Ginsberg, playing with power would be far more appealing than overwhelming others or violating Gandhi's principle of nonviolence, as others were contemplating.[8] Only months after this interview, Ginsberg stumbled upon riots taking place outside the Stonewall Inn in Greenwich Village in New York City. Queers formed kick lines to dance and thwart the police, and the message of gay liberation was heard around the world. They were playing with power in much the same way he had imagined in the *Playboy* interview. "They've lost that sad look," Ginsberg would declare exultantly of the newly liberated protesters.[9]

Out of the ashes of the Old (and New) Left, gay liberation would stress the defense of pleasure as a valid aspect of its agenda. For Ginsberg, whose breakthrough 1955 poem *Howl* celebrated those who "screamed for joy" while "being fucked in the ass by saintly motorcyclists," queer politics rejected the politics of prohibition in favor of the politics of pleasure, authenticity, and social connection.[10] Play and pleasure, resulting in social connection, would be central to the gatherings of a new tribe that shaped the gay liberation movement in the 1970s.[11]

While gay liberationists embraced the politics of pleasure and play, the practice and philosophy behind it was nothing new. Herbert Marcuse wrote about it; Beat movement writers, Yippies, and Situationists famously practiced it—turning pranks into a work of art.[12] The Yippies made use of absurdist parodies and humor as a tactic to protest the Vietnam War. Notable examples of Situationist pranks included disrupting Easter high mass at Notre Dame Cathedral in Paris some four decades before ACT UP New York's foray into Saint Patrick's Cathedral in 1989.[13] Rejecting notions of work and social hierarchy, the Situationists put a premium on free expression, play, and sexual liberation. The philosophy was best embodied within the calls for exalting imagination and desire during the 1968 mass strikes in Paris. Two U.S. journalists witnessed the scene. "This very widespread revolt against the old forms of established authority was accompanied by an acute and profoundly enjoyable sense of liberation," Patrick Seale and Maureen McConville wrote. "All sorts of people felt it in all walks of life. A great gust of fresh air blew through dusty minds and offices and bureaucratic structures."[14]

Building on these traditions, gay liberationists helped fashion an entire movement based on the political efficacy of play in action. Many of those who had been involved with antiwar and civil rights organizing helped realize such a notion. No social actor better embodies the practice than Hibiscus, a.k.a. George Harris III, who moved to San Francisco during the Summer of Love in 1967. Once Harris was there, his political work grew, albeit in a distinctly "only in San Francisco" fashion. He changed his name to Hibiscus and took on a new identity as queer artist and drag performer. On December 31, 1969, he helped form the drag performance group the Cockettes—"a hippie, glitter, genderfuck troop."[15] In many ways, Harris's life would take on the dimensions of a work of art. His story offers a telling chapter in the early history of the politics of play and counterculture movement. Themes of pleasure and possibility, politics and DIY world-making characterize the tragicomic story of Harris's years as a Cockette.

Jesus with Lipstick

Before joining the Cockettes, Hibiscus had lived his life as George Harris III, a privileged resident of Westchester County, New York, who became an actor and then a political pacifist. He recognized the possibilities of activist performance well before he formed the Cockettes. This distinct disposition toward performance was on hand during his drive out West in 1967 with Allen Ginsberg's lover Peter Orlovsky. Before heading west, Harris and company attended an antiwar rally. There, Harris helped create one of the most enduring images of the Vietnam War as he placed a flower in the rifle of a national guardsman. The contrast between the well-coifed, preppy flower child, with well-trimmed bob and roll-neck sweater, and the rigid soldier was captured in a 1967 *Time* magazine photo.[16]

Once in San Francisco, Harris joined the Kaliflower commune, a collective on Sutter Street founded by Beat author Irving Rosenthal, a friend of Allen Ginsberg. Images of 1940s movie icons torn from library books, Vaseline, beads, glitter, and fabrics adorned his incense-filled room. Constantly on LSD, Harris lived an experience that ebbed and flowed between San Francisco street life, magical reality, and 1940s black-and-white celluloid. He grew a beard, threw out his khakis, strung beads in his hair, pierced his nose, and renamed himself Hibiscus. Walking the streets of San Francisco barefoot, clad in skirts culled from garbage bags, remainder bins, thrift shops, and leftover piles—"waste of a culture"—Hibiscus aspired to the life of an angel. Other Cockettes said he looked like "Jesus Christ with lipstick."[17]

Hibiscus's Kaliflower commune organized itself around the ambition to disseminate free art, food, and theater throughout the city. Like the San Francisco Diggers, members of Kaliflower busied themselves with efforts to create a new morality through the simple gesture of dispensing free food and flowers. "There was a powerful new force in the air as one walked down Haight Street and saw people giving away flowers, fruits and candies," wrote one observer.[18] Such a practice was not new. Between their participation in the Beat and hippie countercultures, queer activists had long grappled with an anticapitalist humanist politics. "When I was young the split was more between the grubby, beatnik open hearted . . ." and "the monopolistic queens, say, who had privilege and money," Allen Ginsberg explained in an interview with *Gay Sunshine*, a San Francisco literary journal. For Ginsberg, queer politics had long involved a struggle "between the cold hearted and the warm hearted."[19]

Hibiscus chose to live his life with the financial and social have-nots. In the years before the Cockettes officially became a performance troupe, Hibiscus spent days in Golden Gate Park, sitting naked in the trees, singing show tunes and inviting people into his possibility, to play within the panorama of his nether-reality. It was there that future Cockette Pam Tent happened upon him. "Join us," Tent recalled him gesturing to her, with a delightfully naïve, messianic disposition. So, like many others, she started singing along and was soon a regular part of the performances in the park.[20]

On the final night of the decade, Hibiscus invited his new friends from the park to share a dinner of rice and vegetables and a bottle of wine with his commune. There he announced he'd been invited to perform at the Nocturnal Dream Show, an experimental midnight movie event, at the Palace Theatre in San Francisco's North Beach. Hibiscus proposed that the group take their impromptu performances and transform them into "a new theater for a new decade." "But what do we call it?" Hibiscus asked the group. "Something like the Rockettes?" "No, the Cockettes," another Kaliflower member responded immediately. That was already on everyone's mind, anyway. And the Cockettes were born. Irving Rosenthal, the founder/den mother of Kaliflower, kept a drag room filled with gills and boas and petticoats. Ralph, another commune member, had a key and let everyone in. So Hibiscus and company raided the stash of old 1940s dresses, costumes, and finery. And the company primped and prepped themselves with whatever dresses, gowns, and glitter they could find strewn between the Vaseline, assorted linens, and clutter among the commune on Sutter Street.[21] The 1970s had arrived.

Dosed with LSD and dressed in genderfuck—men with beards in women's clothing—this group of men, along with women and even a few children, stumbled onstage for their impromptu clothing-optional midnight performance to the tune of "Can-Can." And they started dancing. A kick-line formed. "Jumpin' Jack Flash" and "Honky Tonk Woman" followed. Galvanized by the ridiculousness of the semi-clad liberatory theater, the crowd roared for more. Not having a second act, the Cockettes simply performed "Honky Tonk Woman" again, and the rest of the audience leaped onstage to reprise their quasi-nude kick line, many without clothes. The lines between audience and performer, reality and theater, dissolved. More enthusiastic than polished, the Cockettes' romp radiated spontaneous joy—both hopeful and tantalizing—and unofficial play.[22]

Fun was the primary goal of the Cockettes' performance in living. Most of the group assumed the New Year's midnight show was a simple, spontaneous moment, not a plan for a new liberatory theater. Yet, between the kick line and the standing ovation, something changed. "I thought it was a one time deal," Scrumbly, one of the performers, recalled. "The audience reaction made us think again."[23]

Despite the 1940s retro glamour, the Cockettes show embraced the iconoclastic politics of a new kind of play. Troupe members built on their intuitive sense that the most formal of performances was merely a rehearsal, while the rehearsal was always a performance. This play element was not always understood or appreciated, particularly when the Cockettes performed to New York audiences expecting polish and professionalism. Yet disorder was exactly the point for the Cockettes, who were born, lived, and thrived within the ludic politics of play, as opposed to work and professional development. Between dancing and doing what they knew, an authentic politics of play took shape as a rejection of form, in favor of a new form of spectacle that night at the Palace.[24]

To the basic ingredients of faded Hollywood glamour, the Cockettes added the elements of San Francisco gay counterculture: flower power, drag, communal living, and camp. This mix created an exuberant, even anarchistic, anticapitalist queer sensibility. "The weirdest thing about the Cockettes was that they were Communist drag queens," recalled filmmaker John Waters, whose muse Divine later performed with the Cockettes. "Bearded, transvestite, drug crazed, hippie Communists."[25]

By the second Cockettes performance in February 1970, the drag room at Kaliflower Collective was rendered off-limits. So the Cockettes resorted to thrift shops for their costumes. For most of the group, these consisted of makeshift 1940s gowns, adornments of feathers glued to cardboard, sparkles, and glitter.

Different shows had different themes from the old 1940s musicals, all with little to no rehearsal or preparation. Glitter compensated for a lot. And the style had made its mark. Allen Ginsberg, who was dating Hibiscus at the time, became all too familiar with the trails of Cockette glitter. "His bed was a little gritty because he had a lot of it. And it was difficult to sleep on the sheets because there was this sort of like difficult glitter stuff there. And it was always in our lips and in our butt-holes. You know it was always around. You couldn't quite get it out."[26]

Throughout 1970, Cockettes shows drew legions. Yet, when the Palace started charging entrance fees for Cockettes shows, Hibiscus revolted. Ever an advocate of play over professionalism, rather than profits over people, he opened the back door of the Palace for performances so fans without money could attend. Play has to be free, after all.[27] Hibiscus temporarily left the group to form a new company called the Angels of Light, though he rejoined not long after leaving.

For Hibiscus and the Cockettes, the combination of play and performance offered a portal to a new kind of living. Entry to this new world required rejecting monoculture, militarism, and a system that perpetuated sexism, racism, and homophobia. Cockettes shows rejected a linear logic, a de facto revolt against ruthless reality in favor of hazy fantasy.[28]

As the shows became more elaborate, Cockettes performances presaged the extreme costume balls which were to be an element of protests three and four decades later by theatrical direct-action groups for global justice, such as the Billionaires for Bush, the Absurd Response to an Absurd War, the Clandestine Insurgent Rebel Clown Army, and even San Francisco's Gay Shame. "It [Gay Shame] combined the performative qualities of the Cockettes with the ambition to reclaim public space of RTS [Reclaim the Streets] and the militancy of early ACT UP," San Francisco activist Mattilda explained in a 2006 interview with the author.[29]

The aim of this playful theatricality would be to create a brand of protest that merged the joyous, ecstatic spirit of exhilarating entertainment with social activism. Within this festive, revolutionary theater, progressive elements of political change would be linked with notions of social renewal, enticing specta-tors to join not only the performance but the movement. Spectacle ultimately sparked seismic shifts in people's lives. Party as protest was an invitation to a possibility.[30]

The politics of gay liberation during the early 1970s was about a social eros as much as it was about physical eros. Unlike physical eros, social eros represented a connection among spirits moving through a group. Such a connection among souls, as well as bodies, contributed to the sense of profound optimism; Hibiscus's theater for a new decade helped mark the beginnings of a new social reality. Without didactics, this theater served as a call to dismantle sexuality hierarchies, smash patriarchy, and unleash a new model for sexual relations. "Liberation of emotion between men would also lead to a liberation or straightening out of relations between men and women," Allen Ginsberg would explain.[31] Here,

Ginsberg alluded to more liberated models of social relations that reflected new democracies of self, sexuality, and citizenship.

"The very definition of things like gay was under suspicion at that point," recalls San Francisco music journalist Joel Selvin. "Pan-sexuality was what was going on. It was an adventure. It was an experiment. The Cockettes were really a part of that. Their gayness was less significant than their outrageousness."[32]

For Ginsberg, who performed with both the Cockettes and Hibiscus's Angels of Light, these shows functioned as an embodiment of the poetics he had championed since the earliest days of the Beat movement. The name Angels of Light is said to have been from Ginsberg's poem, "Angels of Light dancing by the River Ganges." This sense of pleasure and social eros was ever-present at their events. Ginsberg sang William Blake's *Songs of Innocence and of Experience* with the Cockettes.[33] "When we got on the stage and played together—communication between us got ecstatic and delirious," Ginsberg explained. "And it couldn't be withheld."[34] As far as Ginsberg was concerned, these performances were "part of the large scale spiritual liberation movement and reclamation of self from the homogenization of the military state."[35]

Play, Protest, and the Politics of Pleasure

Throughout the 1970s, queers helped fashion a highly creative approach to sex and sexual self-determination. This model stood in stark contrast to the historical understanding of sexuality in culture and social life. Until the movements for sexual freedom in the late 1960s and 1970s, much of sexuality resided in the private, not public, realm. Pleasure existed counter to social order—the pleasure principle versus the reality principle, as conceptualized by Sigmund Freud. Those who enjoyed pleasure were considered outside the realm of social order and normalcy.[36]

This view also permeates left-wing politics. "The left has not been there as advocates of pleasure in their organizing or their politics," long-term gay activist Eric Rofes explains.[37] In contrast, gay liberationists recognized the importance of pleasure as a vital part of social and political life. In so doing, they rejected Marxist notions that pleasure was a bourgeois indulgence.[38]

To this end, the movement sought to liberate not only queer sexuality, but sexuality in general. Instead of serving as a tool of production or an indicator of social status, sexuality was understood as something pleasurable and relational. Yet others did not see it this way. Throughout the early 1970s, veterans of homophile politics, such as Barbara Gittings, worked with members of Gay Activist Alliance and the Chicago Gay Liberation Front (GLF) to challenge the notion that homosexuality was an illness.[39] "From its outset, the gay liberation movement has identified the establishment of psychiatry as a basic institution involved in the oppression of homosexuals," declared a leaflet written by Chicago GLF for doctors attending the 1970 convention of the American Medical Association.[40] The leaflet called for doctors to reject links between homosexuality and illness. "Join us in the struggle for a world in which all human beings are free to love without fear or shame."[41] While the doctors did not join Chicago GLF, they did heed the call and purge the link between homosexuality and pathology.

Accompanying these struggles, cultural activists and sexual outlaws helped organize to make sense of—and incorporate—notions of play within both private and public spheres of life. The theatrics of Cockettes shows seemed to embody such an ethos. With the memory of Stonewall just a few months old, the Cockettes offered a theater of transgression, their shows performances in sexual liberation. "It was total sexual anarchy," John Waters would recall.[42] "From the very beginning everything was fun—a nice way to be together, be ourselves and do our bit for sexual freakdom," Scrumbly concurred. A distinct anti-authoritarian politics characterized their performances in living. "Anarchy ideally is a wonderful system. If it feels good, go along with the game. And it felt really good, it felt really right. We were having fun. We were getting more sex and meeting great people."[43] More than sexuality, the shows reveled in a hopeful and absurd view of politics.

The Cockettes' ludic disposition involved a distinct philosophical outlook. Their play helped highlight a differentiation between a "realm of necessity" and a "realm of freedom" in which imagination could thrive.[44] Rather than engaging with something, it involved "the play of life." Here, art and aesthetics offered a "manifestation of freedom itself."[45] Take Hibiscus's hallucinogenic life story, which blurred any number of lines between art, experience, and the surreal. "A bizarre morning here in San Francisco," he wrote in a letter home in 1968. "The wind howls as I howl. . . . I remember last night running through Chinatown, flowers and glittering red Chinese banners. I lay on the scaffold, like Christ on his cross, the sunshine, the stars, the moon. So strange to be living in up in the clouds . . . with the angels of light."[46] Such a view breaks down boundaries, while fashioning new forms of social experience, possibility, and world-making.

Ridiculous Dada Fun

Although the Cockettes broke up in 1972, their spirit continued through social and cultural practices, up and down the West Coast in particular. Throughout the 1970s, new stories and manifestations of play found their expression in countless cultural intersections and divergences from social or sexual classifications. A spirit of exploration weaves its way through this history. Members of the collective scattered after the Cockettes project ended, helping spread their defiantly absurd ethos. One former Cockette, Tomata Du Plenty, carried on with the vagabond life, drifting from New York to Seattle to Los Angeles, where he became part of the burgeoning Los Angeles punk scene. There, many of the bands borrowed from the Cockettes' DIY approach to performance. The aim was more to create a liberatory spectacle, not play the proper notes.[47] And like the Cockettes' earlier performances, those punk shows left their mark on the lives of many who saw them.

Don Bolles was an avant-garde drummer who moved to Los Angeles in 1977 to join one of the new punk bands, the Germs. He viewed the band's whole ethos as one of "ridiculous Dada fun." With most every gig, the point was to create an almost "wholesome spectacle." Rather than being musical events, Germs concerts were like "Sufi whirling dervishes."[48] "The Germs were not just about 'music,' " Bolles writes. "Music was our front, but we were dealing in something a lot more elemental, although it was rarely articulated."[49] These concerts built on a spirit of play that was far from serious, yet deeply engaging. Blurring the line between fan and performer, their shows cultivated a highly participatory, nonsensical atmosphere.

The band's origins begin within a series of ludic ambitions. They met by just playing around. "Queen was staying at the Beverly Hilton, and we'd met them in the lobby the day before," Pat Smear, the band's guitar player, recalled. "The next day we went back and we were hanging around the pool watching Freddie [Mercury] on his balcony. . . . We snuck into the room below Freddie's and [Darby Crash] tried to climb the balcony to get into his room, but couldn't." While the groupies did not get into the glam icon's boudoir, they did make a few lasting connections. "We met those two girls from the Valley, total twins, with matching poodle haircuts," Smear remembered. "They gave us a ride home."[50] Kindred spirits Pat Smear, Darby Crash, Lorna Doom, and Belinda Carlisle started hanging out. And they went on to form the Germs.

"We made T-shirts with iron-on letters that said THE GERMS in front, and AFTER YOU on the back," Pat Smear explained. "We were a band long before Lorna even had a bass. We'd make posters and put them around town, not for gigs, just to advertise the band."[51] They could not play, but that was not the point. The driving approach to the project was a cultural ethos used to create music and build community with whatever resources were available. The do-it-yourself core of punk philosophy, doing what you can with what you've got, fueled the Germs.[52] "The LA scene completely took over the musical life of the city for a while—and the people who were part of it in whatever capacity know the kind of hard-won pride that comes from building something from nothing," recalls Don Snowden, a music journalist who covered Los Angeles punk.[53]

"Punk was not just a music, it was an attitude, an ethic, and a sense of community," cultural critic and activist Stephen Duncombe writes. "It allows for the nuances and variations that necessarily arise through the practices of punks doing-it-themselves as they rebel against local powers."[54]

"There was a nascent thing beginning, this vibe in the air, and we knew it wasn't about jocks vs. 'goody-goods'; it was about something subversive. And it was very young," explains Will Amato, a Los Angeles music writer and high-school buddy of the Germs' singer Darby Crash.[55] The Beatles and hippie culture were over. David Bowie's album *Ziggy Stardust and the Spiders from Mars* had captivated a new generation. "It's like homosexual pornography," Amato thought when he first heard it. "But then the texture of Ronson's guitars came out of the speakers, a very manly guitar sound—it really was like a weird drug, you know?"[56]

The name the Germs signified the beginning, the germ of a new idea.[57] The early Germs gigs functioned in much the same way as the first Cockettes shows had. "We just did it, got off stage, took a little more LSD, and went out for food," one of the early Cockettes described their first show at the Palace.[58] Most nights, everyone at Germs shows would meet at Danny's Oki Dog, a fast-food restaurant on Santa Monica Boulevard, after the show.[59] Implicit was the pleasure of playing with an alternate reality with utter engagement, although not being that serious about it.[60] Like the Cockettes shows, the Germs shows interacted vitally with the audience. "Everyone on stage!" Crash screamed, gesturing to the audience in a typical 1979 performance.[61] Between stage dives and Oki Dogs, a community and a scene took shape.

The Germs clearly embodied a DIY ethos that permeated countless social and cultural movements throughout the era.[62] Through DIY social and cultural politics, activists created different kinds of spaces for democratic engagement through embodied, community-building approaches. The point was to cultivate alternate spaces with whatever tools one had. Within such spaces, use was valued over commercial exchange. Participants played with new social realities, creating a space for life, reflection, and pleasure outside of commerce. "DIY as a form of activity creates value outside of capitalism," the authors of "Do It Yourself . . . and the Movement Beyond Capitalism," argue.[63] For Don Bolles, the Germs "was like a total amphetamine mania and psychotic mass breakdowns of the Third Reich, except a lot more fun and without the bloodshed."[64]

As with much of the early punk, the effort was to challenge social, cultural, and even sexual norms.[65] Throughout their first shows, the Germs performances retained a frivolous, playful quality. "When the Germs first started they had a sense of humor to it that made it fun. They were huge Bowie and Iggy fans who first started in the garage with the name Sophistifuck and the Revlon Spam Queens. You couldn't get much more vulgar glam than that," Chris Ashford, an early Germs fan recalled, in a tacit reference to the band's distinctly queer and bountiful wanderlust. "They were the Revlon Spam Queens for at least four or five months during late '76, early '77. They were still in school, and they didn't play at all, they just had matching T-shirts."[66]

"I never knew whether Darby was gay or not. All I remember is that all the girls wanted to sleep with him and didn't get to," Germs guitarist Pat Smear remembered.[67] Still, the lyrics to their first single, "Sex Boy," read like a celebration of polymorphous sexuality. "Every day it's the same, a dozen boys are on my scene," Crash sang.[68] While Crash went as far as recruiting his boyfriend to play drums for the band, sexual ambivalence was always part of the band's anarcho-punk aesthetic.

The Germs were not the only early punk band to embody queer outsider sensibilities. Many of the early punk bands helped create this. While few were particularly conscious about it, the movement was fueled by burning ambitions to challenge social norms in broad, even terms of social struggle. The Dead

Kennedys' influential album *Fresh Fruit for Rotting Vegetables* features a photo of police cars that had been burned during the 1979 riots after the unjustly lenient verdict for Dan White, the former policeman turned city supervisor who murdered Harvey Milk, the San Francisco City Council member and first openly gay man elected to public office in the United States.[69] Many compared the White Night Riots to the events outside the Stonewall Inn some ten years prior.[70] All over California, queer politics and punk overlapped, contributing to and reflecting tumultuous changes in the social landscape. In solidarity with the emerging community surrounding the Germs, Crash supported queer activists in their boycott of the 1979 film *Cruising* for its denigration of leather and S/M subcultures, even though the Germs had contributed to the movie's soundtrack.[71]

As the burning of police cars on the Dead Kennedys album cover suggests, punk overlapped with movement aspirations to change the rules of who played when, under what terms, for how much, and why. Germs shows thrived in the liminal, anarchistic space between performance and violence, destruction and creation.[72] When Germs shows lacked this tension, Crash sought to shift the dynamic. "You guys, you've not having any fun, do damage," Crash implored the audience during another show at the Whisky A Go Go in 1979. "Do damage!" he cried, over and over.[73]

For a while in the 1970s, punk shows conveyed the hopeful ambition that the movement could dismantle a reified world and create something better in its wake. "There was something undeniable about this bunch of losers, an almost giddy feeling of danger, like absolutely anything could happen at their shows," Bolles later recalled. "Somehow this bunch of ridiculous, bratty no-talents could turn any venue that would have them into a total chaos vortex, and anyone could feel it."[74] For the Germs, play arose through a bountiful shift in the possibilities and altered parameters of urban performance. Each gesture at creating something new seemed to be followed by forces of inertia pushing backward. Play was always emphasized over polished performance.

"Whattya wanna hear?" Crash asked the audience during a July 17, 1979, show. The band was playing for gratis in restitution for a window Crash had broken during their previous show at the venue. Shifting the line between audience and performers, concert and carnival, he asked the crowd: "Do you know any songs? Pretend you're at a party. Gimme some beer!"[75]

In the 1970s, punk represented a space for competing social and aesthetic sensibilities. By the end of the decade, the movement's liberationist ethos was forced to contend with a reactionary backlash that included the subcultures of racist skinheads and Nazi punks. Penelope Spheeris captures much of this tension in her 1981 documentary on the scene, *The Decline of Western Civilization*.[76] The film includes Black Flag, Fear, and the fey Darby Crash and his bandmates hanging out and performing. Spheeris contrasts both the misogyny of Lee Ving and his band Fear with the naïve, amateur disposition of the Germs. Compared to Ving, Crash looks practically dandy. Throughout the documentary footage, one gets the sinking feeling that the queerness of the Germs was slowly being consumed within the hardcore turn in the movement and the decade to follow. Many of these conflicts shaped a debate that took place in the DIY public commons that punk helped create. These ideas were hashed out in the Los Angeles streets, graffiti, squats, alternative concert venues, and fanzines written by and for participants of the scene.[77]

In Los Angeles, the scene was characterized by distinct tragicomic dimensions embodied within the highly physical, theatrical, and participatory nature of punk shows. Part of the play of punk shows was the risk and release of the dance. Like much of the play in aesthetic and political experience, this performance blurred the line between spectator and performer. At most shows, audience members engaged in a highly ritualized performance of leaping from the stage onto the convulsing bodies of those "slam dancing" or "pogoing." They hurled their bodies both vertically and horizontally into the air and at each other as the show took place. Historian of play Johan Huizinga suggests that such play is characterized by both anxiety and release.[78] Highly connected, a sweaty social eros took hold as sweaty bodies dance and perspire, bleed and lunge into each other. All the while, everyone depends on one another to keep anyone from falling onto the floor. Diving from the stage into the crowd, one immediately feels a group of hands pushing oneself upward, holding, supporting, tossing one through the hands, into the air, out of danger. "There was a new sense of kinship there," notes Perry Farrell, the founder of Jane's Addiction, an iconic post-punk Los Angeles band with a distinctly queer disposition. "Even with . . . the violence so heavy you could taste it on your tongue, everybody was in it together, and they'd better help one another out. Because no one else was going to."[79]

The Germs had mastered this performance. "The spectacle of Germs shows is suicide magnetic," Will Amato wrote in 1979. "Their white noise version of black death was ring mastered by DC [Darby Crash] who barked out incoherent tirades to exhort the crowd into frenzy."[80] Throughout 1980, Crash agitated for his boyfriend to become the new drummer for the Germs. Crash left for London to hang out with rocker Adam Ant and asked Pat and Lorna to teach the new drummer to play. The Germs' manager quit in April, and the band ran out of gas. In many respects, the Germs story can serve as a case study on play as cultural resistance. It aptly captures both the DIY possibilities as well as the limits of the model. Isolated from more coherent strategies of social change, such cultural politics are reduced to subcultural social activities, their larger efficacy diminished.[81]

As Crash became more and more lost, he became incapable of speaking outside of his subculture. Over time, the band's approach to play took a darker quality. "Everybody's talking about politics and what's going to work and what's not going to work. None of it's going to work," Crash would explain, his once ludic voice reduced to a Macbeth-like sound-and-fury dimension. "It's just a big game . . . either you play my game or you get to play their game, and if you play their game . . . their game's going out."[82] The Germs performed for a legendary four years, offering a blurring of social and sexual boundaries, a will to power and a rejection of monoculture, before they got lost in the fog of their own creation.[83]

Play, Pleasure, and Memory

Crash was a David Bowie fan, and "Five Years," from *Ziggy Stardust and the Spiders from Mars*, was his favorite Bowie song. Friends recalled that in 1975, Crash would say he had just five years to live, just like the song. Much like Hibiscus, Crash infused his life with a messianic death wish. Yet, instead of fashioning himself as Christ on a cross, as Hibiscus had with the Angels of Light shows, Crash built his life around Bowie's glam fantasy of Ziggy Stardust. "That's how he had all those girls weeping onstage 'cause they knew he was gonna die," recalled Geza X, a friend and member of the Mommymen, another Los Angeles band at the time.[84]

The final Germs gig was on December 3, 1980. Don Bowles came back to play the goodbye gig with the band. He remembers it as one of their best. Many do. After most Germs shows, no matter how terrible, most in attendance would converge at the Oki Dog. "The Germs and their fans were known to frequent this establishment, and on just about any night you could watch them give themselves the famous Germs Burn—a cigarette burn on the wrist," remembered Fred Patterson, a writer for the punk magazine *Slash*.[85] And this gig was supposed to be no different. Yet it was a rainy night, and few made it to the restaurant besides Crash. Watching his scene, and the connection to others it represented, seem to fade out, Crash despaired.

His friend Casey Cola was with him four nights later:

Darby and I had been doing consistent drugs for about a month and a half. We'd really been trying to put our lives together. Everything was fucking up with our plan. . . . We looked around the courtyard of the Hong Kong and said, "Man, fuck it, let's do it. Fuck this shit, its not gonna ever change, its not gonna get better. Its going to go on and on, we're going to be doing this same shit next year." We talked about whether we could get enough drugs, and that if he hit me up it wouldn't be murder—I can't do myself, because I have a manual dexterity problem. We were each asking, "Are you sure? Are you sure?" He didn't coerce me, and I didn't talk him into it. We never talked each other into anything. I didn't make Darby die. I got water and a spoon. He wrote a note, which he didn't show me, but which I think said, "My life, my leather, and my love goes to Bosco." He hit me up first and said, "Are you okay?" and I said, "Um, yeah." He put his hand at the small of my back and he said, "Just hold it, just stay there, just wait for me, okay?" He held me up for a second, then he hit a vein and laid himself against the wall and pulled me into him. It was almost like he forgot what we were doing, and he goes, "Wait a minute." And he kissed me and said, "Well bye."[86]

Crash died the morning of December 7, 1980. Rumors abounded. At first, some suggested he had died as part of the losing end of a barbiturate-eating contest. The full narrative of his death only took shape in bits and pieces. The day after his passing, John Lennon was shot outside the Dakota apartment building in New York. Their near-simultaneous deaths marked a synchronistic intersection as the story of a leader of life on the fringe overlapped with the departure of a man who had conceptualized political struggle as a battle between Blue Meanies and those who hoped to sing. Lennon recognized the futility of "flower power" and kept going; Crash saw his struggle against mono-culture as a battle against oblivion and jettisoned himself out of this world. Though the punks and hippies rarely saw themselves as engaged in a joint project, both Lennon and Crash reimagined social experience through play and per-formance, protest and aesthetics. By the 1990s, other punks recognized that these movements shared any number of common linkages in movements born of the generation of 1968.[87] All would contend with the limits and possibilities of their movements and the process that propelled them, eros and thanatos dueling it out. The passion to create included destructive dimensions as well as liberatory possibilities.[88]

While the Germs did not last, their influence has long been recognized as a distinct early chapter in the history of punk as a countercultural movement. Alumni of the Germs spread out through the music scenes of the next two decades. Don Bolles formed the influential goth band 45 Grave. The first Germs drummer, Belinda Carlisle, found fame as lead singer of the New Wave crossover band the Go-Go's. And Pat Smear went on to play guitar for the Seattle grunge band Nirvana. As a member, he witnessed another rock-and-roll suicide, with the death of frontman Kurt Cobain in 1994. Ever the resilient one, Pat Smear would go on join the Foo Fighters. The inspiration for the Germs, Queen singer Freddie Mercury, died of AIDS in the fall of 1991, bringing world attention to those with the virus. Many would remember the joyful, standout performance by the band at the Live Aid concert just five years earlier.

Hibiscus himself succumbed to the virus in 1983, one of the early AIDS deaths. "The article reporting his death in the *Village Voice* was the first time in print I saw the acronym 'AIDS,' followed by its then-obligatory parenthetical expansion, '(Acquired Immune Deficiency Syndrome),'" science-fiction writer Samuel Delany would recall.[89] The AIDS years marked a profound shift in our faith in, and under-standing of, the politics of pleasure.[90]

Mercury, Hibiscus, and Crash all made play and love an enticing political culture. The Cockettes shows were tantalizing social and cultural spaces. Listening to Queen, watching movies of the Cockettes, remembering Darby Crash—queer artists who seemed to embody the boundary-transgressing politics of play—it is easy to recognize the potency of the adage, "free your ass and your mind will follow." The endpoint of such politics is often liberation from pain, as well as liberation from isolation through innovation and community-building. But play comes with its paradoxes: joyous possibility arrives in tandem with the specter of penalty, harm, even death. But who can resist its siren song?

ACKNOWLEDGMENTS

The author would like to thank Jay Blotcher for his close reading and suggestions for this essay, Spencer Sunshine for his insights on connecting queer world-making with Los Angeles punk, and Stephen Duncombe for sending me his essay on punk and DIY culture.

NOTES

1. N. N. Foote, "Sex as Play," *Social Problems* 1 (1954): 159–163; John D'Emilio, "Capitalism and Gay Identity," in *The Lesbian and Gay Studies Reader*, ed. Henry Abelove, Michele Aina Barale, and David M. Halperin (New York: Routledge, 1993), 467–476.

2. Benjamin Shepard, *White Nights and Ascending Shadows: An Oral History of the San Francisco AIDS Epidemic* (London: Cassell Press, 1997); Susan Stryker and Jim Van Buskirk, *Gay by the Bay: A History of Queer Culture in the San Francisco Bay Area* (San Francisco: Chronicle Books, 1996); Don Teal, *The Gay Militants* (1971; rpt. New York: St. Martin's Press, 1995).

3. Stephen Duncombe, *Notes from Underground: Zines and the Politics of Alternative Culture* (New York: Verso, 1997); George McKay, "Notes Toward an Intro," in *DiY Culture: Party & Protest in Nineties Britain*, ed. George McKay (London: Verso, 1998).

4. Allen Ginsberg, interviewed by Allen Young, in *Gay Sunshine Interviews*, ed. Winston Leyland, vol. 1 (1973; rpt. San Francisco: Gay Sunshine Press, 1978). Benjamin Shepard, *Queer Political Performance and Protest: Play, Pleasure, and Social Movement* (New York: Routledge, 2009).

5. Roger Caillois, *Man, Play, and Games,* (New York: Schocken Books, 1979 [1958]).

6. Allen Ginsberg, interview by Paul Carroll, *spontaneous mind: Selected Interviews, 1958–1996* (New York: Perennial/HarperCollins, 2001).

7. Ginsberg, *spontaneous mind*, 183.

8. Jeremy Varon, *Bringing the War Home: The Weather Underground, the Red Army Faction, and Revolutionary Violence in the Sixties and Seventies* (Berkeley: University of California Press, 2004).

9. Teal, *Gay Militants.*

10. Allen Ginsberg, *Howl and Other Poems* (San Francisco: City Lights Press, 1956); Allen Ginsberg, *Gay Sunshine Interviews.*

11. Michel Maffesoli, *The Time of the Tribes: The Decline of Individualism in Mass Society* (Thousand Oaks, CA: Sage Press, 1996).

12. Herbert Marcuse, *Eros and Civilization: A Philosophical Inquiry into Freud* (New York: A Vintage Book, 1955). Re/Search, *Pranks! (Re/Search #11)* (San Francisco: Re/Search Publications, 1987).

13. Greil Marcus, *Lipstick Traces: A Secret History of the Twentieth Century* (Cambridge, MA: Harvard University Press, 1989); Shepard, *Queer Political Performance.*

14. Re/Search, "Pranks!" 176.

15. Joshua Gamson, *The Fabulous Sylvester: The Legend, the Music, the Seventies in San Francisco* (New York: Henry Holt and Company, 2005); Pam Tent, *Midnight at the Palace: My Life as a Fabulous Cockette* (Los Angeles: Alyson Books, 2004).

16. Gamson, *Fabulous Sylvester*; Tent, *Midnight at Palace.*

17. Gamson, *Fabulous Sylvester*; Pickupstricks, "The World's Leading Exponents of Sexual Role Confusion," available at http://www.pickupstricks.com/exponents.htm (accessed June 2, 2009).

18. Alex Forman, "San Francisco Style: The Diggers and the Love Revolution," *Anarchy* 7:7 (July 1967).

19. Ginsberg, *Gay Sunshine Interviews*, 109.

20. Tent, *Midnight at Palace.*

21. David Weissman and Bill Weber, *The Cockettes* (Los Angeles: Strand Releasing, 2002).

22. Tent, *Midnight at Palace*; Weissman and Weber, *The Cockettes.*

23. Tent, *Midnight at Palace*, 35.

24. Gamson, *Fabulous Sylvester*; Pickupstricks, "The World's Leading Exponents"; Tent, *Midnight at Palace.*

25. Gamson, *Fabulous Sylvester,* 49.

26. Tent, *Midnight at Palace*, 37.

27. Caillois, *Man, Play, and Games.*

28. Gamson, *Fabulous Sylvester.*

29. Shepard, *Queer Political Performance.*

30. Claudia Orenstein, *Festive Revolutions: The Politics of Popular Theater and the San Francisco Mime Troupe* (Jackson: University of Mississippi Press, 1998).

31. Ginsberg, *Gay Sunshine Interviews*, 105.

32. Gamson, *Fabulous Sylvester*, 55.

33. Pickupstricks, "The World's Leading Exponents."

34. Ginsberg, *Gay Sunshine Interviews*, 102.

35. Gamson, *Fabulous Sylvester*, 54.

36. Michael Bronski, *The Pleasure Principle: Sex, Backlash, and the Struggle for Gay Freedom* (New York: St. Martin's Press, 1998); Sigmund Freud, *Civilization and Its Discontents* (New York: W. W. Norton, 1961); Tina Takemoto, "The Melancholia of AIDS: Interview with Douglas Crimp," *Art Journal* 62:4 (Winter 2003): 81–90.

37. Shepard, *Queer Political Performance.*

38. Marshall Berman, *Adventures in Marxism* (New York: Verso, 1999).

39. Gary Alinder, "Gay Liberation Meets the Shrinks," in *Out of the Closet: Voices of Gay Liberation*, ed. Karla Jay and Allen Young (New York: New York University Press, 1972), 141–145.

40. Chicago Gay Liberation Front, "A Leaflet for the American Medical Association," in *Out of the Closet*, ed. Jay and Young, 145.

41. Ibid., 147.

42. Gamson, *Fabulous Sylvester*, 55.

43. Tent, *Midnight at Palace*, 18.

44. Herbert Marcuse, *An Essay on Liberation* (Boston: Beacon Press, 1969).

45. Marcuse, *Eros and Civilization*, 187.

46. Weissman and Weber, *The Cockettes.*

47. Marc Spitz and Brendan Mullen, *We Got the Neutron Bomb: The Untold Story of L.A. Punk* (New York: Three Rivers Press, 2001).

48. *Media Blitz: The Germs Story* (Cleopatra Records, 2004).

49. Brendan Mullen with Don Bolles and Adam Parfrey, *Lexicon Devil: The Fast Times and Short Life of Darby Crash and the Germs* (Los Angeles: Feral House, 2002), v.

50. Spitz and Mullen, *We Got the Neutron Bomb*, 67–68.

51. Ibid.

52. Craig O'Hara, *The Philosophy of Punk: More than Noise* (Oakland, CA: AK Press, 1999), 153–186.

53. Don Snowden, "You Should Get to Know Your Town," in *Make the Music Go Bang: The Early L.A. Punk Scene*, ed. Snowden (New York: Macmillan, 1997), 157.

54. Stephen Duncombe, "Punk and DIY Politics," undated manuscript in author's collection.

55. Mullen, *Lexicon Devil*, 7.

56. Ibid.

57. Spitz and Mullen, *We Got the Neutron Bomb*.

58. Gamson, *Fabulous Sylvester*, 54.

59. Mullen, *Lexicon Devil*.

60. Johan Huizinga, *Homo Ludens: A Study of the Play Element in Culture* (1938; rpt. Boston: Beacon Press, 1950).

61. Mullen, *Lexicon Devil*, 291.

62. George McKay, *Senseless Acts of Beauty: Cultures of Resistance Since the Sixties* (New York: Verso, 1996).

63. Benjamin Holtzman, Craig Hughes, and Kevin Van Meter, "Do It Yourself and the Movement Beyond Capitalism," in *Constituent Imagination: Militant Investigations, Collective Theorization*, ed. Stevphen Shukaitis and David Graeber with Erika Biddle (Oakland, CA: AK Press, 2007), 45.

64. Mullen, *Lexicon Devil*, v.

65. Peter Belsito and Bob Davis, *Hardcore California: A History of Punk and New Wave* (Berkeley: Last Gasp of San Francisco, 1983).

66. Spitz and Mullen, *We Got the Neutron Bomb*, 67–68.

67. Ibid., 136.

68. Ibid., 281.

69. Belsito and Davis, *Hardcore California*.

70. Shepard, *White Nights*.

71. Mullen, *Lexicon Devil*, 292.

72. Mikhail Bakhtin, *Rabelais and His World* (Bloomington: Indiana University Press, 1984).

73. *Media Blitz: The Germs Story*.

74. Mullen, *Lexicon Devil*, v.

75. Ibid., 291.

76. Penelope Spheeris, *The Decline of Western Civilization* (Los Angeles: Spheeris Films Inc., 1981).

77. Duncombe, *Notes from Underground*. Also see Stephen Duncombe, *Cultural Resistance Reader* (New York: Verso, 2002).

78. Huizinga, *Homo Ludens*.

79. Dave Thompson, *Perry Farrell: The Saga of a Hypester* (New York: St. Martin's Griffin, 1995), 24.

80. Ibid.

81. Duncombe, "Punk and DIY Politics."

82. Mullen, *Lexicon Devil*, 127.

83. Spheeris, *Decline of Western Civilization*.

84. Spitz and Mullen, *We Got the Neutron Bomb*, 271.

85. Fred "Phast Phreddie" Patterson, "Like Everything Else in Los Angeles, It Is Now a Mini Mall," in Snowden, *Make the Music Go Bang*, 31.

86. Spitz and Mullen, *We Got the Neutron Bomb*, 271–272.

87. Julian Temple, *Joe Strummer: The Future Is Unwritten* (London: Parallel Film Productions, 2007).

88. Bakhtin, *Rabelais and His World*; Freud, *Civilization and Its Discontents*; Richard Schechner, *Performance Studies: An Introduction* (New York: Routledge, 2002).

89. Samuel R. Delany, "Notes on *The Star-Pit*," available at http://www.pseudopodium.org/repress/TheStarPit/SamuelRDelany-NotesOnTheStarPit.html (accessed June 30, 2009).

90. Takemoto, *The Melancholia of AIDS*. Also see Shepard, *Queer Political Performance and Protest*.

10

"We Want Justice!"

Police Murder, Mexican American Community Response, and the Chicano Movement

BRIAN D. BEHNKEN

In August 1971, the National Chicano Moratorium Committee, the leading Mexican American anti–Vietnam War organization, dissolved in the wake of police harassment and brutality.[1] Much of this violence occurred in Los Angeles at the 1970 Chicano Moratorium March, where police killed journalist Ruben Salazar and two others, wounding many more. In May 1972, a Mexican American boycott against the public school system in Houston, Texas, fell apart after nearly three years of successful protest. At about the same time, the Los Angeles–based Brown Berets, perhaps the most militant symbol of the Chicano civil rights movement, succumbed to internal factionalism and disbanded. In late 1972, the Mexican American Youth Organization (MAYO), the Chicano corollary to the black freedom struggle's Student Nonviolent Coordinating Committee, dissolved to make way for a new organization, La Raza Unida Party (RUP). But RUP's tenure as a major Chicano movement organization proved short-lived. The party, suffering from internal divisions, voter intimidation, and electoral losses, was largely defunct by 1974.[2]

It is no small wonder why many historians and the lay public consider the early 1970s the end of the Chicano struggle for rights.[3] By 1972, Chicano activism in numerous local communities seemed to dissipate in the wake of government intimidation, internal bickering, and the conservative reaction to minority radicalism. The demise of so many heretofore vibrant organizations certainly makes this chronology appear accurate. But such a timeframe is inherently problematic for two reasons. First, scholars have largely created this chronology in order to neatly periodize a host of local social movements that occurred spontaneously and at irregular intervals. Thus, it is artificial. Second, and more simply, the Chicano movement did not end in 1972. Rather, in numerous locales it evolved into a more sophisticated and mature civil rights struggle. By examining Chicano responses to police murder, scholars can begin to appreciate this transformation. Across the United States, Mexican Americans suffered from persistent police intimidation, harassment, and violent death. With the Chicano movement, Mexican-descent people began to forcefully respond to police murder. As in the black freedom struggle, Mexican Americans reacted to police violence by working with local government agencies, by protesting, and, on occasion, by rioting.[4]

This chapter examines two instances of police murder in Texas. In 1973, a Dallas police officer executed twelve-year-old Santos Rodríguez. The Chicano community responded by forming a local self-defense unit, demanded that the city implement a police review board, and engaged in a massive march decrying police violence.[5] The march ultimately degenerated into a riot. In 1977, Houston police murdered twenty-three-year-old army veteran Jose "Joe" Campos Torres. Chicanos organized grievance committees, worked with the Houston Police Department to create an internal affairs office, and anxiously watched the trial of the officers responsible for Torres's death. When an all-white jury handed down guilty verdicts but sentenced only two police officers to one-year jail terms, the Mexican American community rioted. In both cities, Mexican Americans from all walks of life and all social classes participated in the demonstrations. While some Chicanos were affiliated with groups like the Dallas Brown Berets, Houston's People United to Fight Police Brutality, and the Revolutionary Communist Party—all radical leftist organizations—most did not identify with this brand of politics. Instead, they were concerned about civil rights, justice, and the inability of community members to protect the freedom of young people like Santos Rodríguez and Joe Campos Torres. By examining the Rodríguez and Torres cases, this chapter elucidates Chicano civil rights activism outside the timeframe that most scholars consider part of the Chicano movement. In so doing, I show that the Chicano movement, and the concept of *chicanismo*, continued well beyond 1972.

The Murder of Santos Rodríguez: Dallas, 1973

Dallas emerged as a major commercial center in the early twentieth century.[6] A distinctly southern metropolis, the city's racial climate was like that of other New South cities. But Dallas's Jim Crow system also extended to its small Mexican-origin population. Throughout much of the twentieth century, the city could claim a Mexican American population of about 5 percent, or approximately three thousand to five thousand people. In the 1950s, however, Mexican immigrants began arriving in greater numbers. By 1970, nearly one million people inhabited Dallas, and approximately forty thousand, or 8 percent, of these were Chicanos.[7] Mexican-origin people played a crucial role in the city's economic and cultural development, but their low status on the socioeconomic ladder meant that many social ills plagued the Mexican American community. The Chicano movement that developed in the late 1960s and early 1970s attempted to deal with these problems. The struggle in Dallas, while not as militant or as well-organized as the Chicano movement in other parts of the country, demonstrates the continued vitality of *chicanismo* after 1972. Indeed, the murder of Santos Rodríguez reinvigorated the movement in Dallas from 1973 to 1975.

Police violence was one of the issues that Chicano activists in Dallas attempted to combat. Outside of Dallas, the 1970 police murders of Dr. Fred E. Logan, Jr. (an Anglo physician beloved by the Chicano community in South Texas), Mario Benavides in Corpus Christi, Ruben Salazar in Los Angeles, and others reminded Mexican Americans that the police did not serve and protect their community. Problems came to a head in Dallas in 1971 when police wounded Tomas Rodriguez and his pregnant wife, Bertha. Police stormed the Rodriguezes' apartment searching for a murder suspect, shot the couple several times, and then arrested Tomas. The Dallas Police Department (DPD) later admitted that they had raided the wrong home. This situation outraged the Mexican American community. Chicanos held a number of rallies and marches to protest police violence, demanding that the city establish a police or civilian review board. They also organized a self-defense unit that they called the Brown Berets to act as an informal police review committee. The police eventually dropped all charges against Rodriguez. But the city enacted no civilian review board, and the police officers went unpunished. The results proved catastrophic.[8]

The inaction of local officials led to an incredibly disgusting example of white racism. On the night of July 24, 1973, DPD Officers Darrell Cain and Roy Arnold witnessed three individuals burglarizing a Fina gas station. A short foot chase ensued, but the culprits evaded the police. Although the suspects fled, the officers thought they recognized two of the robbers as brothers David and Santos Rodríguez. So Cain and Arnold drove to the Rodríguez home. The officers woke the boys' foster grandfather, Jose Minez, and demanded that he allow police to enter the small structure. Minez granted them access to his home, explaining later that "I was afraid. What could an old man do against their guns? I was afraid they would shoot me like they shot Tomas Rodriguez."[9] Cain and Arnold roused the sleeping brothers, handcuffed them, and placed them in their squad car. They then drove back to the gas station and parked at the rear of the facility. Out of sight and under cover of darkness, Cain and Arnold began interrogating the Rodríguez brothers.

David sat in the back seat with Arnold, while Cain sat with Santos in the front. The policemen pointed out a broken window at the gas station and asked the boys to admit their involvement in the burglary. They refused. In an attempt to coerce a confession, Cain began to play a game of Russian roulette with Santos. He withdrew his .357 magnum revolver and pressed it to Santos's head. Cain demanded that he confess. Santos refused, so Cain pulled the trigger. Nothing happened. "This time there's a bullet in there," Cain stated, "so you better confess." "Tell the truth, *hombre*," Arnold demanded from the back seat, "because he means it, this time he's going to shoot you." Officer Cain then pulled the trigger again. This time the gun discharged. Young David could only watch in horror as Cain blew his brother's brains out.[10]

After Santos Rodríguez's murder, events in Dallas progressed rapidly. The police department suspended Cain and Arnold. They also arrested Cain and charged him with murder, but he posted bond and was released. On July 26, Dallas residents learned that fingerprints taken from the gas station did not match those of the

Rodríguez brothers. Community leaders also discovered that Cain had killed an unarmed African American man named Michael Moorehead in 1970. This information infuriated the Mexican American community, because it suggested that Rodríguez's murder could have been prevented had the DPD removed Cain from the police force for killing Moorehead. That this did not happen indicated the stark difference between the value police placed on the lives of their own officers versus the value they placed on the lives of people in the communities they were charged to protect.[11]

Chicano leaders responded to this situation in several ways. First, the Dallas Brown Berets refocused their efforts on protecting the Chicano community from police abuse. Brothers Ricardo and Roberto Medrano, the sons of Dallas activist and labor leader Francisco "Pancho" Medrano, had formed the group after the shooting of Tomas and Bertha Rodriguez. They hoped the Brown Berets would act as an independent version of the never-established police review board. But after the murder of Santos Rodríguez, the group began to focus more explicitly on self-defense. Utilizing a confrontational but egalitarian message, the Brown Berets excoriated American tolerance of police violence and insisted that law enforcement be held accountable for its crimes. They spoke of Mexican American "*carnalismo*" (brotherhood) and unity, arguing that there was "power in togetherness." Promising to "keep a watchful eye on federal, state, city and private agencies which will deal with the Chicano, especially the law enforcement agencies," the Brown Berets vowed "to protect, guarantee, and serve the rights of the Chicano by 'All Means' necessary."[12]

At the same time, Pedro Aguirre, the lone Mexican American serving on the Dallas City Council, began to push the city to institute an internal affairs or police review board. Rene Martínez, another Chicano political leader and the head of Dallas's informal Tri-Ethnic Committee, also demanded that the city establish some form of police oversight commission. These leaders hoped that the city's political structure, which had moderated racial disputes in a forthright and judicious manner since the early 1960s, would fix problems within the police department.[13] Aside from the proposed police review board, Aguirre, Martínez, and others demanded the termination of Police Chief Frank Dyson. The city did nothing.[14]

Frustrated by the city's inaction, Pancho Medrano began organizing meetings with activists in the Mexican American and African American communities. He hoped to arrange a massive march to decry the murder of Rodríguez and, more generally, to protest police violence. He met with Aguirre, Martínez, his sons Roberto and Ricardo, the Reverend Rudy Sanchez (a popular Mexican American minister), George Allen (the only African American on the city council), and other leaders to plan for the protest.[15] Indeed, Medrano had previously organized a march after the shooting of Tomas and Bertha Rodriguez, and he envisioned a similar protest for the slain Santos.[16] Through unified direct action, he hoped to send a powerful message to city leaders that minorities would no longer tolerate police violence. Barely three days after the shooting, civic leaders finalized plans for a protest march to memorialize Santos Rodríguez and denounce police murder.

At noon on Saturday, July 28, 1973, the protest commenced with nearly two thousand Mexican Americans and a handful of African Americans. This group met at John F. Kennedy Plaza and marched peacefully through downtown Dallas to City Hall. There, Martínez, Aguirre, Rev. Rudy Sanchez, and others gave speeches. But a palpable anger hovered over the crowd of protesters. Sensing this tension, the various speakers began cutting their remarks short so the marchers could return to Kennedy Plaza. At approximately 1 P.M., the marchers began the return trek. A reporter asked Rene Martínez how he felt about the protest. "I believe it went well," he stated. "We're not trying to keep emotions down," he said, explaining why the speeches were cut short, "but [to] keep them in order." His optimism proved misplaced.[17]

Unbeknownst to Martínez, Aguirre, Medrano, and the other march organizers, another group of approximately five hundred activists had arrived late at Kennedy Plaza. Finding no march and no leaders, these activists assumed police had suppressed the protest. Angered, they began their own trek to City Hall. This new group met the original group of marchers about halfway to their destination. At this point, during the heat of the day, tensions began to flare. Police officers attempted to move the marchers back to Kennedy Plaza. In response, some of the Chicanos involved in the march began taunting the police, refused to return to Kennedy Plaza, and started marching back to City Hall instead. Once the group arrived, Aguirre climbed atop a parked patrol car and attempted to calm the marchers. But his microphone failed. At about the same time, an African American woman began yelling that the police had killed her son (a claim later proven false). The crowd erupted in violence.

The marchers attacked the police with bottles and rocks, beat several officers, and dispersed them. The crowd also jumped atop the patrol car Councilmember Aguirre had occupied and crumpled the roof and hood of the vehicle. The group then set fire to a police motorcycle. Shortly thereafter, protesters added a second police motorcycle to the pyre. The marchers also began breaking the windows of stores along Main Street. They ultimately looted more than forty businesses and destroyed anything of value in their path, including newspaper vending machines, mail boxes, and street signs. Many in the crowd shouted "We Want Justice!" "Brown Power!" and "We Want Cain!" They continued to taunt and attack police officers whenever they appeared.[18] After nearly an hour, tactical police reinforcements dressed in riot gear and gas masks arrived. Yet they could not stop the riot. Indeed, their efforts often deteriorated into personal skirmishes with individual rioters. Police attacked rioters; rioters attacked the police.[19]

The Dallas riot police ultimately restored order. Their presence seemed to stay many of the marchers/rioters. As the police fought with individual Chicanos, others escaped down side streets and away from downtown. By 5 P.M. the riot was over. The marchers had destroyed portions of Main Street. They left in their wake broken windows, wrecked cars and motorcycles, and burgled stores. Indeed, the marchers-turned-rioters singled out jewelry stores and department stores, taking merchandise and even mannequins. Five policemen were injured in the violence, along with several marchers. Police arrested thirty-six activists involved in the

"Dallas Disturbance," as the riot came to be known. But they released most of these individuals in the following days. Finally, in November, a jury found Darrell Cain guilty of murder and sentenced him to five years in prison.[20]

The Rodríguez incident remained an ugly blight on the city. So, too, was the riot, the only major racial conflagration in Dallas's history. The whole affair seemed to stun city leaders and local people, so much so that the shock actually helped calm the situation in Dallas. But Mexican American and African American desires for change did not end after the riot. Indeed, the communities continued to push the city to enact reforms. In late 1973, Councilmember Aguirre passed a city council resolution that decried the "unequal law enforcement, dual justice, and unequal treatment for the different segments of the community and different races in Dallas."[21] Throughout 1974 Chicano and black leaders continued to demand that the police department implement an internal affairs office, that DPD hire more minority officers, and that the department assign Chicano and black officers to minority neighborhoods. The police department attempted to assuage the community by hiring more black and Chicano officers. DPD also appointed its first minority deputy police chief in 1974. And the department officially began the operation of its own internal affairs office that same year. Throughout 1975, Chicanos continued to protest the murder of Rodríguez and the light sentence Cain had received. They pushed the federal government to investigate the murder. When the U.S. Justice Department declined to review the case in 1978, the campaign to secure justice for Rodríguez came to an end.[22]

The persistence of activism in Dallas after the riot, and the eventual victories activists won in overhauling the DPD, demonstrate the continued vitality of the Chicano movement after 1972. Indeed, Chicano activism in Dallas reached its height only after the murder of Santos Rodríguez. For local residents, this meant that not only did *chicanismo* persist after 1972, it actually increased during this period. And Dallas's populace would not soon forget the Rodríguez incident and the riot. The renowned Chicano poet Ricardo Sánchez memorialized Rodríguez in his poem, "Santos Rodríguez." Two folk songs, "Los Hermanitos Rodríguez" ("The Little Rodríguez Brothers") and "El Chicanito Sacrificado" ("The Martyred Little Chicano"), also narrate the tragic killing of Rodríguez. Finally, when immigrants' rights protests occurred throughout the United States in 2006, a number of pro-testers in Dallas recognized similarities between these demonstrations and the march on behalf of Rodríguez. Rene Martínez opined that the 1973 march "was a wake-up call for the city of Dallas. Some important and dramatic changes did take place after that, from police training to recruiting and many other things." He hoped the 2006 demonstrations would serve as a similar wakeup call.[23]

The Killing of Jose Campos Torres: Houston, 1977

The police murder of Joe Campos Torres in Houston roughly mirrored events in Dallas. Like Dallas, Houston emerged as a commercial nexus in the early twentieth century.[24] Nearby lumber, cattle, petrochemical, and cotton industries benefited from Houston's port and railroad shipping terminals. With economic growth came population growth. Increased immigration, especially Mexican immigration, resulted in the city breaking the one million inhabitants mark in 1961.[25] By 1970, the city's total population exceeded 1.2 million; Mexican Americans made up approximately 144,000, or 12 percent. Mexican Americans bolstered the city's economic, social, and cultural development, but the community experienced many social problems, none more pressing than police brutality. The vibrant Chicano movement that emerged in the late 1960s combated poverty, school segregation, and, most importantly, police murder. Houston's Chicano civil rights struggle, much like the movement in Dallas, remained largely a local phenomenon disconnected from other parts of the country. But this struggle once again demonstrates the persistency of *chicanismo* beyond 1972. Indeed, the movement in Houston spanned half of the 1960s and almost the entire decade of the 1970s. The murder of Torres initiated one of the most intense periods of protest during the Chicano movement there.

Members of the Houston Police Department (HPD) frequently clashed with ethnic minorities in the Bayou City. Numerous anti-police brutality protests had occurred in Houston throughout the 1970s, but most of these came to naught. Then came Jose "Joe" Campos Torres. The U.S. Army had discharged Torres in 1977. A veteran of the Vietnam War and a Houston native, he returned to his hometown shortly after his discharge. After recovering from a stomach ulcer, Torres began looking for work around the city, but evidently had some difficulty due to the economic slump of the late 1970s. He also began drinking heavily. On the night of May 6, Torres was allegedly involved in a fight at a local bar. Houston Police Officers Stephen Orlando and Terry Denson, who were later joined by officers Carless Elliott, Joseph Janish, and Louis Kinney, arrested Torres for drunk and disorderly conduct.[26]

Instead of escorting Torres to the city jail, however, Orlando and Denson drove him to a secluded area that police referred to as "the Hole." Police frequented the Hole to gossip, drink or take drugs, gratify themselves with local prostitutes, and interrogate, harass, or otherwise abuse suspects in custody. There, Denson, Orlando, and the other officers began beating Torres. After nearly an hour of punching and kicking him, they drove their bloody and bruised suspect to a precinct station. But the desk sergeant refused to allow the officers to book Torres and ordered them to take the battered man to the hospital. Instead, Denson and Orlando drove back to the Hole. The officers beat Torres again. They then drove him to a bridge over Buffalo Bayou, roughly extracted Torres from the back seat, removed his handcuffs, and pushed him to the edge of the bridge. Denson exclaimed, "Let's see if the wetback can swim." Then, he pushed the partially conscious Torres off the bridge and into the murky, stagnant water. Although Denson and Orlando claimed that they had watched Torres swim away, this statement proved a lie. Three days later a bystander spotted Torres's bloated body floating face down in the bayou.[27]

Local officials initially attempted to downplay this incident, but the sequence of events leading to Torres's death soon came to light. HPD fired the five officers involved in the murder and the state began preparing a grand jury investigation.[28] Ben T. Reyes, a prominent Chicano politician and one of the few Mexican Americans in the Texas legislature, immediately pressed for a national inquiry. Reyes wrote to Houston Mayor Fred Hofheinz, U.S. Attorney General Griffin Bell, and to U.S. Congressman Henry B. Gonzalez and Congresswoman Barbara Jordan, among others. Reyes demanded justice and promised that Mexican Americans "will not be content with a whitewash of this shocking case."[29] Most national leaders responded politely but declined to get involved. Instead, they awaited the outcome of the two officers' trial in Huntsville, a nearby community.[30]

Chicanos also waited, anxiously, for the outcome of the state trial. The prosecution of Denson and Orlando began in September 1977. Several shocking revelations came to light during the proceedings. First, rookie police officer Carless Elliott testified against Denson and Orlando. Although he did not witness the men push Torres into the bayou, Elliot claimed to have heard the splash as Torres fell into the water. Elliott explained his shock at the trial; "Oh my God," he claimed to have said to himself at that moment, "they've really thrown him in." He also admitted that the two officers had forced him to help destroy investigative notes taken while Torres was in custody.[31] Second, police officer Louis Kinney also testified against Orlando and Denson. He admitted beating Torres. Kinney stated that he, Denson, Orlando, and Elliott had all taken turns hitting and kicking Torres. Kinney gave further evidence as to the severity of Torres's bludgeoning. He reported that at one point during the beating, Orlando withdrew a flashlight and stated, "This is a brand new flashlight, and I want to try it out." "Then he [Orlando] hit him [Torres] four or five times hard on the shins," Kinney stated. After beating Torres, Kinney testified, Orlando said, "I've got this Mexican's blood on my hands. The jail probably won't take him and we'll have to spend all night out at Ben Taub's [the city's main charity hospital]." To avoid wasting time at the hospital, the officers chose instead to dump Torres into the bayou. Kinney admitted that he had feared the worst: "I bet that guy drowned," he testified to having thought. It seems likely that the other officers came to similar conclusions.[32] Finally, Harris County Medical Examiner Dr. Joseph Jachimczyk confirmed what many Houston residents already knew—that Torres did not have a chance of surviving once thrown into Buffalo Bayou. He testified that Torres was "twice drunk," from the alcohol and the beating. He also clarified the nature of the wounds on Torres's body: a cut leg, bruised wrists and hands, a wound to the temple, and a bruised abdomen. When asked if there was any way Torres could have survived the plunge into the bayou, Jachimczyk said, "I wouldn't bet on him making it."[33]

The jury deliberated for several weeks.[34] For many minorities, the results were hardly surprising. The jury convicted Denson and Orlando of negligent homicide, a misdemeanor. Their punishment: a two-thousand-dollar fine and one-year probated jail sentences. Despite the preponderance of evidence presented by the state, including the testimony of the HPD officers, the all-white jury ultimately concluded that sufficient evidence did not exist to convict the officers of a more severe crime. The punishment set the stage for prolonged protests from the Chicano community in Houston.[35]

Two women emerged as the most vocally militant leaders in the Mexican American community. The circumstances of her son's death forced Joe Campos Torres's mother, Margaret, into the spotlight. She denounced the officers, saying "I'm disgusted. . . . Killing my son like that, beating him like he was an animal and then throwing him in the bayou." Margaret Torres raised the specter of self-defense, saying "if we don't get justice, we'll just have to try to defend ourselves." She and other activists also began planning a major protest march to express community anger over the sentences. She also vigorously supported the short-lived People United to Fight Police Brutality, which not only fought against police brutality but also served as a self-defense group similar to the Brown Berets in Dallas. Although less radical, Mamie Garcia, the president of the Houston council of the League of United Latin American Citizens (LULAC), also took a prominent leadership role after the trial ended. Garcia began meeting with Houston Police Chief Byron G. "Pappy" Bond (who retired in June 1977) and later Chief Harry Caldwell in order to promote the creation of a civilian oversight or internal-affairs office. While Margaret Torres was concerned about seeking justice for her son, Mamie Garcia wanted to make sure that there would never be another Torres-style police murder in Houston. LULACers also appealed to federal authorities to intervene. They hoped to convince federal prosecutors to begin a new case and argued that the police had violated Torres's civil rights. "Justice has not been done," explained Mamie Garcia, "and we will no longer sit back. We will take an active role in guaranteeing civil rights."[36]

The protest march engineered by Margaret Torres occurred on Saturday, October 8, 1977. Approximately two hundred demonstrators marched to Moody Park, the heart of Houston's Northside barrio. There, Mrs. Torres condemned the lenient sentences and called for a federal investigation. A week later, another march and protest took place.[37] These demonstrations occurred sporadically throughout late 1977. They ended when the HPD formally began the operation of a new Internal Affairs Division (IAD). Indeed, the Torres case had spurred the creation of the division. Chicano leaders also halted the protests because the federal government had finally intervened. A federal grand jury indicted four HPD officers involved in Torres's death, including Orlando and Denson.[38]

The Mexican American community pinned its hopes on the federal prosecution of Torres's murderers. After a short trial that largely duplicated the first trial, in early February 1978, the federal court found Orlando, Denson, and Janish guilty of conspiring to deprive Torres of his civil rights, a conspiracy that resulted in his death. But at sentencing, U.S. District Judge Ross Sterling largely followed the sentences of the earlier state trial. Sterling ordered the officers to serve one year in prison for felony misdemeanor for beating Torres and ten years for violating Torres's constitutional rights. But Sterling suspended the harsher sentence and substituted the ten years of jail time with five years' probation.[39] This decision angered the Chicano community and set the stage for a riot in Houston.[40]

As they had done previously, Margaret Torres, Mamie Garcia, and other activists planned a number of protests and rallies at Moody Park. They first engaged in a silent march from the Northside barrio to downtown Houston on April 1, 1978. The march ended at the spot along Buffalo Bayou where Torres had died.[41] Another protest occurred about a month later on May 7, 1978. A crowd of several hundred once again heard a number of speakers at Moody Park. But on this occasion, tension filled the air. The presence of several HPD officers only inflamed hostilities. When the officers attempted to arrest one Chicano, the crowd erupted in violence. The protesters gathered around a police car and eventually turned it over. Amid shouts of "Get the pigs!" and "Justice for Joe Torres!" the crowd surged out of the park toward a growing contingent of police officers. The protesters destroyed almost anything in their paths, breaking store windows, looting, and throwing bottles and rocks. A convenience store, bakery, record shop, and laundry were soon in flames. Unknown assailants fired shots at the police as the crowd ransacked a variety of local stores. The police had had enough. Dressed in full riot gear, Houston police officers marched toward the crowd, which retreated as they arrived. Despite sporadic violence throughout the night, the riot was over in a matter of hours.[42]

Police arrested nearly twenty-five people for the violence at Moody Park. Numerous others, including a number of police officers, sustained injuries from the protest. Three randomly chosen individuals were eventually charged with instigating the riot. Their cases generated considerable attention and resulted in the creation of Free the Moody Park 3 and the Committee to Defend the Houston Rebellion, both legal defense funds. These legal defense groups held rallies and protests around the country to push local authorities to release the Moody Park 3. The demonstrations included a short play, "The Houston Rebellion," which recounted the murder of Torres and the Moody Park Riot. After years of turmoil, local authorities cleared the Moody Park 3 in 1985.[43]

The violence at Moody Park, generally referred to as the Moody Park Riot or Moody Park Rebellion, was the outgrowth of the lengthy and complicated handling of the murder of Joe Torres. It was an expression of community anger, to be sure. But more importantly, it was the violent manifestation of a community that had waited patiently for justice. When that justice was not forthcoming, Chicanos reacted with rage. Various Mexican American leaders had done a great deal to quell the community's anger, including forcing the establishment of HPD's Internal Affairs Division and pushing the federal government to initiate its own trial of Torres's murders. The creation of the IAD pleased many Chicanos. But the light sentences and a general perception that authorities and law enforcement were unconcerned did little to convince Houston Chicanos that their rights were protected. When meeting at Moody Park, they demanded those rights, and ultimately demanded them through a violent upheaval.

The protests against the murder of Joe Campos Torres and the Moody Park Riot occurred well outside the accepted timeframe of the Chicano movement. These protests demonstrate the continuation of the ideology of *chicanismo* and the Chicano struggle for rights. Houston, like several other local communities, experienced a movement that lasted far beyond 1972. Indeed, the fate of the Moody Park 3 pushed the movement into the 1980s. Mexican Americans in Houston have kept the memory of Torres alive long after his death. A play called "The Houston Rebellion" reenacted his murder and the riot for nearly a decade after 1978. Torres and the Moody Park Riot have also been the subjects of continued media attention in Houston. In 2008, the thirty-year anniversary of the riot, Houston's National Public Radio affiliate aired a weeklong retrospective on these events, as did other local media outlets. Additionally, black poet-singer-activist Gil Scott-Heron (probably most famous for his song "The Revolution Will Not Be Televised") memorialized Torres with "A Poem for Jose Campos Torres." He wrote:

I had said I wasn't gonna' write no more poems
    like this.
I had confessed to myself all along, tracer of
    life/poetry trends,
that awareness/consciousness poems that screamed
    of pain
and the origins of pain and death had blanketed
    my tablets and therefore
my friends/brothers/sisters/outlaws/in-laws
and besides, they already knew.
But brother Torres,
common, ancient bloodline brother Torres,
is dead.
I had said I wasn't gonna write no more poems
    like this.
I had said I wasn't gonna write no more words
    down
about people kickin' us when we're down
about racist dogs that attack us and
drive us down, drag us down and beat us down.
But the dogs are in the street!
The dogs are alive and the terror in our hearts
    has scarcely diminished.
It has scarcely brought us the comfort we
    suspected:
the recognition of our terror,
and the screaming release of that recognition
has not removed the certainty of that knowledge.

How could it?
The dogs, rabid, foaming with the energy of their
        brutish ignorance,
stride the city streets like robot gunslingers, and
        spread death
as night lamps flash crude reflections from gun
        butts and police shields.
I had said I wasn't gonna' write no more poems like this.
        . . .
The MOTHERFUCKIN' DOGS are in the street!
In Houston maybe someone said Mexicans were
the new niggers.
In L.A. maybe someone decided Chicanos were
        the new niggers.
In Frisco maybe someone said Asians were the
        new niggers.
Maybe in Philadelphia and North Carolina they
        decided they
didn't need no new niggers.
I had said I wasn't gonna' write no more poems like this.
        . . .
Brother Torres is dead.
The Wilmington Ten are still incarcerated.
Ed Davis, Ronald Reagan and James Hunt and
        Frank Rizzo are still alive.
And the dogs are in the MOTHERFUCKIN' street.
I had said I wasn't gonna' write no more poems
        like this.
I made a mistake.[44]

Gil Scott-Heron's poem reads as an angry, ugly indictment of racist law enforcement and the fear generated by police abuse in minority communities. He ties
Joe Torres and Houston to other communities and activists. More importantly,
Scott-Heron acknowledges that police treated ethnic groups such as Chicanos as
"the new niggers." The refrain "I had said I wasn't going to write no more poems
like this" makes clear that he had hoped that a new day had dawned. But as he,
black victims of police violence, and murder victims like Joe Torres and Santos
Rodríguez surely knew, they "made a mistake" in thinking that times had changed.

The Aftermath of Protests in Dallas and Houston

Clearly the events in Dallas surrounding the murder of Santos Rodríguez and those
in Houston stemming from the murder of Joe Torres had numerous similarities.

Both resulted from heavy-handed and violent police actions. Both resulted from the murder of defenseless Chicanos. Both resulted in the formation of radical, defensive groups like the Brown Berets and People United to Fight Police Brutality. And both resulted in riots. But the reaction of the Chicano community in each city differed. Dallas had a rather small Mexican-origin population and this group did not have a long history of Chicano civil rights activism. The absence of a long-standing movement, well-known leaders, and established organizations meant that the Dallas protests quickly degenerated into a riot. The violence was a visceral reaction to the murder of Rodríguez, and once the community had vented its rage, the protests quickly subsided. The situation in Houston proved different. The city had a much larger Mexican-descent population, who had fought numerous local battles throughout the Chicano movement. Houston Chicanos proved more even-handed and patient as they attempted to work longstanding community ties with the local government and even federal authorities. Only when those community ties failed to yield results did Chicanos erupt violently. While the Moody Park Rebellion certainly expressed community anger, it lacked the visceral, spur-of-the-moment quality of the Dallas Disturbance.

The Chicano struggles in Dallas and Houston did win additional rights for Mexican Americans. Most importantly, Chicanos forced the formation of internal affairs departments, which oversee community complaints and investigate all officer-involved shootings. This was an important step in securing justice for not only Mexican Americans, but also for every resident in Houston and Dallas. Indeed, it was during the 1970s and 1980s, in many cases in direct response to police murders of minority suspects, that numerous police departments across the United States inaugurated internal affairs units. Police departments also began to adopt the idea of "community policing" in which community relations officers and storefront police substations were strategically located in minority neighborhoods. Along with police review, this gave departments an increased presence at the neighborhood level, served as a form of civic outreach, allowed officers to respond to criminal activity more quickly, and in both Dallas and Houston gave police the chance to do voluntary community service—from refuse collecting to planting gardens—in minority neighborhoods.[45] Both movements also forced local governments to hire additional minority police officers and promote officers of color. Additionally, the publicity garnered by both murders and the protests that followed brought increased scrutiny from federal authorities. Not only did the U.S. Justice Department investigate these cases, it also initiated the second trial of Joe Campos Torres's murderers. Such federal intervention served as an additional weapon available to Chicano activists, and it encouraged local officials to change police policies so as to avoid involving federal authorities in local issues.

The focus on police professionalization, community police review, and the formation of internal affairs departments became a major concern of the Chicano movement. Throughout and beyond the civil rights era, police harassment, abuse, and murder led directly to major urban riots—from the Watts Riots to the Chicano

Moratorium Riot to the Dallas Disturbance and Moody Park Riot to the 1991 riots in Los Angeles following the acquittal of the police officers who beat Rodney King. Chicanos found police abuse especially irritating because, in many instances, it not only stemmed from the continuation of Anglo racism but also seemed designed to arrest the progress of the Chicano movement. Such was the case in Los Angeles, where police assaulted high school student activists participating in 1967 demonstrations and attacked the Chicano anti–Vietnam War protest in 1970. In both of these cases, officers brutally beat Chicanos who were protesting nonviolently. Three people were killed during the 1970 protest, including Ruben Salazar: a Los Angeles County sheriff's deputy murdered Salazar by shooting him in the head with a teargas canister as he sat drinking a beer at a local bar. Chicanos responded to these events by demanding that the police hire minority officers, implement civilian review or internal affairs departments, and curtail the violence meted out to people of color. In Dallas and Houston, Chicanos followed this example. When police murders touched off protests, Chicanos demanded not only justice for individuals like Santos Rodríguez and Joe Campos Torres, but justice for all underrepresented groups. That they succeeded in pushing the Dallas and Houston police departments to begin the process of reforming themselves remains a testament to the power of the Chicano movement.[46]

Both the Dallas Disturbance and the Moody Park Riot reveal the continuation of the Chicano movement beyond 1972. Coming in 1973 and 1978, respectively, these riots occurred outside the accepted timeframe of the Chicano movement. But these events demonstrate that the spirit of *chicanismo*—and, indeed, the Chicano movement itself—did not end in the early 1970s. Instead, Chicanos continued to protest in the mid- to late 1970s in much the same way that they had in previous years. The Dallas Disturbance came at the heel of the chronology usually attributed to the Chicano movement. The murder of Joe Campos Torres and the Moody Park Riot perhaps best fit the picture of the continuation of Chicano radical activism, because these events occurred well after 1972. Chicanos had long focused on police brutality and murder. That focus did not end in 1972. Rather, it and the Chicano movement continued for many more years.

NOTES

1. A note on terms: Throughout this essay I refer to persons of Mexican heritage as "Chicano," "Mexican American," and occasionally as "Mexican-origin" or "Mexican-descent." I refer to individuals of European ancestry as "white." I also spell names and use accent marks only as the historical actors used them.

2. For the Chicano antiwar movement, see George Mariscal, *Aztlán and Viet Nam: Chicano and Chicana Experiences of the War* (Berkeley: University of California Press, 1999); and Lorena Oropeza, *¡Raza Sí! ¡Guerra No!: Chicano Protest and Patriotism during the Viet Nam War Era* (Berkeley: University of California Press, 2005). For the school boycott in Houston, see Guadalupe San Miguel, *Brown, Not White: School Integration and the Chicano Movement in Houston* (College Station: Texas A&M University Press, 2001). On the Brown Berets, see Carlos Muñoz, Jr., *Youth, Identity, Power: The Chicano Movement* (New York: Verso,

1989); Laura Pulido, *Black, Brown, Yellow, and Left: Radical Activism in Los Angeles* (Berkeley: University of California Press, 2006); and Ernesto Chávez, *"¡Mi Raza Primero!": Nationalism, Identity, and Insurgency in the Chicano Movement in Los Angeles, 1966–1978* (Berkeley: University of California Press, 2002). On MAYO and RUP, see Armando Navarro, *Mexican American Youth Organization: Avant-Garde of the Chicano Movement in Texas* (Austin: University of Texas Press, 1995); Ignacio M. García, *United We Win: The Rise and Fall of La Raza Unida Party* (Tucson: University of Arizona Press, 1989); Armando Navarro, *The Cristal Experiment: A Chicano Struggle for Community Control* (Madison: University of Wisconsin Press, 1998); and Armando Navarro, *La Raza Unida Party: A Chicano Challenge to the U.S. Two-Party Dictatorship* (Philadelphia: Temple University Press, 2000).

3. Almost all of the books cited in the first endnote follow the standard chronology of the Chicano movement. The authors nearly universally end their discussion of the movement in the early 1970s. My conception of the chronology of the Chicano movement has also been influenced by conversations with numerous colleagues. In informal polls with fellow Mexican American historians, 1972 is the year almost all cite as the end of the Chicano movement. Of course, critics may argue that my chronology is just as artificial as the one I criticize—and they would be right. I nonetheless demonstrate the continuation of Chicano activism into the mid- and late 1970s.

4. For background information on Mexican Americans and law enforcement, see United States Commission on Civil Rights, *Mexican Americans and the Administration of Justice in the Southwest* (Washington, DC: GPO, March 1970).

5. Chicanos called this self-defense group the Brown Berets, a nod to the more radical, and by this point defunct, California Brown Berets. On the Brown Berets, see chapter 2 of Chávez, *"¡Mi Raza Primero!"*

6. For general histories of Dallas, see Darwin Payne, *Big D: Triumphs and Troubles of an American Supercity in the 20th Century* (Dallas: Three Forks Press, 2000); Royce Hanson, *Civic Culture and Urban Change: Governing Dallas* (Detroit: Wayne State University Press, 2003); Patricia Evridge Hill, *Dallas: The Making of a Modern City* (Austin: University of Texas Press, 1996); Robert B. Fairbanks, *For the City as a Whole: Planning, Politics, and the Public Interest in Dallas, Texas, 1900–1965* (Columbus: Ohio State University Press, 1998); and Shirley Achor, *Mexican Americans in a Dallas Barrio* (Tucson: University of Arizona Press, 1978).

7. Payne, *Big D*, 394. Population totals for individuals of Mexican descent are difficult to tabulate, because the U.S. Census Bureau classified this group as white.

8. The Rodriguez case originated from the murders of three Dallas police officers and the DPD's attempts to apprehend two Mexican American suspects. "DLS's Polk Takes Rodriguez Case," *Dallas Times Herald*, February 24, 1971; "Police Harassing of Latins Probed," *Dallas Times Herald*, February 24, 1971; "I Only Tried to Protect My Family," *El Sol de Texas*, February 26, 1971; "Chicanos, Anglos, y Negros Protestaron," *El Sol de Texas*, March 5, 1971; "The Rodriguez Story," *Dallas News*, March 10–24, 1971; "Chicanos Protest Shooting," *Dallas News*, March 10–24, 1971; "Guzman y Lopez por Tres Muertes," *El Sol de Texas*, March 12, 1971; Bob Eckhardt to Señor y Señora Tomas Rodriguez, March 12, 1971, Francisco "Pancho" Medrano Papers, Special Collections, University of Texas, Arlington (hereinafter cited as Medrano Papers, UTA); Birch Bayh to Honorable John N. Mitchell, March 15, 1971, Medrano Papers, UTA; "Chicanos y Negros Preparan Fuerte Boicot," *El Sol de Texas*, March 19, 1971; "Chicanos March in Protest of Rodriguez Treatment," *El Sol de Texas*, March 26, 1971; "Chicanos Stage March to Protest 'Injustice,' " *Dallas Morning News*, March 28, 1971; "Dallas Latins March in Protest," *El Sol*, April 2, 1972; "Raza Rallies Against Repression," *Papel Chicano*, n.d. (ca. April 1971); "Social Workers Take Stands on Rodriguez Case," *Papel Chicano*, June 12, 1971; "Brown Berets Forman Comite para Recibir Quejas Sobre los Abusos Policiales," *Papel Chicano*, September 2, 1971; "Forman Comite

Chicano Para Recibir Quejas Sobre los Abusos Policiales," *Papel Chicano*, September 16, 1971; "One Year Later—Rodriguez Family Still Survives," *Iconoclast*, February 25–March 3, 1972; "The Law Fails Rodriguezes," *Iconoclast*, March 31–April 7, 1972.

9. "Santos Rodriguez: Anniversary of a Murder," *Tejano News Magazine*, August 2–16, 1974.

10. "Questioning of Brothers Ends in Dallas Tragedy," *Dallas Times Herald*, July 24, 1973; "Minorities Hope Child's Death Will Bring Change," *Iconoclast*, August 3–10, 1973; "Santos Rodriguez," *Tejano News Magazine*, August 2–16, 1974.

11. "Policeman Involved in Previous Shooting," *Dallas Morning News*, July 25, 1973; "Fingerprints Don't Match," *Dallas Morning News*, July 26, 1973; "Minorities Hope," *Iconoclast*, August 3–10, 1973; "Santos Rodriguez," *Tejano News Magazine*, August 2–16, 1974; Achor, *Mexican Americans*, 148–153; Payne, *Big D*, 416–418.

12. "The Medranos: Family of Activists," *Dallas Morning News*, November 22, 1970; "Dyson Puts Militants 'Off Limits,'" *Dallas Times Herald*, May 21, 1971; "Brown Berets," *Chicano*, June 14–27, 1971; "Brown Berets Forman comite para Recibir Quejas Sobre los Abusos Policiales," *Papel Chicano*, September 2, 1971; "Forman Comite," *Papel Chicano*, September 16, 1971; "Brown Berets Say '*Carnalismo*,'" *Papel Chicano*, September 16, 1971. See also, "Brown Berets Wait, See," *Dallas Morning News*, August 5, 1973; "Chicanos Protest Shooting," scrapbook of newspaper clippings, Medrano Papers, UTA; see also the various news stories relating to these events in *Peoples' Community Voice*, ca.1971, Medrano Papers, UTA.

13. See Brian D. Behnken, "The 'Dallas Way': Protest, Response, and the Civil Rights Experience in Big D and Beyond," *Southwestern Historical Quarterly* III:1 (July 2007): 1–29.

14. "Santos Rodriguez," *Tejano News Magazine*, August 2–16, 1974.

15. Ibid.

16. For information on the Tomas Rodriguez protests, see, "Chicanos, Anglos," *El Sol de Texas*, March 5, 1971; "Guzman y Lopez," *El Sol de Texas*, March 12, 1971; "Chicanos March," *El Sol de Texas*, March 26, 1971.

17. As quoted in "March Began in Peace, Ended in Violence," *Dallas Times Herald*, July 29, 1973.

18. "March Began in Peace," *Dallas Times Herald*, July 29, 1973; "Angry Crowd Burns and Loots in Downtown Dallas Rampage," *Dallas Times Herald*, July 29, 1973; "City March Dissolves into Random Violence," *Dallas Morning News*, July 29, 1973; "Police Security Guards Against Disturbance Repeat," *Dallas Times Herald*, July 30, 1973; "Downtown Area Guarded," *Dallas Morning News*, July 30, 1973.

19. The riot is recounted in the following: "March Began in Peace," *Dallas Times Herald*, July 29, 1973; "Angry Crowd Burns," *Dallas Times Herald*, July 29, 1973; "City March Dissolves," *Dallas Morning News*, July 29, 1973; "Minorities Hope," *Iconoclast*, August 3–10, 1973; "Santos Rodriguez," *Tejano News Magazine*, August 2–16, 1974; Achor, *Mexican Americans*, 148–153; Payne, *Big D*, 416–418; Michael Phillips, *White Metropolis: Race, Ethnicity, and Religion in Dallas, 1841–2001* (Austin: University of Texas Press, 2006), 164.

20. "Fatal Flashback," *Dallas Morning News*, July 24, 1998.

21. As quoted in Roy H. Williams and Kevin J. Shay, *And Justice for All: The Untold History of Dallas* (Fort Worth, TX: CGS Communications, 2000), 148.

22. "New Deputy Chiefs," *Dallas Morning News*, August 23, 1973; "Police Shakeup," *Dallas Morning News*, January 22, 1974. See also, Payne, *Big D*, 418; W. Marvin Dulaney, "Whatever Happened to the Civil Rights Movement in Dallas, Texas?" in *Essays on the American Civil Rights Movement*, ed. W. Marvin Dulaney and Kathleen Underwood (College Station: Texas A&M University Press, 1993), 88–89.

23. See, "Santos Rodríguez," in Ricardo Sánchez, *Hechizospells* (Chicano Studies Center Publications, University of California, Los Angeles, 1976), 196–204, available at

http:// www.dr-ricardo-sanchez.com/santos.html (accessed July 30, 2009); Shirley Achor, "Rodríguez, Santos," in *Handbook of Texas Online*, available at http://www.tshaonline.org/handbook/online/articles/RR/frocr.html (accessed July 30, 2009); "Recalling Protest Over '73 Slaying," *Dallas Morning News*, April 9, 2006 (quotation).

24. For general histories of Houston, see David G. McComb, *Houston: A History* (Austin: University of Texas Press, 1981); Joe R. Feagin, *Free Enterprise City: Houston in Political-Economic Perspective* (New Brunswick, NJ: Rutgers University Press, 1988); Marguerite Johnson, *Houston: The Unknown City, 1836–1946* (College Station: Texas A&M University Press, 1991); Robert D. Bullard, *Invisible Houston: The Black Experience in Boom and Bust* (College Station: Texas A&M University Press, 1987); David G. McComb, *Houston: The Bayou City* (Austin: University of Texas Press, 1969); Arnoldo De León, *Ethnicity in the Sunbelt: Mexican-Americans in Houston* (College Station: Texas A&M University Press, 2001); and San Miguel, *Brown, Not White*.

25. De León, *Ethnicity in the Sunbelt*, 98, 147; McComb, *Houston: A History*, 83–85. Population totals for individuals of Mexican descent are difficult to tabulate, because the U.S. Census Bureau classified this group as white.

26. For information on the Houston Police Department, see Dwight Watson, *Race and the Houston Police Department, 1930–1990: A Change Did Come* (College Station: Texas A&M University Press, 2006). Steven Wilson also examines the Torres case in Steven Harmon Wilson, *The Rise of Judicial Management in the U.S. District Court, Southern District of Texas, 1955–2000* (Athens: University of Georgia Press, 2003), 469.

27. "Officer Charged with Murder," *Houston Post*, May 10, 1977; "Police Officer Charged with Murder of Man," *Houston Chronicle*, May 10, 1977; "Slain Man's Brother Asks 'Why' of Death," *Houston Post*, May 11, 1977; "The Hole," *Houston Chronicle*, May 14, 1977; "Torres," *Houston Chronicle*, May 15, 1977; "The Torres Case," *Texas Observer*, June 17, 1977; " 'Oh, My God, They've Really Thrown Him In,' " *Houston Post*, September 16, 1977.

28. "Bond Fires Five Officers in Torres Death Case," *Houston Chronicle*, May 12, 1977; "5 of 6 Officers Fired in Torres Death Case," *Houston Post*, May 13, 1977; "U.S. Probe of Torres Death Is Sought," *Houston Chronicle*, May 13, 1977.

29. Representative Ben T. Reyes, May 11, 1977. Press release. Ben T. Reyes Papers, Houston Metropolitan Research Center (hereinafter cited as HMRC).

30. For the variety of appeals written on behalf of Torres by local and state leaders, see, Ben T. Reyes to Drew S. Days III, mailgram, May 19, 1977; Drew S. Days III to Ben T. Reyes, June 1, 1977; Hilda D. Garcia (president of Houston's IMAGE chapter) to Griffin Bell, May 11, 1977; Henry B. Gonzalez to Ben T. Reyes, May 18, 1977; Texas Representative Joe L. Hernandez to Griffin Bell, May 19, 1977; Texas Representative Arnold Gonzales to Griffin Bell, May 19, 1977; Congresswoman Barbara Jordon to Griffin Bell, May 23, 1977, all in Reyes Papers, HMRC.

31. "Police Officer Charged," *Houston Chronicle*, May 10, 1977; "Police Officers' Defense: Five Expected to Contend Bayou Drowning Not Intentional," *Houston Post*, May 13, 1977; "Police Rookie Recounts Arrest of Joe Torres," *Houston Post*, September 15, 1977; "The Torres Case," *Texas Observer*, June 17, 1977; " 'Oh, My God,' " *Houston Post*, September 16, 1977.

32. "Ex-Officer Admits Beating Torres," *Houston Chronicle*, September 20, 1977, and "To Save My Hide," *Houston Post*, September 21, 1977. See also "Police Story: Two Hard Towns," *Time*, September 19, 1977.

33. "Body Bruised, Autopsy Shows," *Houston Post*, May 15, 1977; "Official Says Torres Had Little Chance," *Houston Post*, September 23, 1977.

34. "Jury Set to Begin Deliberating Today in Trial of Officers," *Houston Post*, October 4, 1977; "Torres Case Jury Deliberates," *Houston Post*, October 5, 1977; "Jurors Deliberate Fates of 2

Fired Officers Charged in Torres Drowning," *Houston Chronicle*, October 5, 1977; "Torres Case Jurors Meet Again Today," *Houston Post*, October 6, 1977.

35. "Negligent Homicide is Verdict in Torres Case, " *Houston Chronicle*, October 6, 1977; "2 Ex-Officers Convicted of Misdemeanor," *Houston Post*, October 7, 1977; "Bitterness Greets Verdict," *Houston Post*, October 7, 1977; "Orlando, Denson Get Probated Sentence," *Houston Post*, October 8, 1977; "2 Ex-Policemen Get Probation," *Houston Chronicle*, October 8, 1977; "No Evidence, Jurors Claim," *Houston Post*, October 8, 1977; "LULAC Leader Calls Torres Case Verdict 'Unconscionable,' " *Houston Informer*, October 15, 1977.

36. "2 Ex-Officers Convicted," *Houston Post*, October 7, 1977 (first quotation); "Federal Trial Still Possible," *Houston Post*, October 7, 1977; "Mexican-American Groups Looking to Federal Process," *Houston Post*, October 7, 1977 (second quotation); "LULAC Will Lobby for Civil Rights Law," *Houston Post*, October 9, 1977; "About 200 Protest Torres Case Verdict," *Houston Post*, October 9, 1977. See also "LULAC Director to Ask U.S. Probe of Alleged Police Murder of Torres," *Houston Chronicle*, May 11, 1977; "Latins Will Make Proposals to Bond on Police Brutality," *Houston Post*, May 15, 1977; Paul C. Moreno to Griffin Bell, October 18, 1977, Reyes Papers, HMRC; and Henry B. Gonzalez to Ben T. Reyes, October 18, 1977, Reyes Papers, HMRC.

37. "About 200 Protest," *Houston Post*, October 9, 1977; "100 March to Protest Sentences," *Houston Chronicle*, October 9, 1977; "March, Rally in City Protest Verdicts of Torres Case Jury," *Houston Chronicle*, October 16, 1977; "Communities March in Unity Against Police Brutality," protest flyer, ca. October 15, 1977, Reyes Papers, HMRC; "Demonstrate!" protest flyer, ca. October 15, 1977, Reyes Papers, HMRC; "Justice for Joe Torres!!!" protest flyer, ca. October 15, 1977, Reyes Papers, HMRC.

38. On the formation of HPD's Internal Affairs Division, see Watson, *Race And the Houston Police Department*, 116; "Torres Case Lawyers Expects U.S. Indictments," *Houston Chronicle*, October 16, 1977; "The Torres Case—Relief Expressed at Indictments," *Houston Post*, October 21, 1977.

39. "Torres Case Goes to Jury," *Houston Post*, February 7, 1978; "Many Will Await Sentencing to See if Justice Served," *Houston Post*, February 9, 1978; "3 Former Officers Convicted of Violating Torres' Rights," *Houston Post*, February 9, 1978.

40. "Torres' Mother Unhappy," *Houston Post*, March 29, 1978; "Many Critical of Punishment and Comments by the Judge," *Houston Post*, March 29, 1978; "Chicano Leaders Say Sterling Is Prejudiced," *Houston Informer*, April 29, 1978.

41. "McConn Supports Protest," *Houston Post*, March 30, 1978; "McConn Says Police to 'Assist' March," *Houston Chronicle*, March 31, 1978; "Demonstrators Protest Torres Case Sentences," *Houston Post*, April 3, 1978; "End of the Rope," *Time*, April 17, 1978.

42. See *Tejas News*, which devoted the full length of the May 14, 1978, issue to the riot. See also, "Chicano Fete Erupts in Violence," *Houston Informer*, May 13, 1978; "Morales, 2 Others Held on Riot Charges," *Houston Post*, May 13, 1978; "Echoes of the Moody Park Rebellion," *Revolutionary Worker*, June 7, 1998.

43. "Echoes," *Revolutionary Worker*, June 7, 1998. See also, "Support for Houston Rebellion Grows," protest flyer, ca. 1978; "Free the Moody Park 3," protest flyer, c. 1978; "Demonstrate October 29," protest flyer, ca. 1978; "Trial Bulletin, Railroad Starts Monday April 16, Free the Moody Park 3!" ca. 1978. All of these documents are in the Moody Park Riot Papers, HMRC. Two of the Moody Park 3 were convicted of felony riot in 1984 and sentenced to five years' probation. That sentence was overturned in 1985, and the two individuals then pleaded no contest to misdemeanor riot.

44. Gil Scott-Heron, "A Poem for Jose Campos Torres," from *Now and Then: The Poems of Gil Scott-Heron* (New York: Canongate, 2000). For the full lyrics of "A Poem for Jose

Campos Torres," see http://lyricwiki.org/Gil_Scott-Heron:Jose_Campos_Torres (accessed July 27, 2009). Thanks to Gil Scott-Heron for allowing the use of his poem in this article. The Wilmington Ten was a group of civil rights activists, nine African Americans and one white, who were arrested, tried, and found guilty of firebombing a North Carolina grocery store in 1971. The evidence in the trial was largely circumstantial and many Americans think the group was wrongly accused. Their charges were subsequently overturned. For the Houston Public Radio broadcast, see http://kuhf.convio.net/newsaudio/2008/05/080508moodypark3.mp3 (accessed July 27, 2009). See also, "Remembering the Moody Park Riots," KHOU 11 News, May 7, 2008, *http://www.txcn.com/sharedcontent/dws/txcn/houston/stories/khou080506_jj_moodyparkriots.d48cabe1.html* (accessed July 27, 2009).

45. Relatively few works examine the history of police review and internal affairs departments. For a good start, see Richard Chackerian, "Police Professionalism and Citizen Evaluations: A Preliminary Look," *Public Administration Review* 34:2 (March–April, 1974): 141–148; Richard A. Staufenberger, "The Professionalization of Police: Efforts and Obstacles," *Public Administration Review* 37:6 (November–December, 1977): 678–685; Harry W. More and Peter C. Unsinger, eds., *Managerial Control of the Police: Internal Affairs and Audits* (Springfield, IL: Charles C. Thomas Publisher, 1992); and Watson, *Race and the Houston Police Department*, 116.

46. See, Edward J. Escobar, *Race, Police, and the Making of a Political Identity: Mexican Americans and the Los Angeles Police Department, 1900–1945* (Berkeley: University of California Press, 1999), 34–36; Escobar, "The Dialectics of Repression: The Los Angeles Police Department and the Chicano Movement, 1968–1971," *Journal of American History* 79:4 (March, 1993): 1483–1514; Alfredo Mirandé, "The Chicano and the Law: An Analysis of Community-Police Conflict in an Urban Barrio," *Pacific Sociological Review* 24 (January 1981): 65–86; Gregg Lee Carter, "Hispanic Rioting during the Civil Rights Era," *Sociological Forum* 7:2 (June 1992): 301–322; Oropeza, ¡*Raza Sí! ¡Guerra No!*, chapter 5; and Pulido, *Black, Brown, Yellow, and Left*, 173–174, 194.

11

Rising Up

Poor, White, and Angry in the New Left

JAMES TRACY

Third world people have built their own independent movement to fight against racism and for revolution. That's because racism is so deep that it would be foolish for third world people to think white people would fight as hard against racism and exploitation as they would. No one can give oppressed people their freedom. . . . But just because Black and brown people are fighting the hardest doesn't mean that white people don't have a responsibility to join the fight. We've got to struggle against our own racist attitudes and the racism of our people and at the same time actively support the struggle of third world people. We've got to fight for the elimination of capitalism so we can get rid of the basis of racism once and for all, so together we can build a new humane world for all people.[1]

–*Rising Up Angry*, 1972

In the first half of the 1970s, three small organizations with roots in the 1960s New Left attempted to organize working-class white communities toward a radical class politics and prevent white conservative reaction against the gains of the civil rights and black liberation movements. Rising Up Angry (RUA), based in Chicago, the Bronx's White Lightning (WL), and the October 4th Organization (O40) from Philadelphia comprise an important but largely forgotten project within the legacy of the New Left.

In the early part of the decade, recession and reaction dampened the Left's optimism. Attempting to counter the fatigue from more than a decade of mobilization and reaction, these three groups focused their organizing on the uphill battles that lay before them. Their work was characterized by a long-term commitment to radicalizing the white working class; a defined independence from the student milieu; a dedication to organizing within communities rather than on campuses, in factories, or for politicians; and a strategic emphasis on building multiracial coalitions through providing services and waging campaigns rooted in poor people's immediate needs.[2]

In a time of intense racial division within the Left as much as the broader society, these organizations experimented with models for organizing white urban communities in step with radical "Third World" activists. Poor white neighborhoods were changing rapidly, just as their black and Latino counterparts were, both in racial composition and in the crossfire of government "urban renewal" programs.[3] By locating themselves in neighborhoods ripe for racial conflict and largely written off as slums, these three groups took on campaigns related to health, welfare, housing, drug addiction, and police violence, while making direct links to similar struggles led by their counterparts in communities of color.

These groups utilized a model of service-plus-organizing, a strategy partially derived from the survival programs of the Black Panther Party (BPP), such as breakfast programs, legal counseling, and health clinics.[4] RUA organized campaigns against lead poisoning that took medical staff into poor neighborhoods and performed toxicity tests for children out of a van. This approach launched RUA into tenant organizing, using tactics such as rent strikes and landlord pickets. RUA targeted slumlords with holdings in black, Puerto Rican, and white communities— offering an opportunity for joint action and multiracial coalition. The spirit of these survival programs was replicated in similar initiatives on the East Coast. WL offered detoxification programs to recovering addicts, and 040 conducted a People's Bail Project to help indigent community residents get out of jail.

These three groups emerged to fight the dire economic conditions of the era. The early 1970s were yet another slap in the face for working-class Americans, whose children had done the majority of the fighting and dying in Southeast Asia. By 1973, a deep recession had arrived, in part due to the muscle flexing of the Organization of Petroleum Exporting Countries (OPEC). By raising the price of oil, OPEC increased the U.S. trade deficit, and consumer prices rose to their highest level since the end of the Korean War. The combination of high prices and unemployment erased any remaining optimism; by winter 1974, 7.2 percent of the nation's workforce was unemployed.[5] Factory closures began to pick up pace as CEOs, encouraged by the successful off-shoring of semiconductor factories, eyed moving other industries overseas.[6]

These conditions impacted all workers, but African Americans bore an especially difficult burden, as unemployment in black communities jumped from 9.3 percent in 1973 to 15 percent in 1975.[7] Yet many white workers saw nondiscrimination protections and affirmative-action projects as evidence that white workers were being left behind in this recession. The end of the post–World War II labor peace, marked by an emerging trend of plant closures and off-shoring, placed many white workers in an unfamiliar position—uncertain for the first time in decades where the next paycheck would come from.[8]

This tension played out in multiple ways throughout the decade, not the least of which was racist violence in northern states. In 1974, a boycott campaign by

white families protesting the busing of blacks into South Boston schools was punc-
tuated by bloody clashes and white mobilizations resembling lynch mobs. Such
incidents clearly demonstrated that racism was never solely a southern issue, and
that Jim Crow simply wore a different mask up North. Also plain to see was the
manner in which the positions espoused by reactionary street mobs such as the
neofascist group Powder Keg and the slightly more professional Restore Our Alienated Rights (ROAR) fused with the "respectable" positions articulated by members
of the school board, who defended segregation by calling for "neighborhood
schools." Even Boston's famously liberal establishment attempted to reconcile
with the racists. Mayor Kevin White allowed the use of school funds for tutoring
white students who observed the boycott. Senator Edward Kennedy verbally
opposed segregation yet kept silent as the busing protests grew more openly racist
and more brutally violent.[9]

Out of this political-economic uncertainty, which coincided with a revival of
interest in European American ethnicity, elements of the Right and of the Left
were hoping to find loyal recruits among poor working-class whites.[10] Organizations such as RUA, WL, and 040 fought against the reactionary push for the hearts
and minds of poor urban whites by building a base in communities in northern,
white, working-class neighborhoods. From the late 1960s throughout much of the
1970s, these groups tried to tackle racism as an integral part of rebuilding a class
politics. Their projects, formed amid the turbulent 1970s, provide evidence of how
white supremacy can be undermined even as it demonstrates its durability. The
scale and scope of this work sheds light on a largely unexamined dimension of
urban radicalism in the recent past—both its promise and its perils.

Forks in the Road

By the end of the 1960s, most of the divergent parts of the radical Left identified
the enemy as a system of imperialism. The shift was dramatic, because it cast
doubt on the possibility of pressuring American political institutions for change
and took the radical gaze far beyond the borders of the United States. Through this
prism, war wasn't the result of poor policy but an inevitable result of the push for
profits based on the resources stolen from Third World countries, many of which
were successfully decolonizing their lands. Racism was a symptom of U.S. imperialism, and ethnic minorities in the United States were understood as "nations
within nations," entitled to political self-determination.[11]

Radical anti-imperialist organizations opted for different strategies to confront
imperialism, ranging from armed support for national liberation to promoting
shop-floor militancy. Leftist organizations sent cadre into factories to organize at the
point of production or sent them underground to attack the symbols of U.S. power.
Another path meant returning to working-class neighborhoods and walking a
tightrope: energizing dissent through meeting people "where they were at," in hopes
of eventually bridging the gap between local rent strikes and anti-imperialist

international action. The Black Panthers, the Puerto Rican Young Lords, the Chicano Brown Berets, and the Asian Red Guard Party/I Wor Kuen centered themselves in community organizing. Although other tactics and strategies emerged out of these formations, it was their orientation to community as the site of organizing that appealed to founders of RUA, 040, and WL.

This deep radicalization was in part catalyzed by the liberal establishment's strategy of passing reforms, such as the Civil Rights Act of 1964, while simultaneously blocking independent black political participation in the Democratic Party.[12] The Jobs Or Income Now (JOIN) Community Union helped lay the groundwork for the set of white, working-class, and radical organizations to come. JOIN formed in 1964 as part of Students for a Democratic Society's (SDS) community-organizing project in Chicago's Uptown neighborhood. In Uptown, student activists found what they thought was an ideal community to organize—poor whites who moved from the South to northern industrialized cities for work. JOIN hoped to form a link in an eventual "interracial movement of the poor." Doing this would require diminishing the appeal of white supremacist attitudes in the neighborhood, simultaneously building support for the demands of people of color while addressing poor white people's economic demands.[13] Many of JOIN's key student leaders had participated in, or were deeply influenced by, the civil rights movement in the South. These activists found the progressive voices within Uptown. A central JOIN figure, Peggy Terry, a white southern woman who had migrated to Chicago, was already an organizer with the Congress of Racial Equality (CORE). Despite the prevalence of Klan members in her family, Terry worked closely with Dr. Martin Luther King, Jr. toward desegregation of housing and schools in northern cities.[14]

During this time, JOIN activists had become part of a broader conversation questioning whether long-term change could happen through racially integrated organizations. In Chicago, they attempted to put into practice what some black activists had been telling them to do—"organize their own" in order to broaden and deepen the movement's roots. In 1966, this conversation became a demand as white students were expelled from the South by the black leadership of the Students Nonviolent Coordinating Committee (SNCC).[15] The expulsion led to a pronounced race-based "division of labor" where radicals were expected to organize their own (racial) community.

JOIN's actions challenged President Johnson's "War on Poverty" programs for their limitations and exposed the lack of input poor people had in the growing web of programs, whose jobs often reinforced the city's machine politics. "It really was an issue of grassroots organizing versus the top-down, patronizing model favored by the [Chicago Mayor Richard] Daley machine. Our loose alliance with radical Black and Latino groups helped to sharpen our understanding of such programs," said Burton Steck, a JOIN member who also volunteered for voter registration campaigns in the South.[16] JOIN disintegrated for many reasons, not the least of which was class tensions between students and neighborhood people. Yet, when combined with the inspiration of groups such as the Black Panthers, its organizing supplied the foundation for new projects to emerge in the 1970s.[17]

Rising Up Angry

Many of the personalities who had worked in JOIN coalesced to form a radical collective in Chicago called Rising Up Angry, which served as the archetype for this sector of white, working-class radicalism. In July 1969, RUA went citywide and corner-to-corner with its own newspaper (also named *Rising Up Angry*). The newspaper targeted "greaser" youth with articles about cars, sports, and pool next to calls to resist the war, stop fighting with youth of color, and to "fight the real enemy" (i.e., capitalists, racists, and imperialists). Much of the first year was spent simply trying to build a rapport with the various street gangs that dotted Chicago's street corners through activities not normally associated with the radicals of the era: barbeques, softball games, and pool matches. Co-founder and SDS/JOIN alum Mike James photographed the youth in their stylized leather jackets and published the pictures in the "Stone Grease Grapevine" section of the paper, hoping the youth might also come around to reading its political content.

James and many others founded RUA on the assumption that something unique had happened in Uptown during the JOIN years that needed to be both salvaged and reinvented. Student organizers had gained a deeper understanding of the realities of impoverished America. Key neighborhood leaders had become connected to the larger movement against war and inequality, and RUA saw its neighborhood base as central to building an antiracist, class-based movement against American imperialism. RUA focused on neighborhoods in large part because many founding members had become part of the fabrics of the various neighborhoods in which they were organizing or were lifelong residents themselves.

By organizing greasers, RUA had built a largely male membership. Women organizers, such as Diane Fager, Norrie Davis, Janet Sampson, and Christine George, pushed the organization to embrace issues important to women and families as part of its notion of community. Their insights were central to the group's founding a community health clinic and participating in Jane, a clandestine abortion service, in collaboration with the Chicago Women's Liberation Movement.[18] Women in RUA worked to add feminist sensibilities and strategies to the group; they did not form separate caucuses or leave the organization. They hoped that incorporating feminist politics would strengthen the organization and the movement overall, and they saw enough possibility in the rest of the group's approach to push it in a feminist direction from within rather than from without.

By not leaving the male-dominated organization or forming a caucus to strategize from within, the women not-so-subtly rebuked one school of thought within the broader, burgeoning women's liberation movement. Some women in RUA saw separatism as a form of privilege that working-class women could not

afford. "While we worked closely with organizations with women-only membership," explained RUA activist Janet Sampson, "we [RUA women] thought it was much
harder for working-class women to separate from men, who were of course husbands and relatives. By building campaigns based in working-class women's needs
within the organization, we were able to educate men in our communities at the
same time."[19]

One of RUA's hallmark organizing campaigns—challenging slum housing and
lead poisoning—consciously combined race and class in its approach: The group targeted landlords with substandard housing in neighborhoods of color and poor white
communities. This meant collaborating with the Young Lords Organization around
housing and urban renewal issues, believing that tangible organizing campaigns
were the best way to create meaningful alliances. Often, RUA took white youth to
rallies supporting imprisoned radicals of color, such as Panther leader Huey Newton,
hoping that a common mistrust of the police would spark solidarity.[20]

The organization embodied "rainbow" politics—the idea that each ethnic
group would have its own organizations, independent from each other, yet mobilize together through coalitions. The original Rainbow Coalition, formed in 1969
and of no relationship to the one organized later by the Reverend Jesse Jackson,
included the Chicago Black Panthers, the Puerto Rican Young Lords, and the white
Young Patriots. Mixed signals were the Patriots' forte. Peggy Terry's son Doug
Youngblood was one of several Patriots founders who worked previously with the
anti-police-brutality work group of JOIN. The short-lived Patriots proudly used the
confederate flag as an emblem, while consistently agitating against racism through
their work in the Rainbow Coalition. Like so many others on the radical Left in this
era, the Patriots credited the Black Panther Party as its inspiration. "We learned so
much from the Panthers, setting up breakfast programs in our own communities,
health clinics and the like," remarked former Patriot member Carol Coronado.[21]

According to former Panther Bob Lee, the original Rainbow Coalition was a
strategy to reintroduce class politics to a movement that had been catalyzed by
racial struggle and made suspicious of poor whites thanks to the racist violence
that greeted the civil rights movement. The leadership of the Chicago Panthers
believed that work with the Patriots might become the foundation for larger
alliances between poor people. As Lee put it, "The Rainbow was just a code word
for class struggle."[22]

Much of the Rainbow Coalition's short life was spent agitating against the
demolition of poor neighborhoods through urban renewal programs. Its emergence coincided with the intensification of police repression against the movement. The Panthers formally announced the alliance in June 1969, and within a
few weeks, the police shot Lords' Manuel Ramos dead in the streets. By the end of
the year, Chicago Panther Chairman Fred Hampton was murdered in an early-
morning raid on his home—part of a coordinated action between local and state
law enforcement entities. "Repression certainly came down much stronger after
the Rainbow Coalition was formed," recalls former Young Lords chair Cha-Cha

Jimenez.[23] As a result, some members retreated from radical politics while others remained steadfast. The Young Patriots split under the pressure, with one faction, renamed the Patriot Party, attempting to build a national presence. By 1971, the Patriot Party had disintegrated following a weapons bust at their New York City headquarters. In Chicago, a few Young Patriots remained a vocal force until 1973.[24] With its member organizations experiencing such poor fortunes, the Rainbow Coalition dissolved in 1971.

Despite the short life of the Patriots and the Rainbow Coalition, they provided a glimpse of the potential for building unity among dispossessed populations. This example held out hope that poor whites, often alienated from the student Left, could form an independent and progressive political force. Rising Up Angry continued that vision by organizing at nearby Navy and Marine bases, expanding RUA's membership to include a solid core of enlisted people and their families. RUA worked with Chicago Area Military Project (CAMP) and Vietnam Veterans Against the War (VVAW) to stage direct-action protests and help active service personnel channel their dissent or extricate themselves from the military. This antiwar organizing convinced several veterans to join RUA in its efforts to undermine the United States' ability to carry out the war, which made RUA a vital link connecting dissident service-people to the movement. RUA saw its efforts as bolstering the struggle within this country. "We're learning how to disrupt this country. The disruption is nothing compared to what's going to come if this war continues," the *Rising Up Angry* newspaper boasted.[25]

Such brash predictions were common to many anti-imperialist organizations in the early 1970s. As RUA member Peter Kuttner recalled, "part of our challenge [that] was implicit in anti-imperialist politics is the assumption that we wanted our country to lose the war, because U.S. domination was bad for the whole of humanity." In hindsight, Kuttner fears such rhetoric may have created a wedge between the group and the communities they tried to organize.

October 4th Organization

On the East Coast, White Lightning and October 4th Organization provided variations on RUA's themes. Founded in 1971, O40 took its name from the date of a 1779 revolt when a throng of Philadelphians stormed the warehouses of merchants and businesspeople who had hoarded food and clothing in order to inflate prices. The seized supplies were redistributed to the hungry. The group took this example as its inspiration. Like RUA, O40 was also a hybrid organization of student radicals and people from white, working-class neighborhoods. Despite the fact that some activists in either group got their start individually as student radicals, both groups saw the student movement as shallow and believed that student radicals were too disconnected from communities to implement a "serve the people" strategy. They also saw in white, working-class neighborhoods a potential and, for some, a natural base to organize.

O40 was constantly in the streets—not rioting, but talking with white youth and distributing "know your rights" cards to those harassed by the police. By confronting police brutality, they charted a collision course with Philadelphia Mayor Frank Rizzo, a former police officer who used his office to organize whites from the Right. His ascent to power symbolized the final phase in the assimilation of Italian Americans into the larger fabric of white America. Rizzo, as both an officer and the mayor, coordinated police attacks on various New Left and countercultural institutions, notably a violent raid on Philadelphia Panther offices on trumped-up charges in August 1970. His path to power was built on the anxieties of Poles, Ukrainians, Irish, Italians, Germans, and Russians—especially those who couldn't afford the white flight to the suburbs.[26] To them, Rizzo offered validation in the form of (highly masculine) race-baiting resentment and law-and-order politics; the combination made the gruff politician a favorite of Richard Nixon.[27]

Rizzo's backlash succeeded despite—or in some cases because of—the fact that his police force was notoriously violent. O40 sought to exploit popular anger at police violence through their People's Bail Project. Hitting the streets and educating white youths about their rights was also an opportunity to talk about the violence faced by youth of color. O40 member Jack Whalen remembers that it wasn't always an easy sell; some of the whites they spoke with believed that police brutality was somehow justified in communities of color. But this was not a universal view. "For some of the youth we worked with, it was pretty easy to get them to challenge their own racism and become critical of the racism in their own communities. I never thought we should take a dogmatic or confrontational line—just simply reinforce that O40 was against racism and why that was so. It was the consistency of the message and the work with the organization that made the difference over time."[28] This consistency, as we shall see, gave O40 a significant role in the campaign to defeat Rizzo.

In more than one case, police brutality brought neighbors into O40's orbit. In September 1970, Philadelphia police killed Paul Frankenhauser. His family contacted O40 for help, and in April 1971, the group planned a protest to demand that the investigation into his death be reopened. They decided to disrupt one of Rizzo's mayoral campaign rallies in the heart of Fishtown, the white, working-class neighborhood in North Philadelphia where Frankenhauser had lived. Frankenhauser's wife, Joann, accompanied the group. The police had likely anticipated the protest, as members of its civil-disobedience squad were already on the scene. The Frankenhausers and O40 demanded the opportunity to address Rizzo, at which point the police attacked them, shattering the skull of O40 co-founder Robert Barrow.[29]

The group tried to find ways to link neighborhood work, such as police brutality issues, to the Vietnam War. In December 1972, B-52 bombers unleashed thirty bombs over heavily populated sections of Haiphong and Hanoi. The bombings destroyed the nine-hundred-bed Bach Mai Hospital, killing twenty-five doctors. The Pentagon described it as "some limited, accidental damage."[30] O40 went door-to-door collecting pledges for a blood drive for bombing victims. Even among Kensington's more conservative residents, few agreed with bombing a hospital, and the group was able to raise several hundred dollars for the relief of Bach Mai.[31]

In 1978, the group worked in coalition with dozens of other Philadelphia organizations, including the Third World Women's Alliance and the Puerto Rican Socialist Party, among others, to hand Rizzo his pink slip as he attempted to amend the city's charter to allow him to run for a third term. The coalition, People Against Rizzo, prevailed after a massive, door-to-door voter-registration drive that mobilized more than one hundred thousand new voters. Just before the election, Rizzo appealed to white neighborhoods to "vote white," a statement that guaranteed a large black presence at the polls.[32] 040 found that the working-class neighborhoods they canvassed were deeply ambivalent toward Rizzo. Despite his appeal for white solidarity, Rizzo had to contend with the fact that his police routinely beat the same people he turned to for support. Many of these people were further alienated by his attempt to amend the city charter. 040 organizer Sharon McConnell recalled that people responded to the group's canvassing by saying that "Rizzo amending the city charter to run again was just anti-democratic, that no one should have that much power, be in there for so long."[33] 040's canvassing took place within a racial division of labor, as the group tried to organize white voters to break from a demagogue who had, time and time again, appealed to their fear of blacks, Latinos, and radicals to keep himself in power.

None of this work, not even the late 1970s defeat of Rizzo, stemmed the conservative backlash, which relied on white supremacy as a cornerstone and swept many New Left gains to the margins. Rizzo's Philadelphia became a national model for a "white ethnic strategy" embraced by conservative politicians to swing the nation to the Right.[34] This strategy turned to idealized notions of old-world identities and played upon white resentment toward black and brown people's modest and recent political gains. In this sense, the 1970s was a time when the specters of crime, housing integration, and busing were orchestrated toward the politics of resentment. Through them, the Right continued its patient and strategic bludgeoning of progressive gains—a rollback that became an avalanche with the election of Ronald Reagan in 1980.[35]

White Lightning

White Lightning organized in the white, working-class communities of the Bronx in New York City. It too took inspiration from the Panthers, but it collaborated more closely with the Young Lords. WL's initial cadre was drawn from a multiracial group of dissidents at Logos, a residential drug-treatment program that employed a "therapeutic community" model of intense, confrontational, group sessions. In 1970, the group's director decided to eliminate reintegration into the community as the final phase of the program. Embracing the Synanon model, he wanted to convert Logos from a treatment program into a lifelong utopian community.[36]

Synanon's dissenters dubbed themselves Spirit of Logos (SOL). They soon shifted away from demanding rights as participants and toward a systemic analysis of the drug trade. Dr. Mike Smith, who worked at Lincoln Hospital (a dilapidated and disinvested public hospital in the South Bronx), recruited SOL member Gil Fagiani into Think Lincoln, an alliance of black, Puerto Rican, and poor white communities in the Bronx aiming to reform the hospital. Fitzhugh Mullan, then a doctor at Lincoln, described the hospital: "beds in the halls, beds in the corridors, excrement back up in toilets . . . cracking plaster everywhere."[37]

Lincoln quickly became a flashpoint for activism. Beginning in late 1969, the New York Black Panther Party organized there with the Young Lords, forming the Health Revolutionary Movement (HRUM). Soon, the other organizations involved in the larger coalition split along racial lines. Most people of color left Think Lincoln and the Spirit of Logos to join HRUM. The white people involved built White Lightning, initially dubbed the "white section" of SOL. "We were trying to put into practice what many revolutionary black and Latino leaders were asking us to do at the time—go along with a racial division of labor within the movement and organize the white working class," Fagiani recalls.[38] In 1970, following a botched abortion that killed Carmen Rodrigues, a Puerto Rican resident of Logos, the Young Lords carried out a high-profile takeover of Lincoln Hospital, with SOL and the New York Panthers in support.[39] For about a year and a half, Lincoln operated on a uniquely radical axis. The Lords collaborated with Dr. Smith to pioneer a free acupuncture detoxification program—which was later taken up by a Republic of New Afrika–inspired group, the Black Acupuncture Advisory Association of North America—and doctors, nurses, and hospital staff formed worker's councils to try to run the hospital together with radical community groups.[40]

White Lightning continued to confront the drug epidemic following the Lincoln takeover. Their take on the political economy of dope framed the addicted pusher as an exploited worker, and described the "real criminals" as the drug companies, who overproduced for the illegal market, and the cops and organized crime, who profited from trafficking. Like both the Panthers and the Young Lords, WL framed the drug plague as part of creeping "chemical fascism," borrowing the term from an article written by Black Panther Michael Cetewayo Tabor.[41] In 1973, WL played a central role in convening the United Parents Who Care (UPWC) coalition to fight the nascent Rockefeller drug laws, which established lengthy prison terms for drug possession. The coalition was largely made up of socially conservative, white, working-class people. Although WL membership never topped two-dozen people, UPWC attracted hundreds of concerned individuals. Yet, the credibility WL earned through its hard work organizing demonstrations against Rockefeller was under attack. At one point, an FBI agent contacted families and informed them that WL was a communist group.[42] The group also had to contend with Lyndon LaRouche's cryptic and cultish National Caucus of Labor Committees (NCLC), members of which disrupted community meetings with vitriolic rants and physical violence, resulting in many parents being scared off from the coalition.[43]

Its opposition to the drug trade was not the only way WL was involved in organizing against the criminal justice system. The group had a reputation for being allies to Third World struggles in a time when militancy and state violence drew a line in the sand for many white organizers. On August 21, 1971, guards killed Black Panther George Jackson in the San Quentin State Prison yard in California. Three weeks later, in New York, prisoners at the Attica State Correctional Facility seized the institution and demanded improved conditions; twenty-nine prisoners and ten guards died when New York State Troopers violently retook control of the prison (see chapter 1). The New York Panthers invited White Lightning to be part of the security detail in the Harlem demonstrations against Jackson's murder and against the September slaughter at Attica.

Due to their backgrounds as recovering addicts who grew up in the multiracial neighborhoods of the South Bronx, "organizing their own" did not come as easily to members of WL as it did to the other groups discussed here. For members such as Willie Everich and John Duffy, both of whom grew up in intense poverty as some of the very few white people living in what were otherwise communities of color, the strategy of racially specific organizations built division when unity was needed. They went along with it because they felt their allied organizations were not willing to budge on this issue. Their experience of addiction and recovery, however, facilitated strong bonds with a wide range of people and organizations across all lines of color and class. They felt that organizing was at its best when it was multiracial. "SOL evolved organically from a multiracial group of ex-addicts and its basis of unity was their common experience with drugs, inside the therapeutic community and in forming the SOL," Duffy explains. "The bonds of unity between people in the SOL were real and not ideological. The Young Lords Party exerted pressure to split the [SOL] organization. This was based on their experience of being a primarily Puerto Rican organization. We, a couple of the white members who grew up in the South Bronx, disagreed. Our experience growing up was multiracial. The organization was new and we felt that to split it was to weaken it. It was a challenge for a couple of us who grew up in the South Bronx and had very limited experience with other whites."[44]

While Duffy and others agreed to the separation, they recall doing so with great unease. Their upbringing left them alienated from and ill-prepared to organize in "white" mainstream culture, a feeling that intensified as their own class consciousness grew. As groups such as the Lords and the Panthers unraveled in the early to mid-1970s, the "organize your own" mandate became less relevant and harder to implement. By 1975, Duffy and several others made their way into organizations associated with the new communist movement, such as the October League,[45] and now turned their attention to building a revolutionary socialist vanguard party in the United States. Others brought their skills as tenant organizers to populist Bronx neighborhood groups where revolutionary rhetoric was downplayed in the interest of making more tangible improvements in housing conditions.[46]

There Goes the Neighborhood

In addition to their peers in the New Left, most of these organizations came into being about the same time that Saul Alinsky, considered by many to be the "godfather" of modern community organizing, published *Rules for Radicals* (1971). Alinsky's organizing manual was an attempt to transmit his four decades of experience to the next generation and encourage a strategic return to place-based, geographic organizing. His model stressed an elastic ideology based on colorful direct actions that could build organizations and federations with larger influence than those associated with the New Left. Yet getting a community a seat at the table of power often required downplaying or forgetting the agenda of who sat at its head. For that reason, *Rules* was dismissed by many radicals as a textbook for opportunism and reaction.[47] In Chicago, his hometown, Alinsky-influenced organizations regularly won victories that improved housing conditions and provided certain neighborhoods with a voice that the city establishment might hear. But organizing around immediate neighborhood concerns without addressing the racial polarization that characterized Chicago in the 1970s meant leaving the vital issue of white supremacy untouched.[48] Alinksy, meanwhile, although sympathetic to the young radicals, ultimately believed them to be out of touch with the everyday people. "Spouting quotes from Mao, Castro, and Che Guevara . . . [is] as germane to our highly technological, computerized, cybernetic, nuclear-powered, mass media society as a stagecoach on a jet runway at Kennedy airport," he wrote of New Left revolutionaries in the introduction to *Rules*.[49]

To the naked eye, the rent strikes and pickets of RUA, O40, and WL may have looked similar to those of Alinsky-based groups. But their political perspectives, particularly around racism, and their intentional allegiance with revolutionary nationalist groups were far more direct and radical. While Alinsky frequently trash-talked Black Power icons Stokely Carmichael and Maulana Ron Karenga, these working-class white organizations, like many other sections of the New Left, attempted to work under the mandates of radical organizations of color.[50] Each organization rallied its base to call for the release of imprisoned Third World allies such as Huey Newton, Angela Davis, and Los Siete de la Raza.[51] A tract penned by RUA around 1972 and widely distributed by O40 and WL came closest to a coherent theory. In it, the authors distinguish between individual and institutional racism. In line with emerging notions of white-skin privilege, the group also traced racial hatred back to the development of capitalism through the advantages granted to white indentured servants as opposed to African slaves. A central message throughout was to explain to white workers the justifications of "Third World rebellions" and the responsibility of whites to support such actions.[52]

In this era, it was not only Alinsky's models that were becoming dated, but traditional union and united-front strategies as well. The racialized division of labor was an attempt to grapple with the strategic framework and organizational model put forward by groups trying to organize themselves as struggles for

national liberation. But like most strategies utilized by other sections of the New
Left, these attempts fell short of the goal of radically restructuring society. Uphold-
ing the fight against white supremacy did not produce long-term results much different from those of Alinsky-trained groups that sidelined the issue. The failures
of this project reflect the same of other attempts in the 1970s, all part of a spirited
mass movement ill-equipped to stop the conservative backlash that would soon
reshape the nation.

Among many radical organizations, frustrated with its slow pace, neighborhood organizing itself was falling from favor. As the new communist movement
grew and absorbed various elements of the (post–) New Left, local efforts were
subsumed in the push for the elusive vanguard party. By 1975, key leaders of O40
and WL were recruited into groups such as the October League and the Revolutionary Communist Party, with little consideration to whether the original organizations would survive. O40's Dan Sidorick believes that this push to build radical
political parties stunted the long-term benefits of being rooted in a community. "I
think if the party-building efforts had been a little more open to learning from the
experiences of groups like O40 and others, and if they were less sectarian . . . there
might have been some possibility for things to have turned out differently."[53]

The organizations of this near-forgotten project had an uphill battle from
their inception. As groups trying to organize poor white people, and often being
poor themselves, they had to navigate a space between solidarity and self-interest
in a movement largely radicalized through the struggle for racial justice. This
balancing act was made more difficult by their strategic orientation to local,
neighborhood organizing. Their choice to remain rooted in community was in
contrast to a movement that was increasingly interested in national and international formations. Being out-recruited by these bigger groups was not the only
force to deplete the ranks of neighborhood-based New Left groups—as with other
radical groups, burnout, movement fatigue, and the beginning of new families
also thinned these organizations' ranks. The demands of being a full-time revolutionary made sense—as long as the revolution seemed just around the corner. As
Rising Up Angry and White Lightning members exited the 1970s, the "all for the
revolution" model became impossible for them to sustain. White Lightning began
to disband in 1975, and RUA followed suit a year later. Before it officially dissolved,
RUA member Steve Tappis traveled to Philadelphia and the Bronx to get to know
people from WL and O40 more deeply and discuss the possibility of unifying the
three organizations. All had met with each other prior to that, but they had never
worked closely together. Although the idea appealed to some, it never material-
ized: membership of the three groups had shrunk significantly by that point,
making a national entity unfeasible.[54]

Although it lasted longer than the other two groups, O40's success in the
coalition against Rizzo did not extend its life. It disintegrated as key members
turned their attention to personal lives, became trade-union activists, or entered
emerging communist organizations. At a final meeting of the organization in 1978,

remaining members of the organization decided to gather and destroy their archives of newspapers, flyers, and photographs. Even as they disbanded their organization, many in 040 were convinced that radical, maybe revolutionary change was imminent, and they wished to protect each other from authorities' possible reprisals.[55]

By the end of the decade, RUA, 040, and WL were defunct. Yet the three groups had made accomplishments: Their slow, sustained organizing showed in microcosm that poor and working whites could be mobilized for justice by connecting neighborhood work to bigger political questions. They also challenged the Right in competing for the political allegiance of the white working class. On a neighborhood basis, these groups created effective campaigns, principled alliances, and strong roots. By the end of the decade, the Right had consolidated large swaths of power, and those who envisioned a left-wing revolution by the early 1980s were sorely disappointed. For a moment, however, these groups used community organizing, informed by Third World struggles, to form a crucial link in reinventing an inclusive class politics by placing white supremacy in the dustbin of history.

NOTES

1. "Racism is Amerika's Most Powerful Narcotic," *White Lightning* 1:4 (April 1972): 1–2, credited as reprinted from *Rising Up Angry*, issue unknown.

2. I am deeply indebted to Gil Fagiani, a former member of White Lightning, for his insight into aspects of this political trajectory.

3. See, for example, Larry Bennett, *Neighborhood Politics: Chicago and Sheffield* (Oxford: Taylor & Francis, 1997); and Chester Hartman, *City for Sale: The Transformation of San Francisco* (Berkeley: University of California Press, 1997).

4. Paul Alkebulan, *Survival Pending Revolution: The History of the Black Panther Party* (Tuscaloosa: University of Alabama Press, 2007); and David Hilliard, ed., *The Black Panther Party: Service to the People Programs* (Albuquerque: University of New Mexico Press, 2008).

5. Edward Berkowitz, *Something Happened: A Political and Cultural Overview of the Seventies* (New York: Columbia University Press, 2003), 3–6.

6. General Accounting Office report to the Congressional Committees, *Offshoring: U.S. Semiconductor and Software Industries Increasingly Produce in China and India*, GAO-06-423, September 7, 2006, 6; and Gregory S. Wilson, "Deindustrialization, Poverty and Federal Area Redevelopment in the United States, 1945–1965," in *Beyond the Ruins: The Meanings of Deindustrialization*, ed. Jefferson R. Cowie and Joseph Heathcott (Ithaca, NY: Cornell University Press, 2003), 181–199.

7. Applied Research Center, *Race and Recession: How Iniquity Rigged the Economy and How to Change the Rules* (Oakland, CA: Applied Research Center, May 2009), 13–14.

8. For an overview of labor in the 1970s, see Jefferson Cowie, *Stayin' Alive: The 1970s and the Last Days of the Working Class* (New York: The New Press, 2010).

9. For readings on the Boston busing crisis produced at the time, see, for instance, Imamu Amiri Baraka, *Crisis in Boston! A Black Revolutionary Analysis of the Ruling Class Conspiracy to Agitate Racial Violence Around Busing in Boston* (Newark: Vita Wa Watu—People's War, 1974); and author unknown, "Mass Protest Unites Against Racism," *Guardian*,

December 18, 1974. For an overview of how various groups in the new communist move-
ment responded to it, see Max Elbaum, *Revolution in the Air: Sixties Radicals Turn to Lenin,
Mao, and Che* (New York: Verso, 2002), 186–191. For an overview of the crisis, see Ronald P.
Formisano, *Boston Against Busing: Race, Class, and Ethnicity in the 1960s and 1970s* (Chapel
Hill: University of North Carolina Press, 1991).

10. Matthew Frye Jacobson, *Roots Too: White Ethnic Revival in Post–Civil Rights America*
(Cambridge, MA: Harvard University Press, 2006).

11. See, for instance, Komozi Woodard, *A Nation within a Nation: Amiri Baraka (LeRoi Jones)
and Black Power Politics* (Chapel Hill: University of North Carolina Press, 1999).

12. Laura Pulido, *Black, Brown, Yellow, and Left: Radical Activism in Los Angeles* (Los Angeles:
University of California Press, 2006), 90–92.

13. JOIN was a project of SDS's Economic Research and Action Project, which also placed
New Left organizers in twelve other cities. See Jennifer Frost, *An Interracial Movement of
the Poor: Community Organizing and the New Left in the 1960s* (New York: New York
University Press, 2001). For an early, important examination of community organizing
and the New Left, see Wini Breines, *Community and Organization in the New Left 1962–1968:
The Great Refusal* (New Brunswick, NJ: Rutgers University Press, 1989).

14. Peggy Terry, interviewed by Studs Terkel, *Race: How Blacks and Whites Think and Feel About
the American Obsession* (New York: The New Press, 1992), 51.

15. This decision continues to be a controversial, contested one in histories of SNCC. For a
recent treatment, see Wesley C. Hogan, *Many Minds, One Heart: SNCC's Dream for a New
America* (Chapel Hill: University of North Carolina Press, 2007).

16. Burton Steck, telephone interview with author, January 31, 2008.

17. The anti–police brutality workgroup of JOIN became the Young Patriots Organization
(YPO)—which would form the original Rainbow Coalition with the Panthers and the
Lords in June 1969. YPO was best known for using the Confederate Stars and Bars as a
symbol while at the same time urging poor whites to break from racism. Other members
of JOIN went on to become pillars of the national welfare rights movement. For more, see
Amy Sonnie and James Tracy, *The Firing Line: Working-Class Whites, Radical Politics, and the
Original Rainbow Coalition* (Brooklyn: Melville House Publishing, 2010).

18. Janet Sampson, interview with author, December 29, 2007. See also the CWLU Herstory
Project: The Online History of the Chicago Women's Liberation Union, at www
.cwluherstory.com (accessed July 22, 2009).

19. Janet Sampson, telephone interview with author, April 16, 2009.

20. Steve Tappis, interview with author, November 5, 2005.

21. Carol Coronado, interview with author, February 8, 2009.

22. Bobby Lee, interviewed by James Tracy, "The Original Rainbow Coalition," *Area Magazine*
3 (September 30, 2006).

23. Cha-Cha Jimenez, telephone interview with author, February 8, 2008.

24. Coronado, interview with author.

25. Author unknown, *Rising Up Angry*, date unknown, in author's files, courtesy of Gil
Fagiani.

26. Joseph R. Daughen, Peter Binzen, *The Cop Who Would be King: The Honorable Frank Rizzo*
(New York: Little, Brown and Company, 1977). For the raid on three Panther offices, see
Donald Janson, "Panthers Raided in Philadelphia," *New York Times*, September 1, 1970, 1.

27. Rick Perlstein, *Nixonland: The Rise of a President and the Fracturing of America* (New York:
Scribner's, 2008), 612.

28. Jack Whalen, interview with author, San Francisco, February 14, 2009.

29. Jack McKinney, "The Voices of Dissent in Kensington," *Philadelphia Daily News*, October 26, 1972; Philadelphia Black Panther Party, "Rizzo's Reign of Terror," *Black Panther*, May 29, 1971, 5. Barrow survived the injury and now lives in Washington, DC.

30. Andrew J. Rotter, ed., *Light at the End of the Tunnel: A Vietnam War Anthology* (Lanham, MD: Rowman & Littlefield, Revised Edition, 1999), 138–139.

31. Eileen Shanahan, "I.R.S. Disallows Tax Exemptions for Gifts to Hospital Near Hanoi," *New York Times*, July 9, 1975, 19.

32. Gregory Jaynes, "Rizzo Concedes Defeat on Plan to Seek a Third Term," *New York Times*, November 8, 1978, A19.

33. Sharon McConnell, interview with author, December 12, 2007.

34. See Thomas J. Sugrue and John D. Skrentny, "The White Ethnic Strategy," in *Rightward Bound: Making America Conservative in the 1970s*, ed. Bruce J. Schulman and Julian E. Zelizer (Cambridge, MA: Harvard University Press, 2008), 171–191.

35. Thomas Byrne Edsall with Mary D. Edsall, *Chain Reaction: The Impact of Race, Rights and Taxes on American Politics* (New York: W. W. Norton, 1992).

36. Synanon was an internationally utilized recovery method that later devolved into a cult. Former members faced retaliation that sometimes escalated to attempted murder. Rod Janzen, *The Rise and Fall of Synanon: A California Utopia* (Baltimore: The Johns Hopkins University Press, 2001), 40–43.

37. Fitzhugh Mullan, *White Coat, Clenched Fist: The Political Education of An American Physician* (New York: Macmillan, 1976), 11.

38. Gil Fagiani, telephone interview with author, July 21, 2007.

39. Miguel "Mickey" Melendez, *We Took the Streets: Fighting for Latino Rights with the Young Lords* (New York: St. Martin's Press, 2003).

40. John Castellucci, *The Big Dance: The Untold Story of Weatherman Kathy Boudin and the Terrorist Family that Committed the Brink's Robbery Murders* (New York: Dodd, Mead & Company, 1986), 45–48.

41. Michael Cetewayo Tabor, *Capitalism Plus Dope Equals Genocide* (New York: Ministry of Information, Black Panther Party, ca. 1970), New York Black Panther Party Folder, Tamiment Library and Robert F. Wagner Labor Archives, New York University. Also available at http://www.marxists.org/history/usa/workers/black-panthers/1970/dope.htm (accessed July 22, 2009).

42. Fagiani, interview with author.

43. The NCLC, under direct orders from Lyndon LaRouche as part of his "Operation Mop-Up," routinely sent squads to disrupt Left groups such as the Communist Party USA and the Socialist Workers Party. See Nat Hentoff, "Of Thugs and Liars," *Village Voice*, January 24, 1974, 8. More generally, see Dennis King, *Nazis without Swastikas: The Lyndon LaRouche Cult and Its War on American Labor* (New York: League for Industrial Democracy, 1982); and Chip Berlet and Matthew N. Lyons, *Right-Wing Populism in America: Too Close for Comfort* (New York: Guilford Press, 2000), 273–276.

44. John Duffy, email interview with author, February 7, 2007.

45. No relation to October 4th Organization. The October League took its name after the month in which the Bolshevik Party took power in the Russian Revolution. For more on the group and the new communist movement of which it was a part, see Elbaum, *Revolution in the Air*.

46. Bill Whalen, telephone interview with author, June 19, 2008.

47. Saul Alinsky, interview with Eric Nordon, "Empowering People, Not Elites," *Playboy*, March 1972, 16.

48. Alinsky himself acknowledged this challenge frequently but did not see shortcomings in his model as a cause. For a critique of Alinsky's shortcomings on race, see James Williams, "Alinsky Discovered Organizing (Like Columbus Discovered America)," *Third Force*, July/August 1996, 14–17.

49. Saul Alinsky, *Rules for Radicals: A Pragmatic Primer for Realistic Radicals* (New York: Vintage, 1989), xxi.

50. Sanford D. Horwitt, *Let Them Call Me Rebel: Saul Alinsky, His Life and Legacy* (New York: Alfred A. Knopf, 1989), 451.

51. For more on these cases, see Eric Cummins, The *Rise and Fall of California's Radical Prison Movement* (Palo Alto, CA: Stanford University Press, 1994); Bettina Aptheker, *The Morning Breaks: The Trial of Angela Davis* (Ithaca, NY: Cornell University Press, 1997); Marjorie Heins, *Strictly Ghetto Property: The Story of Los Siete de la Raza* (Berkeley, CA: Ramparts Press, 1972); and Peniel E. Joseph, *Waiting 'Til the Midnight Hour: A Narrative History of Black Power in America* (New York: Henry Holt, 2006), 205–240.

52. See "Racism and Dope," *White Lightning* 1:4 (April 1972). Unpacking the function of white supremacy and the role of whites in dismantling it was a central project of many New Left groups into the 1970s, and they often reached different conclusions. Groups such as the Sojourner Truth Organization, the Weather Underground, and the Prairie Fire Organizing Committee made the fight against white supremacy a cornerstone of their work as all-white organizations. Sojourner Truth Organization's early documents and pamphlets have now been digitally archived at www.sojournertruth.net. Also see Weather Underground, *Prairie Fire: The Politics of Revolutionary Anti-Imperialism. Political Statement of the Weather Underground* (n.p.: Communications Co., 1974).

53. Dan Sidorick, telephone interview with author, July 7, 2007.

54. Steve Tappis, interview with author, September 19, 2005.

55. Dan Sidorick, email interview with author, June 22, 2009.

12

The Movement for a New Society

Consensus, Prefiguration, and Direct Action

ANDREW CORNELL

The revolution for life confronts the old order, but confronts lies with openness and repression with community. It shows in its very style how different
it is from the necrophilic American Empire.

–George Lakey, *Strategy for a Living Revolution*, 1973

Throughout the first years of the 1970s, amid an array of political transformations
on the Left, a cohort of young nonviolent militants worked to rejuvenate the tradition of radical pacifism in the United States by combining its core tenets with political and tactical innovations emerging from the struggles of the 1960s. This effort was
most effectively realized in the Movement for a New Society (MNS), an organization
founded in 1971 as a national network of collectives with a hub of more than one
hundred members living cooperatively in Philadelphia. MNS transmitted the practice of revolutionary nonviolence from the 1960s to the 1990s, synthesizing it with
ecology, feminism, and anarchism in the process. Though MNS is rarely remembered by name today, many of the new ways of doing radical politics that it promoted have become central to contemporary anti-authoritarian social movements.
MNS popularized consensus decision making, introduced the spokes-council
method of organization to activists in the United States, and was a leading advocate
of "prefigurative" politics.[1] Members of the organization substantially aided the
antiwar, antinuclear, feminist, gay liberation, and ecology movements by organizing
mass nonviolent direct actions, building support communities for activists, and
providing political education and skills training to organizers involved in hundreds
of grassroots efforts throughout the United States and the world.

MNS insisted on a "macro" view of social relations that explained how different forms of injustice were linked, and sought to implement a multi-pronged
revolutionary strategy combining its radical analysis with direct action and community building at a time when much of the movement was fracturing along lines

of identity and tactics. MNS's holistic and personal approach to revolutionary change attracted many activists exhausted by the pace and disappointed by the shortcomings of 1960s efforts. However, when the political climate changed and members could no longer juggle the multiple aspects of their work as effectively, their cohesion, long-term vision, and influence began to wane, compelling the organization to disband in 1988.

Radical Pacifism and the Movements of the 1960s

MNS grew out of a Quaker antiwar organization in 1971, but it built on principles and traditions that radical pacifists had developed throughout the twentieth century. Beginning in the World War I period, radical pacifism constituted an alternative vision and method for making progressive social change to that of the traditional Left. Though pacifists believed in economic justice, and many belonged to the Socialist Party, class did not form the linchpin of their politics as it did for Marxists. Instead, pacifists sought a more generalized "fellowship" of humanity and an end to war and the social institutions—including capitalism—that they believed underlay the drive to war. Pacifists distinguished their methods from those of the major Left parties by insisting on a correlation between means and end, and by encouraging adherents to live in a fashion as similar as possible to the way they would live in the ideal society they were striving for.[2] From the 1940s to the 1960s, radical pacifism was also colored by anarchism via the writings of the Dutch anarcho-pacifist Bart de Ligt and the antiwar activities of outspoken anarchists in the United States such as Ammon Hennacy, Paul Goodman, and the editors of the journal *Retort*.[3]

Radical pacifists drawn together by their experiences during World War II created the Congress of Racial Equality in 1942 and were important conduits of participatory deliberative styles and the tactics of Gandhian nonviolence to leaders of the civil rights movement, including Martin Luther King, Jr. and members of the Student Nonviolent Coordinating Committee (SNCC). Students for a Democratic Society (SDS) drew on SNCC's participatory structure and the ethos of the counterculture to formulate two of the defining demands of the New Left: the implementation of a participatory democracy and the overcoming of alienating culture.[4] Yet, in the later 1960s, both the black freedom movement and the student movement, smarting from repression on the one hand, and elated by radical victories at home and abroad on the other, moved away from this emergent, anarchistic political space that was distinguished from both liberalism and Marxism. If participatory democracy, prefigurative politics, and cultural transformation together could be seen as a ball about to be dropped, MNS was one of the most important groups diving for it, working hard to keep it in play. The burgeoning women's liberation movement likewise placed a premium on developing egalitarian internal relationships and making changes in daily life; not surprisingly, then, feminism left an enduring impact on MNS.[5]

MNS emerged in 1971 as the new face of the Philadelphia-based A Quaker Action Group (AQAG). AQAG was formed in 1966 to address the shortcomings its predominantly young members attributed to mainstream peace organizations and to the liberalism of many Quakers. Despite the influence of older radical pacifists such as Dave Dellinger, much of the peace movement appeared structurally bureaucratic and tactically timid, eschewing confrontational direct actions for repetitious mass mobilizations. AQAG aimed to orchestrate creative and risky "witnesses" against the devastation of war that would "undermine the legitimacy of the government" and that the mainstream media would find hard to resist covering.[6] Perhaps most famously, members piloted a fifty-foot ship, *The Phoenix*, on three trips to North and South Vietnam in 1967 and 1968 with cargos of donated medical supplies.[7] Within four years, however, AQAG itself seemed sorely inadequate for the task at hand, as the events of 1966–1970 suggested to its members that the movement should aim not only to end the war in Vietnam, but also to fundamentally reshape all aspects of life in the United States. Through an intensive study group convened in 1968, members concluded that resisting war without addressing its ties to other forms of injustice was inadequate and that direct action could not succeed divorced from other forms of movement work.

AQAG presented a statement to the American Friends Service Committee's (AFSC) Conference of Eighty meeting in March of 1971, arguing that the times, and Quaker principles, called for a broad program to combat ecological devastation, militarism, "corporate capitalism," racism, and sexism. The proposal succinctly laid out a new vision for creating "fundamental social change":

> We hope to catalyze a movement for a new society, which will feature a vision of the new society, and how to get there; a critical analysis of the American political-economic system; a focus on expanding the consciousness and organizing the commitment of the middle class toward fundamental change through nonviolent struggle, often in concert with other change movements; the organization and development of nonviolent revolutionary groups and life centers as bases for sustained struggle on the local as well as national and international levels; training for non-violent struggle; and a program rooted in changed lives and changed values.[8]

Although some members expressed considerable sympathy for the proposal, the AFSC declined to adopt the program. Undeterred, the coterie of approximately two dozen activists renamed themselves Movement for a New Society, to reflect the broader aims and the secular status of the new organization. Beginning with small collectives in Philadelphia and Eugene, Oregon, they set to work building membership and developing each aspect of their vision.

1971–1976

Although not officially sanctioned by the AFSC, MNS was able to draw on the support of an established network of Quaker institutions to build the organization's membership. A 1972 issue of the MNS newsletter, for example, noted that the AFSC funded an MNS group in Pasadena, California, and the Portland AFSC chapter was "centered around building MNS in Oregon." MNS was also discussed at some Quaker meetings, and members were frequently able to use these places of worship to conduct training. Steve Chase, a central figure in the Twin Cities MNS, first learned of the organization through an announcement made at the DeKalb, Illinois, meeting house that he had grown up attending.[9] This broader network helped establish the group's legitimacy, spread information, and provide monetary support crucial to bringing in a critical mass of participants early on. However, reliance on such a network for recruiting also contributed to the predominantly white and middle-class character of the organization's membership in its early years.

MNS also undertook recruiting tours that emphasized the community and personal-development aspects of the group's approach at a time when "burn-out" from the frantic pace of 1960s activism was epidemic. Upon returning from a trip through New England, two MNS trainers wrote, "The wholeness of the MNS approach . . . generated excitement. More and more people are questioning the value of their scattered activities. Fewer and fewer are willing to put off their personal growth until 'after the revolution.'"[10]

In MNS's first year, members engaged in innovative direct-action campaigns as a group. Simultaneously, they designed a variety of trainings in nonviolent campaign strategy and group process for members and other activists, worked to deepen and disseminate their political analysis, and established a community of collectively owned houses and workplaces in which they hoped to nurture new cultural values and the "personal growth" of members.

Direct Action

In July 1971, the newly minted group launched itself into the Baltimore harbor in a fleet of canoes and kayaks to blockade a Pakistani ship from docking to take on military supplies. The confrontation grew out of a "study-action team" that began researching the impact of U.S. policies and business ties abroad. The team decided to focus on the Nixon administration's financial and military support for the Pakistani military dictatorship, known for its brutal suppression of political opponents and the people of East Pakistan. Though police and the coast guard defeated its first attempt at blocking a weapons shipment, and hauled the peace fleet out of the water and into jail cells, the action received wide coverage in national print, radio, and television reportage.[11]

Neither discouraged nor satisfied with their results, MNS expanded the campaign. The group joined forces with the Philadelphia Friends of East Bengal, whose members were more directly impacted by the crisis in the subcontinent, and appealed to the International Longshoremen's Association, persuading the union to refuse to load military materiel bound for Pakistan. When MNS and its allies discovered that another Pakistani ship was to take on supplies in Philadelphia in August, they again mobilized a sea blockade, but this time paired it with a picket on the docks. After an intense effort by the MNS fleet to evade police boats and place itself in the freighter's path, the *Al-Ahmadi* managed to dock. However, following the lead of their local union president, the longshoremen refused to cross a picket line that MNS maintained continuously until the ship sailed away empty twenty-eight hours later.[12]

MNS deployed similar tactics in April 1972, when it allied with Vietnam Veterans Against the War and local Quaker groups to block the *USS Nitro* from loading munitions bound for the Gulf of Tonkin. Though MNS ultimately failed to block the ship, the skirmishes on land and sea so inspired the *Nitro*'s reluctant crew that five sailors jumped from the ship and attempted to join the war resisters in their canoes.[13] These actions confirmed MNS strategists' belief that direct action could yield tangible results and educate the public through media coverage, but that to be successful it required the legitimacy of those impacted, and broader support, especially at the point of production. That is, direct action needed to be rooted in organizing campaigns to be effective.

If the port blockades showed the commitment of Philadelphia MNS members to well-planned action, other developments showcased MNS as a national organization that was able to mobilize in solidarity with radical struggles on a moment's notice. When federal officials seemed poised to violently oust American Indian Movement activists in a standoff at Wounded Knee, South Dakota, in March 1973, MNS implemented a phone tree to contact participants throughout the network. Collectives in Madison, Minneapolis, Milwaukee, Des Moines, Denver, Portland, and Philadelphia responded by organizing carloads of activists to converge on Wounded Knee within two days. Upon arrival, MNSers organized "observer teams" to position themselves between the troops and the militants. Although the activists may have forestalled violence in the first days, the government eventually forced their withdrawal.[14] MNS later launched nationally coordinated protests fewer than twenty-four hours after news broke of the Three Mile Island nuclear disaster in 1979.[15]

Macro-Analysis

The variety of events to which MNS responded with creative direct action tactics throughout the 1970s—U.S. imperialism, Native sovereignty, nuclear power, and ecology—indicates the breadth of its developing political analysis and program. This thinking began as discussions and collective writing projects among a circle of AQAG leaders with significant experience in civil rights and antiwar work. Bill Moyers and Richard Taylor, for example, had served on the staff of the Southern Christian Leadership Conference (SCLC), while George Lakey had spent much of 1969 offering nonviolence workshops to and learning from New Left movements throughout Europe. Their efforts, along with contributions from Susan Gowan, George and Lillian Willoughby, and others, resulted in two books that served as the primary statements of MNS's politics: *Revolution: A Quaker Prescription for a Sick Society* (later retitled *Moving Towards a New Society*) and *Strategy for a Living Revolution*.[16] As the organization took shape, the founders made it a priority to expand the

process of collective political development to include any member who was interested. To this end, a group of MNS activists in Philadelphia formed a collective to
develop "macro-analysis seminars"—long-term collaborative study groups modeled
after the popular education initiatives of the civil rights movement and the ideas of
Paulo Freire. The group developed—and frequently updated—a set of readings for a
twenty-four-week seminar that proceeded from analysis to vision to strategy.[17]

Revolutionary nonviolence formed the bedrock of MNS's political analysis
and its strategy. The group believed that war is inherent to capitalism, and that
social inequality is itself a form of violence maintained by the threat of repressive
state violence; this requires those who morally reject violence to become social
revolutionaries. Members synthesized these core principles with recent developments in leftist thought. Foremost, this process entailed a commitment to principles of ecology and environmental sustainability emerging at the time. MNS,
additionally, placed the United States' neocolonial relationship with the less industrialized countries at the center of its indictment of contemporary society. The
group insisted on the need to "de-develop" the United States and other capitalist
countries, as the members of these nations lived at rates unattainable to the
majority of the world's population and unsustainable given the limits of ecology.
Influenced by the nascent women's liberation movement, MNS incorporated a
critique of sexism alongside its indictment of racism from the outset.[18] Bringing
together a mix of Gandhians, anarchists, and unaffiliated democratic socialists,
the group promoted the idea of a "decentralized socialism" that had much in common with the "participatory economics" others were developing at the time.[19]
"Economic enterprises, as we see it, would be socially owned, decentralized and
democratically controlled," explained an introductory pamphlet. "Political decisions would be made by participatory means, starting with the smallest face-to-face
communities of citizens and extending upward to the global level. Nation-states
as we now know them would cease to exist, supplanted by regional groupings,
perhaps of those with common economic interests."[20]

MNS saw that in starting fresh, it had the chance to incorporate in its structure
the principle—expressed most recently by the New Left, but earlier by anarchists and
radical pacifists—that the movement should "prefigure," or model, its goals in its own
work. MNS's introductory pamphlet declared its opposition to "traditional forms of
organization, from ITT [now AT&T] to the PTA [Parent-Teacher Association] . . . for
they exhibit the sexism and authoritarianism we seek to supplant. Our goals must be
incorporated into the way we organize. Thus the movement we build must be egalitarian and non-centralized."[21] Accordingly, the group developed a network structure
that was directly influenced by Shalom, a Dutch anarchist federation that had
impressed Lakey during his travels.[22] The call for participatory democracy in the New
Left and egalitarianism in the women's movement led MNS to make nearly all of
its decisions using a formal consensus process that it developed by borrowing from
both the Quaker tradition and conflict resolution techniques that some of its early
members practiced professionally as mediators.[23]

MNS's commitment to prefiguration extended beyond the organization's structure, but precisely how the principle was to be enacted was continually debated within the network. The idea was most frequently expressed in MNS's injunction to "live the revolution now"—a reformulation of Gandhi's classic instruction for his followers to "be the change you wish to see." In its early statements, however, MNS was clear that "living the revolution" served as only one practical aspect of a multipronged revolutionary strategy. Like many other radical theorists in the early 1970s, the founders of MNS believed that structural contradictions would create a revolutionary situation in the United States by the end of the century. MNS members would serve as a "leaven in the bread" of the mass social movements responding to this crisis, giving them the tools and the nonviolent principles they would need to effectively make a social revolution. In the short-term, MNS believed radicals needed to develop strategic direct-action campaigns to win reforms while simultaneously building alternative institutions based on radical principles. For these efforts to be sustained throughout a long struggle and ultimately to be successful, activists needed training and to experience new kinds of community that would support their work.

Prefigurative Community

Beginning with its first collective statement, MNS emphasized that a major component of its program would be the creation of intentional communities of activists. As first conceived, the movement would be made up of six-to-twelve person Nonviolent Revolutionary Groups (NRGs, or "Energies") that would work on local issues as teams and link with one another locally, regionally, and nationally. "Through NRGs," a founding statement explained, "individuals can seek to live the revolution now by giving up the characteristic scatter of liberal activities which results in fragmented selves and soulless organizations, and substitute concentration and community." In areas where numerous NRGs were clustered, the movement would develop Life Centers, "more sizable, collective living arrangements for ongoing training and direct action campaigns."[24]

Members organized collective living situations in cities such as Savannah and Seattle, and in smaller towns like Ann Arbor and Madison. MNS members typically lived in communal households and participated in one or more collectives focused on an aspect of the organization's work such as direct actions, trainings, or macroanalysis seminars. Citywide meetings and informal social gatherings knit the collectives together. Members dispersed geographically and involved in an expanding array of campaigns shared their ideas and experiences with one another through a lively internal newsletter, variously titled *Dandelion Wine, The Wine*, and *Grapevine*, published monthly by an internal communications collective that rotated yearly between MNS groups in different cities. The entire network met for a week, once a year, at Whole Network Meetings to socialize, strategize, and hash out policies affecting the entire organization. Whole Network Meetings in the mid-1970s brought together 100 to 120 activists, usually about half of those participating in the organization in a given year.[25]

While many cities hoped to develop Life Centers, only Philadelphia was able to maintain a community large and stable enough to offer the number of activities, collectives, and alternative institutions originally envisioned. In January 1976, when an informal census was completed, a ten-block area of West Philadelphia was home to nineteen collective households composed of four to eleven people each, with names such as "The Gathering," "Kool Rock Amazons," and "Sunflower." Members of these households worked in twenty-two different MNS collectives including the Feminist Collective, the Training Organizing Collective, the Simple Living Group, and the Peace Conversion/B-1 Bomber Collective.[26] Households operated independently—choosing their own members and establishing policies about what was purchased jointly and how much members were required to contribute to expenses for the house. Household cultures varied: Some shared religious practices, others shared their entire incomes.[27] Until the mid-1980s, MNS did not pay anyone for their movement work. Members were encouraged to work part-time jobs to earn the "bread money" they needed for monthly household expenses and personal items. Some members worked retail jobs, sometimes at co-operative enterprises, while some took on construction work, taught college courses, or staffed Quaker-related organizations.

MNS strategy prioritized the creation of alternative institutions that modeled egalitarian and anticapitalist values. Philadelphia members created a worker-owned print shop and a member-run food cooperative, for example. Later, the MNS publications committee launched a commercial publishing house, New Society Publishers. These businesses provided jobs to MNS members and services to the movement and others in the neighborhood. After a series of rapes in the West Philadelphia neighborhood where many MNS activists lived, members also helped organize a block association that worked to prevent crime through community building. The block association rejected an increased police presence in favor of teams of neighbors that patrolled on foot armed only with air horns. The association also offered victim counseling, which it believed was "helpful to prevent overreaction in the longer run," meaning the racism underlying the crime-fears of white people living in racially mixed areas of West Philadelphia.[28] Alternative institutions were meant to demonstrate that radical activity could create immediate, concrete improvements in people's daily lives—improvements that, the founders believed, would give activists confidence and were more likely to attract neighbors and those not already radicalized to participate in MNS than its seemingly remote utopian visions.[29]

Beyond serving as a base for alternative institutions, collective living was meant to allow members to live "simply" and inexpensively, permitting them to dedicate more time to movement work and to reduce their environmental impact. Moreover, living in community was expected to promote the personal growth of MNS members. This commitment to individual transformation was perhaps the most ambiguous aspect of the MNS project, as it combined personal empowerment exercises with spirituality and the unlearning of oppressive behavior through a variety of radical therapy practices emergent at the time. Initially, members' commitment to personal growth meant involvement in self-help and personal empowerment activities, such as yoga or learning to become "active listeners," which were intended to help them become more effective in their daily lives and in their organizing work. However, within the organization's first year, MNS members in Philadelphia began an extended process of understanding and rooting out sexism—and later homophobia, class prejudice, and racism—within the organization and in members' personal lives. As these discussions progressed, personal growth came to mean shedding the internalized strictures of an unjust society—racist and ageist conditioning, patriarchal gender roles, and bourgeois "hangups." Because MNS saw the personal as political, it embraced the process of individuals developing aspects of their personality not sanctioned or encouraged by social expectations as a victory in itself. Moreover, MNS activists understood that unlearning oppressive assumptions and behavior was crucial to becoming better organizers.

Further complicating each of these aspects of personal growth was the penchant most MNS members shared for "radical therapy" practices such as Transactional Analysis and, especially, Re-evaluation Counseling (RC, also known as "co-counseling").[30] Invented by former Communist Party member Harvey Jackins, RC seeks to overcome oppression through reciprocal psychological counseling sessions among nonprofessional individuals trained in the process. The theory proposes that all people have been oppressed, and it suggests that to overcome that oppression one must emote about individual painful and shameful experiences, including those from childhood, in order for the co-counselor to remove emotional "blockages" and to establish fully rational thinking. Jackins believed that after dissolving all such blockages, practitioners could inhabit a childlike state of joy and innocence.

Despite the therapy movement's hierarchical structure and revelations that Jackins had engaged in a pattern of sexual improprieties with female co-counselors, RC language and practice came to pervade MNS's work. When deliberating sensitive issues, for example, members might remind each other that it was all right to act "on our feelings" but unhelpful to "act on our distress as it blurs good thinking."[31] In difficult meetings, facilitators often called for breaks to allow members to pair up for brief counseling sessions. In MNS, then, the Gandhian dictum, that the revolutionary must change as she or he changes society, merged with the growing interest in popular psychology, New Age spirituality, and gurus that occupied many former radicals in the 1970s.[32] If the focus on personal development did not depoliticize MNS members, as it did many of their contemporaries, it did shift MNS work toward a more individual and inner-focused direction that would have significant consequences for the organization in years to come.

Beyond developing personal skills, MNS communities were intended to shape movement culture by changing how participants interacted with each other. In an attempt to correct for the harsh style of many contemporary radical initiatives,

MNS sought to model a form of radical politics that shunned aggressive and egoist behavior and included emotional support to one's comrades as central to the mission of social-change organizations. This culture of support manifested itself in many ways: the practice of physical affection, both platonic and romantic, through hugging and snuggling; collective singing and other self-entertainment in the collective homes; and "light and livelies"—seemingly childish games (similar to today's "ice-breakers") to keep energy and spirits up during long meetings. MNS, in summary, saw their form of collective living as an extension of the work undertaken in consciousness-raising groups and as central to realizing the democratic ideal of individuals developing themselves to their greatest potential. A 1974 *Dandelion* article, "MNS Support Communities," explained: "As members of the community gradually free themselves from oppressive roles and patterns of relating to each other (i.e., from sexist, ageist or racist conditioning), they provide an atmosphere of greater equality and openness for others. New members joining the community find themselves in an increasingly creative environment where they are being "asked"—simply by interacting with others—to be fully themselves, fully rational and loving human beings."[33]

Nonviolence Training

The concentration of MNS members in West Philadelphia also made it possible for the Life Center to serve as a training hub for activists from around the world. MNS's primary and most enduring contribution to 1970s social movements was the trainings it provided to activists in democratic group process, strategic campaign planning, and direct-action tactics. Training collectives devised a series of educational workshops that varied in length from one day to two weeks, to an entire year in residence at the Life Center. Other trainers traveled throughout the country, offering "4 × 4" workshops (two intensive four-day sessions with a break in the middle) to groups of nonviolent activists working together on a specific campaign, or simply living in the same town.[34] Although MNS saw training as a means of giving self-directed activists tools they needed to be effective in their local work, trainings also functioned as an important means of recruiting new members to MNS and disseminating the group's vision of change.

As the movement against nuclear power took off in the mid-1970s, MNS was instrumental both in helping participants train for actions and in encouraging the movement to structure itself on the basis of decentralized affinity groups coordinated through a directly democratic spokes-council.[35] George Lakey recalls that MNS first learned of this technique from a Swedish activist attending a training at the Life Center who had used the spokes-council method in actions to block road development in his own country.[36] The anti-nuclear-power movement came to national attention on the heels of a mass nonviolent direct action to resist the development of the Seabrook nuclear power plant in New Hampshire. MNS trainers traveled throughout New England in early 1977, facilitating workshops on nonviolent direct action with members and supporters of the Clamshell Alliance, the largest anti-nuclear organization on the East Coast, which was coordinating the action. On April 30, approximately fourteen hundred people occupied the site of the proposed power plant, with one thousand or more doing support work. The occupiers were arrested en masse on May 1 and held at five armories nearby.[37]

While the mass occupation, which occurred without violence or injury, was a stunning organizational feat in itself, MNS considered what happened next to be just as powerful. In the armories, MNS members and other action coordinators worked to build jail solidarity—the practice of prisoners bargaining collectively for conditions of their release, rather than being treated individually—and an egalitarian community in microcosm for the two weeks the protesters were held. By facilitating collective decision making on legal strategy using spokes-councils, holding trainings, and encouraging dance parties and other celebrations amongst the hundreds of detainees, MNS helped turn the incarceration from a repressive act meant to discourage resistance into one of excitement, empowerment, and networking.[38] The Seabrook occupation marked the first time that three organizational components which have since become de rigueur for anti-authoritarian mass actions—affinity groups, spokes-councils, and consensus process—were used together in the United States. After Seabrook, MNS trainers traveled throughout the country training anti-nuke organizations in consensus and encouraging them to adopt the spokes-council model that had worked so well in New Hampshire.

1976–1982

By 1976, a number of interrelated problems and tensions had begun to develop within the MNS network. Despite the excitement of the burgeoning anti-nuke movement, many members felt frustrated with the organization's lack of strategic direction. While in agreement with MNS's long-term vision, participants were frequently unsure how best to contribute to the variety of local and national campaigns and movements developing at the time. In towns with only a dozen or so MNS members, this led to high turnover, as committed organizers moved on to more clearly defined projects; in Philadelphia, some left the Life Center, but many others stayed on, viewing its internal life as the defining aspect of their involvement with radical social change.

At the 1976 Whole Network Meeting, members worked to address MNS's "Philly-centric" development by adopting a five-year plan, which encouraged Life Center members to move to promising regions to establish MNS on stronger, less centralized footings. Owing to the plan and to interest generated by the important contributions MNS had made at Seabrook and other high-profile events, the movement grew to a peak of approximately three hundred active members by decade's end.[39] This thickening of the ranks would not last, however. By the early 1980s, MNS collectives in cities from Chicago to Baltimore had gone through what Twin Cities MNS member Betsy Raasch-Gilman identified as a series of "boom and bust cycles," owing to unresolved questions plaguing the group's work in most parts of the country: "The tension between utopian community and a group of involved activists; the push for perfection in personal and political relationships; the confusion about membership and strategy all could be traced directly to Philadelphia's model," she claimed.[40]

While many found the sense of community MNS offered to be the most rewarding part of their involvement, it also led to serious tensions that eventually contributed to the organization's demise. MNS's prefigurative community attracted some people whose conception of social change diverged sharply from early members' assumptions, while it kept others with shared political commitments away. MNS's rationale for group living differed in several respects from that of the often-depoliticized communes and intentional communities formed by counterculturalists in the late 1960s, but this was not always obvious. Some visitors believed that an alternative, communal lifestyle constituted a sufficient form of activism. In line with the utopian socialist tradition, they argued that egalitarian communities could serve as a model of the new society which, through their obvious superiority to other ways of life, would naturally attract more participants and inspire imitations.[41] Lakey remembers encountering newcomers to the Life Center in the mid-1970s who saw it as another intentional community and "wanted lifestyle to be *the* leading edge of change." He had to explain to them that "the cutting edge of [MNS's] understanding of revolution is not lifestyle change. We think of it like ashrams in Gandhi's ideas, which were base camps for revolution. So what do you do in the base camp for revolution? You get ready to go on the barricades."[42]

However, not all members and potential participants were as clear in their thinking about intentional communities, and the role of community building eventually became muddled. By the late 1970s, Raasch-Gilman saw MNS members fitting into two different categories: the "hard-bitten shop floor organizers" and the "new age hippie flakes."[43] MNS's commitments to simple living, its expanding intra-movement jargon, and its countercultural social norms created a subculture that served to glue members together but also threatened to alienate non-members in the broader Left and the public at large. It took time for members to see that, rather than creating a model of *the* new society, they were creating one of many possible new lifestyles that grew out of a specific configuration of values they prioritized. One former member reflected, "A lot of what was defining our culture was our rebellion against white culture. So, we *were* a counterculture, but we were actually counter to white culture."[44] This made MNS's internal culture less appealing and transformative to people of color, and some white working-class people, who had a different relationship to the dominant, white, middle-class culture to begin with.

As this subculture solidified, some members noted with growing anxiety that, "the center of gravity was no longer in work in popular movements. . . . A quality of introspection became dominant."[45] As already noted, MNS members had from the outset spent much of their time developing a deeper collective understanding and approach to combating sexism, gay and lesbian oppression, and classism in the organization and in their personal lives. As the decade wore on, however, these conversations sometimes took on a tone "shrill in moral judgment" in which sim-plistic analyses sometimes exacerbated weaknesses in MNS's structure.[46] As a net-work of semi-autonomous collectives, the organization found itself without a formal body to set strategy and help collectives coordinate their activities nationally. As cri-tiques of classism progressed, the macroanalytic theoretical work MNS originally prided itself on was increasingly criticized as middle-class intellectualizing that was alienating to working-class members. Meanwhile, the desire to plan and enact strategic campaigns against specific targets was sometimes written off as "a mascu-line trip" based on a "big-bang theory of revolution."[47] Such criticisms, combined with the growing focus on exemplary community, the requirement of consensus for every decision, and the personal approach to overcoming oppression advocated by Re-evaluation Counseling combined to draw MNS away from strategic action. The group's initial critique of male-dominated organizations and of patriarchal leader-ship styles slid toward rejecting the idea of "leadership" in general.

As MNS was delving into the lived experience of oppression, it devoted less time to structural analysis of the same issues. This left MNS insufficiently pre-pared to strategically respond to developments such as the Reagan administra-tion's assault on the labor movement and the welfare state or the growing right-wing backlash against gains of the civil rights and feminist movements. The difficulty of maintaining a comprehensive political analysis and a corresponding strategic orientation was exacerbated by the group's method of creating litera-ture. Though the founding statements were drafted by individuals or small groups, MNS later decided to produce all official documents via open committees and consensus adoption, slowing intellectual output to an exasperating snail's pace. As Raasch-Gilman admits, "We did so much difficult internal work because we had such a hard time confronting the larger social, political, and economic world in which we lived. It was easier to try to change ourselves and our immediate com-rades than it was to devise long-term campaigns and strategies for changing the outside world."[48]

1982–1988

In 1982, MNS entered into lengthy discussions about the future of the organiza-tion, touched off by a statement issued by the Baltimore-based Pandora's Collec-tive. The booms and busts that had occurred in many cities shook members' faith that the network was healthy and growing steadily. Meanwhile, the inward focus of the previous years left many unsure of what MNS's contribution to broader movements was or should be. Two position papers significantly shaped the dis-cussion and decisions MNS eventually made at its 1982 Whole Network Meeting. The first, drafted by Bill Moyers, encouraged the group to develop from its current "spontaneous" organizational model to an "empowerment" model. The latter would attempt to combine the benefits of traditional hierarchical organizations with those of the spontaneous sort. An empowerment organization, according to

Moyers, would develop the abilities and leadership skills of all members of the group while creating structures allowing it to establish priorities and carry out long-term work on a national level.[49]

A second paper, Steve Chase's "Reorganizers Manual," provided a useful analysis of tensions within MNS. Chase argued that when it was formed, MNS intended to be both an "exemplary" and an "adversarial" organization. It would be exemplary by "living the revolution now" through collective living, democratic group process, rejection of oppressive roles, and support for members' personal growth. It would be adversarial by participating in and training others for strategic campaigns and direct action against exploitative corporations, the government war machine, and other unjust institutions. As Chase saw it, by the mid-1970s MNS had begun to lean much more heavily toward the pole of exemplary organization. The intense scrutiny of structure, of leadership, and of "group dynamics" represented the implicit prioritization of getting the MNS house—the showroom of the new society—in proper order. Political program and strategic intervention in the central political developments of the day, meanwhile, had fallen by the wayside. Chase concluded that this tension left MNS with a fundamental choice about what type of organization it would be: either a loose network of activists supporting each other's work and commitments to live in a principled fashion or a "movement-building" cadre organization committed to strategically developing the power of radical social movements in the 1980s.[50]

After considerable discussion, the network meeting accepted core elements of Moyers and Chase's analyses, agreeing to reshape MNS into a movement-building organization based on an empowerment model. In terms of practical steps, this meant that members committed to carry out three types of work: participation in grassroots organizations; resource-sharing with social movements (such as conducting trainings, raising funds, and promoting them in MNS publications); and building and maintenance of MNS itself. Members accepted the principle of elected national leadership, whose role was to guide and develop a "self-managed" group of revolutionaries.[51]

During the early 1980s, MNS members devoted considerable energy to new efforts, including Take Back the Night marches, women's peace encampments, and a campaign against the deployment of Cruise and Pershing II missiles that was coordinated with European activists. However, when members opened a discussion in the pages of *The Grapevine* in 1986 evaluating the process of becoming a movement-building organization, most were unsatisfied with their progress.[52] As individuals, members of MNS had put in long hours on various campaigns, yet the organization still lacked clear ways of contributing to developing struggles. With a declining focus on macroanalysis seminars and even informal political discussion, MNS's theoretical development had not only stagnated, but it even devolved throughout the 1980s.[53] Furthermore, MNS had made little progress in bringing in new members and of racially diversifying its membership due to the defining role its own movement subculture played in the organization. As Raasch-Gilman concluded, "We couldn't really expand our cultural boundaries, because our cultural boundaries were what made us who we were."[54]

Despite clarifications and recommitments put forward in 1986, MNS was unable to overcome these internal contradictions. At its 1988 network meeting, the forty assembled members agreed to "lay the group down," in the tradition of Quaker committees that have outlasted their usefulness. Doing so, they reasoned, would allow them to devote their energy to new efforts more effectively able to meet the political challenges of the 1990s.[55]

Legacy

The early 1970s are commonly remembered as a time of "burn-out," but the Movement for a New Society offered new directions in making social change that helped to mitigate the loss of energy and direction felt by many activists during that period. For nearly two decades, MNS attempted to put into practice principles innovated by movements of the 1960s: participatory democracy as an ideal and a practice, prefiguring the world one wants to win, confronting multiple forms of oppression simultaneously, and recognizing that the personal is political.

Members typically evaluated their efforts and tried to understand their shortcomings with a focus on their own actions, rather than considering them in the wider political context MNS was operating within. Participants continued to promote fundamental change as the mass movements and radical sentiments they sought to channel into a comprehensive strategy were rapidly dissipating. The organization was launched with the expectation that movements would grow to revolutionary proportions in a matter of years. When this proved wrong, MNS could not adapt its long-term vision and strategy in a fashion that was compelling enough to retain older members and attract new cohorts of activists. Nor was MNS isolated from developments in other movements. The growing emphasis on community and lifestyle within MNS, for example, paralleled what Alice Echols calls the turn from radical feminism to cultural feminism, a version more interested in community than in strategic campaigns.[56] Likewise, Barbara Epstein notes that prominent members of the anti-nuclear Clamshell Alliance, such as Cathy Wolff, "blamed the deterioration of the Clamshell on the turn toward pursuit of community for its own sake."[57]

MNS was not repressed by state forces, nor did it become irrelevant to the popular movements of the period, as happened with many other radical organizations. Rather, it was ultimately unable to overcome the hostile social and political climate of the 1980s as well as the unforeseen challenges that arose from its own innovations in the areas of radical community building and anti-authoritarian leadership, decision making, and structure. Nonetheless, MNS made an impact on the practice of radical activism in the United States disproportionate to its small membership.

MNS linked the broadening objectives of radical politics that characterized 1960s movements to a critique of traditional Left organizational structures. It attempted to demonstrate that when the *goals* of radical politics are expanded to include changes in ecological practices and personal relationships, the *means* of reaching these goals must also be expanded. MNS was an early and consistent advocate of the need for all radical organizations, regardless of the specific campaigns they were engaged in, to collectively challenge sexism, homophobia, classism, and racism in group dynamics. It began experimenting with a network structure before speakerphones were widely available—to say nothing of the internet—and posed the provocative idea of an anti-authoritarian cadre organization. In trying out these new approaches, MNS proved that Left formations can innovate organizations that hew to neither Leninist nor electoral-party models. In some ways, the MNS approach resembled that of the revolutionary syndicalist union Industrial Workers of the World (the Wobblies), founded in 1905. Like the Wobblies, MNS members believed in the need to organize on a mass scale while "building the new world within the shell of the old."[58] Their experiences indicate just how challenging that might be in a period when activists recognize the need to organize people not solely according to their class position, but on the basis of other aspects of identity and social inequality as well.

Since MNS dissolved, its ideas and practices have been taken up by groups such as Earth First!, Food Not Bombs, Anti-Racist Action, and ACT UP, as well as by infoshops, radical periodicals, anarchist collectives, campus organizations, and, perhaps most notably, the global justice movement that arose at the turn of the millennium.[59] Like MNS, these efforts have often been hindered by the insularity of radical communities, a fetishization of consensus process, and confusion about the desirability and the nature of leaders and leadership in radical organizations. But if it never satisfactorily resolved these and related dilemmas, MNS made many other contributions.

Although it is difficult to evaluate the exact extent of the group's influence until we have fuller accounts of the other key organizational initiatives of the 1970s and 1980s, it is clear that MNS was a major innovator and force in promoting multi-issue political analysis, consensus process, collective living and political community in urban areas, models of political commitments in everyday relationships and life choices, network structure, anti-oppression work personally and within organizations, identity-based caucuses, cost-sharing and sliding-scale prices, direct action, and the use of spokes-councils. Through its intensive work and its experiments with new ways of making a "living revolution," the Movement for a New Society kept alive and permanently transformed the practice of revolutionary nonviolence in the United States—lending new tactics, new organizational structures, and new priorities to an array of other radical movements and traditions in the process.

NOTES

1. Prefigurative politics denotes the principle that activists and social-change organizations should model in their present-day lives and work the new values, institutions, and

social relationships they advocate for on a broader scale, as part of their strategy for bringing about that change. See Wini Breines, *Community and Organization in the New Left, 1962–1968: The Great Refusal* (New Brunswick, NJ: Rutgers University Press, 1989), 6; Francesca Polletta, *Freedom Is an Endless Meeting: Democracy in American Social Movements* (Chicago: University of Chicago Press, 2002), 6–12.

2. Cf. Scott H. Bennett, *Radical Pacifism: The War Resisters League and Gandhian Nonviolence in America, 1915–1963* (Syracuse, NY: Syracuse University Press, 2003); Marian Mollin, *Radical Pacifism in Modern America: Egalitarianism and Protest* (Philadelphia: University of Pennsylvania Press, 2006); James Tracy, *Direct Action: Radical Pacifism from the Union Eight to the Chicago Seven* (Chicago: University of Chicago Press, 1996); and Polletta, *Freedom Is an Endless Meeting*, 26–54.

3. See Bart de Ligt, *The Conquest of Violence: An Essay on War and Revolution* (1937; rpt. London: Pluto Press, 1989); Alan Antliff, *Anarchy and Art: From the Paris Commune to the Fall of the Berlin Wall* (Vancouver: Arsenal Pulp Press, 2007), 113–117; Dachine Rainer, "Holley Cantine: February 14, 1916–January 2, 1977," in *Drunken Boat: Art, Rebellion, Anarchy*, ed. Max Bleckman (New York and Seattle: Autonomedia and Left Bank Books, 1994); and Taylor Stoehr, "Introduction," in *Drawing the Line: The Political Essays of Paul Goodman*, ed. Taylor Stoehr (New York: Free Life Editions, 1977).

4. Polleta, *Freedom*, 120–148.

5. See Polletta, *Freedom*, 149–175; Alice Echols, *Daring to Be Bad: Radical Feminism in America, 1967–1975* (Minneapolis: University of Minnesota Press, 1989).

6. George Lakey, interview with author, July 9, 2008.

7. George Lakey, *Strategy for a Living Revolution* (San Francisco: W. H. Freeman and Company, 1973), xiii–xviii.

8. "Program for a New Society: A Statement by A Quaker Action Group," leaflet, Wisconsin Historical Society, Social Action Vertical File, Box 1, Folder: A Quaker Action Group. Hereafter WHS, SAVF.

9. Lynne Shivers, "Short-Term Trainer's Collective at the Life Center," *Dandelion*, December 1971; no title, *Dandelion*, December 1973, no page number; "Movement Building—National," *Dandelion*, October 1972; Betsy Raasch-Gilman, "The Movement for a New Society: One Participant's Account" (unpublished memoir), 17, Swarthmore College Peace Collection, Movement for a New Society Collection, DG 154, Acc. 02A-025, Box 6.

10. Berit Lakey and Paul Morrisey, "Hello . . . Goodbye, I Say Hello," *Dandelion*, June 1973.

11. For an account of the action by an MNS member see Richard Taylor, "Blockading for Bangladesh," *The Progressive*, February, 1972, 20–23. Associated Press coverage of the blockade was picked up by newspapers across the country. See "Flotilla of Canoes Fails to Bar Ship," *Corpus Christi Times*, July 15, 1971, 50; "Union to Load Non-Military Cargo on Ship to Pakistan," *Cumberland (MD) News*, July 17, 1971, 3.

12. Richard Taylor, "Blockading for Bangladesh," *The Progressive*, February 1972, 20–23.

13. Chuck Fager, "22 Canoes vs. Navy," pamphlet, WHS, SAVF, Box 29, Folder: Movement for a New Society.

14. Jim Schrag, "MNS at Wounded Knee: The Network Works," *Dandelion*, June 1973.

15. MNS fundraising appeal, Spring 1979, University of Michigan, Labadie Collection, Vertical File, Folder: Socialism—Movement for a New Society.

16. Susanne Gowan et al., *Moving toward a New Society* (Philadelphia: New Society Press, 1976); and Lakey, *Strategy for a Living Revolution*.

17. "Finding Out," no author, *Dandelion*, October 1973, n.p.

18. "Analysis," *MNS Packet*, WHS, Movement for a New Society Records, 1974–1977, Box 1.

19. On participatory economics, see Michael Albert and Robin Hahnel, *Looking Forward: Participatory Economics for the Twenty-first Century* (Boston: South End Press, 1991). Albert and Hahnel's earlier work, *Unorthodox Marxism: An Essay on Capitalism, Socialism and Revolution* (Boston: South End Press, 1978) was used regularly in the vision section of macroanalysis seminars after 1978.

20. "Vision," *MNS Packet*.

21. "Structure," *MNS Packet*. For the concept of prefigurative politics, see Polleta, *Freedom*, 6–12; Breines, *Community and Organization in the New Left*.

22. George Lakey, interview by author, and Andrew Willis Garcés, tape recording, Philadelphia, June 28, 2008.

23. For a history of the use of consensus decision-making in U.S. social movements, see Polletta, *Freedom*.

24. "Program for a New Society: A Statement by A Quaker Action Group," leaflet, WHS, SAVF, Box 29, Folder: Movement for a New Society.

25. MNS membership numbers are difficult to calculate, because the organization loosely defined membership during its first decade. Often, small groups that expressed interest in MNS's political vision were considered "part of the network" in internal publications, only to disappear from the record soon afterward.

26. Jim Schrag, "Collectives of the Movement for a New Society and 'Friends of MNS' in West Philadelphia," SCPC, MNS Collection, DG 154, Acc. 90A-55, Box 15.

27. "The Philadelphia Life Center," *Dandelion*, Spring 1976.

28. "Neighborhood Block Group Fights Crime, Fear of it," *Dandelion*, October 1973, n.p.

29. "Alternative Institutions," *MNS Packet*; Lakey, interview.

30. Raasch-Gilman, "One Participant's Account," 64–74; Scott Burgwin, "Re-evaluation Counseling as a Tool for Social Change," *Dandelion*, Spring 1976, 1–3. For a critical analysis of Re-evaluation Counseling, see Matthew Lyons, "Sex, Lies, and Co-Counseling," *Activist Men's Journal*, August 1993, available at http://www.culthelp.info/index.php?option=com_content&task=view&id=995&Itemid=12.

31. Bill Moyers, "MNS Historical Development Goal to Start the 1980s: Move from the 'Spontaneous' to the 'Empowerment' Organizational Model," January 31, 1981, SCPC, MNS Collection, DG 154, Acc. 90A-55, Box 10.

32. On former radicals turning to gurus and mysticism, cf. Christopher Lasch, *The Culture of Narcissism: American Life in an Age of Diminishing Expectations* (New York: W. W. Norton, 1979); Jerry Rubin, *Growing (Up) at Thirty-Seven* (New York: M. Evans, 1976).

33. "MNS Support Communities," *Dandelion*, Winter 1974.

34. "Training," *MNS Packet*; Raasch-Gilman, "One Participant's Account," 4–15.

35. The spokes-council, also known as the "small-to-large group decision-making process," is a form of organization in which representatives of affinity groups meet to communicate their group's ideas and to deliberate on issues affecting the larger group, typically using consensus process.

36. Lakey, interview.

37. "MNS at Seabrook," *Dandelion*, Spring 1977, 12–17. For an account of the antinuclear movement, see Barbara Epstein, *Political Protest and Cultural Revolution: Nonviolent Direct Action in the 1970s and 1980s* (Berkeley: University of California Press, 1991).

38. MNS was certainly not the first organization to turn incarceration into an opportunity for movement building. For the free-speech fights of the Industrial Workers of the World, see Melvyn Dubofsky, *We Shall Be All: A History of the Industrial Workers of the World*

(New York: Quadrangle, 1969), 173–197. For a discussion of "the black public sphere of incarceration" during the civil rights movement, see Houston Baker, "Critical Memory and the Black Public Sphere" in *The Black Public Sphere: A Public Culture Book*, ed. Black Public Sphere Collective (Chicago: University of Chicago Press, 1995), 5–38.

39. George Lakey, "The Life and Death of the Movement for a New Society," *Friends Journal*, September 1989, 22.

40. Raasch-Gilman, "One Participant's Account," 31.

41. For a history and contemporary reassertion of this theory of change, see Richard Day, *Gramsci Is Dead: Anarchist Currents in the Newest Social Movements* (London and Toronto: Pluto Press and Between the Lines, 2005).

42. Lakey, interview.

43. Raasch-Gilman, "One Participant's Account," 55.

44. Lakey, interview.

45. George Lakey, "Eleven Years Old: A Perspective on Movement for a New Society in Philadelphia, October 6, 1982, 7, SCPC, MNS Collection, DG 154, Acc. 90A-55, Box 10.

46. Ibid., 14.

47. Ibid.; Raasch-Gilman, "One Participant's Account," 22–26, 55.

48. Raasch-Gilman, "One Participant's Account," 32.

49. Bill Moyers, "MNS Historical Development Goal to Start the 1980's: Move from the 'Spontaneous' to the 'Empowerment' Organizational Model," January 31, 1981, SCPC, MNS Collection, Acc. 90A-55, Box 10. Also see Raasch-Gilman, "One Participant's Account," 113.

50. Michael Siptroth, "Directions," *Dandelion Wine*, July 1982, 20–21; Raasch-Gilman, "One Participant's Account," 103.

51. Raasch-Gilman, "One Participant's Account," 103–105.

52. See the July/August 1986 and September 1986 issues of *Grapevine*.

53. Steve Chase noted, for instance, "Ecology . . . was dropped from our official description of the core elements of our philosophy, along with decentralization, cooperative economics, and racial and cultural diversity, when, in 1984, the majority of MNSers agreed to only describe feminism and revolutionary nonviolence as the core elements of our philosophy." Steve Chase, "Some Thoughts after Taking My Foot Out of My Mouth," *Grapevine*, July/August 1986, 53.

54. Raasch-Gilman, "One Participant's Account," 133.

55. See the September 1988 issue of *Grapevine*; Grace C. Ross, "Ending, Going On: Movement for a New Society," *Peacework*, October 1988, 11.

56. Echols, *Daring to Be Bad*.

57. Epstein, 60.

58. See Dubofsky, *We Shall Be All*; Salvatore Salerno, *Red November, Black November: Culture and Community in the Industrial Workers of the World* (Albany: SUNY Press, 1989).

59. Cf. Benjamin Shepard and Ronald Hayduk, eds., *From ACT UP to the WTO: Urban Protest and Community Building in the Era of Globalization* (New York: Verso, 2002); C. T. Butler and Keith McHenry, *Food Not Bombs*, rev. ed. (Tucson: See Sharp Press, 2000); Starhawk, *Webs of Power: Notes from the Global Uprising* (Gabriola Island, B.C.: New Society Publishers, 2002); George Katsiaficas, Daniel Burton-Rose, and Eddie Yuen, eds., *Confronting Capitalism: Dispatches from a Global Movement* (New York: Soft Skull Press, 2004); and Joshua Kahn Russell and Brian Kelly, "Giving Form to a Stampede: The First Two Years of the New SDS," *Upping the Anti* 6 (May 2008): 75–94.

13

Hard to Find

Building for Nonviolent Revolution and the Pacifist Underground

MATT MEYER

PAUL MAGNO

In activist priest Daniel Berrigan's classic 1972 poem "America Is Hard to Find," he talks about those aspects of contemporary United States reality that escape common recognition. Things of beauty—wild strawberries, swans, heron, and deer—and things that people thrive on—good news, housing, holiness, wholeness, and hope—were all hard to find in an era marked by racism, assassination, and the continuing horror of the Vietnam War. But Berrigan was writing of personal experience as well. The subtitle of his book bearing the same name as his poem is straightforward enough: *Notes from the Underground and Letters from Danbury Prison.*[1] "I shall shortly be hard to find," Berrigan wrote before beginning a clandestine life in April 1970. In part to escape capture from the Federal Bureau of Investigation (FBI) and imprisonment for his part in the Catonsville Nine case of the destruction of draft records, Berrigan's four months of evasion were mostly symbolic in nature.[2] Because, he believed, actions against war and injustice needed to become more militant, dramatic, and serious, all parts of the movement should prepare for escape from capture and for a deeper level of total commitment. "Remember me," Berrigan declared somewhat ironically, as his very public, media-oriented speeches, television appearances, and writings during these four months made it difficult to forget about this Jesuit-on-the-run. "I am free, at large, untamable, and not nearly as hard to find as America."[3]

The exploits of Daniel Berrigan and the Catholic Left of this period are just one aspect of a larger tendency of radical pacifists and peace activists who wanted to move beyond the sit-ins, teach-ins, and demonstrations of the earlier radical groups. Though under-reported and often misunderstood, these efforts make up a major part of that mythological period known as "The Sixties," that time in U.S. history beginning in the early 1950s and going late into the 1970s. The 1970s, in particular, saw small but significant groups of nonviolent activists take the call for revolution seriously—adapting that call to fit their philosophical, strategic, and tactical beliefs. Whether through personal witness or mass action, through secret campaigns or public disobedience, through "dropping out" of the system or naming and fighting that system of imperialism and colonialism, the history of revolutionary nonviolence remains largely hidden.

Many examples of militant nonviolence may be found as individual or exceptional narratives, but these stories must be seen in the context of developing new ideologies and modes of practice. The political trajectory of these pacifist radicals troubles the too-easy attempts to explain movement decline by way of tactical excess. This coterie of pacifist militants invites a redefinition of violence by providing an example of clandestine revolutionary force absent physical harm—using nonviolence as, in Martin Luther King, Jr.'s terms, "the sword that heals."[4] Movement historians and organizers have largely failed to understand that the frustrations of the late 1960s related directly to various but often unconnected actions of the early 1970s, which, in turn, influenced widespread action in the late 1970s and 1980s. By connecting the words and deeds of these nonviolent revolutionaries to the activism of the time, we hope to identify those obscured sites of militancy that shaped nonviolent action during and since the Vietnam War. In their story, we find a sector of the Left that took seriously the challenge to forge a revolutionary response to the horrors of American empire but did so guided by a commitment to pacifism. These activists made connections within and beyond the Left on the basis of shared radical politics; their profound and unswerving understanding of revolutionary nonviolence provided the basis for, rather than an obstacle to, forging coalitions with others.

Theories of Nonviolent Revolution

Though the anarchist and socialist conscientious objectors who had served prison time during World War II used the phrase "nonviolent revolution," the concept did not come into popular usage until the radical upsurge of 1967–1968. World War II conscientious objectors like Dave Dellinger, Ralph DiGia, Bill Sutherland, and others were still active at this time: Sutherland in Tanzania, providing support to the guerilla movements of Namibia, South Africa, Zimbabwe, and Mozambique; DiGia on the national staff of the War Resisters League; and Dellinger as the central architect of the coalitions to end the war in Southeast Asia.[5] With the spotlight upon him due to his involvement in the infamous Chicago Eight case, Dellinger evinced an uncanny and abiding ability to bridge the gaps between generations, diverse communities, and ideologies. He gave shape and substance to the phrase "nonviolent revolution" in his essay "Towards Revolutionary Humanism," published in his 1970 book *Revolutionary Nonviolence*.

"Along with the growing rejection of a society of class divisions and delegated democracy is a rejection of the channels for social change within this society," Dellinger wrote as a summary of late-1960s sentiment. "It's not so much a question of 'lacking patience,' as is sometimes charged, but rather of realizing that the traditional methods do not lead in the right direction. The most that can be accomplished through electoral politics, lobbying, governmental commissions, polite negotiations with the authorities, or nonviolent demonstrations within the framework of law and order," Dellinger asserted, "is to shake loose a few benefits around the edges." At the start of the 1970s, it was clear to Dellinger that the anti-war and civil rights movements had developed well beyond the strategic forms in which they began, and that nothing short of "forceful confrontation" would be sufficient in the new decade. "All of this," he believed, "represents tremendous growth in a few short years, a growth for which the country owes a debt of grati-tude to the Cuban revolutionaries, the incredibly heroic Vietnamese, and the Black insurgency within our own country."[6]

What this revolutionary potential meant, practically, in 1970 was more diffi-cult to develop. Dellinger was quite at ease with labeling as "absurd" the fact that both the "privileged elite" and the "timid moderates" had, by this time, become the major advocates of a pacifism that, in reality, was meant to convey passivity. That provided no comfort for the fact that those who criticized the reformist nature of the nonviolent movements of the 1950s and early 1960s were now call-ing for smashing windows, beating up police, or roughing up antagonists in order to prove one's seriousness about radical change. "These are bad ways to educate people and win them to the real freedom and solidarity of our cause," Dellinger wrote.[7] His praise of Third World revolutions, his action orientation, and his sta-tus in the antiwar movement made Dellinger a comrade and confidante of many of the younger militants, including the nascent Weatherman. Although they strongly disagreed on the role of violence in the U.S. Left, both Dellinger and Weatherman agreed on the need to raise the stakes of antiwar activism to derail U.S. imperialism. In conversation with the would-be guerrillas, Dellinger routinely argued for a nonviolent response. At the same time, his frustration with some pacifists and his connection to the black and youth movements sensitized him to the challenge of the task.[8]

"In the general debasement that the word 'nonviolence' has suffered, it may be necessary for those of us who are anxious to preserve the humanistic sensitiv-ity and content of the revolution to find another word to sum up what we are advocating," he wrote. Calling for the development of a new "socialist humanism," he urged that activists refuse to "retreat" into either liberalism or into the "pseudo-revolutionary 'infantile leftism' which plays at revolution while leaving the movement bereft of allies and credibility, because of the gap between its goals and its methods."[9] Dellinger suggested and struggled for a new movement based on both the militancy and vision of the New Left and the people-centered prin-ciples of mass mobilization and anti-militarism of the older pacifist groups.

On a theoretical level, this call had its own antecedents in the writings of Barbara Deming. A civil rights activist who, like Dellinger, had worked under the tutelage of labor and religious leader A. J. Muste and as staff of the influential *Liberation* magazine, Deming took on the challenge leveraged by Africanist Frantz

Fanon. In his influential *The Wretched of the Earth*, based on his experiences as a psychiatrist and fighter working for the Algerian revolution, Fanon suggested that only through armed struggle could one be psychologically liberated. Deming's essay "On Revolution and Equilibrium," published in *Liberation* in 1968 and widely reprinted in anthologies and pamphlet form over the next ten years by women's groups and peace groups, challenged the notion that the oppressed needed violence as a catharsis. The revolutionary experiment that Deming saw as an urgent task involved nonviolent activists learning to better challenge the "institutions of violence that constrict and cripple our humanity." She wished that those who question nonviolence might better see that one's right to life and happiness can only be claimed as inalienable "if one grants, in action, that they belong to all men [*sic*]."[10] Like Dellinger, Deming worked to build a new movement based on a balance of means and ends and a merger of personal, organizational, and institutional responsibility. She quotes Fanon extensively as an ally in this endeavor. "You'll never overthrow the terrible enemy machine," proclaimed Fanon, "and you won't change human beings, if you forget to raise the standard of consciousness of the rank-and-file."[11] Agreeing on the basic task, Fanon and Deming struggled rhetorically over the most strategic and effective way to do so.

Resistance Communities

One practical, if individualistic, way to opt out of traditional oppressive institutions was the fairly widespread move to alternative "lifestyles"—more rural, more communal, and much less structured than the corporate model. Flowing freely from the hippies and the countercultural scene in art and music, the commune movement took buying a cool record, smoking a joint, or opposing war one step further. Though hardly as proactive as the antiwar, anti-imperialist, or antiracist movements of the early 1970s wanted them to be, the back-to-nature communities did share similar roots and were a concrete means of dropping, in part, "off the radar" of mainstream society. They included overtly Christian collectives, other religious and spiritual groupings, and some more political and nonreligious groups. Founded in 1971 in Tennessee, The Farm commune possibly gained the most attention for its innovative midwifery and childcare practices. The communards were also pioneers of solar energy; like the hundreds of other communes of the era, they were avid environmentalists. Though Timothy Miller correctly points out that The Farm "most perfectly epitomized the spirit" of 1970s communes, it was far from the only or even the most long-lived of these experiments.[12]

A more decidedly leftist and public manifestation of this period's desire to alter living, housing, social, and work relationships came from the groups Movement for a New Society and Community for Creative Nonviolence. During the same years, however, and along very similar political and philosophical lines, came the consolidation of draft resistance communities as both aboveground and underground entities. Some of the draft-card burners and stoic public anti-draft activists who had been in the spotlight since the mid-1960s were now part of a growing network of communes and "safe houses" near the Canadian border. There, draft evaders who had decided to relocate outside of the United States met, often unknowingly, with other fugitives from the injustice of the times.[13] A leading member of one of these collective homes suggested that they had an open door to anyone fleeing or fighting U.S. militarism: "I think we sheltered a lot of these people," remembered Kenoli Oleari, "without having any idea we were sheltering them."[14]

A major "captain" of the East Coast underground railroad for draft-age conscripts was Karl Bissinger of the Greenwich Village Peace Center in New York City. With more than seventy thousand such people living abroad by the time conscription ended on July 1, 1973, and the full draft was revoked in 1975, the government went after the significant network of activists, doctors, legal workers, and draft counselors that had been set up. Aware that FBI agents and other law enforcement officials would regularly attempt to listen in on counseling sessions, Bissinger remembers being careful—at first—regarding what advice to give to whom. As the war dragged on and the number of those seeking advice on illegal options increased, it became harder to keep the lines of international communication and travel open.[15]

By 1973, however, the need for secretive draft resistance tactics had ended. Bissinger, with longtime friends and colleagues Grace Paley, Joseph Chaikin, Robert Jay Lifton, Nobel laureate George Wald, Andrea Dworkin, and others, initiated a campaign to award Vietnam draft resisters the Nobel Peace Prize. As was often the case with this grouping of people, their call was inclusive, for "all those young persons who refused complicity with their government's war in Vietnam—whether through draft refusal, desertion from or opposition within the armed forces."[16] Later that year, the national office of the War Resisters League (WRL), a secular pacifist group founded after World War I that spotlighted the plight of vocal draft resisters, expanded its program to include the issue of amnesty for those who fled. "Instead of closing down or 'downsizing,' as they say today," Bissinger reflected three decades later, "the WRL upsized." He joined the staff to coordinate the campaign.[17] When President Jimmy Carter finally granted pardons for all "draft dodgers" in January 1977, word spread throughout communities in Canada, Sweden, and elsewhere that people could return home.[18]

One WRL-affiliated draft resister active on the national level at this time was Jerry Elmer, who had gotten involved in the late 1960s as a public draft-card burner and become attracted to the public destruction of draft-board files. Inspired by the Baltimore and Catonsville, Maryland, actions in 1967 and 1968, respectively—where activists destroyed office-loads of 1-A files of those about to be conscripted—Elmer and his circle discussed how this strategy could be broadened to include as large a sector of the Left as possible. The Baltimore Four and Catonsville Nine were led by the Catholic Left, with the Berrigan brothers and their supporters at the core. In one case, the draft files were emptied into a trash can, taken to the draft board building's parking lot, and ignited with homemade napalm developed from a "recipe" found in a Green Beret manual.[19]

Baltimore Four and Catonsville Nine member Tom Lewis recalled attending a gathering of antiwar youth in the Midwest in 1967 and returning to Baltimore with the idea of nonviolently attacking draft boards. It resonated with the others at the Baltimore Interfaith Peace Mission, especially Philip Berrigan, and they went to work on it. They concluded that with young men (disproportionately working class, poor, and black or Latino) at risk of being drafted and then maimed or killed in Vietnam, older people also needed to assume some significant risk in confronting the machinery of war. Taking heed of Rev. Martin Luther King, Jr.'s recent antiwar call, linking "the triple evils" of racism, capitalism, and militarism, they thought that there must be some way to provoke a crisis of conscience among apparently apathetic Americans. They had tried civil disobedience to challenge the war, they had appealed to and confronted the churches, and they tried to engage in dialogue with policy-makers. Finally, they listened to the voices of those who were liable to the draft. According to Lewis, some among the younger generation of potential draftees and draft resisters were highly interested in crafting, if not leading, a militant response. Deeply shaken by the government's illegal and immoral actions, this group of largely working-class youth helped the older Catholic activists understand the need for intensified direct action.[20] In October, four of the Catholics entered the draft board at the Baltimore Customs House and poured blood over the draft files. Well before student radicals turned to bombs, then, ordained clergy and practicing Catholics had begun physically dismantling and destroying the accoutrements of war.

In their statement of purpose, released to mainstream and movement press, the activists explained their motivations:

> We shed our blood willingly in what we hope is a sacrificial and constructive act. We pour it on these files to illustrate that with them and with these files begins the pitiful waste of American and Vietnamese blood 10,000 miles away. That bloodshed is never rational, seldom voluntary—in a word—non-constructive. It does not protect life. . . .
>
> We quarrel with the idolatry of property and the war machine that makes property of men. . . .
>
> We charge that America would rather protect its empire of overseas profits than welcome its black people, rebuild its slums and cleanse its air and water. Thus we have singled out inner-city draft boards for our actions.
>
> We invite friends in the peace and freedom movements to continue moving with us from dissent to resistance. We ask God to be merciful and patient with us and all men. We hope he will use our witness for his blessed designs.[21]

The action represented a nonviolent but risky confrontation with the state. Similar to what the Weather Underground and other groups later attempted, the

Baltimore Four endeavored to use direct action to both materially impede and symbolically indict U.S. imperialism. Philip Berrigan, for one, had become immensely frustrated with safe protest and its inability to disrupt the war on Vietnam. For him at this point, "risky" was the only worthwhile nonviolence, both to politically contest the war and to personally underscore unconditional rejection of war in principle. The Baltimore Four action energized sympathizers to some extent, though this energy was expressed largely through organizing around the impending trial of the four the following April. After a jury convicted them in federal court, the four were all sentenced to substantial prison sentences but released pending appeal.[22]

Upon release, Philip Berrigan and Tom Lewis proceeded immediately to organize the action at Catonsville.[23] They faced federal trial for destruction of the Selective Service records at Catonsville, and much stiffer potential sentences, but the impact on kindred spirits was, by now, galvanizing. The following year saw another draft-board action, by the Milwaukee Fourteen, which was followed by a whole array of such actions across the country during the next several years.[24] These actions included not just antidraft targets, but also raids of FBI field offices, break-ins at the corporate offices of Dow Chemical (maker of napalm), and more. By 1975, more than two hundred such actions had been carried out.[25]

In the meantime, other aspects of this nonviolent resistance had also captured the imagination of a public increasingly fed up with the continuing war. In April 1970, after exhausting their appeals, five of the defendants from the Catonsville Nine and Baltimore Four actions went underground rather than surrender to authorities. Most were captured quickly, but Daniel Berrigan eluded the FBI for months, speaking publicly and releasing press interviews from underground, to the embarrassment of the bureau and the excitement of the antiwar Left.[26]

In his letters from the underground, Berrigan articulated strategic and tactical questions that were on the minds of many at that time: When one took part in nonviolent yet illegal civil disobedience, was it necessary—in attempting to maintain the moral high ground and to win over undecided sectors of the population—to face the jail time inherent in such actions? Was going underground itself a departure from pacifist principles? These debates about whether there was value in building a clandestine movement raged throughout the early 1970s. In responding to these debates through letters published in a variety of movement magazines, Berrigan defended the need for an underground while still eschewing the use of violence:

> For white Americans like ourselves an attempt to create an underground presence which will be nonviolent and politically audible is indeed a chancy one. We are neither Black Panthers, Frenchmen opposing Vichy, the German confessing church in the thirties, Algerians under occupation, [nor] members of the National Liberation Front [of Vietnam]. It would be disastrous to apply to our situation the realities of colonialism or occupation; and any analogies between ourselves and the third world, or ourselves

and historic minorities in our own country, must be explored with extreme
reserve.

At the same time, analogies are not to be despised. Our government is
not merely courting disaster in its irresponsible war abroad, it is setting its
face more and more firmly against peaceable change as long as that change
threatens the status quo. Such a political atmosphere, if pushed far enough,
favors the change it so dreads; it bursts the pods of discontent, resistance,
and violence, and scatters the seed far and wide. A profound and widespread sense of fraternity is created across time and distance, between
disenchanted Americans and the suppressed masses of Asia, Africa, and
Latin America.[27]

Berrigan's own activities and statements while underground, and throughout
the 1970s and beyond, provide testament to that growing fraternity. His own solidarity with the Panthers was noted in most of his at-large communiqués, calling
the courtroom dramatics of the accused Panther Twenty-One signs of "the unkill-
able resources of the spirit." He spoke of the jailing of Panther co-founder Bobby
Seale as a symbol of the war at home, suggesting that Seale, along with Philip Berrigan and the other Catonsville co-defendants, be termed not political prisoners but
"hostages of war."[28] And, in a letter to the Weather Underground printed in the
June 21, 1971, edition of the *New York Times*, Berrigan wrote that Weather's
decision to forcefully rebel against the system was "one of the few momentous
choices in American history."[29]

Berrigan was clear, forthright, and consistent that sabotage was a necessary, if
somewhat dangerous, tool for change. Steadfast in his radical pacifism, however,
Berrigan challenged the Weather People (as he called them) about the corrupting
seduction of violence, not as a method, but as an end in itself. Writing that
the quality of life within the communities of the underground or the alternative
movements was the main thing radicals had to offer the mainstream, Berrigan
suggested that what he and Weather shared in common was the ability to give
people hope. His tactical disagreement, therefore, emerged from a strategic
unity.[30]

The Weather Underground responded favorably to Berrigan's overtures and
released a message of support to Berrigan just after he was captured. One person
cited in their note, and a key figure in this history, was Catonsville Nine defendant
Mary Moylan, who, like Berrigan, had gone underground. Unlike Berrigan,
however, Moylan did not receive much attention from either the movement or the
media. And, also unlike Berrigan, she was not quickly captured. Called "remarkable" by Weather leader Bernardine Dohrn, Moylan joined Weather and remained
in clandestinity for almost ten years. Weather celebrated Moylan's persistence,
viewing her as an exemplary model of revolutionary militancy. "Jonathan Jackson
made his heroic attempt to free the San Quentin prisoners and the Soledad Brothers," Weather noted. "The Palestinians have freed Leila Khalid. Timothy Leary has

escaped from San Luis Obispo and joined us in the Underground. Mary Moylan and many tribes of revolutionaries can't be found. . . . We are free outlaws."[31]

The extent of the freedom experienced in the 1970s underground is still an open question. It is not so clear whether life underground ended up creating liberating communities for the wider movement to emulate or join. Prolonged underground militancy did not seem to interest most on the Left, nonviolent or otherwise. There were still some in the radical pacifist circles of 1970 who saw even the destruction of draft files as anathema, because such actions required "raiding, looting, and secrecy."[32] Most young nonviolent activists of the 1970s, however, found small group actions involving property destruction and short-term clandestine planning to be not only appropriate, but, in the words of Jerry Elmer, "morally imperative."[33] From destroying war-related documents to bombing ROTC buildings on college campuses, the first half of the 1970s was filled with hundreds of often-unclaimed secret actions that challenged U.S. imperial designs.[34]

For most of these actions and much of this time, there is a hidden nature to the names and numbers of those who were involved. Also hidden in this history is the ideological focus of those who took part in these events. The network of those supporting or spreading news of most of these actions, however, suggests more than a tentative link between clandestine militancy and the nonviolent Left. Many of this period shied away from labeling themselves either pacifists or proto-guerrillas. So long as actions did not involve the taking of human life, individuals or small, local collectives felt moved to engage in nonpublic property destruction of an often dramatic nature. No single organization or publication was at the center of these actions, though the independent *WIN Magazine*, growing out of the 1960s New York Workshops in Nonviolence and motivated by the energy of the younger resistance movements, reported and commented on much of this tumult.[35]

Case Studies in Revolutionary Nonviolence

Three events involving nonviolent revolutionaries between 1970 and 1972—in Media, Pennsylvania; Camden, New Jersey; and Harrisburg, Pennsylvania—proved particularly disastrous for the U.S. government. While millions watched the boxing match between Muhammad Ali and Joe Frazier on television on March 8, 1971, an unknown group of radicals let themselves in to the FBI's Media field office. By morning, the file cabinets were empty. By the end of the month, an organization calling itself the Citizens' Commission to Investigate the FBI had sent documents from those files to the nation's major newspapers. The now-public documents were later reviewed in congressional offices in Washington, DC, breaking open the FBI's Counter Intelligence Program (COINTELPRO), which was a coordinated effort to disrupt and discredit progressive organizations within the United States. Most notorious for its use of assassination and frame-up tactics against the Black Panther Party and the American Indian Movement, COINTELPRO was also involved in attempts to get the Reverend Martin Luther King, Jr. to commit suicide or scale back his widespread critiques of U.S. racism, militarism, and materialism.[36]

By 1972, the full contents of the Media papers had been published by the peace movement press, in the March 1972 issue of *WIN Magazine*—well before Congress began investigating the FBI. And though activists had long suspected that the FBI and related government agencies were involved in questionable methods against the Left, the full extent of these efforts was not clear before the Media break-in. In 1975, the U.S. Senate convened its Select Committee to Study Governmental Operations with Respect to Intelligence Activities—leading to widespread condemnation of the FBI. The Senate committee, known as the Church Committee after its chairperson, Idaho's Frank Church, reviewed the work of the CIA and other government groups. But its conclusions regarding COINTELPRO were particularly damning. COINTELPRO's techniques, the Church Committee report stated, would be "intolerable in a democratic society even if all of the targets had been involved in violent activity." But COINTELPRO went further, seeking, as Church put it, to prevent the "exercise of First Amendment rights of free speech and association."[37]

The FBI, for its part, fought hard to counter the effects of COINTELPRO's revelation—and to find out who was responsible for Media. Lifelong pacifist and civil rights activist John Grady was quietly but widely considered to have been one of the masterminds behind the Media action. Former FBI agent Terry Neist, citing Grady's leadership, noted that the break-in was taken very personally by the agency and was considered a "disastrous" setback. The FBI clearly believed that those responsible for the Media action were also involved in some of the draft-board break-ins as well as the action in Camden that took place later that year.[38]

Six years and thirty-three thousand investigative pages later, however, the FBI gave up on solving the break-in. More recently, *Los Angeles Times* reporter Allan Jalon called the Media events "one of the most lastingly consequential (although underemphasized) watersheds of political awareness in recent American history."[39] On par with the release of Daniel Ellsberg's Pentagon Papers, which helped speed the end of the Vietnam War, the Media action vindicated those calling for or engaged in small, secret acts of nonviolent sabotage.[40]

Not two months following the Media raid, in nearby Camden, New Jersey, another event challenged both the government's power and the movement's understanding of what was possible through collective action. In what became known as the Camden Twenty-Eight case, a large grouping of mainly Catholic Left activists went to their local draft board office to destroy the files. Several things distinguished this group from other antidraft actions of this period. First, the group decided from the outset not to submit themselves to easy arrest by taking the documents outside of the offices for a ceremonial burning, or to stay long while in the process of destroying the records. Secondly, the larger number of participants suggested a "conspiracy" far beyond the small number of those willing to face long jail terms and a full-scale disruption of their lives. (Twenty of the group were arrested on the scene, and the other eight were arrested days later as con-spirators.) The tactics of clandestine property destruction had gained acceptance among radical elements of the pacifist Left, an acceptance that was growing stronger. Unknown to the participants, however, the action's planning group had been infiltrated by a person willing to inform the FBI of their goings-on.[41]

Not only did the May 4, 1972, Camden action go forward with the knowledge of the FBI and the involvement of an informant, the FBI ended up supplying most of the burglary tools involved. The FBI also allowed the activists two hours inside the draft board, where they destroyed various files, before moving in to make the arrest "in the act." At trial, the jury learned of the FBI machinations, including hearing from its penitent informant, Robert Hardy. Hardy told of how the FBI had facilitated the raid—instead of stopping it, as he had hoped and had been prom-ised it would. In a landmark verdict, the jury refused to convict, finding all defendants not guilty. Supreme Court Justice William Brennan later called the 1973 process "one of the great trials of the twentieth century."[42]

According to the historian Howard Zinn, a witness for the defense at Camden, the trial's success owed in part to the judge allowing discussion of the war—something forbidden from previous trials of draft-board vandalism. "Some showed Vietnam villages bombed, in flames; others showed sections of Camden looking like a bombed out city. . . . Another defense witness, surprisingly, was Major Clement St. Martin, who had been in charge of the state induction center in Newark, New Jersey, from 1968 to 1971. He described in detail how the draft system discriminated systematically against the poor, the black, and the uneducated, and how it regularly gave medical exemptions to the sons of the wealthy. Major St. Martin said he thought all draft files should be destroyed. Asked, under cross-examination, if he thought private citizens had a right to break into buildings to destroy draft files, he replied: 'Probably today, if they plan another raid, I might join them.'"[43]

Exasperated by the resilience of the draft-board and FBI-office raiders, and those who would defend them, FBI Director J. Edgar Hoover began targeting this sector of the movement more directly. After developing an informant at Lewisburg Prison who gained Philip Berrigan's confidence, the federal police agency in 1971 announced a startling conspiracy implicating members of the Catholic Left, called the East Coast Conspiracy to Save Lives. They were accused of plotting to kidnap National Security Advisor Henry Kissinger and use explosives on the federal Forrestal Building in downtown Washington, DC. Richard Nixon's Justice Depart-ment, under John Mitchell, secured a grand-jury indictment in Harrisburg, Pennsylvania, a venue deemed naturally conservative and thus sympathetic to the government, despite the rapidly eroding public support for its war effort.[44]

The Harrisburg conspiracy case proved a call to action, and by trial the fol-lowing year, more than 125 local Harrisburg Defense Committees had been estab-lished in more than twenty states. But the fourteen months between Hoover's initial proclamation and the start of trial were trying for the movement's rank and file. Many were summoned to grand-jury appearances and refused; others were distressed by the charges leveled. Still others struggled with the now-obvious romantic relationship between defendants Philip Berrigan (a priest) and Liz McAlister (a nun). Still, when in January 1972 the trial of the Harrisburg Seven commenced, it was a phenomenon. Harrisburg was swarming with enthusiastic supporters, including Daniel Berrigan, then just released from prison himself. A legal team including prominent attorneys such as civil rights and constitutional law icon Leonard Boudin and former Attorney General Ramsey Clark (whose Justice Department had sent the Catonsville defendants to prison) sat at the defense table.

The government's case rested completely on its provocateur informant, Boyd Douglass. Douglass took the stand for the prosecution and remained on the stand for fourteen days, half of them in relentless cross-examination by the team of defense attorneys. By the time he was done, his credibility was greatly diminished. When it was the defense's turn to open its case, Ramsey Clark rose and announced, "The defendants will always seek peace, the defendants continue to proclaim their innocence, and the defense rests." As a stunned courtroom struggled to fathom this development, Judge R. Dixon Herman charged the jury and sent it out to deliberate. Sixty hours later, they reported themselves deadlocked, ten to two against conviction, save on the charge of smuggling letters into prison.[45]

Monumental defeats for the government, the Harrisburg and Camden trials were the high-water mark of this movement. They coincided with and informed a turning point in public sentiment decisively against the Vietnam War. Nevertheless, the war continued until the middle of the decade under the guise of "Vietnamization," and the nonviolent Left went through a period in which many involved felt drained and disoriented.[46] Routine jail terms helped contribute to this feeling; Philip Berrigan, whose leadership had been so catalytic, remained in prison until early 1973. When he got out, Berrigan returned to Baltimore and began a new project.

In 1973, Philip Berrigan and Elizabeth McAlister announced their marriage and established Jonah House. Their commitment, and that of their new community, was to engage in and cultivate nonviolent resistance, first to the war on Indochina, and later to the nuclear arms race. To do so, Jonah House undertook an effort to share its vision with sympathizers along the eastern seaboard. An ongoing interplay of travel and action ensued over the next several years to promulgate that vision, premised on intentional community committed to resistance.[47] By 1975, as the Vietnam War ended and the activists' attention turned to nuclear war, the nascent network cultivated by Jonah House sprouted into the Atlantic Life Community, akin to the earlier East Coast Conspiracy to Save Lives alleged by the FBI, but consciously rooted in "community" as a virtue and principle. In their judgment, community would give their nonviolent resistance a sustainability lacking in earlier resistance movements. As Berrigan and McAlister explained in the introduction to their 1989 book *The Time's Discipline*, "We have learned that community, when properly understood, is not merely a vivid foretaste of the people of God, not only the most formidable critic and opponent of a criminal state. It is also a constant test of personal and interpersonal integrity. In no other setting are we held so closely accountable to God, to the victims and to one another."[48]

Throughout the late 1970s, members of Jonah House's community traveled up and down the east coast, often a few weekends a month, sharing with others this basic idea of the need to build resistance communities. Reflecting on faith and justice, and examining one's responsibility to share and embody risk on nonviolent terms with the poor of the world, became the cornerstone of these communities. It was in this context, Philip Berrigan insisted, that a revolutionary movement ought to form its core radical politics.[49] The methodology that Jonah House proposed and conducted did not rely on mass organizing and did not aim deliberately at political impact. Yet its radicalism was quite pronounced. The biblically inspired technique of "going out two-by-two" and "evangelizing" small circles of dedicated individuals, necessarily backed by public confrontation with official violence, led the resisters inevitably to court and jail, helping to forge a ubiquitous radical challenge to U.S. imperial conduct after the Vietnam War. Having laid the groundwork for this perspective in the wake of the Vietnam War and against the backdrop of the aggressive first-strike nuclear war policy developed during the Carter and Reagan administrations, Jonah House could look on (and participate in with satisfaction) many such manifestations of "discipleship."[50] The influence of militant, direct-action-oriented nonviolent struggle continued in the work of the Plowshares movement (emerging in the 1980s and still enduring), the Sanctuary movement and the White Train campaign (both significant in the 1980s), School of the Americas Watch (during the 1990s and continuing), and Witness Against Torture (begun in 2005).

Beyond the Catholic Left, the tactics, philosophy, and vision of the radical nonviolent movement of the early 1970s led directly to the vibrant direct-action movements of the latter part of the decade. From the Clamshell Alliance and the movement against nuclear power at Seabrook, New Hampshire, to the Abalone Alliance and its commitment to radical egalitarian democracy in California, the coming together of affinity groups in the late 1970s can be seen as a direct outgrowth of the decentralized, small-group dynamics of the radical pacifist underground. Though explicitly open in their approach, these loose campaign- and region-based coalitions consistently engaged in actions that involved secretive elements, planned and executed by collectives that assessed the level of legal risk they were willing to take for a given cause. The Livermore Action Group, the Women's Pentagon Action, and other ad hoc groupings combined revolutionary analysis with specific targets in the military industrial complex that appeared strategic at the time.[51] The War Resisters League's 1976 (bicentennial) Continental Walk for Disarmament and Social Justice sought directly to bridge grassroots peace and justice radicalism, and to help develop new momentum out of the militancy of early 1970s antiwar protest. By literally walking through and talking with organizers, students, and others in cities from one coast to the other, walk coordinators worked for an enhanced understanding of how a massive nonviolent movement could bring down a repressive, war-mongering state.[52] Hundreds of anti-nuclear and "meet human needs" actions became the center-point of multi-issue coalitions that were prevalent from the mid-1970s through the early 1980s.[53]

By the late 1970s, radical feminism became a bridge for joining politically revolutionary ideals with culturally radical lifestyles. The shifts from 1960s counterculture to 1970s feminist philosophy and action represent the conscious merger of culture and politics in post–New Left radicalism. Barbara Deming was a major part of this progression, focusing her writings from the mid-1970s onward on the need to center any revolutionary activity in opposition to patriarchy and support for feminism.[54] Feminism fused the effects of direct action with the liberating potential of grassroots collective organizing. Eco-feminist Ynestra King identified this hybrid of culture and politics, spirituality and sustainability, as the signal contribution of revolutionary nonviolence. "If you maintain a consistent critique of domination, if you are concerned about peace, ecology, and gender, you have to have a politics with a cultural base, one that calls into question old ways of living. The politics of nonviolence is the only thing that makes sense, in terms of thinking about militarism as a manifestation of dominance, and advancing an intentional feminist strategy."[55]

An End to Limits?

Some historians have called the 1970s a decade when the majority of the United States began to learn the lesson of limits. From the unsuccessful war in Southeast Asia to the Watergate scandal to domestic economic concerns, American hopefulness and bravado appeared to be on the decline.[56] Some, however, also assess that the development of the new feminist, antinuclear, solidarity, and peace movements prove that the New Left that emerged during the 1960s had, in fact, gained lasting successes.[57] The truth, the evidence suggests, lies somewhere in between.

That the nuanced lessons of that era for today's movements and historians are "hard to find" may be a testament to their subtlety. Clearly many important elements of this period, such as the expansion of belief and practice in a revolutionary brand of nonviolence, are absent from most writings and reflections about this period. The tactics of clandestinity, sabotage, property destruction, and direct action held particular appeal and had unprecedented support from wide circles of progressive people. The philosophies of pacifism, feminism, environmentalism, and spiritual discipleship engaged and interested broad sectors of the activist community. The pacifist 1970s show that revolutionary nonviolence holds a key to building a mass movement capable of exciting people towards that goal. Studying their historical example and legacy troubles any attempts to assess the impact of social movements by numbers alone, as small groups, operating underground or in obscurity, provided the vital building blocks in this movement.

Dave Dellinger, in his groundbreaking but long out-of-print book *More Power Than We Know*, suggested that the methods the resistance communities of this era used were not wrong, but underutilized. The task, he argued in that book and throughout his life, is to build on these methods—to expand, supplement, and experiment with them. In order to end not just war but all its causes, we must find ways to generate "more love, not less; more participatory democracy, not less; more respect for human rights. . . . In a word, we need more force and less violence."[58]

NOTES

1. Daniel Berrigan, *America Is Hard to Find: Notes from the Underground and Letters from Danbury Prison* (New York: Doubleday and Company, 1972), 15–16.

2. Staughton Lynd and Alice Lynd, eds., *Nonviolence in America: A Documentary History* (Maryknoll, NY: Orbis Books, 1995), 115.

3. Berrigan, *America Is Hard to Find*, 54.

4. Martin Luther King, Jr., *Why We Can't Wait* (New York: Harper and Row, 1964), 23–28.

5. Robert Cooney and Helen Michalowski, eds., *The Power of the People: Active Nonviolence in the United States* (Culver City, CA: Peace Press, 1987); Bill Sutherland and Matt Meyer, *Guns and Gandhi in Africa: Pan-African Insights on Nonviolence, Armed Struggle, and Liberation* (Trenton, NJ: Africa World Press, 2000).

6. Dave Dellinger, *Revolutionary Nonviolence* (New York: Dobbs-Merrill, 1970), 273.

7. Ibid., 272.

8. Conversations between Dellinger and Meyer, November 10–12, 2000, Vieques, Puerto Rico, at the International Tribunal on Human Rights Violations. Dellinger's discussions and relationships with Weatherman and his orientation to black and youth movements of the era are discussed throughout his book, *More Power Than We Know: The People's Movement Toward Democracy* (New York: Anchor Press, 1975).

9. Dellinger, *More Power Than We Know*, 27.

10. Barbara Deming, "On Revolution and Equilibrium," *Liberation 4* (February 1968), reprinted in Deming, *Revolution and Equilibrium* (New York: Grossman Publishers, 1971), 178.

11. Frantz Fanon, *The Wretched of the Earth* (New York: Grove Press, 1963), 136.

12. Timothy Miller, *The 60s Communes: Hippies and Beyond* (Syracuse, NY: Syracuse University Press, 1999), 118; see also Elias Katz, *Armed Love* (New York: Holt, Rinehart, and Winston, 1971).

13. Miller, *The 60s Communes*, 131.

14. Ibid., 132.

15. Matt Meyer, interview with Karl Bissinger, April 1, 2008; see also Lawrence Baskir and William Strauss, *Chance and Circumstance: The Draft, the War, and the Vietnam Generation* (New York: Random House, 1978).

16. Karl Bissinger et al., "Nobel Peace Prize," *New York Review of Books* 20:15 (October 4, 1973).

17. Michael Maronna, "Work As Though You Had Hope: An Interview with Karl Bissinger," *The Nonviolent Activist*, July–August 1996, 12.

18. A thorough analysis of the scope of Carter's pardon, one of his first acts as president, is covered in former Secretary of the Navy James Webb's "The Insult of Carter's Mass Pardon," *Wall Street Journal*, February 23, 2001.

19. Jerry Elmer, *Felon for Peace: The Memoir of a Vietnam-Era Draft Resister* (Nashville: Vanderbilt University Press, 2005), 82.

20. Paul Magno, interview with Tom Lewis, February 18, 2008.

21. Quoted in Murray Polner and Jim O'Grady, *Disarmed And Dangerous* (Boulder, CO: Westview Press, 1997), 177–178.

22. Philip Berrigan, *A Punishment for Peace* (New York: Macmillan Company, 1969).

23. Magno, interview with Lewis.

24. Jim Forest, "Looking Back on the Milwaukee 14," available at www.incommunion.org/forest-flier/jimsessays/looking-back-on-the-milwaukee-14 (accessed July 3, 2009).

25. Tom Pelton, "Tom Lewis, One of the 'Catonsville Nine,' Dies after Life of Activism," *Baltimore Sun*, April 6, 2008.

26. Berrigan, *America is Hard to Find*, 6.

27. Ibid., 54.

28. Ibid., 67.

29. Ibid, 93.

30. See, for example, Ethan Vesely-Flad, "Surveillance = Security?" *Fellowship Magazine* September/October 2005, available at http://www.forusa.org/fellowship/sept-oct_05/editorialethan.html (accessed June 30, 2009).

31. Bernardine Dohrn, Bill Ayers, and Jeff Jones, *Sing A Battle Song: The Revolutionary Poetry, Statements, and Communiqués of the Weather Underground 1970–1974* (New York: Seven Stories Press, 2006), 155. Enraged by the "rampant clericalism and patriarchalism" in the way the Berrigan brothers were the center of attention, alienated by the world of 1980 in which she resurfaced to serve her prison term, Moylan never returned to the movement her example helped to inspire. In the words of a friend, her life underground had itself become an "extended imprisonment." Though she tried to continue work for progressive causes until the time of her death, she was, like others of this period, "shattered and ground under by the trample of events." See Rosemary Radford Ruether, "To Mary Moylan, Another Casualty of War," *National Catholic Reporter*, November 10, 1995, available at http://thechristianradical.blogspot.com/2008/04/to-mary-moylan-another-casualty-of-war.html (accessed June 30, 2009).

32. Elmer, *Felon for Peace*, 84.

33. Ibid., 85.

34. See Dan Berger, *Outlaws of America: The Weather Underground and the Politics of Solidarity* (Oakland, CA: AK Press, 2006), for an overview.

35. WIN Magazine files, Swarthmore College Peace Collection. After a hiatus, WIN is now a publication of the War Resisters League. See www.warresisters.org/win.

36. Ward Churchill and Jim Vander Wall, *Agents of Repression* (Boston: South End Press, 1988); Ward Churchill and Jim Vander Wall, *The COINTELPRO Papers: Documents from the FBI's Secret War Against Dissent* (Boston: South End Press, 1990).

37. U.S. Congress, Senate Select Committee to Study Governmental Operations with Respect to Intelligence Activities, *Final Report—Book III, Supplementary Detailed Staff Reports on Intelligence Activities and the Rights of Americans*, 94th Cong., 2d sess., 1976.

38. From http://www.camden28.org/thefbi.htm. For more on Grady's role in the revolutionary nonviolence movement, see Patrick O'Neill, "Peace Activist John Grady Dies at 77," *National Catholic Reporter*, November 22, 2002.

39. Allan Jalon, "A Break-In to End All Break-Ins," *Los Angeles Times*, March 8, 2006.

40. Daniel Ellsberg, *Secrets: A Memoir of Vietnam and the Pentagon Papers* (New York: Viking, 2002).

41. See "The Camden 28 Newsletter" files, The Vietnam Center and Archive, Texas Tech University (http://www.vietnam.ttu.edu/virtualarchive).

42. Edward McGowan, *Peace Warriors: The Story of the Camden 28* (New York: Circumstantial, 2001).

43. Howard Zinn, "A Break-In for Peace," *The Progressive*, July 2002.

44. A fascinating account of the background to the trial can be found in Amy Posey and Lawrence Wrightsman, *Trial Consulting* (New York: Oxford University Press, 2005), 173–178.

45. Zinn, "A Break-In for Peace."

46. Paul Magno, interview with Philip Berrigan, March 15, 1989.

47. Philip Berrigan and Elizabeth McAlister, *The Time's Discipline: The Eight Beatitudes and Nuclear Resistance* (Baltimore: Fortkamp Publishing, 1989), Appendix A.

48. Ibid, xviii.

49. Magno, interview with Berrigan.

50. In the lingo of the Catholic Worker movement as a whole, the concept of discipleship and service is key. See Jim Forest's "The Catholic Worker Movement," and Tom Cornell's "A Brief Introduction to the Catholic Worker," both at http://www.catholicworker.org. See also Mel Piehl, *Breaking Bread: The Catholic Worker and the Origins of Catholic Radicalism in America* (Philadelphia: Temple University Press, 1982).

51. Barbara Epstein, *Political Protest and Cultural Revolution: Nonviolent Direct Action in the 1970s and 1980s* (Berkeley: University of California Press, 1991), 9.

52. Vickie Leonard and Tom MacLean, eds., *The Continental Walk for Disarmament and Social Justice* (New York: War Resisters League, 1977).

53. See, for example, Cooney and Michalowski, eds., *The Power of the People.*

54. Barbara Deming, *Remembering Who We Are* (Tallahassee: Pagoda Press/Naiad Press, 1981).

55. Quoted in Epstein, *Political Protest and Cultural Revolution*, 188.

56. Stephanie Slocum-Schaffer, *America in the Seventies* (Syracuse, NY: Syracuse University Press, 2003), 206.

57. Van Gosse, *Rethinking the New Left: An Interpretative History* (New York: Palgrave Macmillan, 2005), 201.

58. Dellinger, *More Power Than We Know*, 193.

14

"The Original Gangster"

The Life and Times of Red Power Activist Madonna Thunder Hawk

ELIZABETH CASTLE

There are those of us who are content to assimilate or whatever, but there
are those of us who want to maintain the culture our ancestors died for. . . .
We have the right to be who we are.

—Madonna Thunder Hawk, 2008

One surprisingly sunny day during the 1973 American Indian Movement (AIM)
occupation of Wounded Knee, South Dakota, Madonna Thunder Hawk, who
served as a medic and leader in the community, experienced a powerful moment
of clarity about her purpose. She plainly felt the spirit of her ancestors and imagined how they had stood their ground in a losing battle to protect their right to be
who they were and to protect the land. Wounded Knee brought that insight and
experience of freedom that would stay with her and guide her choices when the
real work of moving Red Power beyond powerful rhetoric to meaningful community change occurred in the years to come.

For most, the history of the Red Power movement ended with the 1973 occupation of Wounded Knee. The rather hidden history of the struggle for Indian self-
determination and revitalization unfolded between 1974 and 1980. During that
time, women sustained their families and communities through the endless legal
trials following Wounded Knee, the growth of the international indigenous movement, the establishment of alternative schooling for Native children, the fight to
protect reproductive health against illegal sterilization, and natural resource pollution by companies exploiting Indian land. The central organizations formed to
contend with all of these issues were the Wounded Knee Legal Defense/Offense
Committee, the We Will Remember Survival School, the International Indian Treaty
Council, Women of All Red Nations, and the Black Hills Alliance. One woman connected all of these South Dakota–based groups: Madonna Thunder Hawk.

The history of the Red Power movement has been overly associated with the famous occupations of Alcatraz and Mount Rushmore and the military conflict of Wounded Knee. While these events were vital to showing the world that Native people were still alive and fighting for survival, much of the substantial work of Red Power did not begin until Wounded Knee *ended*.[1] Many women on the front lines of Indian activism in the 1970s could have been featured in historical writing, but it is precisely because Thunder Hawk insists she was "just one of the people" that her story is so emblematic. She is both ordinary, one of countless grassroots activists and community residents, and extraordinary, in that no one else has quite walked her path.[2] She may never have given a "chiefly" speech that, one day, will be reduced to a trendy bumper sticker, but her life's work reflects the greatest-kept secret to the world outside of Indian Country: women are the core and the strength of Native society. This is not a modern social phenomenon but one that extends back prior to European invasion. However since contact, unseeing missionary eyes have recorded a history that erased, or made invisible, the most critical elements of balance in gender relations and the central importance of women to tribal societies.[3]

Native and women's history has been slow to reveal the historical experiences of the separate but equal gender roles occupied by Native women in most traditional societies. Former principal chief of the Cherokee nation and Red Power activist Wilma Mankiller, a late twentieth-century example of public leadership, assessed the impact and response of Native women to colonization: "From the time of European contact, there had been a concerted attempt to diminish the role of indigenous women. But even with the sustained efforts by the federal government and various religious groups to assimilate them, women continue to play a critical role in many indigenous communities in formal and informal leadership positions in every sector of tribal society and the larger culture around them."[4] As Mankiller points out, the treacherous federal policies administered largely through religious institutions systematically reduced Native's women's autonomy and collapsed it into the patriarchal tradition of Euro-America—at least that has been the view from the outside. Native women have consistently remained the backbone of indigenous cultures, and the Red Power Movement of the 1960s and 1970s inspired the reclamation of Native identity, spirituality, and traditional gender practices.

Therefore, nothing was unusual about Thunder Hawk's involvement in every major occupation that is typically associated with•Red Power activism: Alcatraz Island (1969–1971), Mount Rushmore (1970 and 1971—a patriotic symbol to many non-Natives, while a desecration of a sacred site to the Lakota), the Bureau of Indian Affairs (1972), and Wounded Knee (1973). Far more significant than these physical occupations of sites with dual symbolic importance was how she inculcated the ideal of Red Power in the lives of Native people after Wounded Knee. Between 1973 and 1980, she co-founded a survival school, Women of All Red Nations (WARN), and the International Indian Treaty Council and helped organize the Black Hills International Survival Gathering.[5] During these years, she was sent all over the world by invitation to speak on behalf of the movement.

When I first interviewed Madonna Thunder Hawk in 1998, we were sitting in the living room of her home on the east end of the Cheyenne River Sioux Reservation, in the Swift Bird district. Since then we have shared an innovative intellectual partnership that has grown into nonprofit work and informed grassroots activism. Our interviews over the years have become discursive conversations as well as interrogations into the historical meaning of her life's work. This chapter is a combined effort of our work together, moving in and out of oral history testimony and analysis of the hidden history of indigenous radicalism.

One of her main motivations to participate in this ongoing dialogue was the desire to see a more complex history of women reflecting indigenous values and priorities in contemporary society. She has expressed frustration by what she has observed in academia and the fact that too often curricula have relied solely upon *Lakota Woman* (1991), the autobiography of Mary Brave Bird (also known as Mary Crow Dog), written with Richard Erdoes. In the absence of an overall history of women in the Red Power Movement, many have taken Brave Bird's personal experience in the movement as the exclusive story of all women.[6]

"I guess I'm not your typical Indian woman," Thunder Hawk offered reflectively as she began another guest lecture to one my classes. Each time she speaks, she offers new insight into the meaning of her life of activism and organizing: "It was my grandmother who told me there was such a thing as treaty rights. But in her day and even in my day growing up you didn't talk about that—'Oh, that's a thing of the past.' Even our own people, 'That's a thing of the past. Don't make trouble. What's the matter with you?' But that's being colonized too, you know, that self-hatred that comes out."

Her grandmother's words were a constant source of strength that sustained her activism and nourished her intellect. Indeed, it was her female ancestors who ingrained in her a duty to "do what's right" no matter the circumstance—whether she had to speak out against her own people, the federal government, or the media-recognized male leaders of the movement.

Contrary to popular masculine conceptions of the Lakota, fueled by the ubiquitous headdresses and warriors-on-horses imagery, the culture is not patriarchal—though this is relatively unknown to most outside of Lakota Country. Even more problematic is the trend of men adopting sexist practices from mainstream white culture and claiming them as "traditional Lakota ways." This, to some degree, goes unchallenged by both men and women.[7]

During a 2008 filming of Thunder Hawk visiting Mount Rushmore to describe the occupations she was a part of in 1970 and 1971, she stated, "This is our land, y'all [standing in front of Mount Rushmore, widely and protectively gesturing to the land behind her]. Keep that in mind. Don't ever forget it. I will tell you what my grandmother told me—'The Black Hills belong to us, and don't you forget it.' No profound words from no stoic chief—it was *the women*!" What Thunder Hawk wants us to know is that, despite the highly masculinized stereotypes of Lakota men, women are equal partners in protecting land—and in her family, they were the ones who led the fight and resisted. She is also lightly referencing the inside joke that you never "give an Indian man a microphone," because he will never stop talking.

Thunder Hawk hails from the Feather Necklace *tiospaye* (extended family). She was born in 1940 on the Yankton Sioux Reservation but grew up in the old Bureau of Indian Affairs agency town on the fertile grounds near the Missouri River, on the Cheyenne River Sioux Reservation, in north-central South Dakota.[8] While Thunder Hawk's early life was very typical of the lives of Native people of her generation—the historical violence of boarding schools, the blatant anti-Native racism, the intrusion of the federal government, the misdirected rage—few responded with such explicit forms of resistance as the women in her family.

> You know, now that I'm older and have thought about it, it seems like our family—the strong people in our family—were all women. You know, it's not that there weren't a lot of the grandpas and uncles and all that were around in our family. But I guess you can say this is a matriarchal family, but I don't think we were that different from everyone else, because it's always been that way, and it still is, where the women are the center of the family. For real. It's not just something from our past history. It's because there's neo-colonialism still going on in Indian country that people don't know this. A lot of it's been twisted; for example, the Tribal Councils are male-dominated by choice, because that's what non-Indians expect—but just on the top, the surface—but underneath, it's still women, you know. It starts with the family. [Women are] in control of the family and how things go, and they're the mainstay. So—and it's not a competition-type thing either, because you look at our Indian colleges on the reservations, the students are predominantly female. And you go to any of the tribal offices, the pro-grams, the majority are women employed and the directors are—the major-ity of them are women. So it's not such a competition thing between men and women with our people as looking at it in terms of survival as a people, that whatever's the most efficient way to get things done [is best].

In Thunder Hawk's lifetime, a harsh test of that gender balance and commu-nity resilience was the devastating impact of the 1944 Pick-Sloan Act. The U.S. Army Corp of Engineers decided it was necessary to dam and flood reservations all along the Missouri River to protect predominately white towns from flooding. Millions of acres of prime reservation land were lost forever as the government flooded towns and a few burial grounds.[9] Though no quantitative study has been conducted, qualitatively, through countless interviews, women have located this event as that which plunged their nations into welfare dependency in the 1950s, as the ability to produce, collect, or hunt their own food was dramatically reduced by the loss of these fertile lands.[10]

Later in life, Thunder Hawk connected her unbridled anger, and her urge to "slug any cowboy who looked at me wrong," to this event. She was known for her deadly elbow punch, which she used to survive boarding school, as well the occasional bar fight. As a student, she was "one step ahead of getting kicked out" of every school she attended, more for her ostensibly disruptive attitude than her "bad" behavior. She questioned an educational environment that mandated complicity and docility. Every Native person living has been affected in some way by the boarding school experience. Corporal punishment was used to keep children from speaking their language or "acting" Indian culturally or spiritually, and sexual abuse was commonplace, which greatly disrupted the Native sense of self and affected the intergenerational ability to parent. Young children were forcibly taken from their homes and not returned until they had completed school. For many, it forever broke their family and community bonds.[11] While the stories of victimization were severe, there were always stories of resistance. Thunder Hawk remembers her time at boarding schools as marked by constant rebellion.

The federal government's plan to relocate Native people from the reservations to urban areas to further assimilate them into the American experience, while simultaneously gaining access to remaining reservation land, backfired.[12] The relocation policy brought Native people together in urban areas, where they shared common experiences of colonization and organized a movement of resistance. Thunder Hawk went on relocation to Cleveland, Ohio, and later moved out to the Bay Area, where she was drawn into the emerging social movements.

Thunder Hawk became involved in the American Indian Movement during its early years and recalled Indian communities from all across the country asking AIM to come and support them in their struggles. Cheyenne River Lakota tribal president T. O. Traversie disparaged AIM as being "only the have-nots, young people, and old people." Thunder Hawk laughs, remembering this interview, and replied, "Who else is there?" His point, however, demonstrates how AIM and the Red Power movement differed from other organizing at the time: They were indeed a movement of the people. If an event or meeting was held, entire extended families came; they had to plan for elders, infants, and everyone in between.

When the movement was constrained within the legal system starting in late 1973, the days of AIM as a protest movement shifted. After the tanks rolled away, the government's next quasi-legal tactic of suppression was the most insidious and effective: the entrapment of AIM in court for months, or even years, on end. Sitting in court or jail with no protest actions left many frustrated and restless, for they were accustomed to the excitement of being on the move. Responding to the shift from open war in the fields of Wounded Knee to subterfuge in the federal courts, AIM was quick to respond with an impressive volunteer team of lawyers and legal workers. Headed up by Ken Tilsen, they formed the Wounded Knee Legal Defense/Offense Committee (WKLD/OC) during the March 1973 occupation to respond to the mounting court cases.[13]

The aftermath of Wounded Knee brought both great violence and great hope. Without a dramatic confrontation to focus the eyes of the world on the area, the revenge violence on Pine Ridge made it the most dangerous place to live in America in 1974 and 1975. Some residents of Pine Ridge described the vigilante GOON squad (the "Guardians of the Oglala Nation") as little more than a terrorist operation funded by the federal government. There was no one but AIM to stand in its way—and at times, meet violence with violence. Murders occurred on a near-weekly basis, gaining little attention until the deaths of FBI agents Ron Williams and Jack Coler in 1976.[14]

With the violence as an ugly backdrop, the court cases spread like shrapnel in multiple cities in South Dakota, Iowa, Nebraska, and Minnesota, requiring a goodly supply of the hardest resource to come by: money. While many involved had the time, talents, and courage necessary to defy the FBI, getting the capital to keep bailing out the hordes of people thrown in jail for every sort of offense required genius. So, as the major network cameras turned away from the battle-field spectacle of the painted warriors of Wounded Knee, a new kind of war was already raging in the courtrooms and the unlit gravel roads of Pine Ridge. The new warriors were those involved with WKLD/OC.

The offices were in a constant state of activity, be it determining whether a visitor was a friendly or an infiltrator or managing the serious and sometimes comical conflicts around personal relationships between the lawyers, legal volunteers, Native activists, and the media-recognized Red Power leaders. Madonna Thunder Hawk never had a break from keeping the movement on track, or somewhat managed. Her role in WKLD/OC could best be described as interpersonal liaisons manager. In other words, she had to sort out the culture and gender clashes that were common as such a diverse group came together.

While families were caught up on the trial process, someone was needed to look after the children they left behind. These extended Indian families had been the mainstay supporters of the movement. There were no lone, stoic warriors here. Proactive measures were needed to protect the family and community from persecution.

Survival Schools

Not all was grim in the struggle that lay ahead. Another movement on the rise gave hope to building sovereign Native minds out of the destruction the boarding schools caused: the alternative education of young Indian people. This hope came in the form of the "survival school" phenomenon that emerged during the Red Power movement in the 1970s as an explicitly political and pragmatic response for Native cultural and intellectual revitalization. Whatever their geographic location, activist families were persecuted, and their children suffered. In response, these families applied the passionate ideals of self-determination by combating colonization on the front lines, through educating Indian children with indigenous values and knowledge. Because education for Indian people had been the primary site of assimilation, the ultimate expression of Red Power resistance was creation of an "alternative" form of education in line with cultural practice, language, and values. Survival schools were designed to instill cultural pride and tribal awareness, and offer tribally specific history and language as an alternative to the public or Bureau of Indian Affairs school system at the time, which did not offer these things.

Determined to never again have their young people suffer the damage of the boarding schools, women assessed what was best for their communities in the process of reclaiming education. The schools they started fell largely into two main types—one was an indigenous version of the public school experience, and the other was a less-structured group-home experience. Approximately sixteen of these schools appeared in urban areas and reservations across the country throughout the 1970s. Unlike other alternative-education institutions for indigenous people at the time, these schools were explicitly associated with the movement. They formed themselves into the Federation of Native-Controlled Survival Schools, with a shared affirmation of Native self-determination and indigenous knowledge and culture at the center of their efforts.

One of the earliest of these schools was established by the Ojibways, who founded the American Indian Movement in the Twin Cities. Established in January 1972, the first to open was the AIM Survival School, located at 1209 Fourth Street, SE, in Minneapolis. In March 1974, its name was changed to The Heart of the Earth Survival School, providing a curriculum of routine academic subjects—Indian history, literature, art, music, and the Anishinabeg language—to 135 students.[15] The Red School House—often incorrectly and diminutively called the "Little" Red School House, to the chagrin of its founders—also opened in 1972 and was located just across town at 643 Virginia Street in St. Paul. Charlotte Day, known to many as the "grandmother" of the St. Paul chapter of AIM, was central to the establishment of this school. It offered culturally based education services to students from kindergarten to twelfth grade. Both schools received federal monies through the United States Office of Education and followed the nationally accepted curriculum of the public school system.[16]

The most radical edge of these schools was embodied by the We Will Remember Survival School (WWRSS), which was established for the children of the many defendants of the Wounded Knee trials. Rejecting the path of the more conventional survival schools (if there was such a thing as "conventional" survival school), this group of young people was entirely in control of the school and learned *how to learn*, as they were given the freedom to think for themselves, without the enforced guidelines that the government imposed when a school accepted federal monies. This also meant that the experience was marked by a certain degree of chaos and excitement that comes when a group of young people is in charge of itself.[17]

The WWRSS grew primarily out of the combined efforts of the dynamic duo of Madonna Thunder Hawk and Lorelei De Cora. Though Thunder Hawk was thirteen years older, the pair had been side by side since their arrest for looting and liberating the trading post at the beginning of the Wounded Knee occupation. Inside Wounded Knee during the occupation, they had run the medical clinic and were considered grassroots leaders whom fellow occupiers turned to when they felt they were not being heard by the media-recognized leaders. In April 1974, they had established the Cultural Learning Center with a small grant of eleven thousand dollars provided by the American Friends Service Committee and were living in Rapid City in the condemned flood-disaster house that the city allowed them to use.[18]

In hindsight, there is a noticeable pattern in the beginnings of many Red Power projects. While other movement organizations, primarily those of the New Left, created programs to better the world, indigenous organizing often emerged from circumstances of need and survival, because of the pressing need to take care of their own. As historical actors are asked to reflect on the reasons for their actions, the most common refrain is, "We did what we had to do." This was also how the WWRSS came about; Thunder Hawk remembered the school's beginnings as just another step in the survival process:[19]

I mean it first started with our own kids, my own children and relatives. And then pretty soon some other kids were hanging around. A lot of these kids were looking for a night's sleep in safe surroundings. We didn't recruit students, nothing like that. They showed up at our door with a backpack, and I don't even know how the word spread. I don't know if they were runaways, or dropouts or what. But no parents, truant officer, social worker, police officer, no one ever came to my door and said, "What are you doing with all these kids here? Who gave you permission? Where's your papers?" Well, it just proves what we were saying about the school systems and everything. These kids were throwaways, you know, push-outs as far as the system was concerned. And if their parents had drinking problems or whatever, it just made it easier for them, for us to take their responsibility and take care of the kids.

But at the same time, our main focus was the kids. We didn't have a lot of money and the best meals and all that. But those young people knew when they went to bed, no one was going to beat them up or molest them. There was always food; it might have been pretty slim sometimes, but there was always food. It was like they found some place where they were safe and treated well.

From its practical and protective origins, the survival-school model was important because it was the ultimate rejection of the boarding schools' cultural genocide. In the 1970s, young Native students were no longer subjected to boarding schools as a matter of course and could attend public schools, but the racism they faced was often equally intolerable. Many generations of boarding schools had significantly impacted the ability of Native families to pass on healthy parenting skills, let alone cultural knowledge. This was where survival schools could be a place of cultural replenishment. The survival-school model offered a powerful way to revitalize Indian identity through an educational experience.

Women of All Red Nations

The idea for Women of All Red Nations (WARN) was born in late 1977 during a meeting of a handful of key indigenous women organizers in San Francisco, after they returned from the International Non-Governmental Organization (NGO) Conference on Discrimination Against Indigenous Populations in the Americas, held in Geneva, Switzerland, sponsored by the Sub-Committee on Racism, Racial Discrimination, Apartheid, and Decolonization of the Special Committee of NGOs on Human Rights. Phyllis Young, Pat Bellanger, and other women attended the Geneva conference as representatives of the International Indian Treaty Council (IITC). IITC was formed as a means to bring the issue of human rights and treaty violations committed by the U.S. federal government against American Indians to the United Nations. IITC, which had formed in 1974 following Wounded Knee, achieved NGO status and sought to create coalitions with other indigenous groups around the world (see chapter 6). During the Geneva experience, the ITTC women realized they were the only indigenous group that did not have a "women's society" representing the issues of importance to women as the culture-keepers and centers of family and community.

WARN was formally founded in 1978 at a meeting at the Mother Butler Center in Rapid City, South Dakota, by a group of women including Madonna Thunder Hawk, Lorelei Means De Cora, Agnes Williams, Phyllis Young, Lakota Harden, Pat Bellanger, and Janet McCloud and a collective of other female leaders under the philosophy that "Indian women have always been in the front lines in the defense of our nations." For many of the activists, however, the choice to work together as women was as much a pragmatic response to government infiltration and effective state repression as it was an attempt to organize consciously around shared women's concerns.

At the founding conference, WARN decided to address sterilization abuse, political prisoners, education for survival, the destruction of family and theft of Indian children, and the destruction and erosion of an indigenous land base.[20] Its first major publication, called the *WARN Report I*, asked: "What are you doing to fulfill your duties as a sovereign Native American woman? What are you doing to channel the strength of the Great Power within you and all around you, your family, your nation, your planet? That's what working on the local-national-international level means. As you read through this booklet, we'd like you to be thinking about these things, and about how you can join hands with other women to work on those local, national, and international levels to bring about meaningful action against the genocidal processes we face at every turn."[21]

The newly formed group issued a challenge to Native women. Rather than take the approach of victimhood, WARN demanded accountability for the "great power" women wield and how that power should be utilized to fight against geno-cidal processes to protect family and community. It was a call to recognize that they had *responsibilities* to fight for family and community. Those obligations were critical to a definition of community that was simultaneously local and global, and that included Mother Earth.

In general, women active in the Red Power movement could rarely afford the time to work in more direct coalition with women's liberationist groups. The pragmatic considerations of their tiny population and the severe lack of resources made focusing on their own organizing critical. Conflict arose when they had to work in close association with feminist groups, such as at fundraisers, confer-ences, or gatherings. In these situations Native women encountered behavior by non-Indians, particularly white women, that reminded them that as indigenous people, "we were still invisible." As a speaker for a university program for Interna-tional Women's Day, Thunder Hawk heard fellow speaker (and New York Congress member) Bella Abzug claiming women's place alongside men in "fighting on the frontier on the trek west." When Thunder Hawk, the last speaker in the line-up, finally had her chance to speak, Abzug had already left for another engagement. Deflated and feeling Abzug's comments as a stinging reminder that white women narrowly and ignorantly defined the terms of the feminist movement, Thunder Hawk asked the audience, "Who were your ancestors fighting [on the trek west]? Well, that would be the Indians, wouldn't it—and you didn't even hear her say it."

While Abzug reminded Thunder Hawk that white privilege and general igno-rance blinded even the most educated or politically experienced when it came to understanding Indians, this was not atypical of Indian encounters with other feminist activists, many of which occurred at the Black Hills International Survival Gathering.

Consistent experiences like the one she had with Abzug made Thunder Hawk feel she simply lacked the patience to speak to audiences about the Native struggle. However, it was critical that she travel internationally to raise awareness for the movement and to help raise the always-needed bail money. She felt she was not a natural speaker and was reluctant at first. Though she was asked to visit various countries, including Iran, Libya, Japan, Mexico, and Panama, she said the place that had the most impact on her was Northern Ireland, which she visited as a guest of Sinn Fein in 1974. By speaking to social clubs in Dublin and Derry, she gained insight into a much wider definition of what it meant to be indigenous.

> There were all these parallels to what had gone on with us, our people. Man, it was just an incredible experience. Then from Dublin, I went from there to Northern Ireland and ended up in Derry with the coolest bunch of people. I just felt at home. I mean even their humor was the same; nobody understands Indian humor. They were the same way as us. When they had meetings and had to restrict the booze, all of that because—well, they're Irish! They had the same problems we do. I think that's what really helped

me for the long haul. I think back to our ancestors, and then I think back to the Irish. All these hundreds of years of colonization and they are still Irish. Why? They got their vision and they stayed with it.

That's when I really developed this whole global view. I didn't have the word *indigenous* then, but for the indigenous around the world, regardless of what color, it is a struggle for the land and who you are.

In the same manner in which Malcolm X's Hajj showed him that the unity of Islam undermined the false construction of race, Thunder Hawk connected the land struggle and the fight for cultural preservation as inherent to all indigenous peoples, regardless of racial identity or skin color. This realization was crucial to the cross-racial organizing she did to prevent Union Carbide and other corporations from drilling for uranium in the Black Hills.

The late 1970s was a crucial time of organizing in the Black Hills area of South Dakota. AIM was based primarily in Rapid City to handle the Wounded Knee trials, and during that time, it became publicly known that Union Carbide was planning to lease some sites to conduct exploratory drilling for possible uranium mining. Thunder Hawk recalled: "Well, right away, that got everybody's attention. Again, the Black Hills still belong to the Great Sioux nation legally, despite having been stolen by the United States government in 1877. So it isn't just something that we're saying, 'Well, this is our land and it's sacred.' It was more like, 'Well, here we go again. On top of everything else, now we've got to do the work of the government, which should be at least protecting the land they stole. This is an issue that we are going to have to fight."

That fight was an example of what Thunder Hawk described as "cowboy and Indian" politics. The landowners, with small homesteads in the Black Hills, were "shocked and appalled" that the government would allow this, and they looked to the very people they usually battled against—the Indian activists. Colleen Ragan, a member of the Black Hills Alliance, remembered how they would recruit in the Black Hills area to gain support: "We are talking about uranium tailings under people's houses, in the water, cattle breakin' their legs in exploratory holes that nobody knew about. Russell Means starting talking about doing speeches out in the white community about how you're the new Indians, they are taking your land. Oh, they don't need your land? Perhaps your water or your mineral rights. Get used to it! This is how they treated us, this is how they're treating you—how do you like it?"[22]

The ranchers did not like it at all—and were willing to involve themselves in a coalition established in 1978 known as the Black Hills Alliance (BHA). The BHA was Native-led and dedicated to protecting the Black Hills from exploitative and destructive uranium mining, for environmental and spiritual motivations. Producing a newsletter, the BHA was run on a daily basis by the energetic Mark Tilsen, son of the lawyer Ken Tilsen and the organizer Rachel Tilsen. Working alongside Mark was a crew of women that included Thunder Hawk, Lakota Harden, Lilias Jones, and Colleen Ragan, to name a few.[23]

Thunder Hawk found it possible to work in coalition with those with whom she had significant philosophical and political differences. "We saw the value of coalitions and alliances with different people," she said. "We could be issue-oriented, rather than dwell on anything else. The issue was the most important thing, and the bottom line is how do we stop this desecration of the land? So those cowboy and Indian differences didn't even become an issue."

The BHA and WARN organized a major event, the first of its kind, when they hosted the Black Hills International Survival Gathering from July 18 to 27, 1980. The event was held on the ranch land of Marvin Kammerer, featuring huge tents on the open plains, and was attended by an estimated ten thousand people from all over the world. BHA's goal for the gathering was to create a rural solar- and wind-power awareness campaign and invite other groups who were dedicated to living sustainably on the earth. One group, the Women's Feminist Health Collective (WFHC), attended to provide workshops on women's health topics, including birth control, self-examination, lesbian health issues, and childbirth. WFHC member Carol Downer recalls how their plan to teach women how to conduct vaginal self-examinations, to be done in an open tent as other sessions were, was approved in the planning stages but banned once they had arrived at the gathering. Downer remembered Thunder Hawk's behavior as particularly hostile to their participation. Downer stated that the WFHC felt they could not compromise their agenda by censoring their workshops. They chose to pull out of the program and simply be attendees.[24] Thunder Hawk's perspective was that the group should have respected the cultural mores of the Lakota as well the conservatism of the local ranchers, who would be alienated by the exposed vaginal exams.

The Original Gangsta Granny

The story of Madonna Thunder Hawk's activism has no end point. In her elder years, which she enjoys for the status it affords her as an Indian woman, she is no less engaged in shaking up Indian Country than she was forty years ago. She remembers the controversy she created in the mid-1990s when she spoke out against the $100 million casino resort development with railroad access being planned by actor Kevin Costner and his brother Dan. After his performance in *Dances with Wolves*, Costner apparently had little conflict over commercially exploiting the same Black Hills he was giving lip-service to protecting in the media. "Dunbar, Co." (named after his heroic white film character, John Dunbar) decided to withdraw the project due to the negative publicity generated by Thunder Hawk, who plainly called out his duplicitous game.[25]

Madonna Thunder Hawk returned home in the 1990s to the Cheyenne River Reservation to work on "decolonizing" her people from the grassroots before it could become the latest academic trend. She did so by taking positions on the school board and housing board and demonstrating, through her leadership, indigenous values and protocols that have underpinned Lakota society for generations. Using her "elder card" to gain access, she frequently addressed the tribal council and urged them to develop more community-based projects and to think "green" in developing wind energy. She established the Swift Bird Oyate Center in her district of the reservation. Preferring to be "poor and free," as she describes her lifestyle, she has taken paid work positions only when they advanced the cause she was involved in at the time; otherwise, she insists that being accountable to employers compromises her ability to be accountable to her community. She has continued her community organizing and hell-raising because she feels it is the closest way to re-create the experience of living free in Wounded Knee. She has had to "hustle," as she describes it, to get by in her never-ending quest for gas money and has received support from the radical activist community over the years. In 2006, she began work as the tribal liaison for the Lakota People's Law Project, which allows her for the first time in her life to be paid for what she says she would be doing anyway—traveling around Indian Country to talk to the typically voiceless and to bring their concerns to light. At this time in her life, after years of being called a militant, radical, terrorist, and communist, she accepts just two titles: "warrior woman" and "granny." Her oldest *takoja* (grandson) expanded that title to "original gangsta granny," not for any association with negative violence, but rather as the definition of a woman who stood her ground as an Indian before it was hip to be Native—and one who never compromised, despite the pressures, in her fight for indigenous life.

> The years go by so quickly, but I just feel like working as a community organizer was the closest thing I could get to as an individual to carry on a lot of the issues and the principles we had as a movement. We were a movement of people. It wasn't a certain generation, or radicals over here and elders over there. It was a movement of people. That's basically the bottom line for me.
>
> It influenced my family, my children. I saw them as individuals . . . it would've been easier for me to travel around and play militant and stick my kids in school, and let someone else take care of them. But as a result of that, we had our own school, because that's what my children wanted. It brought my thinking in how work with people, alliances with non-Indians. Up until that point it was foreign to me. I mean, I didn't even think of it like that. But since then, it's been a good life, because you're constantly striving to keep your principles intact, to be accountable. If you're working for an issue, then you're accountable to the people that it affects. And of course you stay true to your family, because the bottom line is your family. But yeah, that's what Red Power did for me.

Thunder Hawk's life and experience provide insight into the difficult realities of Indian Country, and the central place gender occupies in preserving indigenous cultural practices, worldviews, and cosmological beliefs. Her life and work have been a fight for the cultural right to be, a struggle that is deeply connected to rebalancing gender relations in Native society. From early on in Madonna's organizing life, having learned directly from well-known community organizer Saul Alinsky while on relocation in San Francisco, she emphasized the need for group empowerment and achievable goals. Consistently prioritizing the importance of community accountability, she felt process was as important as the outcome, and the outcome should be attainable. She expressed this commitment through always seeking to connect the rural residents of the reservation to national or international policies and issues. For instance, in the 1976 film *Indian Country?*, produced during the bicentennial to juxtapose more assimilated Native people against the "militants" of AIM, she criticized the National Indian Policy Review Committee's work, stating that it held little value if the residents in outlying districts of her reservation had never heard of it.[26]

While she has been fiercely committed to social justice, she has not been dogmatic in her approach. She has been happy to see "young people on the move," seeing youth as the only phenomenon powerful enough to create social change. She always sympathized with the "underdog" as she described it, believing that *everyone*, no matter how life had rendered them, had something to contribute. The centrality of "women's work" to indigenous communities was what kept them together and was not secondary to the role of men as leaders—who more often than not appeared as media window dressing. It was women's work and commitment that maintained the Red Power Movement beyond the 1973 Wounded Knee occupation when it was left for dead by the media. This was not the result of any essentialist "natural" power of women but because they were the ones most often doing the work in maintaining the relationships that are so critical to developing social movements. And Madonna's particular experiences, from traveling to Ireland to working with white ranchers, show a fascinating commitment to creative thinking about politics and alliances that brings her understanding of sovereignty to bear on local issues, be they in her own backyard or across the world. The local is indeed the global in the scope of the "original gangtsa granny."

NOTES

Unless otherwise noted, all quotations from Madonna Thunder Hawk are taken from fourteen separate interviews conducted by the author between 1998 and 2008. The collection will be available online as part of a Ford Foundation–supported collection on the website www .warriorwomen.org.

1. Only two books offer a narrative of the Red Power Movement, and these focus on the years from 1969 to 1973. See Paul Chaat Smith and Robert Warrior, *Like a Hurricane: The Indian Movement from Alcatraz to Wounded Knee* (New York: New Press, 1997); and Troy Johnson, *The American Indian Occupation of Alcatraz Island: Red Power and Self-Determination* (Lincoln: University of Nebraska Press, 2008). Neither work addresses the importance of gender relations and the centrality of women's activism in the Red Power Movement.

2. Madonna Thunder Hawk has resisted being focused on as a singular activist, knowing that she comes from a group of women who relied heavily upon on each other for success and survival. These women include her sister, Mabel Ann Chasing Hawk, and her kinship sisters in struggle, Lorelei Means DeCora, Andria Syke Robideau, Minnie Two

Shoes, Mary Quintana, and Phyllis Young. This is by no means a full list of the women she worked alongside, but a short list of the most referenced.

3. European colonization is based on a patriarchal monotheism, which has presupposed the inferiority of women since invasion, to the present day. As an American-style patriarchy has developed, women have responded with movements for women's rights, called at different times *women's suffrage, women's liberation,* or *feminism.* Because of the success of colonization, all women of color suffer under this patriarchy, but typically their method of response is imbedded in the cultural context to which they connect the most. A number of historians have located Native women's history in the context of indigenous cultural radicalism. See, for example, Teresa Amott and Julie Matthaei, *Race, Gender, & Work: A Multi-Cultural Economic History of Women in the US* (Boston: South End Press, 1991), 31–61; Wynne Hanson, "The Urban Indian Woman and Her Family," *Social Casework: The Journal of Contemporary Social Work* (1980); M. Annette Jaimes with Theresa Henley, "American Indian Women: At the Center of Indigenous Resistance in Contemporary North America," in *The State of Native America: Genocide, Colonization, and Resistance,* ed. M. Annette Jaimes (Boston: South End Press, 1992), 311–344; Clara Sue Kidwell, "What Would Pocahontas Think Now?: Women and Cultural Persistence," *Callaloo* 17:1 (1994): 149–159; Beatrice Medicine, "The Role of Women in Native American Societies," *The Indian Historian* 8:3 (1976): 50–53; Devon Abbott Mihesuah, *Indigenous American Women: Decolonization, Empowerment, Activism* (Lincoln: University of Nebraska Press, 2003); Theda Perdue, *Cherokee Women* (Lincoln: University of Nebraska Press, 1998); Marla N. Powers, *Oglala Women: Myth, Ritual, and Reality* (Chicago: University of Chicago Press, 1986); Karen Anderson, *Changing Woman: A History of Racial Ethnic Women in Modern America* (New York: Oxford University Press, 1996); Nancy Shoemaker, "The Rise or Fall of Iroquois Women," *Journal of Women's History* 2:3 (1991): 39–57; Lisa J. Udel, "Revision and Resistance: The Politics of Native Women's Motherwork," *Frontiers* 22:2 (2001): 43–62; Robert A. Williams, Jr., "Gendered Checks and Balances: Understanding the Legacy of White Patriarchy in an American Indian Cultural Context," *Georgia Law Review* 24 (1991): 48–72; Shirley Hill Witt, "The Brave-Hearted Women," *Civil Rights Digest* (Summer 1976): 39–45.

4. Wilma Mankiller, *Every Day Is a Good Day: Reflections by Contemporary Indigenous Women* (Golden, CO.: Fulcrum Publishing, 2004), 9.

5. It is important to emphasize that WARN was not established until 1978. One book has mistakenly set the founding earlier, and this error has been repeated in subsequent references to WARN. See Alvin M. Josephy, Jr., Troy R. Johnson, and Joane Nagel, eds., *Red Power, American Indians Fight for Freedom,* 2nd ed. (Lincoln, NE: Bison Books, 1999).

6. Mary Brave Bird, who took the name of her husband, Leonard Crow Dog, is commonly known as Mary Moore on the Rosebud reservation, where she grew up. A common critique among Native activists is that the book portrays her as a more pivotal historical character in the movement than she was.

7. This is a difficult claim to source using existing literature, as it is based quantitatively and qualitatively on seventy oral history interviews that I have completed during the past ten years. It is generally agreed upon that the tribal relationships of men and women in pre-invasion indigenous societies were not exclusively based on a religious or social hierarchy, but rather on egalitarian recognition of the separate, but equally necessary, roles of women and men. Not to say that there were no hierarchies, but in various tribes you would find women holding high political or spiritual positions. One theme that has emerged over time in my work as an interviewer, historian, and professor in the heart of Lakota country is how contemporary Lakotas *remember* their own history in a way that generally contradicts existing anthropological research about gender relations.

8. *Tiospaye* is a Lakota word meaning extended family. An agency town is a reference to where the Bureau of Indian Affairs first set up its services when reservations were established. The majority of resources were available there.

9. Michael Lawson, *Damned Indians: The Pick-Sloan Plan and the Missouri River Sioux, 1944–1980* (Norman: University of Oklahoma Press, 1982).

10. Of all the interviews I conducted for my book, *Women Were the Backbone, Men Were the Jawbone: Native Women's Activism in the Red Power Movement* (Oxford University Press, forthcoming), every woman with Lakota cultural connections discussed the devastating impact of the Pick-Sloan Act on their tribe and personal life.

11. The literature exposing the history of the boarding-school policy has dramatically increased in the last ten years. This history has also received recognition by Amnesty International as a human rights violation, and the Canadian government has officially apologized for its policy. Every interview I have ever conducted includes a traumatic boarding-school experience. See, for example, David Wallace Adams, *Education for Extinction: American Indians and the Boarding School Experience* (Lawrence: University of Kansas Press, 1997); Margaret Archuleta, Brenda J. Child, K. Tsianina Lomawaima, eds., *Away from Home: American Indian Boarding School Experiences, 1879–2000* (Phoenix: Heard Museum, 2000); and Ward Churchill, *Kill the Indian, Save the Man: The Genocidal Impact of American Indian Residential Schools* (San Francisco: City Lights Publishers, 2004).

12. The relocation program following World War II was another dramatic pendulum-swing in federal Indian policy, from self-determination back to assimilation. Scholar Donald Fixico is the expert on the termination and relocation policies. See his books *Termination and Relocation: Federal Indian Policy, 1945–1960* (Albuquerque: University of New Mexico Press, 1990); and *The Urban Indian Experience in America* (Albuquerque: University of New Mexico Press, 2000). Troy Johnson's first chapter in *American Indian Occupation of Alcatraz Island* directly connects the outgrowth of activism to the relocation program.

13. Ken Tilsen donated the WKLD/OC papers to the Minnesota Historical Society. See also John William Sayer, *Ghost Dancing the Law: The Wounded Knee Trials* (Cambridge, MA: Harvard University Press, 1997), for a full history of WKLD/OC.

14. Pine Ridge residents have claimed that during the period known as the "Reign of Terror," approximately sixty tribal members were murdered, homicides that have gone unsolved to this day. There is little evidence other than consistent oral-history testimony and that it was referenced in Peter Matthiessen, *In the Spirit of Crazy Horse* (New York: Penguin, 1992).

15. It survived the transformation from a private AIM school to alternative-school status, to its current charter-school designation in 1999.

16. Data on the Twin Cities schools was drawn from archival documents, including the school newsletter, located in the Ethnic Studies Library, University of California, Berkeley.

17. I have interviewed Mark Tilsen (2005), Marcella Gilbert (2003, 2008), Roddy Little (2008), and Lakota Harden (2001, 2004), all of whom attended WWRSS and commented on the freedom as well as the chaos that came with a large degree of self-supervision as young people.

18. Cultural Learning Center, fundraising document, produced in 1975, personal archival collection of Madonna Thunder Hawk.

19. The survival schools created during the Red Power Movement shared some of the same motivations of racial-group empowerment in their formation as those schools established by black and Latino groups. The primary difference for Native activists was utilizing these schools as a means of recovery from the damage of boarding schools. In order to establish some universalities in the experience, these schools formed the

Native-Controlled Federation of Survival Schools. The We Will Remember Survival School was different from the others because Thunder Hawk, Lorelei DeCora, and Ted Means rejected any state funding, which they felt would compromise their goals and they might be forced to follow state curriculum guidelines.

20. The founding conference for WARN was held in September 1978 in Rapid City. The program from the conference reflected these areas of priority. These documents are held in the private collection of Madonna Thunder Hawk and will be scanned and made available through www.warriorwomen.org.

21. *WARN Report* 1 (1979): 4. The *WARN Report* can be found in the Native American Studies Library at the University of California, Berkeley.

22. Colleen Ragan, interview with author, March 6, 2009.

23. See Zoltan Grossman, "Unlikely Alliances: Treaty Conflicts and Environmental Cooperation between Native American and Rural White Communities," *American Indian Culture and Research Journal* 29:4 (2005): 21–43. Scanned copies of the BHA newsletter and the handbook for the Black Hills International Survival Gathering held in 1980 will be available at www.warriorwomen.org.

24. Carol Downer, e-mail interview with author, July 30, 2008.

25. Throughout 1994, this story was covered in the *Rapid City Journal*. See also Ginia Bellafante and Elizabeth Taylor, "Broken Peace," *Time*, July 31, 1995, available at http://www.time.com/time/magazine/article/0,9171,983255,00.html (accessed July 24, 2009); and "Actor Kevin Costner's Bison Indian Center Provides Insight on American West," *Voice of America News*, August 23, 2003, available at http://www.voanews.com/english/archive/2003–08/a-2003–08–23–6-Actor.cfm?moddate=2003–08–23 (accessed July 26, 2009).

26. *Indian Country?*, VHS, 26 minutes, 1972, Cinema Guild, New York, Producer Brenda Horsfield. The commission was established by Congress, who declared "it is timely and essential to conduct a comprehensive review of the legal and historical developments underlying the Indians' unique relationship with the federal government in order to determine the nature and scope of necessary revisions in the formulations of policies and programs for the benefit of the Indians." Most grassroots organizers on reservations foresaw no worthwhile results for the "average reservation Indian," which they felt was a necessity for any further research or reports conducted on or about Native people. Lloyd Meeds, "The Indian Policy Review Commission," *Law and Contemporary Problems* 40:1 (Winter 1976): 9–11.

NOTES ON CONTRIBUTORS

BRIAN D. BEHNKEN is an assistant professor in the Department of History and the U.S. Latino/a Studies Program at Iowa State University. He received his Ph.D. from the University of California, Davis. He specializes in twentieth-century Mexican American and African American history, focusing on comparative race relations and civil rights. Behnken is the author of several articles, the monograph *Fighting Their Own Battles: African Americans, Mexican Americans, and the Struggle for Civil Rights in Texas* (forthcoming), and editor of the collection *The Struggle in Black and Brown: African American and Mexican American Relations during the Civil Rights Era* (forthcoming).

DAN BERGER studies and writes about race, media, prison, and American social movements since World War II. He is the author of *Outlaws of America: The Weather Underground and the Politics of Solidarity* (2006) and co-editor of *Letters From Young Activists* (2005). His writings have appeared in numerous scholarly journals and progressive publications. Berger was a Mellon Dissertation Fellow in 2009–2010 and received his Ph.D. from the University of Pennsylvania in 2010. He is the George Gerbner Postdoctoral Fellow at the Annenberg School for Communication, University of Pennsylvania (2010–2012).

ELIZABETH CASTLE is an assistant professor of American Indian Studies at the University of South Dakota and co-founder of the Warrior Women Project (www.warriowomen.org). She previously held a position as an academic specialist at the Regional Oral History Office at the University of California at Berkeley. In 2003–2005, as the recipient of a University of California President's Postdoctoral Fellowship, she worked under the mentorship of Professors Bettina Aptheker and Angela Davis at the University of California at Santa Cruz. Her book *Women Were the Backbone, Men Were the Jawbone: American Indian Women's Activism in the Red Power Movement* will be published by Oxford University Press. While completing her Ph.D. in history at the University of Cambridge, she worked for President Bill Clinton's Initiative on Race as a policy associate.

ANDREW CORNELL is a Ph.D. candidate at New York University, where he is completing a dissertation on anarchist movements in the United States during the mid-twentieth century. He has worked as an organizer in labor, global justice, and antiprison movements, and his writing appears in *Left Turn*, *Perspectives on Anarchist Theory*, *MRzine*, and *The University Against Itself: The NYU Strike and the Future of the Academic Workplace* (2008).

ROXANNE DUNBAR-ORTIZ is professor emerita of ethnic studies at California State University, Hayward. She received her Ph.D. in history from UCLA. She is a longtime activist on behalf of indigenous sovereignty and is the author of many books on the subject. Additionally, she is the author of three memoirs, most recently *Blood on the Border: A Memoir of the Contra Years* (2005). She is a regular contributor to *Monthly Review*, among other publications.

VICTORIA LAW is a writer, photographer, mother, and a co-founder of Books Through Bars—New York City, an organization that sends free radical literature and books to prisoners nationwide. She is editor of the 'zine *Tenacious: Writings from Women in Prison* and also the author of *Resistance Behind Bars: The Struggles of Incarcerated Women* (2009).

PAUL MAGNO is a longtime member of the Catholic Worker Movement and lives in Washington, DC. He participated in the Pershing Plowshares action at Easter/Passover/Earthday 1984 and served twenty months in federal prison as a result. He received his bachelor's degree from Georgetown University in 1978; his further education at the hands of many nonviolent revolutionaries, some referenced herein, continues today.

MATT MEYER is founding chair of the Peace and Justice Studies Association, former national chair of the War Resisters League, and currently the educational director of a small alternative high school in New York City. Meyer is the author of *Time Is Tight: Urgent Tasks for Educational Transformation—Eritrea, South Africa, and the U.S.A.* (2007), and co-author of *Guns and Gandhi in Africa: Pan African Insights on Nonviolence, Armed Struggle, and Liberation* (2000). He is the editor of *Let Freedom Ring: Documents from the Movement to Free U.S. Political Prisoners* (2008) and of the recently published two-volume set, *Seeds of New Hope: Pan African Peace Studies for the 21st Century* (2009 and forthcoming). On the local level, he is a member of Resistance in Brooklyn.

SCOTT RUTHERFORD is currently studying history at Queen's University in Kingston, Ontario, Canada. His dissertation, tentatively titled "Canada's Other Red Scare," examines the relationship between Third World decolonization movements and the growth of indigenous "Red Power" movements in Canada from 1965 to 1975. He is the co-editor of *New World Coming: The Sixties and the Shaping of Global Consciousness* (2009).

LIZ SAMUELS is currently a medical student living in Boston. She received a bachelor's degree from Reed College in 2004. She has been a member of Critical Resistance since 2005 and does harm reduction and health work in communities most impacted by the prison industrial complex. Samuels is particularly interested in helping to develop and expand work for health justice as a part of a larger effort toward liberation, self-determination, and the abolition of the prison industrial complex.

BENJAMIN SHEPARD is an assistant professor of human service at New York School of Technology/City University of New York. He received his Ph.D. from the CUNY Graduate Center. He is the author/editor of six books, including *Queer Politics and Political Performance: Play, Pleasure, and Social Movement* (2009), *White Nights and Ascending Shadows: An Oral History of the San Francisco AIDS Epidemic* (1997), and *From ACT UP to the WTO: Urban Protest and Community Building in the Era of Globalization* (2002), a nonfiction finalist for the 2002 Lambda Literary Awards. His forthcoming works include part two of this study on play: *Play, Creativity, and the New Community Organizing* and *Community Projects as Social Activism,* and with co-author Greg Smithson, *The Beach Beneath the Streets: Exclusion, Control, and Play in Public Space.* His writing has appeared in several anthologies and popular and academic journals. A former freelance journalist, he has also done organizing work with ACT UP, SexPanic!, Reclaim the Streets New York, CitiWide Harm Reduction, Housing Works, and the More Gardens Coalition, among other groups.

MEG STARR is a founder of the New York–based antiracist and anti-imperialist collective Resistance in Brooklyn. She has been active in Puerto Rican solidarity organizing for more than twenty-five years, serving as a central organizer for both the New Movement for Puerto Rican Independence and Socialism and the Free Puerto Rico Committee. An early-childhood educator and curriculum designer, Starr is author of the award-winning children's book *Alicia's Happy Day* (2001).

MICHAEL STAUDENMAIER is a long-time anarchist and independent scholar from the Midwest. His political work has focused on antifascism, prison issues, educational alternatives, Latin American solidarity, and developing revolutionary theory and strategy. His writings have appeared in a range of anarchist publications over the past decade, including *Arsenal, Onward,* the *Northeastern Anarchist,* the *Fifth Estate,* and *Upping the Anti.* He is currently writing a book-length history of the Sojourner Truth Organization.

JAMES TRACY is the editor of *The Civil Disobedience Handbook: A Brief History and Practical Advice for the Politically Disenchanted* (2001) and the author of *Sparks and Codes* (2007). A community organizer in California, he is currently completing a book on radical working-class white organizations in the 1960s and 1970s who worked in tandem with radical organizations of color.

FANON CHE WILKINS is associate professor of African American history and culture in the Graduate School of American Studies at Doshisha University in Kyoto, Japan. He is a graduate of Morehouse College and holds master's and Ph.D. degrees in history from Syracuse University and New York University, respectively. He is the co-editor of *From Toussaint to Tupac: The Black International Since the Age of Revolution* (2009). Beyond his academic work, which largely examines the global contours of twentieth-century black radicalism, Wilkins divides his time between photography, DJing, and riding anything that requires a board.

INDEX

1970s, the: 2008 presidential campaign, 1–2; alternative political communities, 5, 29–30, 231–232, 237–243, 261–262; anti-imperialism, 7, 10, 64, 155, 157, 163–168, 216–217; armed struggles, 4, 5, 9, 28, 39, 87–88, 113n19, 136, 143–145, 164–165, 252–253; clandestine organizations, 9, 11, 135–136, 143–145, 148–149, 164, 250–251, 256–258, 263; community-building, 5, 12, 177–178, 186, 216–218, 242–243, 245, 278–280; conservatism and, 2–3, 6–7, 9–10, 222; as contemporary reference point, 1–2, 9–10; electoral politics, 9–10, 251–252; grassroots social movements, 2, 4, 10, 11, 113n19, 136, 217, 231, 263, 268; limits as framework, 4, 6–9, 263–264; as the "long sixties," 4–5; neoliberalism and, 7, 203; periodization, 4, 195–196; personal transformation and, 6, 238–240, 242–243, 245–246; politics of resentment, 8, 108, 214–216, 221–222, 225; poor people's movements, 17n48, 27, 33–34, 51, 118–119, 214–219, 226–227, 228n17; race and, 8, 22–23, 25, 57–60, 156–157, 165, 214–216; racism and, 23–24, 25, 45, 51, 55n82, 56n83, 78–79, 132n14, 132n18, 214–216, 219–220, 225; radical pacifism, 10, 28, 146–147, 231–233, 236, 250–251, 257–258, 262; sexism and, 37n48, 45, 49, 51–52, 85, 236, 246; spirituality and, 5, 6, 8, 83, 178, 182–183, 238–239, 253, 261–263, 266n50; transracial/national solidarity, 11, 22–23, 25, 87–88, 99–101, 157, 163–168, 215, 219–220, 276–277; vanguard political formations, 5, 60, 70, 151n31, 156, 158, 162, 169; Vietnam War as oppositional framework, 3, 6, 14n10, 57–58, 83, 137, 140, 144, 151n31, 179, 251–252; whiteness and, 8, 155–157, 165–166, 214–216, 224, 225, 230n52, 276; women and, 4, 37n48, 39, 45, 49, 51–52, 85, 236, 246, 267–269, 275–277
Abalone Alliance, 262
Abernathy, Ralph, 65
abolitionist organizing, 11, 21–23, 28–33, 37n48
Aborigines Advancement League (AAL), 112n9
Absurd Response to an Absurd War, 182
Abzug, Bella, 276
Acoli, Sundiata, 71n9
ACORN (Association of Community Organizations for Reform Now), 17n48

ACT-UP (AIDS Coalition to Unleash Power), 179, 182, 246
Adams, Howard (Hank), 79, 83, 116
Ad Hoc Committee on Prison Reform in the Northeast, 31
Africa Information Service, 110
African Liberation Day, 108
African Liberation Support Committee, 108, 109
African National Congress (ANC), 123, 127, 133n22
African Party for the Independence of Guinea and Cape Verde (PAIGC), 112n11
African Society for Cultural Relations with Independent Africa (ASCRIA), 106
Afrikan People's Party, 74n40
Afro-Asian Peoples Solidarity Organization (AAPSO), 133n24
Afro-Caribbean Circle, 101
Afro-Caribbean Self-Help Organization, 101
Aguirre, Pedro, 198, 199, 200
Ahmad, Muhammad, 64
Ahrens, Lois, 49
AIDS Coalition to Unleash Power (ACT-UP), 179, 182, 246
Akwesasne (encampment community), 61
Alaska Native Claims Settlement Act (ANCSA), 62
Alba, Panama, 147
Alcatraz (encampment community), 61, 116, 117, 118, 123, 268, 282n12
Alderson Federal Women's Prison, 22
Algerian National Liberation Front (FLN), 144
Alinsky, Saul, 225–226, 230n48, 280
Alston, Ashanti, 23–24
alternative political communities, 5, 29–30, 231–232, 237–243, 261–262. See also Movement for a New Society (MNS)
Amato, Will, 185, 188
American Friends Service Committee (AFSC): AQAG and, 233; Conference of Eighty meeting (1971), 233; MNS and, 233–234; prison abolition organizing, 29–30, 33
American Indian Movement (AIM): alternative structures of governance of, 58–60, 271–272; Anicinabe Park occupation and, 80, 86–87; anticolonialism/decolonization struggles, 59–60, 153n53; COINTELPRO and, 258–259; Crazy Horse and, 57, 59, 71n10; decline of, 69–70;

American Indian Movcment (AIM)
  (*continued*)
  Dennis Banks and, 79–80, 81–82, 86,
    90n20, 91n40; global framework and, 80,
    86–87, 93, 118–119; impact of previous
    generations of activism on, 59, 60–62;
    influence of Black Power on, 116–117;
    International Indian Treaty Council (IITC),
    63, 118–119, 123, 267, 268, 275; land-based
    struggles and, 58–60, 59, 71; Maoism and,
    71n6, 87, 93; multiracial coalitions and, 141,
    153n53; national liberation and, 58–60,
    153n53; prisoner activism and, 24; Russell
    Means and, 62, 71n10, 116; survival schools,
    272–275, 282n15; Trail of Broken Treaties
    march (1972), 62, 117; urban focus of, 61,
    62–63; Wanrow case support, 40;
    Wounded Knee Resistance and, 62–63,
    117–118
anarchism, 10, 184, 186, 187, 231, 232, 236
ANC (African National Congress), 123, 127,
  133n22
ANCSA (Alaska Native Claims Settlement
  Act), 62
Anderson, Mark, and Carmen Robertson, 86
Angel, Michael, 83
Angels of Light, 182, 183, 189
Anicinabe Park occupation (1974), 79–82,
  85–86, 88–89. *See also* First Nations
  activism; indigenous peoples movements
anti-apartheid movement, 99, 109, 110, 123
anti-authoritarian social politics, 26, 184, 231,
  236, 241, 245
Anti-Depression Program of RNA, 66
anti-imperialist solidarity/movements: PFOC
  and, 157; STO and, 155, 157, 163–168, 172n33;
  white-skin privilege analysis and, 155,
  156–157, 162, 165, 169; white working-class
  organizing and, 155, 216; WUO and, 157
anti-interventionist movements, 10
anti-Klan organizing, 13n2, 25, 165, 166–167,
  168, 170n4
antinuclear movement: Clamshell Alliance,
  240–241, 245, 262; MNS and, 235, 240–241;
  Seabrook Nuclear Power Plant action, 4,
  240, 241, 262; STO and, 168, 173n50; Three
  Mile Island, 235
anti–police violence protests: anti–police
  brutality organizing, 221–222; Dallas
  Disturbance (1973), 198–199, 199–200, 207,
  208; impact on police departments, 200,
  207–208; JOIN and, 219; Jose Campos
  Torres case, 196, 200–206, 206–208;
  League of United Latin American Citizens
  (LULAC), 202; Moody Park rebellion,
  203–206; People United to Fight Police
  Brutality, 196, 207; police racism and, 197,
  206, 208; Ruben Salazar murder, 208;
  Santos Rodríguez case, 195–196, 196–200,
  206–208, 209n8
Anti-Racist Action, 246
antisterilization campaigns: indigenous
  peoples, 60, 267, 275; in Puerto Rico, 141,
  146, 148, 163
antiviolence organizing, 22–23, 25, 32

antiwar organizing, 2, 3, 35n9, 141, 220, 233,
  51I4n50. *See also* draft-board actions; draft
  resistance; Vietnam War
Aptheker, Bettina, 28
A Quaker Action Group (AQAG), 232–233
Armed Revolutionary Independence
  Movement/Movimiento Independista
  Revolucionario Armado (MIRA), 140, 151n25
armed struggles: Pan-Africanism and, 113n19;
  people's war theory, 5, 87, 136, 144, 145;
  Puerto Rican independence movement
  and, 143–144, 145, 164, 173n40; right to
  self-defense *vs.*, 40, 41, 73n25; women and,
  39, 50. *See also* Black Liberation Army
  (BLA); clandestine organizations; Fuerzas
  Armadas de Liberación Nacional/Armed
  Forces of National Liberation (FALN);
  George Jackson Brigade (GJB); self-defense;
  Weather Underground (WUO)
Arm the Spirit (newspaper), 67
ASCRIA (African Society for Cultural Relations
  with Independent Africa), 106
Ashford, Chris, 186
Association of Community Organizations for
  Reform Now (ACORN), 17n48
Atlanta Lesbian Feminists Alliance
  (ALFA), 43
Atlantic Life Community, 261
Attica prison uprising, 11, 21–23, 27–28, 34n4
Australian Conference of Aborigines, 126
Autunno Caldo (Hot Autumn), 158
Ayers, William (Bill), 1, 265n31

Baker, Ella, 141
Ballantyne, Edith, 127
Baltimore Four action, 254–256
Baltimore Interfaith Peace Mission, 255
Banks, Dennis, 79–80, 81–82, 86, 90n20,
  91n40
Baraka, Amiri, 64, 70, 108
Barrow, Kai Lumumba, 45, 46
Barrow, Robert, 221
battered women's movement: battered
  women's defense and, 43, 50; *Easterling v.
  State* (1954), 52n14; indigenous peoples
  movements and, 39–41, 56n83; political *vs.*
  personal arguments, 46–48; politicization
  of battering/spousal abuse, 48–52; race
  and, 45, 51–52; rape *vs.* domestic abuse,
  46–48; shelters, 48–50; social service
  orientation of, 49–52, 56n83; *State v. Koss*
  (1990), 55n75. *See also* sexual violence
  activism
Battered Women's Syndrome, 50
Beat movement, 177, 179, 180, 183. *See also*
  Ginsberg, Allen
Bellanger, Pat, 275
Bellecourt, Clyde, 141
Bellecourt, Vernon, 80, 91n31
Benavides, Mario, 197
Bennett, Ramona, 116
Berrigan, Daniel: "America Is Hard to Find,"
  250; Catonsville Nine action, 250, 254–256,
  257, 261; underground, 256–258, 265n31;
  WUO and, 257–258

Berrigan, Phillip, 255, 256, 257, 260–261, 261–262
Biberman, Dana, 141–142
bicentennial protests, 32, 135, 143, 152n42, 262, 280
Bicentennial without Colonies protests (1976), 135
Billionaires for Bush, 182
Bissinger, Karl, 254
Black African Nations Towards Unity (BANTU), 31
Blackearth, Damesha, 45
Black Hills Alliance (BHA), 267, 277
black internationalism: black freedom movements and, 98–99; indigenous peoples movements and, 133n22; Pan-Africanism *vs.*, 98–99, 110n2; UN and, 68. *See also* Sixth Pan-African Congress (Sixth PAC)
Black Liberation Army (BLA), 5, 27, 68, 69, 145, 153n53, 154n63. *See also* Shakur, Assata
Black Muslims, 23–24, 25
black nationalism: Black Power *vs.*, 111n4; black women and, 44–45, 45–46; feminist movement and, 44–45; impact on 2008 presidential campaign, 1; internationalism and, 68, 98–99, 110n2; prison abolition and, 11; white pacifists and, 11. *See also* Republic of New Afrika (RNA); Sixth Pan-African Congress (Sixth PAC)
Black Panther Movement (London), 101
Black Panther Party (BPP): COINTELPRO and, 258–259; contemporary prosecution of former Panthers, 13n2; Fred Hampton murder, 219; Inez Garcia case, 41–42; influence on AIM, 116–117; Joan Little case, 43; Panther Twenty-One, 257; police repression and, 219; political prisoners and, 35n9, 257; prisoners' rights organizing, 23–24, 74n40; Rainbow Coalition and, 219–220; RNA compared to, 59; service-plus-organizing model, 215. *See also* Jackson, George
Black People's Liberation Party, 101
Black Power: British Black Power organizations, 101; civil rights organizing and, 111n7; as global concept, 99–100, 109, 113n19; impact of previous generations of activism on, 2; impact on First Nation activism, 77; militancy and, 73n25, 111n4; nationalism and, 98–99, 111n4, 112n9, 136, 138; Nixon on, 113n19; Pan-Africanism and, 9, 111n4, 113n19; political mobilization of white ethnicity and, 8; Red Power and, 116–117; Sixth PAC and, 98–99, 100–105, 109
Black Pride (magazine), 67
Black Reconstruction (Du Bois), 156–157
Black Solidarity Day, 68, 75n49
Black Workers Party, 139
Block, Diana, 46, 47
Blood in My Eye (Jackson), 21, 24, 37n59
Boggs, James, 58
Bolles, Don, 185, 186, 187, 190
Boone, John, 31
Boston bus boycott (1974), 215–216

Boudin, Leonard, 261
Bowie, David, 186, 189
Brave Bird, Mary (a.k.a. Mary Moore), 269, 280n6
Bring the Ruckus, 173n50
Brown, Bo, 35n17
Brown, Elaine, 41–42
Brown, H. Rap, 64
Brown Berets, 24, 63, 195, 197, 198, 207, 209n5, 217
Browne, Roosevelt, 100, 112n9
Bureau of Indian Affairs (BIA), 117
Burton, E. C., 90n20, 91n40
Bush, George W., 2, 132n14, 145

Cabral, Amilcar, 112n11, 123
California Institute for Women, Frontera, 26
Call to the Sixth Pan African Congress, 97, 99, 100, 102–105
Camden Twenty-Eight case, 259–260
Cameron, Louis, 80, 81, 82, 83, 84
Campos, Pedro Albizu, 137–138, 145, 146–147, 149
Canada. *See* Anicinabe Park occupation; First Nations activism; indigenous peoples movements
Caribbean activism, 77, 88, 100, 105–107, 111n8
Carlisle, Belinda, 190
Carmichael, Stokely, 103, 104, 225
Carroll, Peter N., 3
Carson, Clayborne, 111nn6–7
Carter, James (Jimmy): draft resistance pardons, 254; energy resource policy of, 6, 118; FALN and, 144–145; international human rights and, 121; limits as framework and, 6; neoliberalism and, 2–3, 6, 7; presidential campaign, 2, 144–145; UN initiatives on racism and, 132n14; U.S. political prisoners and, 75n45, 121, 148
Catholic Left, 12, 250–251, 255, 259, 260, 266n50
Catonsville Nine action, 250, 254–256, 257, 261
Center for Battered Women (Austin), 47, 49, 50, 56n83
Center for Black Education (CBE), 104, 110
Central Intelligence Agency (CIA), 3, 259
Chaka, Bill, 108
Chandra, Romesh, 127
Chase, Steve, 234, 244, 249n53
Chasing Hawk, Mabel Ann, 280n2
Chicago Area Military Project (CAMP), 220
Chicago Eight case, 251
Chicago Women's Liberation Movement, 218
chicanismo, 196, 200, 201, 205, 208
Chicano Moratorium March (1970), 195, 208
Chicano movement, 195–213; 1970 murders by police, 197; African Americans and, 198–199; and anti–police violence movements, 195–196; anti-Vietnam War protest (1970), 195, 206, 208; Brown Berets, 195, 198; Chicano Moratorium March (1970), 195, 208; chronology of, 195–196, 208, 209n3; civil rights activism, 195–196, 201, 207; Dallas Disturbance (1973), 198–199, 199–200, 207, 208; impact on

Chicano movement (*continued*)
 police departments, 200, 207–208; Jose
 Campos Torres murder, 196, 200–206,
 206–208; La Raza Unida Party, 195; League
 of United Latin American Citizens, 202;
 Moody Park rebellion, 203–206; National
 Chicano Moratorium Committee, 195;
 People United to Fight Police Brutality, 207;
 Santos Rodríguez murder, 195–196,
 196–200, 206–208, 209n8
Chisholm, Shirley, 10
Church, Frank, 259
Church Committee, 3, 259
Citizens' Commission to Investigate the
 FBI, 258
civil rights movement: Black Power and, 99,
 111n7; Chicano movement and, 195–196,
 201, 207; gender and, 92n56; impact on
 indigenous peoples movement, 61, 70,
 78–79; impact on Puerto Rican
 independence movements, 138;
 Pan-Africanism and, 11; white working-class
 organizing and, 214–216, 217
Clamshell Alliance, 240–241, 245, 262
Clandestine Insurgent Rebel Clown Army, 182
clandestine organizations: BLA, 5, 27, 68, 69,
 145, 153n53, 154n63; FALN, 5, 16n41, 135–136,
 140, 142–148, 153n50, 154nn61–63, 164; GJB,
 5, 16n41, 24, 35n17, 145; Jane (abortion
 service), 218; Macheteros, 148–149, 152n45;
 MIRA, 140, 151n25; New World Liberation
 Front, 145; people's war and, 9, 136, 143, 144,
 145, 148–149, 164; PSP and, 164; radical
 pacifism and, 250–251, 256, 258, 260;
 revolutionary nonviolence and, 250–251,
 256, 258, 260; SLA, 9, 16n40, 145; WUO, 1, 5,
 13n1, 145, 153n53, 157, 173n29. *See also* armed
 struggles; revolutionary nonviolence
Clark, Ramsey, 32–33, 261
class-based organizing, 25, 101, 105, 107, 155,
 157, 218–219. *See also* white working-class
 organizing; workplace organizing
Clutchette, John, 27
Coates, Ken, 78, 82
Cockettes, 177, 179–183, 184, 186, 190
co-counseling (Re-evaluation Counseling),
 239, 243
COINTELPRO (Counter Intelligence Program),
 3, 115, 258–259. *See also* Federal Bureau of
 Investigation (FBI)
Cola, Casey, 189
Collazo, Oscar, 140, 148
Combahee River Collective (Boston), 51
El Comité, 139–140
Committee for Prisoner Support in
 Birmingham (CPSB), 29
Committee for Puerto Rican Decolonization,
 140, 141, 153n57
Committee in Solidarity with Puerto Rican
 Independence (CISPRI), 154n62
Committee of Concerned Citizens (CCC), 81
Committee to Free the Five, 142
Communist Party of Canada (Marxist-
 Leninist) (CPC-ML), 93n71
Communist Party USA, 35n9, 65, 167, 229n43

community-based organizing, 216–218
Community Change Project, 56n83
Community for Creative Nonviolence, 253
Conference of Eighty meeting (1971), 233
Congress of African People, 108, 109, 110,
 112n9
Congress of Racial Equality (CORE), 217, 232
Continental Walk for Disarmament and Social
 Justice, 262–263
Convention on Tribal and Indigenous
 Populations (1953), 122
Cordero, Andrés Figueroa, 140, 148
Corretjer, Juan Antonio, 144, 145, 147, 149
Costner, Kevin, 278
Cox, Courtland, 105, 107
Crash, Darby, 185–190
Crazy Horse, 57, 59, 71n10
Cristóbal, Angel Rodríguez, 142–143
Critical Resistance, 10, 34
Crockett, George, 73n27
Crusade for Justice, 69
Cuba, 77, 83, 88, 102, 127, 129, 137, 142, 144, 252
CUNY open admissions battle (1969), 138–139,
 147

Dallas Brown Berets, 195–196
Dallas Disturbance (1973), 198–199, 199–200,
 207, 208
Davis, Angela, 10, 28, 35n9, 225
Davis, Norrie, 218
A Day in Solidarity with Puerto Rico rally
 (1974), 135
Dead Kennedys, 187
death penalty, 3, 33, 43–44, 68
The Decline of Western Civilization
 (documentary film), 187–188
decolonization movements: AIM and, 59–60;
 Anicinabe Park occupation, 79–82, 85–86,
 88; Canada and, 77–78; Committee for
 Puerto Rican Decolonization, 140, 141; First
 Nations activism and, 77–78, 80, 82–83,
 87–88; gender analyses and, 84–86;
 indigenous peoples movements and, 77–78;
 internationalism and, 65, 77–78, 82–83,
 87–88; national liberation movements and,
 57–60, 58, 69–70; Pan-Africanism *vs.* black
 internationalism and, 98–99, 110n2; Red
 Power and, 77–78, 82–83; RNA and, 59–60;
 state power and, 69–70; transracial
 nationalism and, 101, 108–109, 114n46.
 See also American Indian Movement (AIM);
 Anicinabe Park occupation; Republic of
 New Afrika (RNA)
De Cora, Lorelei Means, 272–275, 280n2
Deganawidah-Quetzalcoatl University
 (encampment community), 61
de la Cruz, Joe, 123
Delany, Samuel, 190
Dellelo, Bobby, 25
Dellinger, Dave, 141, 233, 251–253, 264, 264n8
Deloria, Phillip (Sam), 123
Deloria, Vine, Jr., 72n12, 116, 131n2
Deming, Barbara, 252–253, 263
DiGia, Ralph, 251
Diop, Alioune, 102

DIY culture: Cockettes, 177, 179–183, 184, 186, 190; the Germs, 177, 185–186, 187–190; politics of, 177–178, 186, 188; punk, 184–188, 190. *See also* gay liberation movement
Dohrn, Bernardine, 257
domestic spying, 3, 259
domestic violence. *See* battered women's movement
Douglas, Rosie, 88
Douglass, Boyd, 261
Downer, Carol, 278
draft-board actions: Baltimore Four, 254–256; Catonsville Nine, 250, 254–256, 257, 261; Milwaukee Fourteen, 255
draft resistance, 9, 250, 253–256, 258, 259–260
drug law activism, 3, 31, 222–223
Du Bois, W.E.B., 98, 156–157, 170n2, 170n7
Duncombe, Stephen, 185
Durham, Douglas, 91n40
Durham, Jimmie, 123, 127
Dworkin, Andrea, 254
Dylan, Bob, 6

Earth First!, 246
East Coast Conspiracy to Save Lives, 260, 261
Easterling v. State (1954), 52n14
Echols, Alice, 245
ECOSOC (Economic and Social Council of the United Nations), 119–120, 123–124, 126, 128, 133n21, 133n24
education, political: Bring the Ruckus, 173n50; Center for Black Education, 104, 110; macro-analysis seminars, 235–236; nonviolence training, 231, 240–241; prisoners' education, 23–24, 30–31; survival programs, 24, 215, 268–269, 272–275, 282n19; worker self-education, 50, 173n50. *See also* Movement for a New Society (MNS)
Edwards, Brent Hayes, 110n2
Elbaum, Max, 142
electoral politics: 1972 Chisolm presidential campaign, 10; 2008 presidential elections, 1–2, 192; Dellinger on, 251–252; Harvey Milk, 2, 4, 187; law-and-order platform and, 8, 88; politics of resentment and, 8, 222; PSP and, 143; race and, 9–10, 58; radical politics and, 9–10
Ellsberg, Daniel, 7, 259
Elmer, Jerry, 254, 258
encampment communities, 61, 116, 117, 118, 123, 244, 268, 282n12
Epstein, Barbara, 245
Ervin, Lorenzo Komboa, 25
Escobar, Elizam, 140

Fager, Diane, 218
Families and Friends of Prisoners Collective (Massachusetts), 22
Fanon, Frantz, 83, 84, 105, 252–253
The Farm (Tennessee), 253
Farrell, Perry, 188
Federal Bureau of Investigation (FBI): Camden Twenty-Eight case, 259–260; Church Committee report, 3, 259; Citizens'

Commission to Investigate the FBI, 258; COINTELPRO, 3, 115, 258–259; domestic spying, 3, 259; Harrisburg conspiracy case, 260–261; Media, PA, break-in, 258–259; pardons by Reagan, 3
Feliciano, Carlos, 140, 151n25
Felt, Mark, 3
feminism/feminist movement: Atlanta Lesbian Feminists Alliance (ALFA), 43; battering/spousal abuse and, 39, 45, 46–48, 48–52, 56n82; black nationalism and, 44–45; intersectional analyses of, 4; Lesbian Feminist Organizing Committee, 40; MNS and, 232, 249n53; policing/incarceration and, 52; racism within, 45, 51, 55n82, 56n83; radical feminism *vs.* cultural feminism, 245, 263; Red Power movement and, 276, 278, 281n3; RUA and, 218–219; separatism and, 218–219; sexual assault and, 39; Triangle Area Lesbian Feminists, 43; white working-class organizing and, 218–219; women-of-color feminism, 4, 35n9, 51, 55n82, 56n83. *See also* women's movement
Ferguson, Herman, 64
First Nations activism: Anicinabe Park occupation, 79–82, 85–86, 88; decolonization and, 77–78, 80, 82–83, 87–88; definition of First Nations, 89n1; gender analyses of, 84–86; impact of Black Power movements on, 77; impact of Cuban revolutionaries on, 77; internationalism and, 77–78, 82–83, 87–88. *See also* indigenous peoples movements
Flores, Irvin, 140, 148
Folsom Prison, 25, 35n17
Food Not Bombs, 246
Ford, Gerald, 7, 9
Fourth World (Hall), 82–83
Francis, Daniel, 85–86
Frank, Phyllis B., 56n83
Frankenhauser, Paul, 221
Franklin, C. L., 65
Free Puerto Rico Committee, 154n62
Free South Africa Movement, 110
Frente Sandinista de Liberacion Nacional (FSLN), 127
Fresh Fruit for Rotting Vegetables (Dead Kennedys), 186–187
Fuentes, Luis, 138
Fuerzas Armadas de Liberación Nacional/Armed Forces of National Liberation (FALN), 5, 16n41, 135–136, 140, 142–148, 153n50, 154nn61–63, 164
Fuller, Hoyt, 107, 109

Gant, Liz, 100–101
Garcia, Inez, 41–43, 54n56
Garcia, Mamie, 203, 204
Garrett, James, 100–102, 104, 106, 107
Garry, Charles, 42
Garveyism, 64, 101
Gay Activist Alliance, 183
Gay Liberation Front (GLF), 183–184

gay liberation movement: Cockettes and, 177, 179–183, 184, 186, 190; DIY culture and, 177–178, 186, 188; Gay Activist Alliance, 183; Gay Liberation Front, 183–184; Gay Shame, 182; the Germs, 177, 185–186, 187–190; Harvey Milk murder, 2, 4, 187; impact of previous generations on, 179; politics of play and pleasure, 12, 177–179, 181, 182, 183–184, 188–189, 190–191; prison organizing of, 31; punk and, 184–188, 190; sexual self-determination, 182–183, 183–184; social eros of, 182–183; Stonewall Inn riots, 177, 178, 187; White Night Riots, 187. *See also* play, politics of

Gay Shame (San Francisco), 182

gender: civil rights organizing and, 92n56; decolonization movements and, 84–86; First Nations activism and, 84–86; prison movements and, 31, 37n48; Red Power and, 84–85; stereotyping in civil rights movement, 92n56. *See also* sexism; Thunder Hawk, Madonna; women; women's movement

George, Christine, 218

George Jackson Brigade (GJB), 5, 16n41, 24, 35n17, 145

the Germs, 177, 185–186, 187–190

Gilbert, Barbara Jean, 47–48

Ginsberg, Allen, 178, 180, 182–183

Gittings, Barbara, 183

global organizing: Afro-Asian Peoples Solidarity Organization (AAPSO), 133n24; black internationalism, 68, 98–99, 110n2, 133n22; Black Power and, 99–100, 109, 113n19; Caribbean activism, 77, 88, 100, 105–107, 111n8; decolonization movements, 65, 77–78, 82–83, 87–88; indigenous peoples and, 11, 65, 77–78, 82–83, 84, 87–88, 118–124, 126–131, 133n22; International Indian Treaty Council (IITC), 63, 118–119, 123, 267, 268, 275; Pan-Africanism and, 98–99, 110n2; of Puerto Rican independence movements, 11; Red Power and, 116–117; transnational solidarity, 11, 97–99, 99–102, 219–220, 276–277; transracial nationalism, 101, 108–109, 114n46, 127. *See also* internationalism; Sixth Pan-African Congress (Sixth PAC); United Nations (UN)

Gonzáles, Juan, 146

Goodman, Paul, 232

Gosse, Van, 9

Gottesman, Kathie, 45

Gowan, Susan, 235

Grady, John, 259

Graebner, William, 16n40

Gramsci, Antonio, 155–156, 158, 170n6

grassroots social movements, 2, 4, 10, 11, 113n19, 136, 217, 231, 263, 268

Greenwich Village Peace Center, 254

Guardians of the Oglala Nation (GOONs), 62, 118, 272

Guzmán, Pablo, 146

Hall, Anthony, 82

Hamerquist, Don, 169, 170n2, 170n6, 172n22

Hamm, Ralph, 24, 31

Hampton, Fred, 219

Harden, Lakota, 275

Hardy, Robert, 260

Harper, Vern, 84, 85, 93n71

Harrington, Michael, 7

Harris, George, III (Hibiscus), 179–183, 184, 189, 190

Harrisburg conspiracy case, 260–261

Harvey, David, 16n42

Health Revolutionary Movement (HRUM), 223

Hearst, Patricia, 9, 16n40

Hennacy, Ammon, 232

Henry, Richard and Milton. *See* Obadele, Gaidi; Obadele, Imari Abubakari

Hibiscus (George Harris III), 179–183, 184, 189, 190

Hill, Sylvia, 100, 105

Hodgson, Derik, 86

Huizinga, Johan, 188

Ibn-Tamas, Beverly, 50

If They Come in the Morning (NUCFAD), 35n9

Ignatiev, Noel, 156–157, 159, 169, 170n6, 171n9, 174n53

Imaginary Indian (Francis), 85–86

Indian Country? (documentary film), 280, 283n26

Indian Law Resource Center, 126

indigenous peoples movement, 57–70, 77–89, 115–131, 267–280; Aboriginal revolutionary organizing, 112n9; AIM, 60–64; Anicinabe Park occupation, 79–82, 85–86, 88; antisterilization campaigns, 60, 267, 275; black internationalism and, 133n22; COINTELPRO and, 115; cold-war binary politics and, 127, 129; Convention on Tribal and Indigenous Populations (1953), 122; Cornwall International Bridge blockade, 117; decolonization movements and, 77–78; definitions of indigenous, 89n1, 120–122; early mobilization efforts, 115–118; ECOSOC and, 119–120, 123–124, 126, 128, 133n21, 133n24; encampment communities, 61, 116, 117, 118, 123, 268, 282n12; International Conference on Indigenous Peoples of the Americas (1977), 120, 123–126; International Indian Treaty Council (IITC), 63, 118–119, 123, 267, 268, 275; internationalism and, 65, 77–78, 82–83, 87–88, 118–124, 126–131, 133n22; land-based struggles, 60–64; Longest Walk protest march (1978), 118; Maoism and, 71n6, 87, 93n71; against mercury contamination, 79, 80, 91n30; Nixon on, 62; pan-Indian organizing, 115–118; political prisoners and, 35n9; poor people's movements, 118–119; quincentenary debate, 129–130, 132n18; against racism, 78–79; Reagan administration and, 115, 117, 126, 127–128, 133n23; sexual violence/battered women's self-defense and, 39–41, 56n83; stereotypical representation and, 84–87; Trail of Broken Treaties march (1972), 62, 117; UN Decade to Combat Racism, Racial

Discrimination, and Apartheid, 123, 132n18; vanguard political formations and, 60; women and, 84–85, 92n60, 116; Working Group on Indigenous Populations, 128–129, 133n20; Zapatistas (EZLN), 130, 134n34. *See also* First Nations activism; Thunder Hawk, Madonna; United Nations (UN)
Industrial Workers of the World/Wobblies (IWW), 159, 246
Inmates for Action (IFA), 24, 29, 32, 34n4
Instead of Prisons (PREAP), 10, 28–29, 30, 34
intentional communities, 5, 231, 232, 237–240, 242, 246n1, 253, 261. *See also* Movement for a New Society (MNS)
International Commission of Jurists (ICJ), 123
International Indian Treaty Council (IITC), 63, 118–119, 123, 267, 268, 275
internationalism: black internationalism, 98–99, 110n2, 133n22; decolonization movements and, 65, 77–78, 82–83, 87–88; First Nations activism and, 77–78, 82–83, 87–88; indigenous peoples movements and, 77–78, 82–83, 87–88, 118–124, 126–131, 133n22; national liberation movements and, 65, 77–78, 82–83, 87–88; Pan-Africanism and, 98–99, 110n2; Puerto Rican independence movements and, 136. *See also* global organizing; Sixth Pan-African Congress (Sixth PAC); United Nations (UN)
International Labor Organization (ILO): Convention on Tribal and Indigenous Populations (1953), 122
Inuit Circumpolar Conference, 126
Ironstand, Lyle, 88
It Seemed Like Nothing Happened (Carroll), 3
I Wor Kuen (IWK), 139

Jackins, Harvey, 239
Jackson, George, 21, 24, 36n36, 59, 224. *See also* George Jackson Brigade (GJB)
Jackson, Maynard, 7
Jalon, Alan, 259
James, C.L.R., 99, 104–105, 106, 113n29, 156
James, Mike, 218
Jane (abortion service), 218
Jane's Addiction, 188
ji Jaga, Geronimo, 64
JOIN (Jobs or Income Now) Community Union, 217–218, 228n13, 228n17. *See also* Rising Up Angry (RUA)
Jonah House, 261–262
Jones, Jim, 8
Jones, Leroi. *See* Baraka, Amiri
Jones, Lilias, 277
Jordan, Susan, 42–43, 50

Kaliflower commune, 180, 181
Kammerer, Marvin, 278
Karenga, Maulana Ron, 64, 225
Kelsie, Jenna, 47
Kennedy, Edward, 216
Kenora, Ontario. *See* Anicinabe Park occupation
Kickingbird, Kirk, 127
Kind and Usual Punishment (Mitford), 33

King, Martin Luther, Jr., 10, 217, 232, 251, 255, 258–259
King, Ynestra, 263
Kingfisher, Pamela, 70
Kissinger, Henry, 6, 260
Kochiyama, Yuri, 141
Kuttner, Peter, 220
Kwayana, Eusi, 106, 107

La Alianza de Pueblos y Pobladores, 58
Lakey, George, 231, 235, 236, 240, 242
Lakota People's Law Project, 279
Lakota Woman (Brave Bird and Erdoes), 269, 280n6
land-based struggles, 57–70; AIM and, 60–64; dissolution of the state and, 69–70; international law and, 60, 68, 70; mercury contamination and, 79, 80, 91n30; racial solidarity and, 57–60, 70; radical black prisoners and, 67–68; reclamation as political strategy, 11, 58–60; reparations movement, 65–66, 68; RNA and, 64–69; urbanization and, 57–58, 61–62, 116, 131n1
La Raza Unida Party (RUP), 195
The Late Great Planet Earth (Lindsey and Carlson), 8
Lavall, Jeanette Corbiere, 92n60
law-and-order politics: abolitionist organizers and, 23; death penalty, 3, 33, 43–44, 68; Dellinger on, 252; LEAA and, 50, 55n71; politics of resentment and, 8; prison movements and, 23, 33–34
Law Enforcement Alliance of America (LEAA), 50, 55n71
Lawrence, Bonita, 85
Lawrence, Ken, 170n6
League of Revolutionary Black Workers (LRBW), 139, 158–159
League of United Latin American Citizens (LULAC), 203
Lebrón, Lolita, 137, 140, 148, 150nn8–10
Lee, Bob, 219
Leeks, Linda, 45
Leninism: Communist Party of Canada (CPC-ML), 93n71; imperialism/anticapitalism and, 165; STO and, 156, 162, 165–166, 169, 170n2, 170n4; trade union consciousness, 170n2; vanguard political projects, 70, 158, 162; *What Is to Be Done?* (Lenin), 156. *See also* Marxism; Sojourner Truth Organization (STO)
Lennon, John, 190
Lesbian Feminist Organizing Committee, 40
Lewis, Tom, 255, 256
Lifton, Robert Jay, 254
Liga Socialista Puertorriqueña/Puerto Rican Socialist League (LSP), 144, 153n53
limits as framework, 4, 6–9, 263–264
Lindsey, Hal, and Carole Carlson, 8
Little, Joan, 43–44, 53n40, 54n56
Livermore Action Group, 262
localism, 12
Logan, Fred E., 197
The Longest Walk protest march (1978), 118

Look Lai, Willy, 111n8
López, José E., 146
López Rivera, Oscar, 146

Macheteros, 148–149, 152n45
Magno, Paul, and Matt Meyer, 250–264
Major, Harvey, 86
Malcolm X, 57, 65, 277
Malcolm X Liberation University, 108
Malcolm X Society, 65
Mankiller, Wilma, 268
Manuel, George, 82–83, 123
Maoist frameworks, 71n6, 87, 93n71, 225
Maracle, Lee, 85
Marcuse, Herbert, 179
Mari Brás, Juan, 142, 152n37
Martell, Esperanza, 140
Martínez, Rene, 198, 199, 200
Martínez Cobo, José R., 119, 120, 123
Marxism, 104–105, 107, 108, 136, 155–156.
    See also Leninism
Massachusetts Coalition of Battered Women's
    Service Groups, 51
Mattilda, 182
May 19th Communist Organization, 75n53,
    152n44, 153n53, 165, 168, 173n39
Mayor, Federico, 134n30
McAlister, Elizabeth, 261
McCaffrey, Katherine, 142–143
McCain, John, 1
McCloud, Janet, 116, 275
Means, Russell, 62, 71n10, 80, 84, 116, 277
Medrano, Pancho, 198–199
Medrano, Ricardo and Roberto, 198
Melendez, Mickey, 141
Men Against Sexism (MAS), 31
Menchú Tom, Rigoberta, 129, 130, 133n28
Mercury, Freddie, 190
Mexican American Youth Organization
    (MAYO), 195
Meyer, Matt, and Paul Magno, 250–264
Midewiwin, 83
militancy: people's war theory and, 5, 136, 144,
    145; white working-class organizing and,
    216–217. *See also* armed struggles; union
    organizing
Milk, Harvey, 2, 4, 187
Miller, Jerome G., 26–27, 33
Miller, Timothy, 253
Milwaukee Fourteen action, 255
Minter, William, 114n50
Miranda, Rafael Cancel, 140, 148
Mitford, Jessica, 32–33
Moore, Carlos, 102
Moore, Queen Mother Audley, 65
Moorehead, Michael, 197, 198
Morales, Evo, 130
Morales, William (Guillermo), 9, 16n41, 144,
    147–148, 154n61, 154n63
More Power Than We Know (Dellinger),
    264
Movement for a New Society (MNS), 231–246;
    active listening, 239; AFSC and, 233–234;
    anarchism and, 231, 232, 236; anti-
    authoritarian social politics and, 26, 231,
236, 241, 245; antinuclear movement and,
235, 240–241, 245; Clamshell Alliance,
240–241, 245; class analysis and, 232;
consensus process, 231, 236, 241, 243, 246,
248n35; direct action campaigns, 231,
234–235; early mobilization of, 233–234;
ending of, 232, 243–246; feminism and, 232;
Gandhi's influence on, 232, 237, 239, 242;
IWW comparison, 246; jail solidarity, 241,
248n38; legacy of, 245–246; macro-analysis
and, 231–232, 235–237, 244; membership,
237, 242–243, 246n25; as movement-
building organization, 244–245;
nonviolence training, 231, 240–241; NRGs,
237; participatory structures, 232, 236, 245,
264; personal as political process, 239;
Philadelphia Friends of East Bengal, 234;
port blockades, 234–235; prefigurative
communities, 231, 232, 237–240, 242, 246,
246n1; Quaker traditions in, 232–233, 234,
235, 236, 245; race and, 236, 239, 244;
radical pacifism and, 232–233, 236; RC, 239,
243; recruitment tours, 234; revolutionary
nonviolence, 231, 236, 240–241; right-wing
backlash and, 243; Seabrook Nuclear Power
Plant action, 4, 240, 241, 262; sexism and,
236, 239, 242–243, 246; spokes-council
method, 231, 240, 241, 246, 248n35; tensions
within, 241–245; unions and, 234–235;
VVAW and, 220, 235; Whole Network
Meetings, 237, 241, 243–244
Movimiento de Liberación Nacional/National
    Liberation Movement (MLN), 69, 136, 138,
    145–146, 149n5, 152n45, 154n62, 164, 167,
    168, 173n42
Movimiento Independista Revolucionario
    Armado/Armed Revolutionary
    Independence Movement (MIRA), 140,
    151n25
Movimiento Pro Independencia/Movement
    for Independence (MPI), 140
Moving Towards a New Society (Gowan et al.),
    235
Moyers, Bill, 235, 243–244
Moylan, Mary, 257–258, 265n31
Moynihan, Daniel Patrick, 7
multiracial coalitions: abolition movement
    and, 28–29; AIM and, 141, 153n53; prison
    movement and, 22–23, 25, 32, 67–68;
    Puerto Rican independence movements
    and, 140–142, 143; transracial nationalism,
    101, 108–109, 114n46, 127; white working-
    class organizing and, 215, 217–218, 219–220,
    222–225. *See also* global organizing

National Alliance Against Racist and Political
    Repression (NAARPR), 35n9
National Black Feminist Organization, 51
National Black Human Rights Coalition, 68
National Chicano Moratorium Committee,
    195
National Coalition of Blacks for Reparations
    in America (N'COBRA), 65
National Conference Against Repression
    (1982), 76n54

National Conference of Black Lawyers, 65, 68
National Congress of American Indians, 123
National Indian Brotherhood, 82, 123
National Indian Youth Council (NIYC), 115–116
National Indian Youth Movement, 61
National Lawyers Guild, 141
national liberation movements, 57–70,
    135–149; Aboriginal revolutionary
    organizing, 112n9; AIM and, 58–60; as
    anticolonial movement, 153n53; cross-
    organization cooperation, 64–65, 67–68,
    69–70, 76n54; decline of, 69–70;
    decolonization movements and, 57–60, 58,
    69–70; Garveyism and, 64, 101; impact of
    Black Power on, 112n9, 136, 138; impact of
    previous generations of activism on,
    104–105; internationalism and, 65, 77–78,
    82–83, 87–88; Marxism and, 104–105; the
    national question, 165–166, 173n42; Pan-
    Africanism vs. black internationalism,
    98–99, 110n2; reparations and, 65–66; RNA
    and, 58–60, 64–69; Sixth PAC and, 100–102;
    state-building and, 65–67, 69–70; STO and,
    163–168; transracial nationalism, 101,
    108–109, 114n46, 127; UN and, 68;
    urbanization and, 57–58, 60–61, 116, 131n1;
    as vanguard political formations, 151n31;
    Zapatista National Liberation Army (EZLN),
    130, 134n34. See also land-based struggles;
    Puerto Rican independence movements
National Prisoners Coalition, 38n76
National Prisoners Reform Association
    (NPRA), 24, 26, 31
National Tribal Chairmen's Association
    (NTCA), 117
National United Committee to Free Angela
    Davis and All Political Prisoners (NUCFAD),
    35n9
Nation of Islam (NOI), 23–24
Native American Solidarity Committee, 40
Native Peoples Caravan, 84, 85, 88, 93n71
Neist, Terry, 259
New Afrikan People's Organization (NAPO),
    65–66, 68
New Beginnings Movement, 111n8
New Catholic Left, 12, 250–251, 255, 259, 260,
    266n50
new-communist movements, 136, 155–157, 158,
    162, 164–165, 171n13, 224, 226
New England Prisoners Association (NEPA),
    29, 32
New Progressive Party/Partido Neuvo
    Progresista (PNP), 143, 152n42
New World Liberation Front, 145
Nixon, Richard M.: antiwar movements and,
    3; on Black Power/Black Capitalism, 113n19;
    human rights and, 2; indigenous peoples
    and, 62, 86, 115, 117, 118; mobilization of
    resentment and, 8, 221; neoliberalism and,
    7; political polarization and, 7–8, 13n5;
    resignation of, 8–9, 86, 118
Nkrumah, Kwame, 100
Non-Aligned Movement (NAM), 127
nonviolence. See pacifist movement;
    revolutionary nonviolence

nonviolence training, 231, 240–241
Nonviolent Revolutionary Groups (NRGs), 237
Nordic Sami Council, 123
Notes from a New Afrikan P.O.W. (journal), 68,
    75n44
Nyerere, Julius, 108, 114n46

Obadele, Gaidi, 65–66, 67, 72n10, 73n27,
    74n34, 74n41
Obadele, Imari Abubakari, 68, 71n10
Obama, Barack, 1, 2, 9–10, 132n14
October 4th Organization (O4O), 214–216,
    220–222. See also white working-class
    organizing
October League (OL), 5, 156, 224, 226, 229n45
Ojibway Warriors Society (OWS), 78, 79–82,
    83–84, 93n71
Oleari, Kenoli, 254
Ontario Human Rights Commission, 78

pacifist movement: black nationalism and, 11;
    Catholic Left, 12, 250–251, 255, 259, 260,
    266n50; impact of previous generations of
    activism on, 232; prison abolition and, 11,
    28–33; radical, 10, 28, 146–147, 231–233, 236,
    250–251, 257–258, 262. See revolutionary
    nonviolence
Pagán, Dylcia, 147
Palestine Liberation Organization (PLO), 127,
    128
Paley, Grace, 254
Pan-Africanism: anticolonial struggles and,
    103; armed struggles and, 113n19; black
    internationalism and, 98–99, 110n2; Black
    Power and, 9, 111n4, 113n19; decolonization
    movements and, 98–99, 110n2; Marxism
    and, 104–105, 107; national liberation
    movements and, 98–99, 110n2;
    socioeconomic class mobilization and, 107.
    See also Sixth Pan-African Congress (Sixth
    PAC)
Pandora's Collective, 243
Panther Twenty-One, 257
Partido Africano da Independência da Guiné e
    Cabo Verde (PAIGC), 123
Partido Nuevo Progresista/New Progressive
    Party (PNP), 143, 152n42
Partido Socialista Puertorriqueño/Puerto
    Rican Socialist Party (PSP): armed struggle
    and, 5, 136, 164, 165; debates within,
    142–143, 145; FALN and, 145; multiracial
    solidarity and, 140–142, 143; political
    prisoner activism, 140
Patrice Lumumba Coalition, 110
Patriot Party, 220
Patterson, Fred, 189
Patty's Got a Gun (Graebner), 16n40
Peltier, Leonard, 118
Pentagon Papers, 7, 259
People's Bail Project, 215, 221
People's Temple, 8
people's war theory, 5, 136, 144, 145
People United to Fight Police Brutality, 196,
    207
Perlstein, Rick, 13n5

Pershing II missiles, 244
pet rocks, 3
Philadelphia Friends of East Bengal, 234
play, politics of, 12, 177–179, 181, 182, 183–184,
    188–189, 190–191
Plowshares movement, 262
"Poem for Jose Campos Torres" (Scott-Heron),
    205–206
Polaroid Revolutionary Workers Union, 110.
    See also Sojourner Truth Organization
    (STO)
political prisoners: Carter administration on,
    75n45, 121, 148; indigenous peoples
    movements and, 35n9; movement
    solidarity and, 35n9, 46, 68; National
    United Committee to Free Angela Davis
    and All Political Prisoners (NUCFAD), 35n9;
    prison movements and, 35n9, 75n45;
    Puerto Rican independence movements
    and, 35n9, 142, 145–146, 148; Reagan on,
    154n61
politics of resentment, 8, 108, 214–216,
    221–222, 225
Pontiac Brothers (death penalty case), 68
poor people's movement model, impact on:
    battered women's movement, 51;
    contemporary organizations and coalitions,
    3, 17n48; indigenous peoples movement,
    118–119; JOIN Community Union, 217–218,
    228n13, 228n17; prison organizing, 27,
    33–34; service-plus organizing, 214–215, 216;
    welfare rights movements, 3, 17n48, 228n17;
    white working class organizing, 214–215,
    216, 217, 219, 226–227, 228n17. See also
    October 4th Organization (O4O); Rising Up
    Angry (RUA); White Lightning (WL); white
    working-class organizing
Popular Movement for the Liberation of
    Angola (MPLA), 109
Powder Keg, 216
Prairie Fire Organizing Committee (PFOC), 67,
    69, 74n40, 153n53, 154n62, 165, 170n6,
    173n39, 230n52
Pratt, Elmer "Geronimo" (Geronimo ji Jaga),
    64
Price, Julia Parker, 48
Prison Action Conference (1972), 32
Prisoners Against Rape, 31
Prisoners' Solidarity Committee (PSC), 32
prison movement, 21–34; Afrikan People's
    Party, 74n40; Attica prison uprising, 21–23;
    backlash and decline of, 33–34; BPP and,
    74n40; class and, 25, 27, 33–34; culture of
    solidarity and, 24–26; Folsom Prison, 25,
    35n17; gay prisoners' rights, 31; gendered
    analyses and, 31, 37n48; indeterminate
    sentencing and, 26, 27, 36n36; labor-
    centered organizing, 26; law-and-order
    politics and, 23, 33–34; multiracial
    coalitions and, 22–23, 25, 32, 67–68; New
    Afrikan prisoners, 67–68; PFOC and, 74n40;
    Pontiac Brothers (death penalty case), 68;
    poor people's movement model and, 27,
    33–34; prison abolitionist praxis, 11, 21–23,
    27–33, 37n48; prisoners' rights organizing,

23–26, 67–68; prison reform, 21, 22–23,
    26–27; publications of, 67; racism analyses
    of, 23–24, 25, 28–29; San Luis Obispo
    Prison, 25, 257–258; San Quentin prison
    uprising (1968), 25, 224, 257; sexual
    violence and, 30–31, 43–44, 54n56; Soledad
    Prison, 24, 25, 27, 28, 257; STO and, 74n40;
    unions and, 23, 25, 26, 27, 28, 32; work
    strikes, 22, 24, 25–26. See also political
    prisoners
Prison Research Education Action Project
    (PREAP), 28–30
Prisons of Grass (Adams), 83
Proud Flesh (online journal), 35n14
Provisional Government of the Republic of
    New Afrika (PG-RNA), 66–67. See also
    Republic of New Afrika (RNA)
Puerto Rican independence movement,
    135–149; anticolonialism as nationalism
    and, 135–136, 145, 153n53; antisterilization
    campaigns, 141, 146, 148, 163; armed
    struggle and, 143–144, 145, 164, 173n40;
    bicentennial protests, 135, 143, 152n42;
    Black Workers Congress, 139; bombings,
    143–144, 145, 164; campus demonstrations,
    135; El Comité, 139–140; Committee for a
    Puerto Rican Decolonization, 140, 141,
    153n57; Committee in Solidarity with
    Puerto Rican Independence (CISPRI),
    154n62; CUNY open admissions battle,
    138–139, 147; Day in Solidarity with Puerto
    Rico rally (1974), 135, 141–142; FALN and, 5,
    16n41, 135–136, 140, 142–145, 146–148,
    153n50, 154nn62–63, 164; Fraunces Tavern
    bombing, 144, 145; Free Puerto Rico
    Committee, 154n62; global organizing
    strategies of, 11; human rights campaigns,
    146; impact of Black Power movement on,
    138; internationalism and, 136; IWK and,
    139; Latin Women's Collective, 139–140;
    legacy of, 148–149; Lincoln Hospital
    takeover, 139, 223; LSP, 144; Macheteros,
    148–149, 152n45; Marxism and, 136;
    militancy in, 136; MIRA, 140, 151n25; MLN,
    69, 136, 138, 145–146, 149n5, 152n45,
    154n62, 164, 167–168, 173n42; Mobil Oil
    building bombings, 143–144; MPI, 140;
    Nationalist Party, 136–138, 140, 145, 147, 148,
    153n54; national liberation vs. solidarity
    movements, 135–136, 151n31; the national
    question, 165, 173n42; new-communist
    movement and, 136, 139–140; people's war
    theory, 5, 136, 144, 145; PNP, 143; political
    prisoners and, 35n9, 140, 142, 145–146, 148;
    Por Los Niños/For the Children (NYC), 138;
    PPRWO, 139; Puerto Rico Libre!, 140, 141;
    retraimiento (non-collaboration), 147, 148,
    153n54; RU, 139; school reform campaigns,
    138, 139, 148, 150n11; Statue of Liberty
    occupation (1977), 135, 147, 148; STO and,
    163–164, 166–167; suppression of, 142–143;
    Vieques campaigns, 135, 142, 146–147, 148;
    Young Lords, 136, 139, 140, 146, 164, 217, 219,
    222, 223, 224. See also Campos, Pedro Albizu;
    Lebrón, Lolita

Puerto Rican Nationalist Party, 136–138, 140, 145, 147, 148, 153n54
Puerto Rican Revolutionary Workers Organization (PRRWO), 139
Puerto Rican Socialist Party/Partido Socialista Puertorriqueño (PSP), 164
Puerto Rican Solidarity Committee (PRSC), 141
Puerto Rico Libre!, 140, 141
Pulido, Laura, 85
punk culture, 184–188, 190

Queens House of Detention uprising (1970), 25
queerness. *See* DIY culture; gay liberation movement
Quintan, Mary, 280n2

Raasch-Gilman, Betsy, 241–242, 243, 244–245
race: battered women's movement and, 45, 51–52; culture of solidarity and, 25; feminist movement and, 51, 55n82; land-based struggles and, 57–60, 70; multiracial prison activism, 22–23, 25, 32; politics of resentment and, 8; poor people's movement model and, 214–215, 216, 217, 219, 226–227, 228n17; prison organizing and, 23–24, 24–26; racial solidarity and, 65–67, 69–70; sexual violence analyses and, 45; state-building and, 65–67, 69–70; transracial nationalism, 101, 108–109, 114n46, 127; white-skin privilege analysis and, 156–157, 162, 165, 169, 225. *See also* Black Power; Red Power; white working-class organizing
racism: feminist movement and, 51, 55n82; indigenous peoples movements against, 78–79, 274–275; police violence and, 197, 206, 208; prison organizing and, 23–24, 25, 28–29; UN initiatives on racism and, 123, 124, 126, 132n14, 132n18. *See also* whiteness; white working-class organizing
Ragan, Colleen, 277
Rainbow Coalition, 219–220, 228n17
Ramos, Howard, 77–78
Ramos, Manuel, 219
rape, 30–31, 43–44, 46–48. *See also* sexual violence activism
Reagan, Ronald, 3, 7, 69, 115, 117, 126, 127–128, 133n23, 154n61
Red Power: Black Power and, 116–117; decolonization movements and, 77–78, 82–83; early mobilizations of, 116–117; gender and, 84–85; global organizing and, 116–117; Maoism and, 87; militancy and, 267–268; survival schools and, 268–269, 272–275, 282n19; WARN, 40, 267, 275–278; women and, 267–270, 276, 280n1, 282n10. *See also* American Indian Movement (AIM); Anicinabe Park occupation; indigenous peoples movements; Thunder Hawk, Madonna
Re-evaluation Counseling (RC), 239, 243
reparations movement, 65–66, 68. *See also* land-based struggles

Republic of New Afrika (RNA): alternative structures of governance, 59; anticolonialism/decolonization and, 59–60, 153n53; Anti-Depression Program, 66; Dessie Woods case and, 45; early mobilization efforts, 64–65; FBI and, 74n34; feminism and, 45, 46; land-based struggles, 58–60, 69–70; Malcolm X and, 59; national liberation movements and, 58–60, 153n53; New Communities and, 66; prisoner activism of, 66, 67–68; reparations organizing, 65–66
Restore Our Alienated Rights (ROAR), 216
retraimiento (non-collaboration), 147, 148, 153n54
Revolutionary Action Movement, 64
Revolutionary Communist Party (RCP), 156
revolutionary nonviolence: Abalone Alliance, 262; antiwar organizing and, 233; Atlantic Life Community, 261; Baltimore Four action, 254–256; Camden Twenty-Eight case, 259–260; Catholic Left, 12, 250–251, 255, 259, 260, 266n50; Catonsville Nine action, 250, 254–256, 257, 261; Citizens' Commission to Investigate the FBI, 258; Clamshell Alliance, 240–241, 245, 262; clandestine organizations and, 250–251, 256, 258, 260; Community for Creative Nonviolence and, 253; Continental Walk for Disarmament and Social Justice, 262–263; Dellinger and, 141, 233, 251–253, 264, 264n8; Deming and, 252–253, 263; discipleship, 261–262, 266n50; draft resistance, 9, 250, 253–256, 258, 259–260; East Coast Conspiracy to Save Lives, 260, 261; FBI and, 256, 258–261; Gandhian principles of nonviolence, 232, 237, 239, 242; Harrisburg conspiracy case, 260–261; impact and legacy of, 262–263; jail solidarity, 241; Jonah House, 261–262; Media, PA, break-in, 258–259; MNS and, 253; pacifist underground, 253–258; radical pacifism, 10, 28, 146–147, 231, 232–233, 236, 250–251, 257–258, 262; Sanctuary movement, 262; small-group actions, 258; theories of, 251–253; White Train campaign, 262. *See also* Berrigan, Daniel; Berrigan, Phillip
Revolutionary Nonviolence (Dellinger), 251–253
Revolutionary Union (RU), 139, 195. *See also* Revolutionary Communist Party (RCP)
"On Revolution and Equilibrium" (Deming), 253
Reyes, Ben T., 202
Rising Up Angry (RUA), 214–217, 218–220, 221, 225–227. *See also* white working-class organizing
Rivera, Geraldo, 146
Rizzo, Frank, 8, 221–222, 226
Robertson, Carmen, and Mark Anderson, 86
Robideau, Andria Syke, 280n2
Rodney, Walter, 97, 98, 107, 109
Rodríguez, David, 195–213, 197

Rodríguez, Santos, 195–196, 196–200, 206–208, 209n8
Rodriguez, Tomas and Bertha, 197
Rofes, Eric, 183
Rohrich, Katherine, 48
Rosado, Julio, 138
Rosado, Luis, 139
Rosen, Ruth, 4
Rosenthal, Irving, 180
Ross, Kristin, 84
Rubin, Jerry, 6

Sadauki, Owusu, 108
Salazar, Ruben, 197, 208
Sampson, Janet, 218, 219
Samuels, Liz, 11, 21–38
Sánchez, Ricardo, 200
Sanctuary movement, 262
San Francisco Women Against Rape, 46
San Luis Obispo Prison, 25, 257–258
San Quentin prison uprising (1968), 25, 224, 257
Sayer, John, 84
Schneider, Elizabeth, 48, 50
School of the Americas Watch, 262
school reform organizing: bilingual education, 137, 139, 148, 150n11; CUNY open admissions battle, 138–139, 147
Scott, Agnes, 48
Scott-Heron, Gil, xiv, 3, 6, 68, 205–206
Seabrook Nuclear Power Plant action, 4, 240, 241, 262
Seale, Bobby, 257
self-defense: battered women support vs., 46–48; Brown Berets, 24, 63, 195, 197, 198, 207, 209n5, 217; Easterling v. State (1954) decision, 52n14. See also armed struggles; clandestine organizations
seventies, the. See 1970s at the first entry of the index
sexism: battered women's movements and, 49, 51; MNS and, 236, 239, 242–243, 246; prison abolition and, 28–29, 31, 37n48. See also feminism/feminist movement; gender
sexual violence activism, 39–52; Dessie Woods case, 44–46, 54n46, 54n56; indigenous peoples movement and, 39–41, 56n83; Inez Garcia case, 41–43; Joan Little case, 43–44, 53n40; Prisoners Against Rape, 31; prison guard abuse of women, 43–44; prison movement and, 30–31, 43–44, 54n56; rape, 30–31, 43–44, 46–48; Yvonne Wanrow case, 39–41. See also battered women's movement
Shabazz, Betty, 64
Shakur, Assata, 9, 16n41, 68, 139
Shakur, Zayd, 16n41
Shalom, 236
Shanna, Atiba (a.k.a. Yaki Yakuba), 67–68, 75n44
Sherman, John, 16n41
Sixth Pan-African Congress (Sixth PAC), 97–110; African support for, 98, 100–102, 106, 108–109; anti-apartheid movement

and, 99, 109, 110, 123; Call to the Sixth Pan African Congress, 97, 99, 100, 102–105; Caribbean support for, 102, 105–106, 107; C.L.R. James and, 104–105; Europe-based support for, 100–102; history of, 97–99, 100–102, 111n3, 127; impact of previous generations of activism on, 98–99, 104–105; lessons and legacies of, 97–99, 108–110; Marxism and, 107, 108; national liberation movements and, 100–102; New Left and, 98; SNCC and, 98–99, 103–104; socioeconomic class mobilization and, 98, 101, 105–109; Tanzanian government and, 100–101, 106, 107–108; transracial nationalism and, 101, 108–109, 114n46. See also Pan-Africanism
SLA (Symbionese Liberation Army), 9, 16n40, 145
slave trade/slavery: imprisonment as, 28, 36n28, 68; reparations movement, 65, 66; RNA and, 59, 65, 66; UN treaties on, 122, 129, 132n18
Smear, Pat, 185, 186, 190
Smolick, M. Sharon, 30
SNCC (Student Non-Violent Coordinating Committee), 11n6, 64, 98–99, 103–104, 217, 228n15, 232
Snowden, Don, 185
Sojourner Truth Organization (STO), 155–169; anti-imperialism, 155, 157, 165–166, 172n33; anti-Klan organizing, 165, 166–167, 168, 170n4; antinuclear movement and, 168, 173n50; Free Puerto Rico Committee, 154n62; impact of previous generations of activism on, 155–156; Iranian student movement and, 163, 166; legacy of, 168–169, 172n33; Leninism and, 156, 162, 165–166, 169, 170n2, 170n4; LRBW and, 158–159; Marxist-Leninist frameworks, 155–156; May 19th Communist Organization and, 165, 168; Motorola Organizing Committee, 159, 161; national liberation and, 11, 153n53, 163–168; the national question, 165–166, 173n42; non-union/union organizing approach, 161–162; oppressed worker campaigns, 161–162; organic intellectuals and, 156, 170n6; organizational structure of, 159–162; PFOC and, 165, 168, 171n9; Puerto Rican Independence movement and, 163–164, 166–167; race and, 11, 155, 156–157, 158–159, 169; recruitment concerns, 162; Rock Island blockade, 168–169; SDS and, 155; self-education efforts, 50, 173n50; solidarity work, 163–168; splits within, 162–163, 168–169, 172n32; Stalinism and, 155, 156, 165, 167, 170n4; Stewart-Warner factory organizing, 159–162, 172n23, 172n25; trade unions and, 156, 158, 159, 161, 162, 170n2; white-skin privilege theory, 155, 156–157, 162, 165, 169, 230n52; women, organizing of, 161–162; worker autonomy and, 162; working-class consciousness and, 155–156, 170n2
Soledad Brother (Jackson), 24
Soledad Prison, 24, 25, 27, 28, 257

Soto, Tom, 32
South American Indian Council (CISA), 126
Southern Africa Support Project, 110
Southern Christian Leadership Conference (SCLC), 43, 65, 235
South West Africa People's Organization (SWAPO), 123, 127, 133n22
Spheeris, Penelope, 187
Spirit of Logos (SOL), 222–223
spirituality, 5, 6, 8, 83, 178, 182–183, 238–239, 253, 261–263, 266n50
spokes-council method of organization, 231, 240, 241, 248n35
Stalinism, 155, 156, 165, 167, 170n4
Starr, Meg, 135–154
state-building projects, 65–67, 69–70. See also Republic of New Afrika (RNA)
state power/state violence: battered women's movement and, 49–52, 56n83; decolonization movements and, 69–70; domestic violence and, 51; prisons as microcosm of, 22; sovereignty movements and, 57–60
Stateville Prisoners Organization, 67–68
State v. Koss (1990), 55n75
Statue of Liberty occupation (1977), 135, 147, 148
Steck, Burton, 217
St. Martin, Clement, 260
Stonewall Inn riots, 177, 178, 187
Strategy for a Living Revolution (Lakey), 231, 235
Strucker, John, 160, 171n21
student/campus-based organizing: MAYO, 195–196, 196–200, 206–208, 209n8; SDS, 141, 155, 217, 218, 228n13, 232; SNCC, 11n6, 64, 98–99, 103–104, 217, 228n15, 232; working-class organizing and, 214–215
Student Non-Violent Coordinating Committee (SNCC), 64, 98–99, 103–104, 111n6, 217, 228n15, 232
Student Organization for Black Unity, 110
Students for a Democratic Society (SDS), 141, 155, 217, 218, 228n13, 232
Sullivan, Gail, 51
Sundiata, Mtyari, 69
Sunni-Ali, Fulani, 69
Survival of American Indians Association (SAIA), 115–116
survival programs, 24, 215, 268–269, 272–275, 282n19
Sutherland, Bill, 251
SWAPO (South West Africa People's Organization), 123, 127, 133n22
Sweet Honey in the Rock, 45
Swift Bird Oyate Center, 279
Sykes, Abbas, 100–101
Symbionese Liberation Army (SLA), 9, 16n40, 145

Tanzania, 64, 100–101, 106, 107–108, 251. See also Sixth Pan-African Congress (Sixth PAC)
Taylor, Richard, 235
tenant organizing, 215, 219
Terry, Peggy, 217
Think Lincoln alliance, 139, 223

Third World Women's Alliance, 51, 222
Thirteenth Amendment, 28, 36n28, 68
Thomas, Kathy, 50
Thunder Hawk, Madonna: AIM and, 271, 272–274, 280, 283n26; alliance building and, 276–278; Andria Syke Robideau and, 280n2; BHA and, 267, 268–269, 277–278; boarding-school experience, 271, 282n11; on complex history of indigenous women, 269, 281n3; Cultural Learning Center, 274; decolonizing efforts and, 278–280; early biography, 270; Feather Necklace tiospaye (extended family), 270, 282n8; as grassroots activist, 268, 269, 278–280; International Indian Treaty Council (IITC), 267, 268, 275; internationalism and, 276–277; International Women's Day speech, 276; Lakota People's Law Project, 279; Lorelei Means De Cora and, 272–275, 280n2; Mabel Ann Chasing Hawk and, 280n2; Mary Quintana and, 280n2; Minnie Two Shoes and, 280n2; Mount Rushmore, 268, 269–270; Phyllis Young and, 280n2; Pick-Sloane Act (1944) and, 270–271; Red Power women's activism, 26, 267–270, 280n1, 281n3, 282n10; relocation, 271, 282n12; San Francisco and, 280; Swift Bird Oyate Center, 279; WARN, 267, 268, 275–278, 281n5, 283n20; WKLD/OC and, 267, 271–272, 282n14; Women's Feminist Health Collective and, 278; women's movement and, 269, 276, 278, 281n3; WWRSS and, 267, 268–269, 272–274, 283n19
Tijerina, Reies López, 58
Tilsen, Ken, 271
Tilsen, Mark, 271
Tilsen, Rachel, 271
Time's Discipline (Berrigan and McAlister), 261–262
Todd, Cheryl, 44
Tomata du Plenty, 184
Toronto Warriors Society, 83–84
Torres, Jose "Joe" Campos, 196, 200–206, 206–208
Torres, Margaret, 203, 204
Trail of Broken Treaties march (1972), 62, 117
TransAfrica, 110
Transition House, 49
transracial nationalism, 101, 108–109, 114n46, 127
Traversie, T. O., 271
Triangle Area Lesbian Feminists, 43
Trujillo, Sandra, 140
Turner, James, 105
Two Shoes, Minnie, 280n2
Tyson, Timothy, 92n56

union organizing, 157–161, 225–226, 234–235; Autunno Caldo (Hot Autumn), 158; IWW on, 159, 246; LRBW and, 158–159; neoliberalism and, 2; non-union/union organizing approaches, 161–162; prisoner activism and, 23, 25, 26, 27, 28, 32; trade union consciousness, 156, 158, 159, 161, 162, 170n2; United Prisoners

union organizing (*continued*)
Union, 25, 27. *See also* Sojourner Truth
Organization (STO); white working-class
organizing; workplace organizing
United Nations (UN), 118–131; black
internationalism and, 68; black liberation
movements and, 68; cold-war binary
politics and, 127, 129; Commission on
Human Rights, 119–120, 124, 130, 131n8,
133n20, 275; Convention on Tribal and
Indigenous Populations (1953), 122; Decade
to Combat Racism, Racial Discrimination,
and Apartheid, 123, 124, 126, 132n18;
declarations on the rights of indigenous
peoples, 63, 124–126, 130, 131n5, 133n20;
ECOSOC, 119–120, 123–124, 126, 128, 133n21,
133n24; indigenous peoples and, 9, 63,
119–129, 275; International Conference on
Indigenous Peoples of the Americas (1977),
120, 123–126; NAM and, 127;
nongovernmental status and, 119–120;
Permanent Forum on Indigenous Issues
(PFII), 134n35; prison movement and, 68,
75n45; Puerto Rican independence
movement and, 9, 63, 68, 75n45, 136;
quincentenary debate, 129–130, 132n18;
Working Group on Indigenous Populations,
128–129, 133n20; World Conference Against
Racism (2001), 132n14
United Native Americans (UNA), 116
United Parents Who Care (UPWC) coalition,
223
United Prisoners Union, 25, 27
urbanization, 57–58, 60–62, 116, 131n1

Van Deburg, William, 111n4
vanguard political formations: cadre
organization *vs.*, 169; indigenous militants
and, 60; Leninism and, 70, 158, 162;
national liberation movements as, 151n31;
new-communist movement and, 156;
October League, 5, 156, 224, 226, 229n45;
RCP and, 156
Vaughn, Ed, 108
Vieques campaigns, 135, 142, 146–147, 148
Vietnam Moratorium, 141
Vietnam Veterans Against the War (VVAW),
220, 225
Vietnam War: Chicano Moratorium March
(1970), 195, 208; Chicano movement and,
206, 208; draft-board actions, 250,
254–256, 257, 261; draft resistance, 9, 250,
253–256, 258, 259–260; National Chicano
Moratorium Committee, 195; national
liberation movements and, 57, 83, 136,
151n31; Notre Dame Cathedral disruption,
179; as oppositional framework, 3, 6, 14n10,
57–58, 83, 137, 140, 144, 151n31, 179, 251–252;
port blockades, 235; revolutionary
nonviolent resistance movement and, 233;
RUA and, 220, 221; Vietnamization, 261;
Vietnam Moratorium, 141; VVAW, 220,
235
Ving, Lee, 187–188
Vita Wa Watu (journal), 68, 75n44

Wald, George, 254
Walpole State Prison, 22, 24, 25, 26, 31
Wanrow, Yvonne, 39–41, 54n56
War Resisters League (WRL), 251, 254, 262
Waskow, Arthur, 32–33
Watergate, 3
Waters, John, 181, 184
Watson, John, 159
Weather Underground Organization (WUO), 1,
5, 131n1, 145, 153n53, 157, 173n29
welfare rights movements, 17n48, 228n17
We Still Charge Genocide (NAPO), 68
West Indian Afro-Brotherhood, 101
We Will Remember Survival School (WWRSS),
267, 268–269, 272–274, 283n19
Whalen, Jack, 221
What Is to Be Done? (Lenin), 156
whistleblowers, 7
White, Kevin, 216
White Buffalo Calf Shelter (Rosebud
Reservation), 56n83
White Lightning (WL), 214, 215, 216, 222–225,
225–227. *See also* white working-class
organizing
whiteness: political mobilization of white
ethnicity and, 8, 108, 216, 221–222, 225;
politics of resentment and, 8, 214–216;
white liberal feminism, 4; white-skin
privilege, 155, 156–157, 162, 165, 169, 225,
276; white working-class radicalism, 217,
218, 220, 224, 230n52. *See also* October 4th
Organization (O4O); race; Rising Up Angry
(RUA); Sojourner Truth Organization
(STO); White Lightning (WL); white
working-class organizing
White Night riots, 4, 187
white-skin privilege analysis, 155, 156–157, 162,
165, 169, 225
White Train campaign, 262
white working-class organizing, 214–227;
anti-imperialist organizing, 216;
anti–police brutality organizing, 221–222,
228n17; antiwar organizing and, 221–222;
Boston bus boycott (1974), 215–216; Chicago
Area Military Project, 220; community-
based organizing and, 214, 216–218; as
context for mobilization, 214–216; factory
organizing and, 214–215; feminist
separatism and, 218–219; JOIN and, 217–218,
219, 228n13, 228n17; militancy and, 216–217;
multiracial coalitions, 215, 217–218,
219–220, 222–225; neighborhood-based
organizing and, 220–222; non-
student/campus-based organizing and,
214–215, 220; People's Bail Project, 215, 221;
political mobilization of white ethnicity,
216, 221; politics of resentment and, 215;
race and, 215–216, 216–217; racism and,
214–216, 219–220, 221, 225, 228n17; Rainbow
Coalition, 219–220, 228n17; self-education
efforts, 50, 173n50; service-plus-organizing
model, 215; student/campus-based
organizing and, 220–221; survival programs
and, 215; tenant organizing, 215, 219; Think
Lincoln alliance, 139, 223; VVAW and, 220,

235; white supremacy and, 170n6; YPO and, 219–220, 228n17. *See also* October 4th Organization (O4O); poor people's movement model, impact on; Rising Up Angry (RUA); Sojourner Truth Organization (STO); White Lightning (WL); workplace organizing
Whittington, Les, 87
Willemsen-Diaz, Augusto, 122–123
Williams, Agnes, 275
Williams, Henry Sylvester, 98
Williams, Robert F., 64, 73n25
Willoughby, George and Lillian, 235
Wilmington 10, 212n44
Wilson, Richard, 62–63, 117–118
Witness Against Torture, 262
Witt, Shirley Hill, 127
Wobblies (Industrial Workers of the World), 159, 246
Wolfe, Tom, 6
Wolff, Cathy, 245
women: armed struggles and, 39, 50; black nationalism and, 44–45, 45–46; California Institute for Women, Frontera, 26; factory organizing, 159–160; indigenous peoples and, 39–41, 56n83, 84–85, 92n60, 116, 269, 281n3; Latin Women's Collective, 139–140; prison guard abuse of, 43–44; prison organizing and, 26, 37n48; Red Power and, 267–270, 276, 280n1, 282n10; workplace organizing and, 159–160, 161–162. *See also* battered women's movement; feminism/feminist movement; sexism; sexual violence activism; Thunder Hawk, Madonna; women's movement
Women Armed for Self-Protection, 39
Women of All Red Nations (WARN), 40, 267, 275–278
women-of-color feminist organizing: battered women/spousal abuse and, 51, 56n83; Combahee River Collective (Boston), 51; political prisoners and, 35n9; racism within women's movement and, 51, 55n82, 56n83
Women's Advocates, 49
Women's Feminist Health Collective (WFHC), 278
Women's International League for Peace and Freedom (WILPF), 123, 127
women's movement: class-based organizing and, 218–219; domestic violence analysis and, 39, 46–48, 48–52; importance of the 1970s to, 4; indigenous women and, 40, 41, 52, 56n83, 84–85, 92n60, 116, 269, 276, 278, 281n3 ; Jane (abortion service), 218; liberal

feminism and, 39; personal *vs.* political analyses and, 46–48; racism within, 45, 51, 55n82, 56n83; on rape *vs.* domestic abuse, 46–48; right to self-defense and, 39, 42–43, 43–44, 45; separatism and, 218–219; sexual assault and, 39. *See also* feminism/feminist movement
Women's Pentagon Action, 262
Women's Self-Defense Law Project, 48
Woods, Dessie X., 44–46, 54n46, 54n56
Working Group on Indigenous Populations, 128–129, 133n20
workplace organizing, 155–169; anti-imperialist struggles and, 155, 216; Autunno Caldo (Hot Autumn), 158; factory occupations, 158; non-union/union approaches to organizing, 157–161, 161–162; women and, 159–160, 161–162; work strikes, prison-based, 22, 24, 25–26. *See also* Sojourner Truth Organization (STO); white working-class organizing
World Conference Against Racism (2001), 132n14
World Council of Churches, 123
World Council of Indigenous Peoples, 126
World Peace Council (WPC), 123, 127
Wounded Knee (1890 massacre), 87, 117, 131n6
Wounded Knee Legal Defense/Offense Committee (WKLD/OC), 63, 267, 271
Wounded Knee standoff (1973), 4, 62–63, 80, 84, 91n40, 117–118, 123, 235, 267–274, 279. *See also* Thunder Hawk, Madonna
The Wretched of the Earth (Fanon), 105, 253

Yakuba, Yaki (a.k.a. Atiba Shanna), 67–68, 75n44
Young, Andrew, 75n45, 127
Young, Phyllis, 275, 280n2
Young Lords: history of, 136, 139, 140, 164; police repression and, 219; prisoner activism and, 24; PSP and, 140; Rainbow Coalition and, 219–220; RUA and, 219; tenant organizing and, 219; WL and, 222, 223, 224
Young Patriots Organization (YPO), 219–220, 228n17

Zapatista National Liberation Army (EZLN), 130, 134n34
Zedong, Mao, 71n6
Zeller, Barbara, 147
Zeskin, Leonard, 169
Zinn, Howard, 260
Zwickel, Jean, 146–147